Frommer's®

Istanbul

1st Edition

by Lynn A. Levine

Here's what the critics say about Frommer's:

"Amazingly easy to use. Very portable, very complete."

—*Booklist*

"Detailed, accurate, and easy-to-read information for all price ranges."
—*Glamour Magazine*

"Hotel information is close to encyclopedic."

—*Des Moines Sunday Register*

"Frommer's Guides have a way of giving you a real feel for a place."
—*Knight Ridder Newspapers*

WILEY
Wiley Publishing, Inc.

About the Author

Lynn A. Levine is author of *Frommer's Turkey* and has contributed to a number of other titles, including *Frommer's Italy from $90 a Day* and *Frommer's Southeast Asia*. Her work has appeared in the *Boston Globe*, *Elle*, *MSNBC/Newsweek Budget Travel*, *Travel Holiday*, and the *UN Chronicle*. When not writing about travel, she is a communications consultant for UNICEF, the United Nations Development Program, and the International Fund for Animal Welfare. She also runs the website www.talkingturkey.com.

Published by:

Wiley Publishing, Inc.

111 River St.
Hoboken, NJ 07030-5744

ISBN: 978-0-470-25708-1

Editor: Melinda Quintero
Production Editor: Michael Brumitt
Cartographer: Andrew Murphy
Photo Editor: Richard Fox
Production by Wiley Indianapolis Composition Services

Front cover photo: Inside the Blue Mosque.
Back cover photo: The Mısır Çarşışı (Egyptian Spice Market).

For information on our other products and services or to obtain technical support, please contact our Customer Care Department within the U.S. at 800/762-2974, outside the U.S. at 317/572-3993, or fax 317/572-4002.

Wiley also publishes its books in a variety of electronic formats. Some content that appears in print may not be available in electronic formats.

Manufactured in the United States of America

5 4 3 2 1

Contents

Where to Stay 59

 Where to Dine 84

 Exploring Istanbul 111

 Istanbul Strolls 176

List of Maps

Acknowledgments

Special thanks are in order for a handful of incredibly wonderful and supportive individuals. Thanks to Sırma, Sıla, Aydın, Suha, Süleyman, and Hakan for their professional assistance and personal friendship. Each has been instrumental in supporting me in my work on this guide and in introducing me to the soul of Turkey. Warm thanks also go out to the people and the country of Turkey for exposing me to countless true friendships made during the course of working in Turkey. Special thanks are in order for Melinda Quintero, my editor, for her astute edits and tireless perfectionism, and for making us both look good.

An Invitation to the Reader

In researching this book, we discovered many wonderful places—hotels, restaurants, shops, and more. We're sure you'll find others. Please tell us about them, so we can share the information with your fellow travelers in upcoming editions. If you were disappointed with a recommendation, we'd love to know that, too. Please write to:

Frommer's Istanbul, 1st Edition
Wiley Publishing, Inc. • 111 River St. • Hoboken, NJ 07030-5744

An Additional Note

Please be advised that travel information is subject to change at any time—and this is especially true of prices. We therefore suggest that you write or call ahead for confirmation when making your travel plans. The authors, editors, and publisher cannot be held responsible for the experiences of readers while traveling. Your safety is important to us, however, so we encourage you to stay alert and be aware of your surroundings. Keep a close eye on cameras, purses, and wallets, all favorite targets of thieves and pickpockets.

Other Great Guides for Your Trip:

Frommer's Turkey, 5th Edition

Frommer's Star Ratings, Icons & Abbreviations

Every hotel, restaurant, and attraction listing in this guide has been ranked for quality, value, service, amenities, and special features using a **star-rating system.** In country, state, and regional guides, we also rate towns and regions to help you narrow down your choices and budget your time accordingly. Hotels and restaurants are rated on a scale of zero (recommended) to three stars (exceptional). Attractions, shopping, nightlife, towns, and regions are rated according to the following scale: zero stars (recommended), one star (highly recommended), two stars (very highly recommended), and three stars (must-see).

In addition to the star-rating system, we also use **seven feature icons** that point you to the great deals, in-the-know advice and unique experiences that separate travelers from tourists. Throughout the book, look for:

Finds	Special finds—those places only insiders know about
Fun Fact	Fun facts—details that make travelers more informed and their trips more fun
Kids	Best bets for kids, and advice for the whole family
Moments	Special moments—those experiences that memories are made of
Overrated	Places or experiences not worth your time or money
Tips	Insider tips—great ways to save time and money
Value	Great values—where to get the best deals

The following **abbreviations** are used for credit cards:

AE	American Express	DISC	Discover	V	Visa
DC	Diners Club	MC	MasterCard		

Frommers.com

Now that you have the guidebook to a great trip, visit our website at **www.frommers.com** for travel information on more than 4,000 destinations. With features updated regularly, we give you instant access to the most current trip-planning information available. At Frommers.com, you'll also find the best prices on airfares, accommodations, and car rentals—and you can even book travel online through our travel booking partners. At Frommers.com, you'll also find the following:

- Online updates to our most popular guidebooks
- Vacation sweepstakes and contest giveaways
- Newsletter highlighting the hottest travel trends
- Online travel message boards with featured travel discussions

Best of Istanbul

First-time visitors to Istanbul often leave home with foggy yet preconceived notions about this storied and mysterious destination. And while visitors will have their own opinions and ideas on what to look forward to, in Istanbul, they all have a ring of truth. Istanbul, like Turkey, is simultaneously many and often bewilderingly contradictory things: ancient and modern, western and Oriental, religious and secular, conservative and progressive, wondrous and ordinary, familiar and exotic. But there is one undeniable common denominator among all of these disparate and contradictory traits: Istanbul is growing more and more interesting by the day. Juxtaposed against the unstoppable machine of progress are layers upon layers of ancient civilization, where housing renovations or urban renewal projects invariably uncover groundbreaking evidence of Istanbul's stature throughout the centuries. If you need proof that Istanbul is as momentous as Rome, as captivating as Paris, and—if you know where to go—as exotic as Bangkok, then you've picked up the right book.

A city that straddles Europe and Asia, Istanbul is a symbol of greatness, coveted historically by everyone from Xerxes all the way down the historical dateline through World War I, when Russia was green with envy over the possibilities of what free passage through the Bosphorus Straits could do for its economy.

The traditions inherited from the past 2,500 years of history (although recent discoveries backdate the city by thousands of years) are most evident in the Old City, known as Old Stamboul or the Historic Peninsula. A stroll through this open-air museum reveals ancient Roman hippodromes, underground cisterns, and architectural icons, all representing the greatest excesses of the Byzantine Empire and the mystique and power of the Ottoman Empire. As a religious center (the heart of the Greek Orthodox Church as well as the Islamic faith for centuries), this old section of Istanbul is the custodian of two of the world's most important cultural heritages and home to some of the world's most opulent displays of art and wealth. Early Greek civilization left us the building blocks for Rome and Byzantium, which swathed these earlier foundations in rich mosaics and left their mark with monuments such as the Hippodrome and Ayasofya. Even Sultan Fatih Mehmet II was astounded at the beauty of the city he had finally conquered. The Ottoman dynasty redirected the city's fortunes into the imperial majesty of undulating domes and commanding minarets, and the sumptuousness of Topkapı Palace.

Across the Golden Horn is the modern heart of the city, custodian of the latter centuries of the Ottoman Empire and heir to the future of the country. This, the "modern" city, pulsates with all the electricity of a cutting-edge international metropolis. Although the political capital sits safely in the heartland, this part of Istanbul projects itself into the world as Turkey's ambassador of art, entertainment, music, and education. Meanwhile on the Asian side of the Bosphorus sprawl residential neighborhoods and commercial centers more reminiscent of Europe than the area's counterpart on the European side.

Together, these and Istanbul's other neighborhoods provide a home to 23 million-plus of the 74 million people living in Turkey, many of whom are modest village folk who've migrated to the big city out of economic need. Over pricey brunches, the residents of the more prosperous neighborhoods along the Bosphorus revile the poor wedged into the squalid back streets of Süleymaniye, Çarşamba, and Tarlabaşı, while the religious fundamentalists of the Fatih and Üsküdar neighborhoods stare out through their veils in disapproval.

As a complex society in transition, and a microcosm of the tug-of-war between East and West, Istanbul is still a work in progress. It is a work of monumental proportions. Istanbul is so exotic, wonderful, complex, and utterly captivating, that once experienced, it'll be impossible to break free from its spell.

1 The Most Unforgettable Travel Experiences

- **Taking a *hamam:*** The Turkish bath, rising out of the Islamic requirement of cleanliness, is not just practical; it's relaxing as well. A good *hamam* experience includes the proper traditional ambience and a heavy-handed scrubbing. For historical value and pomp, you can't beat the **Çemberlitaş Hamamı,** or for luxury, one of the many deluxe hotel *hamams.* See p. 142.

- **Attending a performance of the Ottoman Mehter Band:** The under-appreciated Military Museum in Harbiye puts on two half-hour daily performances of what was once the avant-garde of the fearless and brutal Ottoman army. It's a powerful performance of sound and visuals, and truly not to be missed.

- **Wandering the streets behind the Egyptian Spice Market:** It's just as much fun outside as it is inside the market, where purveyors of produce set their prepared foods out on the streets for the local lunch crowd. Bring wet wipes.

- **Discovering the Grand Bazaar:** Nobody should pass through Turkey without spending a day at the mother of all shopping malls. The atmosphere crackles with the electricity of the hunt—but are you the hunter or the hunted? The excitement is tangible, even if you're on the trail of a simple pair of elf shoes or an evil-eye talisman. When the salesman turns away from you in disgust, you've learned the bottom price for an item. See chapter 9.

- **Taking a boat ride up the Bosphorus:** Nowhere else in the world can you cross to another continent every 15 minutes. Connecting trade routes from the East to the West, it's no surprise that any conqueror who was anybody had his sights set on the Bosphorus. Floating in the wake of Jason and the Argonauts and Constantine the Great, sit back and enjoy the breezes, the stately wooden manses, the monumental Ottoman domes, and the fortresses that helped win battles. See p. 151.

- **Stumbling over a small herd of sheep in Balat:** This is one of the countless neighborhoods in Istanbul in transition, where old dilapidated structures are getting the recognition they deserve. It's really just a matter of time before Starbucks moves in, but while I can't promise you sheep on your visit, if you go there soon, you will witness the character of the city before it started looking European. See chapter 8.

Turkey

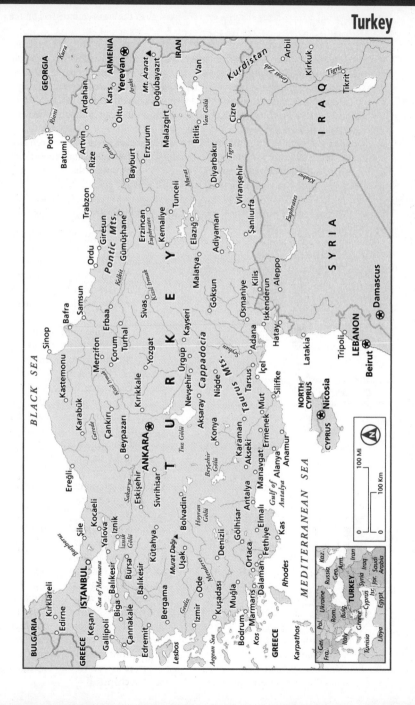

Midnight Express: Fact or Fiction?

The 1978 movie *Midnight Express,* directed by Alan Parker and scripted by Oliver Stone, elicits strong resentment in Turkey for the portrayal of Billy Hayes, who, in spite of a well-publicized crackdown on drug smuggling, took a dumb risk and lost. The movie, which won the director an Oscar, is a hideously graphic (and mostly fictional) account of human rights violations in a Turkish prison. The truth is that the *real* Billy Hayes acknowledges the inaccuracy of many of the scenes in the movie; he was in a low-security prison, and no guard was killed in order for him to escape. Actually, the Turkish government released him.

The name of the movie derives from the midnight train service from Istanbul to Edirne, which, at the time, briefly traveled through Greek territory. During the 1960s and 1970s, the Turkish government reacted to international criticism (particularly from the U.S.) of its harsh sentencing guidelines with a discreet and diplomatic trick. Foreigners convicted of drug-related offenses were divested of their passports and released during appeal. Then they were quietly ushered onto the Midnight Express train, where, once in Greece (and with the complicity of Greek guards on the train), they hopped off the train and were jailed until they could obtain new passports from their consulates. The Turks were thus able to maintain a hard-line stance without jeopardizing diplomatic relations.

- **Soaking up the atmosphere at the Pierre Loti café:** The views of the Golden Horn from this hilltop make the trip to Pierre Loti worth the detour. Take a walk through the picturesque cemetery adjacent to the cafe; then wander down to Eyüp to see parades of princely looking boys on the eve of their circumcision ceremony. See p. 146.

- **Sharing tea with the locals:** Tea is at the center of Turkish culture; no significant negotiation takes place without a cup or three. But more than commerce, tea stops the hands of time in Turkey; it renews the bonds of friends and family. Having tea is inevitable, as is the invitation to share a glass with a total stranger. Accept

the invitation: There's more to a glass than just a hot drink.

- **Buying a carpet, whether you plan to or not:** Come on, you know you want to. And whatever it is that you buy, whether you overpay or not, whether your salesman is naughty or nice, I guarantee you will be talking about the experience for years to come. See p. 199.

- **Rejuvenating your spirit at the ceremony of the Whirling Dervişes at Galata Mevlevihanesi:** The same repetitive whirling and soothing tones of the sufi mystics designed to create a sense of union between the derviş and God will undoubtedly entrance you as well. See p. 167.

2 The Best Museums, Mosques & Churches

- **Blue Mosque:** This landmark mosque assumes a stance of authority over Sultanahmet Park. Just under the dome, hundreds of stained-glass windows sparkle like jewels until you are convinced that you're in the presence of a celestial being. The blue of the mosque actually changes to yellow, orange, and red, depending on the time of day and the entrance you choose to use. See p. 118.

- **Ayasofya:** When faced with the dome of this masterpiece, it's tempting to mimic the actions of Mehmet the Conqueror almost 600 years ago and drop to your knees in a gesture of utter humility. The sensation is intensified by the low level of filtered light that finds its way in, temporarily blinding you to everything except the source of illumination. See p. 114.

- **Topkapı Palace:** Perspective check—this was once somebody's *house*. Actually, it was the home of a whole lot of people—up to 5,000 at a time, all in the service of one man. The sultan surrounded himself with the most beautiful women in the world. He

collected the most precious treasures of the East. He assembled the most sacred relics of the Muslim faith under this roof. Six hundred years of Ottoman history lies behind these grand ornamental gates. See p. 127.

- **Istanbul Archaeology Museum:** This is one of those must-see museums that all too many overlook. It's actually the largest museum in the country, chronicling in stone both the lives of Byzantium's emperors and of Istanbul. Recovered artifacts date back to 6000 B.C. (stick a shovel in the ground, though, and historians are forced to reset the clock of Istanbul's story) and proceed through the centuries. A separate building houses the Museum of the Ancient Orient, exhibiting artifacts obtained during the course of the Ottoman period. See p. 125.

- **St. Savior in Chora:** An empire's devotion to the faith is mirrored in the opulence of the finest preserved collections of Byzantine mosaics just about anywhere. See p. 140.

3 The Best Things to Do for Free (or Almost)

- **Toasting the lights of the Old City at dusk:** It's a magical sight to watch the lights of the Old City come to life. From a rooftop bar (okay, not necessarily free) in Beyoğlu, you can watch the monuments light up one by one. If you're on the ground in Sultanahmet, it's impossible not to enjoy the poetry of the seagulls in flight circling under the spotlights of the Blue Mosque.

- **Crossing the Galata Bridge on foot:** Fishermen line the railings above, while dinner (or tea, or backgammon)

is served below as the majestic and inspiring silhouettes of the Süleymaniye, Rüstem Paşa, and Yeni Camii loom in the distance. If you wait until after sunset, you get to see the seagulls circling the minarets.

- **Strolling along the city's defensive walls:** Ancient history is juxtaposed against the present-day neighborhoods at Yedikule, Edirnekapı, and Ayvansaray, each reflecting its own interpretation of Turkey's past, present, and future.

Tips Best Views

Istanbul is a city of rooftops, attracting refugees from the sticky Mediterranean summers up above the eaves for a breath of fresh sea air. Are the views the bonus, or are the breezes? You decide.

For the cost of a cocktail or a meal, you'll be seduced by views of the city, each revealing an angle of Istanbul you may not have otherwise noticed. The rooftop bars and restaurants of Beyoğlu take advantage of panoramas that include the Old City, the Bosphorus, the Golden Horn, and everything in between. Check out the bar at **Mikla** (or spring for a meal; p. 98), Panorama, the **Marmara Hotel's** top-flight restaurant, or **360 Istanbul** (p. 214), whose very name begs the question: Need I say more? On the Asian side, from Kanlıca, the view is down the Bosphorus to the Fatih Bridge; farther south from Çengelköy the waterfront cafes and restaurants bask in the nighttime glow of the Bosphorus Bridge.

Now, the freebies (or almost free). One of the finest panoramas in the Old City is from the north side of the courtyard of the **Süleymaniye Mosque and Complex** (p. 147). The prolific architect, in service to Süleyman the Magnificent and considered the Ottoman era's preeminent architect, strategically sited his crown jewel on the city's highest point to take advantage of the commanding vistas. From the rear of the courtyard, the view is a straight shot over the Galata Bridge and up the Bosphorus.

For those naughty enough to go to Istanbul without any plans to visit Topkapı Palace, there are amazing views of the Marmara Sea along the path leading from the outer, public courtyard down to the parking lot. Dozens of boats each day park themselves on this side of the peninsula awaiting clearance into the traffic-choked Bosphorus Straits.

4 The Best One-of-a-Kind Places to Stay

- **Çırağan Palace** (© 0212/258-3377; www.ciraganpalace.com): More than just Istanbul's poshest hotel, the Çırağan Palace is a destination in its own right. The grandeur of the lobby—tinted by light coming through the stained glass and imbued with the fragrance of fresh roses—hardly prepares you for what's to come. Expect regal gardens, a delicious Bosphorus-side pool, big fluffy beds, and flawless service. Make sure you splurge for that sea view, or all bets are off. See p. 149.

- **Four Seasons Hotel** (© 0212/638-8200; www.fourseasons.com): Nothing drives home the magnitude of this hotel's history more than watching a former political prisoner once incarcerated here break down and cry in the hallway. Some original tile and marble details were preserved and reused in the renovation, and you might encounter the rough etchings of an inmate's name in one of the columns. But these days the unqualified opulence and comfort of this grand hotel couldn't be further

If you've already paid the admission fee for **Topkapı Palace** (p. 127), the numerous corners with views of the Marmara Sea and the Bosphorus are yours to enjoy. The really staggering ones are in the rear (fourth courtyard), which all at once faces the Marmara Sea, the Bosphorus, and Asia. A great photo op would be under the small Iftariye Pavilion, where during Ramadan the sultan would break his fast with the *iftar* meal. Because the pavilion faces north, the views include the Golden Horn. If you've bought your ticket to the Harem, you'll see that the sultan's favorites also got some pretty good real estate, residing in apartments from which, on a clear day, they could see as far as the Princes' Islands.

You may want to sit down and enjoy the vistas over a cup of tea, coffee, or Turkish wine. From the Malta Köskü in **Yıldız Park** (p. 151), the cool breezes waft over the treetops down to the Bosphorus. If you're into the romance of tragedy, the lore surrounding **Pierre Loti** (p. 146) up along the Golden Horn is the place to absorb the meaning of love lost while contemplating the rebirth of the waterway formerly blighted by industry (and isn't it all so photogenic?).

From the wharf up in **Ortaköy** (p. 47), you can see the floodlit Ortaköy Mosque dangling off its pier, and the twinkling lights of Asia on the opposite shore.

In the evenings, the domes and minarets of the **Old City** light up, acting as a magnet for scores of seagulls. If you haven't already fallen in love with Istanbul, this is the view that will do it. Grab a seat at one of the east-facing pubs along the **Galata Bridge,** or just stand immobilized by the majesty over on the wharf of **Karaköy.**

from its bread-and-water past. The new **Four Seasons the Bosphorus** (© 0212/638-8200) promises the royal treatment—but without the historic background. See p. 63.

- **Les Ottomans** (© 0212/359-1500; www.lesottomans.com): You'll find rooms truly fit for royalty here, if you can get a reservation. Every detail, from the chandeliers, to the salon chairs, to the bedding, is a unique creation that screams "one of a kind."

This very personalized nature of the hotel foreshadows the high standard of hospitality. See p. 81.

- **Sumahan** (© 0216/422-8000; www.sumahan.com): A traditional *hamam* is the bonus feature in four of the hotel's rooms, while the rest of them make due with luxurious slate marble bathroom suites. Enough with the bathrooms; the hotel itself is a restored factory for the production of grain alcohol. See p. 82.

5 The Best Food Experiences

- **Noshing waterside at Eminönü:** For 12 to 14 hours a day, the Tarıhı Eminönü Balıkçısı grills fresh fish quayside, wrapped in a roll and presented for a spectacular 3YTL ($2.60/£1.15) by a gracious man in

The Best Turkey Websites

The **World Wide Web** makes it simple to do additional research before you leave home. These sites provide a range of information, from destination overviews to up-to-date listings on everything from restaurants, hotels, and local events, as well as valuable links to other sites:

- **www.kultur.gov.tr** is the official site of the Turkish Ministry of Culture, and an excellent source for information and links to the country's major arts events.
- **www.tourismturkey.org** is the website of the Ministry of Tourism.
- **www.turkishdailynews.com** and **www.turkishpress.com**, the sites for Turkey's two English-language dailies, allow you to plug into real-time issues.
- **www.mymerhaba.com** is for expatriates by expatriates, but we like to eavesdrop on them, too.
- **http://cat.une.edu.au** provides a wealth of coordinated information on all archaeological works being conducted in Turkey. Information is arranged by age and by ancient site.
- **www.istanbul2010.org** is the go-to site for all things cultural happening in Istanbul leading up to the city's reign as cultural capital of Europe.
- **www.byzantium1200.com** is a nonprofit research project whose goal is to create computer models of Constantinople and its monuments during the Byzantine era. Models are constructed based on all available information, including scholarly and historic accounts as well as historical paintings, and depict buildings, structures, and monuments as they would have appeared in 1200 had they been optimally maintained (by 1200, much of the city was, in reality, in an irretrievable state of decay). Byzantium 1200 also puts out a companion guide to the Byzantine sites in Istanbul called *Walking Thru Byzantium*.

traditional costume. Grab your sandwich and step aside; the condiments are to the right on the railing. See p. 90.

- **Develi:** No visit to Istanbul is complete for me without a visit to Develi. Dine on their spicy *lahmacun, içli köfte,* raw *çiğ köfte,* and you'll be stuffed before the pistachio kebap arrives. See p. 98.
- **Melting Kanlıca yogurt in your mouth:** For more than 100 years, creamy rich yogurt has been a specialty of the tiny Bosphorus front village of Kanlıca, on the upper Asian

side. It's a hell of a haul for a cup of yogurt, but oh, what glorious spoonfuls they are. See p. 173.

- **Morning *simit* from a street vendor:** I grew up on sesame bagels, so call me biased, but these doughy little morning delicacies really do hit the spot. Spread some cheese on one (or slather with butter and jam) and weep. See p. 97.
- **Eating your way through Ortaköy:** This neighborhood is particularly vibrant on a summer evening, with the lights twinkling beneath the Bosphorus Bridge. The streets behind

the mosque are a food fair of Turkish fast-food stalls selling such things as stuffed mussels (for the fearless) and potatoes to drown in your preferred toppings. See p. 97.

- **Dining at Asitane:** Many restaurants bill themselves as "Ottoman," but few of them can actually boast of having translated the recipes from the kitchens of Topkapı. See p. 96.

- **Lunch at a *lokanta:*** These unassuming eateries have some of the best home-style food around. Casseroles and stews such as *moussaka* or *orman kebap* (lamb stew with potatoes and carrots) are the types of labor-intensive dishes the tourist places can't be bothered to prepare. See p. 90.

6 The Best Stuff to Bring Home

- **Carpets and *kilims:*** No matter how lame your bargaining skills, it's still cheaper than Bloomingdale's—and boy, do they look good unrolled under (or on) your coffee table. Turkey's tribal carpets and *kilims* represent a cultural tradition that goes back for centuries.

- **Pottery and ceramics:** These arts thrived under the Ottomans, whose skilled craftsmen perfected the coral red and cobalt blue of the Iznik tile. No one has ever been able to reproduce the intensity of these colors, until now. The only authentic reproductions come out of the **Iznik Foundation**'s workshop and showroom (p. 201) in Iznik, but they are distributed widely at finer-quality shops. Ordinary but equally stunning porcelain designs on white clay come from Kuthaya (the painting is done at private workshops) and are sold throughout Turkey.

- **Textiles:** Check the manufacturer's label on your fine linens, terry-cloth supplies, and cotton T-shirts. I bet you didn't realize it, but Turkey exports a huge amount of textiles, supplying the raw materials for well-known retailers such as OP, Calvin Klein, Walt Disney, and Banana Republic. Many Istanbul residents head out of town to Bursa (p. 200) or Pamukkale to stock up on plush towels and terry-cloth robes, but

you can also find top-quality clothing and bath towels at Home Goods in Akmerkez, and at any branch of Mudo (among others).

- **Copper:** Turks use copper for everything, probably because it looks so good (particularly the white copper). Tea servers with triangular handles pass you by countless times a day; the wide copper platters that double as tables represent typical Turkish style. Those shiny white bowls you see in a *hamam* are copper, too. For the best prices and widest selection, head to **Çadırcılar Caddesi,** near the Grand Bazaar. See p. 201.

- **Gold and silver:** The price by weight is the same, but with labor so cheap you're bound to get a deal. Shopping thoroughfares glitter with the stuff— some of it attractive, some of it hideous. The **Istanbul Handicrafts Center** (p. 201) has an atelier where artisans craft their own work. Museum gift shops are also great sources of unique jewelry.

- **Foodstuffs:** The exoticism of the East is in full bloom at Istanbul's **Egyptian Spice Bazaar,** where you can find over five different types of saffron at prices that will ensure that you take home a sample of each. Specialty stores and *şarcüteris* (small groceries selling deli-style meats and cheeses) in the **Galatasaray Fish Market** in

Fun Fact A Bridge Too Far

Although the movie *Midnight Express* is set in 1970, a poster seen on the wall during Billy Hayes's visit to the airport loo shows a shot of the Bosphorus Bridge—which was built in 1973.

Beyoğlu marinate a variety of delectable little morsels in sealed jars ready-made to take home. Although this isn't Tuscany, you wouldn't know it by the quality of the olive oil; head over to the local supermarket and stock up on a few of the higher-end bottles. Don't forget the wine; several Turkish vintages are walking away with industry awards, such as Doluca's özel Kav Bogazkere-Oküzküzü 2000 and 2001, Kavaklidere's Selection Kirmizi 1997 and özel Kirmizi 2003 and 2002.

2

Planning Your Trip to Istanbul

While planning your trip and consulting this guide, you should know a few things about the nature of travel and tourism in Istanbul and Turkey in general.

It is no surprise to any of us that hotels, restaurants, and museums raise their prices regularly (and in some cases, annually). However, this natural inflation is compounded by Turkey's current popularity as a tourist destination, and indeed the Ministry of Culture and Tourism accordingly recalibrates the entry fees for museums at the start of each tourist season. Thus, sparsely visited museums such as Askeri Müzesi (Military Museum) charge lesser fees in the hopes of attracting more visitors, while the fees for "must-sees" such as Topkapı Palace and the Ayasofya continue to climb to accommodate what the market will bear. Hotels (some of which are now excluding breakfast from the package) and restaurants (which shamelessly have begun to charge a "cover" for bread and water) are also taking advantage of the increased level of demand. I have tried to balance this unavoidable fact by selecting honest and reliable establishments led by professional businessmen and women, and to weed out the "get-rich-quickers." This in itself is not always possible, as ownership of hotels, restaurants, cafes, and even websites changes and evolves, often without the corresponding name change.

Furthermore, Turkey is undergoing a level of development and renewal that it has not seen in decades. Foreign direct investment, improvements in the tax collection system, an unprecedented commitment to the country's as-of-yet unexcavated cultural goods, and elevated museum entrance fees are being plowed back into the economy, while projects anticipating Istanbul's reign as European Cultural Capital (2010) and Turkey's continued bid for membership in the E.U. are giving the entire country a major face-lift. The country is changing at an incredible clip, and unfortunately it's impossible for a guidebook to stay ever-on-top of things.

Finally, there is an unavoidable (and inconvenient?) truth to writing up those rare and secret "finds." Once the secret is out, the floodgates open, and the secret becomes a cliché. The lag time varies, but the process is sadly inevitable. Hotels double their rates, carpet shops double or triple their profits, and restaurants start to cut corners. Some of these establishments ride the coat tails of Frommer's trusted listing for years, proffering outdated guides to "illustrate" the endorsement.

What does this mean for you while you plan and fantasize about your trip? In the end, we do our best and expect that you will do yours. In exchange for our experienced and researched advice, we hope that you will be smart travelers, savvy shoppers, selective with your praise and criticism, and that you will continue to let us know what you think.

1 Visitor Information

Everyone's first stop for comprehensive information on Turkey as well as visa requirements should be the Turkish Embassy website specific to your country (**www.turkey.org** or **www.tourismturkey.org** in the U.S., **www.turkishembassy.com** in Canada, **www.turkishembassy.org.au** in Australia, and **www.gototurkey.co.uk** in the U.K.). The embassy also administers a "consulate online" in English at **www.trconsulate.org** providing up-to-date information and, although completely unnecessary, visas in advance of arrival.

The Turkish Ministry of Culture (**www.kultur.gov.tr**) has an excellent website that contains cultural information, events, regional resources, and current-events articles. Two other great sites for current information are **www.gatetoturkey.com**, which also puts out *The Gate* magazine available in Istanbul airports, and **www.mymerhaba.com**, created by expats for expats living in Turkey.

In the U.S., the **Turkish Government Tourist Office** has a presence in both New York and Washington, D.C.: 821 United Nations Plaza, New York, NY 10017 (© **212/687-2195**) and 2525 Massachusetts Ave., Suite 306, Washington, DC 20008 (© **202/612-6800**), where you can stock up on maps, brochures, ferry schedules to Greece, and access to practical information via an interactive computer database.

TURKISH EMBASSIES & CONSULATES

IN THE U.S.   For residents of Washington, D.C., Maryland, Virginia, West Virginia, and The Bahamas: Turkish Embassy, 2525 Massachusetts Ave. NW, Washington, DC 20008 (© **202/612-6700**, fax 202/612-6744; Consular Section: © 202/612-6741; fax 202/319-1639; www.turkey.org).

For residents of Alabama, Arkansas, Louisiana, Missouri, New Mexico, Oklahoma, Tennessee, and Texas: Turkish Consulate, 1990 Post Oak Blvd., Suite 1300, Houston, TX 77056 (© **713/622-5849;** fax 713/623-6639).

For residents of Alaska, Arizona, California, Colorado, Hawaii, Idaho, Montana, Nevada, Oregon, Utah, Washington State, Wyoming, and the Pacific Islands: Turkish Consulate, 6300 Wilshire Blvd., Suite 2010, Los Angeles, CA 90048 (© **323/655-8832;** fax 323/655-8681; www.trconsulate.org).

For residents of Illinois, Indiana, Iowa, Kansas, Michigan, Minnesota, Mississippi, Nebraska, North Dakota, Ohio, South Dakota, and Wisconsin: Turkish Consulate, 360 Michigan Ave., Suite 1405, Chicago, IL 60601 (© **312/263-0644;** fax 312/263-1449).

For residents of Connecticut, Delaware, Florida, Georgia, Kentucky, Maine, Massachusetts, North Carolina, New Hampshire, New Jersey, New York, Pennsylvania, Rhode Island, South Carolina, Vermont, and Puerto Rico: Turkish Consulate, 821 United Nations Plaza, New York, NY 10017 (© **212/949-0160;** fax 212/983-1293).

IN CANADA   Turkish Embassy, 197 Wurtemburg St., Ottawa, ON K1N 8L9 (© **613/789-4044;** fax 613/789-3442; www.turkishembassy.com). Also, Turkish Embassy Tourism Section, 360 Albert St., Suite 801, Ottawa, ON K1N 8L9 (© **613/789-4044;** fax 613/789-3442).

IN AUSTRALIA & NEW ZEALAND Turkish Embassy, Canberra, 6 Moona Place, Yarralumla, ACT 2600 (© **02/6234-0000;** fax 02/6273-6592; www.turkishembassy.org.au).

IN THE U.K.   Turkish Embassy, 43 Belgrave Sq., London SW1X 8PA (© **020/7393-0202;** fax 020/7393-0066; www.turkishembassylondon.org).

The Turkish Consulate General is at Rutland Lodge, Rutland Gardens, Knightsbridge SW7 1BW (© 020/7589-0360; fax 020/7584-6235; www.turkish consulate.org.uk). The Turkish Culture and Tourism Office is at 170–173 Piccadilly, London W1J 9EJ (© 020/7629-7771; fax 020/7491-0773; www.goto turkey.co.uk).

2 Entry Requirements

VISAS

An entry visa for Turkey is required for citizens of the U.S. (US$20 for a single entry for stays up to 3 months), Canada (US$60 or 45€ on arrival, valid for 90 days and multiple entries), the U.K. (£10 on entry; £50 in advance for multiple entries up to 3 months), and Australia (A$68 on arrival), while a valid passport is sufficient for citizens of New Zealand.

There is no need to acquire an entry visa prior to departure, because obtaining one on arrival is a no-brainer. While it is standard practice for consulates to provide visas in advance, obtaining a visa at the airport will actually be less of a hassle than applying for a visa in your home country. Upon arrival, go to the visa window next to and before clearing Customs and fork over the required cash. Actually, in many cases it will be more expensive if you apply for a visa in advance. (See "Arriving at the Airport," later in this chapter.)

CONSULATES IN ISTANBUL

The **United States,** Istinye Mah., Kaplıa calar Mevkii 2 (© 0212/335-9000); **Canada,** Istiklal Cad. 373/5 (© 0212/251-9838); **United Kingdom,** 34 Meşrutiyet Cad., Tepebaşı (© 0212/334-6500); **Australia,** Askerocağı Cad. 15, Şişli (© 0212/243-1333).

CUSTOMS
ON ENTRY

The Turkish government has established a list of items that may be brought into the country duty-free. In addition to personal effects, travelers are permitted one video player; one laptop computer; one portable radio/tape player; one pair of binoculars (no night vision allowed); one camera and five rolls of film; one typewriter; personal sporting equipment; necessary medical items; gifts not exceeding $300; spare car parts; and various other relatively improbable items for the average tourist. (A complete list is available through the Turkish Embassy website.) Sharp instruments and weapons may not be brought into the country without special permission (diving and camping knives included). Obviously, the importation, buying, selling, and consumption of marijuana and other narcotics is *strictly* forbidden. You shouldn't need to watch *Midnight Express* to figure that one out (see "*Midnight Express:* Fact or Fiction?" in chapter 1).

ON EXIT

For valuables purchased during your stay, be prepared to provide receipts or other proof of purchase—particularly for that 4×6 prize silk Hereke—to avoid problems with Turkish Customs when you leave and to aid in declarations in your home country. Forget about having your carpet salesman lie on the official Certificate of Origin, because the U.S. immigration police are prepared to consult their little carpet blue book if you try to slip through without paying up. Be aware that the authentic 16th-century porcelain soup tureen that you bought or those authentic ancient coins attached to your new necklace are either fake or unable to make the journey with you; it is illegal to take antiquities or anything of historical value out of the country. To enforce this, the Turkish government requires that anything dating to the end of the 19th century be authenticated by a museum official before its exportation can even be considered. It is also illegal to carry out tobacco seeds and plants, or hides, skins, or clothing made from wild animals. For items dating prior to the 20th century, permission plus a certificate of authenticity from a museum official is needed. Minerals require special documentation obtainable from the General Directorate of Mining Exploration and Research in Ankara (© 0312/287-3430; www.mta.gov.tr).

3 When to Go

After a decade of some ups and mostly downs, Turkey's tourism industry is galloping at a nice clip, thank you very much. Almost 10 international hotel chains opened properties in Istanbul in 2007 alone, and the Hilton group is planning 25 additional hotels in Turkey in the coming years. So basically, if you're looking for a quiet bargain, the window of opportunity has long since passed. For the inconvenience of traveling on full flights, staying in hotels booked to capacity and paying top dollar for almost everything (except where the dollar sign has changed to the euro or British pound sterling), visitors will be greeted by a country of intriguing contradictions positively overflowing with optimism for a more prosperous future.

Nevertheless, the seasonal ebbs and flows of tourism in Turkey follow some general patterns. The absolute best time to go is during the "shoulder season" months of April, May, mid- to late September, and October, when families with kids are on a school schedule, leaving the museum sites to smart travelers like you. Spring and fall are also better seasons weather-wise, when instead of the scorching summer months or the dismally gray and rainy winter ones, the sun is shining and the air is pleasantly balmy.

Istanbul has seen temperatures ranging from 18°C to 40°C (0°F–104°F), but it's unlikely that you'll encounter such extremes. Summer lasts roughly from mid-June to mid-September. The city sees a sloshy .7m (27 in.) of rain annually, mostly between October and March. In spite of the cold temperatures that sweep in from the Black Sea in winter, large accumulations of snowfall are a rarity, although light dustings do occur.

Average Daytime Temperature (°F/°C)

	Jan	Feb	Mar	Apr	May	June	July	Aug	Sept	Oct	Nov	Dec
Temp (°F)	41	43	45	54	61	70	73	73	68	61	54	46
Temp (°C)	5	6	7	12	16	21	23	23	20	16	12	8

ISTANBUL CALENDAR OF EVENTS

Islam follows the lunar calendar, which is shorter than the Gregorian calendar by 11 days. The result is that Muslim religious holidays fall on different dates each year. The dates for religious holidays listed here are accurate for 2008 and 2009.

For an exhaustive list of events beyond those listed here, check http://events.frommers.com, where you'll find a searchable, up-to-the-minute roster of what's happening in cities all over the world.

April

International Istanbul Film Festival, Istanbul. This festival lasts 2 weeks, from the last Saturday of March to mid-April, offering movie buffs the rare opportunity to view Turkish movies with English subtitles. For schedules and tickets, contact travel

Muslim Holy Month of Ramadan

One of the five obligations required by Islam is the observation of Ramadan (*Ramazan* in Turkish, but the former is more popularly used, even in Turkey), the Muslim holy month of fasting. For 1 full lunar month, Muslims are prohibited during daylight hours from eating, drinking, smoking, or succumbing to sexual thoughts or activity. Instead, they adapt to an altered schedule, rising before daylight for breakfast or *sahur,* the last meal they will have before sundown. The fast is broken at sundown with an early evening meal, or *iftar.* Because of the extended daylight hours in summertime, this 30-day marathon is particularly arduous, but even in the wintertime, the sleep deprivation, hunger, thirst, and nicotine withdrawal are an admirable display of determination.

Ramadan evenings include festivities and fun. In Istanbul the Hippodrome is transformed into a street fair lined with colorful booths selling dried fruits, kebaps, and sweets, and the lawn is carpeted with picnickers. While highly atmospheric, forget about moving freely around Sultanahmet while this circus is going on.

There are some small considerations for potential visitors in exchange for all of this cultural overload. Expect a slight alteration in the way people and places operate: Museums and holy sights will be crowded; restaurants that are normally open might be closed; shops that are normally closed might be open; menu items that are normally available might be unavailable due to the general lack in demand, and the traffic preceding the evening meal will slow you down considerably. Also potentially bothersome are the drummers who systematically wander the streets waking Muslims (and everybody else) for *sahur,* or the predawn meal. Oh. And no one will offer you tea.

The dates of Ramadan for 2008 are September 1 to October 1; in 2009 the dates are August 21 to September 20.

agencies in Istanbul or the festival itself (© **0212/334-0700;** www.iksv.org). Early April.

Tulip Festival, Istanbul. The tulip, widely accepted as having been exported to Holland and cultivated by appreciative Turkish 17th-century society, is celebrated annually in Istanbul. April.

National Sovereignty and Children's Day, Istanbul and Ankara. This day celebrates the anniversary of the first Grand National Assembly, which met in Ankara in 1920 and was later decreed by Atatürk as Children's Day. The day is marked by parades and processions by schoolchildren. Banks and public offices are closed. April 23.

May

Youth & Sports Day. Atatürk arrived in Samsun on this day in 1919, which signifies the beginning of the Independence War. Students nationwide participate in athletic games, gymnastic events, and parades. May 19.

Fatih Festivities, Istanbul. This festival commemorates the conquest of Byzantium in 1453 by Sultan Fatih Mehmet with local celebrations. May 29.

June

International Istanbul Music Festival. This world-class festival features big names in classical, opera, and ballet. Past artists have included La Scala Philharmonic, the Royal Concertgebouw Orchestra, the Tokyo String Quartet, Itzhak Perlman, Idil Biret, and Burhan Öçal. For schedules and tickets, contact the Istanbul Foundation for Culture & Arts (© **0212/ 293-3133;** www.iksv.org). Mid-June to mid-July.

Kırkpınar Oil Wrestling Tournaments, Edirne and in villages around the country. This revered national sport involves the fittest of Turkish youth and astonishing amounts of olive oil to prevent the opponent from getting a good grip. The event is usually accompanied by a colorful market and fair. Late June to early July.

July

International Jazz Festival, Istanbul. Performances are held at various locations around the city. For schedules, dates, and tickets, contact the Istanbul Foundation for Culture & Arts (© **0212/293-3133;** www.iksv.org).

Folklore and Music Festival, Bursa. One of Turkey's best folk-dancing events of the year, this festival features dance groups from around the country, lasts 1 week, and includes concerts and crafts displays. For more information and specific dates, contact the Bursa Foundation of Culture, Art and Tourism (© **0312/427-1853**) or the Bursa Tourism Information Office (© **0224/ 251-1834**).

August

Zafer Bayramı (Victory Day). This national holiday commemorates the decisive victory over the invading Greek armies during the War of Independence in 1922. Parades run through the main streets, and if you go soon, you may still brush elbows with some surviving vets. August 30.

September

International Istanbul Biennial. The Istanbul Foundation for Culture & Arts (www.iksv.org) puts on this major visual arts event organized around a current political or philosophical theme. Artists are selected from over 45 countries, whose innovative exhibitions are displayed around town, in clever venues such as 500-year-old warehouses, deconsecrated churches and synagogues, and even commuter ferries. September 12 to November 8, 2009.

Şeker Bayramı (or Ramadan Baramı). This is the 3-day celebration punctuating the end of Ramadan. Presents and sweets are given to the children (*şeker* means sugar in Turkish), and the Turkish Delight industry makes a killing. September 30 to October 3, 2008; September 19 to September 22, 2009.

October

Cumhuriyet Bayramı (Republic Day). This event celebrates the proclamation of the Republic of Turkey in 1923. Parades, public speeches, and fireworks displays are just a few of the organized events, but individual Turkish families do their own celebrating as well. October 29.

November

Anniversary of Atatürk's Death. Turkey comes to a grinding halt at exactly 9:05am, when the population pays its respects to the father and founder of the Republic. Rather than a moment of silence, the streets and waterways echo with the blare of car horns and foghorns. Atatürk-related activities are planned for the day, such as conferences, speeches, and exhibitions, in addition to a memorial concert at the Atatürk Cultural Center opera house. November 10.

December

Kurban Bayramı. In the Koranic version of an old favorite, it was Abraham's son Ismael, not Isaac, who was spared the knife. Kurban Bayramı celebrates Abraham's willingness to sacrifice his son, with 4 days of feasting and a death sentence to an alarming number of sheep, the likes of which one only sees around Thanksgiving. In fact, the 4-day festival of sacrifice is the culmination of the Hajj (holy pilgrimage), and much of the meat is given to the poor. December 7 to December 11, 2008; November 27 to December 1, 2009.

4 Getting There

BY PLANE

FROM THE UNITED STATES & CANADA Turkish Airlines (℡ 800/ 874-8875; www.turkishairlines.com), **American Airlines** (℡ 800/433-7300; www.aa.com), and **Delta Airlines** (℡ 800/221-1212; www.delta.com) offer the only direct nonstop service to Istanbul from the U.S. Turkish Airlines flies direct to Istanbul's Atatürk Airport (IST) from New York (JFK) and Chicago (ORD), with access to connecting flights from other U.S. cities on American Airlines. Meanwhile, Turkish Airlines announced that it would be instituting direct flights to Istanbul from Washington, D.C., in 2008, so keep your eyes open for this new service. Delta provides direct service from Atlanta (ATL) and New York (JFK). These airlines are just the tip of the iceberg; most major international airlines flying to Istanbul offer flights from U.S. cities much too numerous to inventory, either as part of their own network or in partnership with an American airline. Choosing one involves a change of planes in the airline's home country hub, but this slight inconvenience is often accompanied by cheaper, more comparable fares.

The following telephone numbers are for the U.S. and Canada. Log on to the airline websites for your local contact number. **Air France** (℡ 800/237-2747; www.airfrance.com), **Alitalia** (℡ 800/ 223-5730; www.alitalia.com), **Austrian Airlines** (℡ 800/843-0002; www.austrian air.com), **British Airways** (℡ 800/247-9297; www.british-airways.com), **Continental** (℡ 800/231-0856; www.continental.com), **Iberia** (℡ 800/574-8742; www.iberia.com), **KLM/Northwest** (℡ 800/255-2525; www.nwa.com), **Lufthansa** (℡ 800/645-3880; www.luftansa.com), **Swiss International** (℡ 877/359-7947; www.swiss.com), **United** (℡ 800/UNITED; www.united.com), and **US Airways** (℡ 800/428-4322; www.usairways.com) all provide service to Istanbul, usually with a stop at their hub in their home country. In addition, Lufthansa flies to Ankara (ANK) and Antalya (AYT), and Austrian Airlines flies to Ankara (ANK). More often than not, Turkish Airlines will provide the connecting flights to other Turkish destinations.

There are currently no direct flights to Turkey from Canada, but negotiations are on for Turkish Airlines to establish direct service, so keep your eyes open for this development. For now, **Air France, Alitalia, British Airways, Delta, KLM/ Northwest,** and **Lufthansa** all provide connecting service out of Toronto (YYZ). From Montreal (YUL), flights are available on **Air France, Alitalia, British Airways, Delta, Iberia, Northwest,** and **Lufthansa.** Vancouver (YVR) is serviced by **British Airways, KLM/Northwest** (via Seattle), and **Lufthansa.**

FROM THE UNITED KINGDOM The only nonstop service to Istanbul out of London is provided by **British Airways** (© 0845/77-333-77) and **Turkish Airlines** (© 20/7766-9300), which also flies nonstop from Manchester (© 161/489-5287). **Air France** (© 0845/082-0162), **Alitalia** (© 0870/544-8259), **Austrian Airlines** (© 0845/601-0948), **KLM/Northwest** (© 08705/074-074), **Lufthansa** (© 0845/7737-747), and **Olympic** (© 8706/060-460; www.olympicairlines. com) offer connecting service through their home port, providing service from many other major cities in the U.K. as well.

There are also charter airline options. **Onur Air**, Şenlikkoy Mah. Çatal Sok. 3, Florya (© **0212/663-9176;** www.onur air.com.tr), offers service from several U.K. cities into Dalaman (DLM), Bodrum (BJV), Izmir (ADB), and Antalya (AYT) via Istanbul; and from various cities throughout Europe. **SunExpress** (© **0232/444-0797;** www.sunexpress. com.tr) flies twice-weekly from London's Stansted Airport to Izmir in summer only. **British Airways** (© **0870/850-9850** in the U.K.) flies direct from Gatwick to Izmir 4 days a week.

FROM AUSTRALIA & NEW ZEALAND There are few choices for connecting flights to Turkey. In partnership with Turkish Airlines, **Qantas** (© 13-13-13 in Australia, or 64-9/357-8900 in Auckland; www.qantas.com) will get you from Sydney, Auckland, and Brisbane, connecting you to a Turkish Airlines flight into Istanbul. **Olympic Airways** (© 612/9251-2044 in Australia; www.olympicairlines.com) has overnight flights from Sydney and Melbourne via Athens. Other flights from Sydney are offered on **British Airways** (© 1300/767-177 in Australia, or 0800/274-847 in Auckland), **Singapore Airlines** (© 612/9350-0100;   www.singaporeair.com), **KLM/Northwest** (© 008/221-714), and **Lufthansa** (© 1300/655-727). From New Zealand, Singapore Airlines flies out of Auckland and New Plymouth; from

Australia, British Airways flies out of Brisbane and Melbourne; and Lufthansa services Brisbane.

FLYING FOR LESS: TIPS FOR GETTING THE BEST AIRFARE

Consolidators, also known as bucket shops, are wholesale brokers in the airline-ticket game. Consolidators buy deeply discounted tickets ("distressed" inventories of unsold seats) from airlines and sell them to online ticket agencies, travel agents, tour operators, corporations, and, to a lesser degree, the general public. Consolidators advertise in Sunday newspaper travel sections (often in small ads with tiny type), both in the U.S. and the U.K. They can be great sources for cheap international tickets. On the downside, bucket shop tickets are often rigged with restrictions, such as stiff cancellation penalties (as high as 50%–75% of the ticket price). And keep in mind that most of what you see advertised is of limited availability. The ones specializing in travel from the U.S. to Turkey are **Club America** (© 212/972-2865); **Picasso Travel** (© 800/742-2776; www.picasso travel.com); and **Tursan Travel** (© 800/875-0075; www.tursantravel.com).

Air Tickets Direct (© 800/778-3447; www.airticketsdirect.com) is based in Montreal and leverages the Canadian dollar for low fares; they also book trips to places that U.S. travel agents won't touch, such as Cuba. **Skyscanner** flight search (www.skyscanner.net) is another one of those new and indispensable tools for searching for competitive fares for airline service all over the globe. It even searches charter airlines.

Visitors arriving via London, Bologna, Vienna, Amsterdam, and Milan now have the option of flying one of a number of budget airlines into Istanbul's **Sabiha Gökcen Airport** (SAW; © 0216/585-5000; www.sgairport.com), about 40km (25 miles) from the center of Istanbul. At the time of this writing, these included **Pegasus** (© 0216/588-0160, international sales agent in Istanbul; www.flypgs.com) from London, Bologna, and Vienna; **Easyjet** (no phone; www.easyjet.com) from London (Luton Airport); **Condor** (© 800/364-1667 in the U.S. and Canada; www.condor.com) from Amsterdam; and **Myair** (© 207/365-1597 in the U.K.; www.myair.com) from Milan.

ARRIVING AT THE AIRPORT

Before 2001, flights into and out of Istanbul's Atatürk Airport operated out of a dingy old terminal. This old terminal is now the domestic terminal, and a new contiguous, state-of-the-art international terminal makes deplaning, passing through Customs, and heading into the city as effortless as can be expected in a transport hub that welcomed 6.5 million visitors in 2007.

There are two main bonuses of arriving at this airport. First, although an entry visa is required by most of us, obtaining one is as simple as stepping up to the visa window located adjacent to the passport control area. The second is that the airport is but a 10- to 20-minute ride into town, depending on what type of transport you've arranged and your ultimate destination.

GETTING INTO TOWN FROM THE AIRPORT

At the time of this writing, most hotels were competing for your business by offering additional services—such as free pickup at the airport. Check with your hotel to see if yours is one of them.

Because taxi fares into both the Old City and Taksim are still very affordable, I recommend this door-to-door option first over the alternatives suggested below. A taxi into Sultanahmet from Atatürk Airport should cost around 16YTL ($14/£6) and a ride into Taksim around 25YTL ($22/£9.50), depending on traffic and whether or not you go the scenic route.

By Bus: If your destination is around Taksim, there is the reliable and convenient **Havaş shuttle bus** (© 0212/444-0487 toll-free), departing every 30 minutes from just outside the airport exit (9YTL/$7.85/£3.40; trip time 40 min.). You could also take the cheaper and rarer green municipal **bus no. 97** (1.30YTL/$1.15/50p), but because Havaş is so convenient and reliable, the public bus is not an option I recommend.

It's unlikely that guests heading to the deluxe hotels along the Bosphorus will be taking public transportation into town. Nevertheless, Havaş also runs a shuttle from Atatürk Airport to the entrance of Akmerkez at Etiler (10YTL/$8.70/£3.80; trip time 45 min.), where taxis are regularly awaiting passengers.

By Metro/Tramway: If you're on a budget and feeling like going the whole nine yards of independent travel, take advantage of the newly completed train connection between the airport (entrance is downstairs next to the international arrivals terminal; 1.30YTL/$1.15/50p) and the Old City all the way up to Kabataş and Taksim. This service connects the airport to Zeytinburnu, where you will need to transfer aboveground to the tramway into the historic part of the city (stops include Beyazit, Cağağoğlu, Sultanahmet, Gülhane, Sirkeci, Eminönü). The tramway continues all the way to Kabataş, with stops at Karaköy, Tophane, and Findikli; from the last stop, there's a brand-new funicular transporting passengers up one of Istanbul's steeper hills to Taksim. The whole trip costs 1.30YTL ($1.15/50p) if you use the Akbil; otherwise it'll be 1.30YTL ($1.15/50p) per transfer. The trip will take a little over an hour. Remember though, you'll be hot, tired, hungry, and luggage laden for this convoluted, albeit convenient, journey.

For more information on taking and paying for public transportation, turn to p. 48.

BY TRAIN

Direct trains from Europe depart daily from Bucharest and Budapest and take about 27 and 40 hours, respectively—and that's without any border delays. It is your responsibility to obtain visas where required (either transit or tourist, depending on your travel plans) for every border that you will cross. If you're coming from Greece, trains leave regularly for Alexandropolis, where you must go through Customs. You can catch a bus to Istanbul from the Alexandropolis train station. Depending on how long you get hung up at the border, it can take anywhere from 6 to 8 hours to get to Istanbul. Visas are readily available at the border crossing.

Of course, the **Orient Express** is still an option (© **800/524-2420** in the U.S. and Canada, 0845/077-2222 in the U.K., 1-800/000-395 in Australia, and 00-800/8392-3500 in New Zealand; www.orient-express.com). Departing from Paris once a year in late summer (Aug. 29, 2008) and passing through Zurich, Innsbruck, Vienna, Budapest, and Bucharest, the journey takes 6 days/5 nights and costs a meager $8,350 (£4,175).

Sirkeci Station (© **0212/527-0050**) has been serving train passengers arriving (and departing) Istanbul from European cities for well over a century and has served as a model for railway stations throughout central Europe. A tram stop is immediately outside the station entrance, but don't rely on this if you're first arriving, as there is no ticket kiosk at this stop.

BY CAR

With global warming issues and petrol prices in the stratosphere, driving to Turkey makes bad sense. But some people just insist on the comfort of their own vehicle, so be prepared for the red tape of sorting out multiple transit visas and at least 4 days of hard driving. There are two traditional routes to take: The "northern" one through Belgium, Germany, Austria, Hungary, Romania, and Bulgaria. Or the "southern" one through Belgium, Germany, Austria, and Italy with a car ferry connection to Turkey. Drivers planning to stay longer than 3 months must have an **International Driving Permit (IDP),** which also comes in handy in out-of-the-way places where the local police can't decipher your national version. You'll also be required to provide proof of third-party insurance at the Turkish border.

5 Money & Costs

CURRENCY

On January 1, 2005, the Turkish Central Bank lopped six zeros off a currency that saw phenomenal inflation in the previous decade or so, making the handling of Turkish money even easier. But those were the old days. With a national economic growth rate rivaling that of China's, Turkey's economy is stronger than it's ever been. Meanwhile, those millionaire bank notes of yesteryear have been replaced with the **New Turkish Lira** (*yeni turk lirası* or YTL).

Bank notes come in denominations of 1, 5, 10, 20, 50, and 100YTL, while coins, called the New Kuruş (Ykr), come in 1, 5, 10, 25, and 50 kuruş pieces. There is also a 1YTL coin. As of this writing, 1YTL cost about 38p, while the U.S. dollar had plummeted from $1 = 1.35YTL (where it hovered for the previous editions of *Frommer's Turkey*) to 87¢ = 1YTL. Prices quoted in this book are based on these rates of exchange. Because there is no consistency to which currency prices are quoted in Turkey (£, YTL, euro, US$), the currency in which the original fees were quoted appear first

What Things Cost in Istanbul	U.S.$	U.K.£	YTL
Just because you're in Istanbul, don't assume that you will pay for everything in YTL. You'll find that many hotels, restaurants, cultural programs, and even the salesmen in the Grand Bazaar all name prices in (and accept) US$, euros, and YTL.			
Daytime taxi from airport to Sultanahmet	13.92	6.08	16.00
Nighttime taxi from airport to Sultanahmet	20.88	9.12	24.00
Havaş bus from airport to town	7.83	3.42	9.00
Double at Çırağan Palace with sea view	765.00–1,015.00	382.50–507.50	
Double at the Apricot Hotel	83.00–111.00	42.00–56.00	59.00€–79.00€
Dinner for one at the Four Seasons	43.50	19.00	50.00
Dinner for one at a *köftecisi* around town	13.05	5.70	15.00
Bosphorus cruise (round-trip) on public ferry	10.88	4.75	12.50
Bosphorus cruise with tour group	26.10	11.40	30.00
Ticket on bus, tram, or metro	1.13	0.49	1.30
Admission to Topkapı Palace and all exhibits	26.10	11.40	30.00
Taxi from Sultanahmet to Taksim	8.70	3.80	10.00
Glass of tea at Meşale tea gardens	1.74	0.76	2.00
One 9×12 wool-on-wool carpet	As much as you are willing to spend in your preferred currency		

in the listings, followed by the conversion into £ and/or US$. In cases where our conversions don't add up, it's because prices were quoted in multiple currencies at the time of research. Oh, and we also round off (to the nickel/5 pence for amounts under 10 and by the dollar or pound for amounts over 10). *Note:* Where applicable, the dollar or pound is exchanged to the euro in this book based on a rate of $1.40 = 1€ and £1 = 1.40€.

Until about 2 years ago, local prices were frequently quoted in U.S. dollars. But the weakness in the dollar has prompted a shift to the euro, which has resulted, for Americans at least, in a remarkable loss of value. Hotel rooms previously costing $80 per night now cost 80€, or $112, with no commensurate upgrade in services.

Although I have tried to be as accurate as possible in quoting prices in this book, please be aware that a number of things are working against me. Obviously, the fluctuation of exchange rates plays an enormous role. But equally capricious is the erratic nature of on-the-spot price quotes and market demand. Recent shocks in petroleum prices have also resulted in titanic increases in the cost of transportation in Turkey. Finally, don't be surprised if prices change in the time between when I research and write this book and when you read it.

For the most up-to-date currency conversions, check **www.xe.com/ucc** before departing.

ATMS

For years, the easiest way to get money away from home was to head to the friendly neighborhood ATM. Unfortunately, a recent innovation by U.S.-based banks has been to charge a commission of up to 5% on withdrawals *in addition to the per transaction fee of $3.* On principle, I'll probably just carry around cash, but for those of you willing to succumb to endless, creative bank fees, all cities and major tourist destinations in Turkey have bank machines on the Cirrus (© **800/424-7787;** www.mastercard.com) and PLUS (© **800/843-7587;** www.visa.com) networks. Look on the back of your card to make sure your credit card is on these networks. ATMs are plentiful and tend to be clustered together around town, including in the arrivals terminal of Istanbul Atatürk Airport, around Taksim Square, and between the Ayasofya and the Blue Mosque.

Among the most reliable of the local banks are **Akbank, Türk Iş Bankası, Garanti Bankası, Yapı Kredi Bankası,** and **Ziraat Bankası.** Ask your bank before leaving whether you need a new personal identification number (PIN), as most ATMs in Turkey accept numbered passwords only, and some limit their input to four digits. Also, be aware that the ATMs are often fickle or empty, so always carry around alternatives in the form of cash or traveler's checks for emergencies.

TRAVELER'S CHECKS

In Turkey, as in many other European countries, local merchants are loathe to accept traveler's checks, as banks charge large fees to cash them out. Banks tend to charge high commissions or hide the commission in higher rates, as do the exchange offices around town. Hotels are most amenable to exchanging your traveler's checks, but hotel exchange rates are notoriously unfavorable. The post office will probably be your best bet for exchanging them for cash.

You can buy traveler's checks at most banks. Most are offered in denominations of $20, $50, $100, $500, and sometimes $1,000. Generally, you'll pay a service charge ranging from 1% to 4%.

The most popular traveler's checks are offered by **American Express** (© **800/807-6233** or 800/221-7282 for cardholders—this number accepts collect calls, offers service in several foreign languages, and exempts Amex gold and platinum cardholders from the 1% fee); **Visa** (© **800/732-1322**)—AAA members can obtain Visa checks for a $9.95 fee (for checks up to $1,500) at most AAA offices or by calling © **866/339-3378;** and **MasterCard** (© **800/223-9920**).

Be sure to keep a copy of the traveler's checks serial numbers separate from your checks in the event that they are stolen or lost. You'll get a refund faster if you know the numbers.

CREDIT CARDS

Private bank accounts are not the only method where banks have been creative with mining additional fees. Purchases on credit card accounts are now also subject to a percentage fee, usually around 5%. In an annoying twist, these very same credit cards offer some of the most competitive exchange rates. It's up to you to do the math, though. Nevertheless, it's highly recommended that you travel with at least one major credit card. You must have a credit card to rent a car, and hotels and airlines usually require a credit card imprint as a deposit against expenses.

ATM cards with major credit card backing, known as **"debit cards,"** are also a commonly acceptable form of payment in most establishments.

EXCHANGE BUREAUS

Because of the bank fees associated with withdrawing cash abroad, you may want to carry your own currency with you to Istanbul and exchange it there. Turkish currency exchange offices are called *dövis* and, like anywhere in the world, offer variable and not-so-competitive rates of exchange. I tend to use the *döviz* located in Sultanahmet on Divanyolu near the tramway stop, or one of the several located along Istiklal Caddesi near Taksim Square. There are also currency exchange windows in the airport arrivals terminal.

6 Travel Insurance

The cost of travel insurance varies widely, depending on the cost and length of your trip, your age and health, and the type of trip you're taking, but expect to pay between 5% and 8% of the vacation itself. You can get estimates from various providers through **InsureMyTrip.com**. Enter your trip cost and dates, your age, and other information, for prices from more than a dozen companies.

U.K. citizens and their families who make more than one trip abroad per year may find an annual travel insurance policy works out cheaper. Check **www.money supermarket.com**, which compares prices across a wide range of providers for single- and multitrip policies.

Most big travel agents offer their own insurance and will probably try to sell you their package when you book a holiday. Think before you sign. **Britain's Consumers' Association** recommends that you insist on seeing the policy and reading the fine print before buying travel insurance. **The Association of British Insurers** (© 020/7600-3333; www.abi.org.uk) gives advice by phone and publishes Holiday Insurance, a free guide to policy provisions and prices. You might also shop around for better deals: Try **Columbus Direct** (© 0870/033-9988; www.columbusdirect.net).

Before you do all this, check your existing insurance policies and credit card coverage. You may already be covered for lost luggage, canceled tickets, or medical expenses.

TRIP-CANCELLATION INSURANCE

Trip-cancellation insurance helps you get your money back if you have to back out of a trip, if you have to go home early, or if your travel supplier goes bankrupt. Allowed reasons for cancellation can range from sickness to natural disasters to the State Department declaring your destination unsafe for travel. (Insurers usually won't cover vague fears, though, as many travelers discovered who tried to cancel their trips in Oct 2001 because they were wary of flying.) In this unstable world, trip-cancellation insurance is a good buy if you're getting tickets well in advance—who knows what the state of the world, or of your airline, will be in 9 months? Insurance policy details vary, so read the fine print—and especially make sure that your airline or cruise line is on the list of carriers covered in case of bankruptcy. For more information, contact one of the following recommended insurers: **Access America** (© 866/807-3982; www.accessamerica.com); **Travel Guard International** (© 800/826-4919; www.travelguard.com); **Travel Insured International** (© 800/243-3174; www.travel insured.com); and **Travelex Insurance Services** (© 888/457-4602; www.travelex-insurance.com).

MEDICAL INSURANCE

For travel overseas, most U.S. health plans (including Medicare and Medicaid) do not provide coverage, and the ones that do often require you to pay for services upfront and reimburse you only after you return home.

As a safety net, you may want to buy travel medical insurance, particularly if you're traveling to a remote or high-risk area where emergency evacuation might be necessary. If you require additional medical insurance, try **MEDEX Assistance**

(© 410/453-6300; www.medexassist. com) or **Travel Assistance International** (© 800/821-2828; www.travelassistance. com; for general information on services, call the company's **Worldwide Assistance Services, Inc.,** at © 800/777-8710).

Canadians should check with their provincial health plan offices or call **Health Canada** (© 866/225-0709; www. hc-sc.gc.ca) to find out the extent of their coverage and what documentation and receipts they must take home in case they are treated overseas.

Travelers from the U.K. should carry their European Health Insurance Card (EHIC), which replaced the E111 form as proof of entitlement to free or reduced cost medical treatment abroad (© 0845/ 606-2030; www.ehic.org.uk). Note, however, that the EHIC only covers "necessary medical treatment," and for repatriation costs, lost money, baggage, or cancellation, travel insurance from a reputable company should always be sought (www.travelinsuranceweb.com).

CAR-RENTAL INSURANCE

If you hold a private auto insurance policy, this does not necessarily mean that you are covered abroad for loss or damage to the car, or liability in case a passenger is injured. Meanwhile, car-rental insurance probably does not cover liability if you caused the accident. Check your own auto insurance policy, the rental company policy, and your credit card coverage for the extent of coverage: Is your destination covered? Are other drivers covered? How much liability is covered if a passenger is injured? (If you rely on your credit card for coverage, you may want to bring a second credit card with you, as damages may be charged to your card and you may find yourself stranded with no money.)

If you do opt for the car-rental insurance, plan on spending around about $20 or £10 a day.

7 Health

STAYING HEALTHY

There are no severe health risks in travel to Turkey, nor are vaccinations required. **Food poisoning and diarrhea** are probably the most prevalent illnesses associated with travel to Turkey. Although water from the tap is chlorinated and generally safe to drink, even the locals drink bottled water. Avoid nonpasteurized dairy products and shellfish during the hot summer months, and maintain a healthy suspicion of street vendors. In the event that you become ill, drink plenty of (bottled) water and remember that diarrhea usually dissipates on its own. Pepto Bismol (bismuth subsalicylate) can often prevent symptoms, but if the problem becomes truly inconvenient, pharmacists are generally sympathetic and bilingual, and will be able to provide an effective remedy. (**Ercefuryl** works wonders.)

Although the persistence and tenaciousness of Turkish **mosquitoes** might cause you to suffer, it is unlikely that malaria will. Keep in mind that you're more likely to catch deadly mosquito-borne diseases in your own backyard than abroad. If you are experiencing symptoms, seek prompt medical attention while traveling as well as for up to 3 years after your return. Don't forget to pack a proven insect repellent (especially for those nights lounging outdoors in a tea garden or spent on the rooftops of Istanbul).

Rabies is endemic in parts of Turkey, and joggers have been known to be bitten by infected strays. But this is extremely rare. Best to stay away from animals altogether, advice that, given the sweet temperaments of the street dogs and cats, I myself am incapable of following. If you're concerned, consult your doctor for pre-exposure immunization.

WHAT TO DO IF YOU GET SICK AWAY FROM HOME

Any local consulate can provide a list of area doctors who speak English. If you do get sick, you may want to ask the concierge at your hotel to recommend a local doctor, even his or her own. This will probably yield a better recommendation than any information number would. Local doctors advertise their services through discreet signs near their offices, and most speak English. If you can't find a doctor who can help you right away, try the **emergency room** of one of the private hospitals under "Fast Facts: Istanbul," p. 54.

If you suffer from a chronic illness, consult your doctor before your departure. Pack **prescription medications** in your carry-on luggage, and carry them in their original containers, with pharmacy labels—otherwise they won't make it through airport security.

8 The Safe Traveler

Newbie Western travelers to Turkey are often plagued by worries over safety: It is a Muslim country, after all, and there is a war going on nearby, right? Well, no actually. Yes, Turkey's population is mostly Muslim, but I don't need to remind you that all Muslims aren't terrorists, do I? Tsk tsk, if I do. Indeed, I guarantee that one of the first impressions that will overwhelm you upon arriving in Turkey is its complete and utter normalcy.

Second, there's a war going on, right? Sure, but it's 1,600km (1,000 miles) away as the crow flies. And as we've all so regrettably learned, distance doesn't contain conflict, and the violence in Iraq menaces us all just as much in London, Toronto, New York as it does in Istanbul.

Okay, but what about the PKK? Sigh. Radicals committed to violence (in this case, right-wing Kurdish nationalists) are attacking Turkish soldiers in the southeast of the country. Infrequently, the violence erupts beyond these borders. In my opinion, such an attack targeting foreign tourists would be a strategic mistake; still, it might be a good idea to check in with your appropriate travel advisories. In the U.S., log onto **http://travel.state.gov/travel**; in the U.K.: **www.fco.gov.uk**; in Canada: **www.voyage.gc.ca**; in Australia: **www.smartraveller.gov.au**; in New Zealand: **safetravel.govt.nz**.

For particular concerns for single female travelers, see the box "Important Tips for Women Travelers," below.

9 Specialized Travel Resources

TRAVELERS WITH DISABILITIES

Although ramps have begun to appear in select Turkish hotels and museums, don't expect seamless access. However, Turkish hospitality being what it is, it'll be the odd tour guide or group leader who won't bend over backward to accommodate your individual needs.

GAY & LESBIAN TRAVELERS

The fact that homosexuality is legal in Turkey is an interesting result of centuries of segregation of the sexes, veneration of female virtue, and lazy afternoons spent in the *hamam* (Turkish bath). Nevertheless, we're talking about a fairly conservative culture, so discretion is advisable, even if Turkish men are into more public displays of affection with each other than with their wives.

The International Gay and Lesbian Travel Association (IGLTA; ✆ **800/448-8550** or 954/776-2626; www.iglta.org) is the trade association for the gay and lesbian travel industry, and offers an

Bait and Switch   It's hard to believe, but in the major tourist areas of Turkey, particularly in the streets of Sultanahmet, an entire industry thrives on the acquisition and manipulation of emotions for economic gain. Foreign women, receptive, even eager for new and exotic experiences, are just ripe for the picking. Although less than attractive ones are particularly vulnerable, any single girl with cash in the bank and foreign nationality is a target.

Sultanahmet is filled with professional "gigolos" practiced in the art of courtship and persuasion. The better ones come armed with scripts; the statements "You foreigners don't know how to trust anyone!" and "You foreigners think that we (Turks) are all thieves and barbarians" effectively disarm even the most remotely liberal.

Inevitably the topic of how bad things are economically will be carefully broached: how he can't pay his bills, how worried he is over his debts, and how any moment the authorities will repossess his furniture. Some invent elaborate stories of woe and before you know it, the woman is offering, no—insisting, that he accept her help.

Some seducers even take this kind of behavior to its limits by pursuing the game as far as the wedding contract. But the most deplorable of the lot have been known to forge the marriage certificate with the assistance of those in the neighborhood even less scrupulous than themselves.

But this kind of behavior doesn't represent all of Turkey, and overall women traveling alone in Turkey are treated with an almost exaggerated courtesy. In some cases, a woman will be in a better position to experience the openness of the Turkish people than if traveling en masse. With all of this warmth and hospitality, it's difficult to know how to temper one's instincts toward friendliness without affirming the general opinion among the more conservative class of Turks that all Western women are prostitutes. Even an innocent greeting or seemingly harmless camaraderie can be misinterpreted, so it's important to find a balance between polite formality and the openness that North American, European, and Australian women find so normal.

Dining   Practically speaking, no matter how modern the country may seem on the surface, don't be surprised if you're the only female in a restaurant. Eateries often have an *aile salonu* (family salon), an unintimidating dining area provided for men, women, couples, and anyone else not wishing to dine among groups of smoking, drinking, mustached Turks.

online directory of gay- and lesbian-friendly travel businesses and tour operators.

Gay.com Travel (© **800/929-2268** or 415/644-8044; www.gay.com/travel or www.outandabout.com), is an excellent online successor to the popular *Out &*

About print magazine. It provides regularly updated information about gay-owned, gay-oriented, and gay-friendly lodging, dining, sightseeing, nightlife, and shopping establishments in every important destination worldwide. British travelers should click on the "Travel" link at **www.uk.gay.com** for advice and gay-friendly trip ideas.

The Canadian website **GayTraveler** (**www.gaytraveler.ca**) offers ideas and advice for gay travel all over the world.

The following travel guides are available at many bookstores, or you can order them from any online bookseller: *Spartacus International Gay Guide, 35th Edition* (Bruno Gmünder Verlag; www.spartacusworld.com/gayguide), *Odysseus: The International Gay Travel Planner, 17th Edition* (www.odyusa.com); and the *Damron* guides (www.damron.com), with separate, annual books for gay men and lesbians.

SENIOR TRAVEL

Always mention the fact that you're a senior when you first make your travel reservations. For example, many hotels offer seniors' discounts. Don't be shy about asking for discounts, but always carry some kind of identification, such as a driver's license, that shows your date of birth.

Members of **AARP,** 601 E St. NW, Washington, DC 20049 (*©* **888/687-2277;** www.aarp.org), get discounts on hotels, airfares, and car rentals. AARP offers members a wide range of benefits, including *AARP: The Magazine* and a monthly newsletter. Anyone over 50 can join.

Many reliable agencies and organizations target the 50-plus market. **Elderhostel** (*©* **800/454-5768;** www.elderhostel.org) arranges worldwide study programs for those aged 55 and over. **ElderTreks** (*©* **800/741-7956** or 416/558-5000 outside North America; www.eldertreks.com) offers small-group tours to off-the-beaten-path or adventure-travel locations, restricted to travelers 50 and older.

Recommended publications offering travel resources and discounts for seniors include the quarterly magazine *Travel 50 & Beyond* (www.travel50andbeyond.com) and the best-selling paperback *Unbelievably Good Deals and Great Adventures That You Absolutely Can't Get Unless You're Over 50 2005–2006, 16th Edition* (McGraw-Hill), by Joann Rattner Heilman.

10 Sustainable Tourism

One of the things that continually amaze me about Turkey is its ability to leapfrog over many of the challenges that traditionally, the "West" has had to grapple with. Turkey seems to be a caldron of budding (and more recently, established) entrepreneurship, and all things organic, natural, vegetarian, healthy, and environmentally sound are no exception. But as elsewhere, achieving these things is still a struggle. So what to expect?

Expect levels of pollution commensurate with any major international metropolis. Many of Turkey's vehicles still run on diesel fuel, although *kürsünsüz* (unleaded) is also pervasive. The newer green city buses are also considered *ekolojik.*

Expect fresh fruits and vegetables that taste like fruits and vegetables. To palettes dulled by hardy, homogenized, and flavorless fresh produce, even the produce grown using chemicals tastes better than what we're used to. Still the trend toward organic produce has begun, and Istanbul now boasts two organic outdoor markets, one in Şişli and one up along the Bosphorus (two noticeably higher income areas).

As far as energy goes, the cost of petrol in Turkey is sky high, costing upwards of $100 (£50) to fill the tank of a compact Honda. Natural gas is a bit cheaper. Turkey does customarily use solar energy mainly as a way to provide hot water. But solar panels are more of a provincial thing, the drawback being limited hours where hot water is available. Istanbullus are less and less likely to tolerate anything but "24-hour hot water"—a sign that was a prevalent hotel marketing tool a mere 8 years ago, but that has since gone by the wayside as a relic of less modern times.

Each time you take a flight or drive a car CO_2 is released into the atmosphere. You can help neutralize this danger to our planet through "carbon offsetting"—paying someone to reduce your CO_2 emissions by the same amount you've added. Carbon offsets can be purchased in the U.S. from companies such as **Carbon fund.org** (www.carbonfund.org) and **TerraPass** (www.terrapass.org), and from **Climate Care** (www.climatecare.org) in the U.K.

Although one could argue that any vacation that includes an airplane flight can't be truly "green," you can go on holiday and still contribute positively to the environment. You can offset carbon emissions from your flight in other ways.

Choose forward-looking companies that embrace responsible development practices, helping preserve destinations for the future by working alongside local people. An increasing number of sustainable tourism initiatives can help you plan a family trip and leave as small a "footprint" as possible on the places you visit.

Responsible Travel (www.responsible travel.com) contains a great source of sustainable travel ideas run by a spokesperson for responsible tourism in the travel industry. **Sustainable Travel International** (www.sustainabletravelinternational.org) promotes responsible tourism practices and issues an annual Green Gear & Gift Guide.

You can find eco-friendly travel tips, statistics, and touring companies and associations—listed by destination under "Travel Choice"—at the TIES website, www.eco tourism.org. Also check out **Conservation International** (www.conservation.org)— which, with *National Geographic Traveler,* annually presents awards to those travel tour operators, businesses, organizations, and places that have made a significant contribution to sustainable tourism. **Eco-travel.com** is part online magazine and part ecodirectory that lets you search for touring companies in several categories (water-based, land-based, spiritually oriented, and so on).

In the U.K., **Tourism Concern** (www.tourismconcern.org.uk) works to reduce social and environmental problems connected to tourism and find ways of improving tourism so that local benefits are increased.

The **Association of British Travel Agents** (ABTA; www.abtamembers.org/responsibletourism) acts as a focal point for the U.K. travel industry and is one of the leading groups spearheading responsible tourism.

The **Association of Independent Tour Operators** (AITO; www.aito.co.uk) is a group of interesting specialist operators leading the field in making holidays sustainable.

11 Staying Connected

TELEPHONES
To call Istanbul from abroad:
1. Dial the international access code: 011 from the U.S.; 00 from the U.K., Ireland, or New Zealand; or 0011 from Australia.
2. Dial the country code: 90.
3. Dial the city code **212** for the European side and **216** for the Asian side and then the number. If the number you are trying to dial is a mobile number (beginning instead with 555, 542, or 532 and their derivatives), then use this number instead of the city code.

To make international calls from Istanbul: First dial 00 and then the country code (U.S. or Canada 1, U.K. 44, Ireland 353, Australia 61, New Zealand 64). Next you dial the area code and number. For example, if you wanted to call the British Embassy in Washington, D.C., you would dial 00-1-202-588-7800.

To make local calls while in town: In order to call the Asian side from the European side, you must dial 0216 and then the number. From the Asian side, you do not add a 0 when calling the European side. For calls to the same side, dial the city code, but not the 0.

For directory assistance: Dial ℂ **115** (in Turkish) if you're looking for a number inside Istanbul. Unfortunately, there is no international directory.

For operator assistance: If you need operator assistance in making a call, dial ℂ **115** if you're trying to make an international call and ℂ **131** (in Turkish) if you want to call a number in Turkey.

Toll-free numbers: Numbers beginning with 0800 within Turkey are toll free, but calling a 1-800 number in the States from Turkey is not toll free. In fact, it costs the same as an overseas call.

National numbers: More and more prevalent is the local 444 number (no area code). These numbers connect you to service call centers for national businesses for the cost of a local call.

CELLPHONES
The three letters that define much of the world's wireless capabilities are **GSM** (Global System for Mobile Communications), a big, seamless network that makes for easy cross-border cellphone use throughout Europe and dozens of other countries worldwide. In the U.S., T-Mobile and AT&T use this quasi-universal system; in Canada, Microcell and some Rogers customers are GSM, and all Europeans and most Australians use GSM. GSM phones function with a removable plastic SIM card, encoded with your phone number and account

information. If your cellphone is on a GSM system, and you have a world-capable multiband phone such as many Sony Ericsson, Motorola, or Samsung models, you can make and receive calls across developed areas around much of the globe. Just call your wireless operator and ask for "international roaming" to be activated on your account. Unfortunately, per-minute charges can be high—usually $1 to $1.50 in western Europe and up to $5 in places such as Russia and Indonesia.

VOICE OVER INTERNET PROTOCOL (VOIP)
If you have Web access while traveling, you might consider a broadband-based telephone service (in technical terms, **Voice over Internet protocol,** or **VoIP**) such as Skype (www.skype.com) or Vonage (www.vonage.com), which allows you to make free international calls if you use their services from your laptop or in a cybercafe. Check the sites for details on restrictions.

INTERNET/E-MAIL
WITHOUT YOUR OWN COMPUTER
To find cybercafes in your destination, check **www.cybercaptive.com** and **www.**

cybercafe.com. Internet cafes are generally bunched around Taksim Square, on the upper floors of the side streets perpendicular to Istiklal Caddesi, and more sparsely, now that all hotels provide Internet access as a rule in Sultanahmet.

Most major airports have **Internet kiosks** that provide basic Web access for a per-minute fee that's usually higher than cybercafe prices.

WITH YOUR OWN COMPUTER
More and more hotels, resorts, airports, cafes, and retailers are going **Wi-Fi** (wireless fidelity), becoming "hot spots" that offer free high-speed Wi-Fi access or charge a small fee for usage. Most laptops sold today have built-in wireless capability. To find public Wi-Fi hot spots at your destination, go to **www.jiwire.com**; its Hotspot Finder holds the world's largest directory of public wireless hot spots.

For dialup access, most business-class hotels throughout the world offer dataports for laptop modems, and a few thousand hotels in Europe now offer free high-speed Internet access.

Wherever you go, bring a **connection kit** of the right power and phone adapters, a spare phone cord, and a spare Ethernet network cable—or find out whether your hotel supplies them to guests.

12 Packages for the Independent Traveler

Package tours are simply a way to buy the airfare, accommodations, and other elements of your trip (such as car rentals, airport transfers, and sometimes even activities) at the same time and often at discounted prices.

One good source of package deals is the airlines themselves. Most major airlines offer air/land packages, including **American Airlines Vacations** (© 800/321-2121; www.aavacations.com), **Delta Vacations** (© 800/654-6559; www.delta vacations.com), **Continental Airlines**

Vacations (© 800/301-3800; www. covacations.com), and **United Vacations** (© 888/854-3899; www.unitedvacations. com). Several big **online travel agencies**—Expedia, Travelocity, Orbitz, Site59, and Lastminute.com—also do a brisk business in packages.

ESCORTED TOURS
Escorted tours are structured group tours, with a group leader. The price usually includes everything from airfare to hotels, meals, tours, admission costs, and local transportation.

Despite the fact that escorted tours require big deposits and predetermine hotels, restaurants, and itineraries, many people derive security and peace of mind from the structure they offer. Escorted tours let travelers sit back (or stand up and walk) and enjoy the trip without having to drive or worry about details. They take you to the maximum number of sights in the minimum amount of time with the least amount of hassle. They're particularly convenient for people with limited mobility and they can be a great way to make new friends.

On the downside, you'll have little opportunity for serendipitous interactions with locals. The tours can be jam-packed with activities, leaving little room for individual sightseeing, whim, or adventure—plus they often focus on the heavily touristed sites, so you miss out on many a lesser-known gem.

CULTURAL TOURS

Istanbul's Old City is, essentially, one big open-air museum, and it would be difficult not to have a learning experience while traveling in such a historically rich area. For their Turkey trips, **Intrepid Travel** (in the U.S. © **877/847-8192;** www.intrepidtravel.com) manages to effectively combine authentic experiences with an optimal cultural overview.

If you're planning to drag along unwilling offspring, try booking through **Thomson Family Adventures** (© **800/ 262-6255** or 617/864-4803; fax 617/ 497-3911; www.familyadventures.com) for kid-friendly trips without adult compromise. Thomson takes an added interest in your children, establishing departure dates according to the school calendar, and they provide fun educational activities prior to departure.

Depending on your commitment to the educational aspect of your vacation, you may want to connect with one of the outfitters geared specifically toward this type of travel. **IST Cultural Tours** (© **800/833-2111**), organizes painstakingly researched tours for the traveler who's looking for a more in-depth cultural experience, and a partnership with the History Channel ensures a high level of quality. **Far Horizons** (© **800/552-4575;** www.farhorizon.com) offers eight archaeological tours for small groups, including a 10-day voyage by sea. Tours hook up with local professionals such as archaeologists, scientists, and experts as guides.

Using a local travel agent can make anybody a bit skittish, but an expert in the region is the English-proficient **Credo Tours** ⊛ (© **0212/254-8175** in Istanbul; fax 0212/237-9670; www. credo.com.tr), specializing in creating theme tours on special request. A recent program organized visits to select fine arts galleries and exhibitions during the 2007 Biennale. Faxes and e-mails are answered within 24 hours, and there is no request that is too unusual.

3

Suggested Istanbul Itineraries

Frankly, 3 days is scarcely enough time to explore very much of anything anywhere, let alone Istanbul, the seat of three world empires. Expect only to cover the bare basics of Istanbul, and to leave thoroughly exhausted, with an aching back and calloused feet. But you will also leave culturally enriched and pining for more.

This chapter gives you a rough outline of what you can see, on a load of caffeine, in 1, 2, or 3 days in Istanbul. Consider these itineraries as a suggestion of Istanbul's greatest hits, the top sights you will want to cover regardless of the length of your trip.

1 The Best of Istanbul in 1 Day

The Byzantine, Roman, and Ottoman kings, Caesars, and sultans were quite obliging when they clustered their lives in, around, and on top of each other's centers of power. The headliners of each are conveniently located in and around the Old City neighborhood of Sultanahmet, which is where we will begin the day. By following this tour, you will beam yourself back and forth between empires with visits to the unforgettable and obligatory stops at the Hippodrome, the Ayasofya, the Yerebatan Cistern, the Blue Mosque, Topkapı Palace, and the Grand Bazaar. If Sunday or Monday is the one day you've allotted for Istanbul, it will be necessary to modify this tour, as the Grand Bazaar is closed on Sundays, while Monday is the day that most of the museums go dark. Unfortunately, because of an upsurge in tourism, you will not be alone at any of these sites. The sequence followed here attempts to mitigate the competition with busloads of tourists, but still, you'll have to be patient and gauge extra time for standing in line. Because of the longer days of summer, this day can be stretched out a bit, as museum hours generally extend to 7pm, as opposed to 4:30 or 5pm in winter. **Start:** *Hippodrome.*

❶ Hippodrome ⟡

A place for public spectacle, the Hippodrome hosted Roman and Byzantine celebrations and revolts, as well as Ottoman royal games and imperial weddings. Its narrative is as grand as it is gruesome. This is the place to get your historical and geographical bearings; remember this spot, as you will want to come back to one of the park benches and watch the people stroll by. During Ramadan, the

municipality dresses up the Hippodrome in a nostalgic costume of Ottoman storefronts, and in anticipation of sunset, a family-style carnival begins. See p. 15.

❷ Topkapı Palace ⟡⟡⟡

The center of Ottoman might for almost 5 centuries, Topkapı Palace is a place of Oriental mystique, conjuring images of turbaned sultans and their harems, of paşas and eunuchs, and of an empire that wielded transcontinental influence at a time when the West was still living in the dark ages. The Treasury Room alone is enough to desensitize a woman to diamonds, rubies, and pearls. Try to get here when it opens, as the busloads descend by 9:30 or 10am.

> **③ KONYALI** 🏮
> At the halfway mark of your visit to Topkapı Palace—the farthest courtyard from the entrance—rejuvenate yourself at the spectacularly sited and storied Konyalı Restaurant. See p. 93.

④ Soğukçeşme Sokagı

Take a walk through the typical, cobbled 19th-century Ottoman lane that runs parallel to the palace wall (to the right of the main gate of Topkapı Palace as you're leaving). This evocative and flowering mews passes a picturesque collection of Ottoman houses. Look closely, and you will see interesting juxtapositions of antiquity and relative modernity before the street slopes gently down behind the imposing backside of the Ayasofya. See p. 158.

⑤ Ayasofya 🏮🏮🏮

The crowning monument to the Byzantine Empire (and not to mention Justinian's reign) has endured for more than 1,000 years, serving Byzantine emperors and Ottoman sultans. Her very structure set the standard for all monumental Ottoman architecture that followed. It wasn't until recent years, after having had her interior whitewashed to create an acceptable prayer space for the Ottoman Muslim rulers, that her astonishing collection of gilded mosaic panels was once again exposed to daylight. See p. 114.

⑥ Yerebatan Sarnıcı 🏮🏮

Who'd have thought that the underbelly of a city could look so good? Hundreds of marble columns support soaring masonry arches, all theatrically alight to emphasize the gravitas, the mystery, and the beauty of what once served as the royal plumbing. See p. 141.

⑦ Blue Mosque 🏮🏮🏮

Named for the predominance of blue in the exquisite Iznik tiles, the mosque whose construction was ordered by Sultan Ahmet was designed to rival the Ayasofya in architectural glory. On weekend afternoons, you may see little mini-sultans parading around the grounds—these boys are celebrating the week preceding their circumcision rite. See p. 118.

⑧ Grand Bazaar 🏮🏮🏮

And now for the treat you've all been waiting for: the bazaar to end all bazaars—a veritable candy store of more than 4,000 shops, 24 *hans* (privately owned inns or marketplaces), 65 streets, 22 gates, 2 *bedestens* (covered markets), restaurants, mosques, fountains, and teahouses within an area of 31 hectares (76 acres). See p. 121.

⑨ Süleymaniye Camii ve Külliyesi 🏮🏮

Another masterpiece of the dream team of Süleyman the Magnificent and his chief architect, Sinan, this mosque complex was their crowning achievement. It is here that Sinan finally manages to outdome the Ayasofya, but beyond this enormous feat of engineering, the mosque is perfectly sited, sitting atop the third of Istanbul's seven hills. There are commanding views from the rear of the grounds that arrive well up to the Princes' Islands. You should get here before sunset to profit from the view. See p. 147.

⑩ Süleymaniye Hamamı 🏮

End this exhausting, and culture-filled day of exploration like a sultan. Indulge your senses at the adjacent Turkish bath, another architectural icon by the great Sinan, where an attendant will rub, scrub, and rinse away all of your cares. See p. 143.

Istanbul in 1, 2 & 3 Days

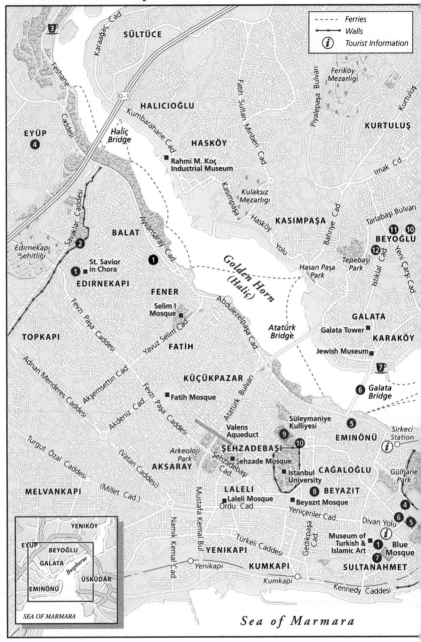

Ferries
Walls
(i) Tourist Information

SÜLTÜCE
HALICIOĞLU
EYÜP 4
Haliç Bridge
HASKÖY
Rahmi M. Koç Industrial Museum
Kulaksız Mezarlığı
KASIMPAŞA
Feriköy Mezarlığı
KURTULUŞ
Tarlabaşı Bulvarı
BEYOĞLU 11 10
12
Tepebaşı Park
Hasan Paşa Park
Golden Horn (Haliç)
BALAT
St. Savior in Chora
1 2
EDIRNEKAPI
Edirnekapı Şehitliği
FENER
Selim I Mosque
Atatürk Bridge
GALATA
Galata Tower
Jewish Museum
KARAKÖY
TOPKAPI
FATİH
KÜÇÜKPAZAR
Fatih Mosque
7
6 Galata Bridge
Valens Aqueduct
Süleymaniye Külliyesi 5
9 EMINÖNÜ
Sirkeci Station
(i)
Arkeoloji Park
ŞEHZADEBAŞI
Şehzade Mosque
10
İstanbul University
CAĞALOĞLU
AKSARAY
LALELI
Laleli Mosque
Ordu Cad.
Beyazıt Mosque
8 BEYAZIT
Gülhane Park
MELVANKAPI
Divan Yolu
4
Yeniçeriler Cad.
6 5
YENIKAPI
Türkeli Caddesi
Museum of Turkish & Islamic Art
1
7
Blue Mosque
SULTANAHMET
KUMKAPI
Kumkapı
Kennedy Caddesi
YENIKÖY
EYÜP
BEYOĞLU
GALATA
EMINÖNÜ
ÜSKÜDAR
SEA OF MARMARA

Sea of Marmara

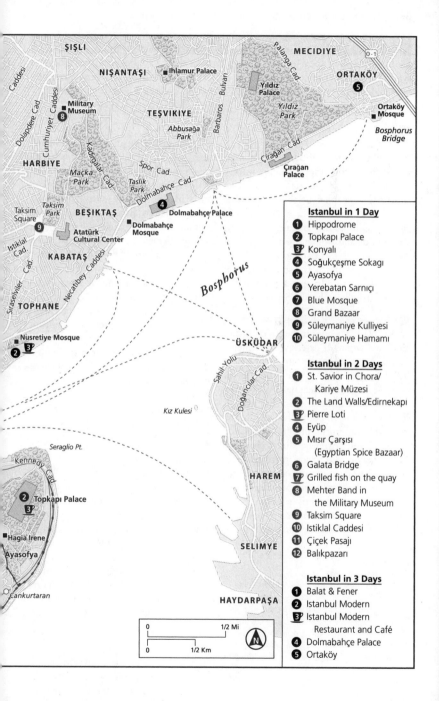

ŞİŞLİ

NİŞANTAŞI ■ Ihlamur Palace

MECIDIYE

O-1

ORTAKÖY ❺

Yıldız
Palace

TEŞVIKIYE

Abbusağa
Park

Yıldız
Park

Ortaköy
■ Mosque

Military
Museum ❽

Bosphorus
Bridge

HARBIYE

Maçka
Park

Spor Cad.

Çırağan Cad.

Taslik
Park

Çırağan
Palace

Taksim
Park

BEŞİKTAŞ

Dolmabahçe Cad.

❹ Dolmabahçe Palace

Taksim
Square ❾

Atatürk
Cultural Center

■ Dolmabahçe
Mosque

İstiklal
Cad.

KABATAŞ

Necatibey Caddesi

Bosphorus

Siraselviler Cad.

TOPHANE

■ Nusretiye Mosque
❷ ③

ÜSKÜDAR

Sahil Yolu

Doğancılar Cad.

Kız Kulesi

Seraglio Pt.

Kennedy Cad.

HAREM

❷ Topkapı Palace
③

SELIMYE

■ Hagia Irene

Ayasofya

Cankurtaran

HAYDARPAŞA

0   1/2 Mi
0   1/2 Km

N

Istanbul in 1 Day
❶ Hippodrome
❷ Topkapı Palace
③ Konyalı
❹ Soğukçeşme Sokagı
❺ Ayasofya
❻ Yerebatan Sarnıçı
❼ Blue Mosque
❽ Grand Bazaar
❾ Süleymaniye Kulliyesi
❿ Süleymaniye Hamamı

Istanbul in 2 Days
❶ St. Savior in Chora/
   Kariye Müzesi
❷ The Land Walls/Edirnekapı
③ Pierre Loti
❹ Eyüp
❺ Mısır Çarşısı
   (Egyptian Spice Bazaar)
❻ Galata Bridge
⑦ Grilled fish on the quay
❽ Mehter Band in
   the Military Museum
❾ Taksim Square
❿ Istiklal Caddesi
⓫ Çiçek Pasajı
⓬ Balıkpazarı

Istanbul in 3 Days
❶ Balat & Fener
❷ Istanbul Modern
③ Istanbul Modern
   Restaurant and Café
❹ Dolmabahçe Palace
❺ Ortaköy

2 The Best of Istanbul in 2 Days

On day 2 (having spent your first day following the 1-day itinerary), you'll have to work a little harder to cover the mosaic of Byzantine, Ottoman, and Republican sites scattered to the four corners of Istanbul. *Start: St. Savior in Chora/Kariye Müzesi.*

❶ St. Savior in Chora/ Kariye Müzesi ⚜⚜⚜

Some of the finest late-Byzantine mosaics anywhere are on display in this former monastic church located in relative obscurity in a quiet neighborhood near the Theodosian Land Walls. The radiance of the shimmering mosaics seems to instill pride and wonder, particularly in a new class of visitors hailing from Eastern Europe. This church is also a tile in the modern-day custodial mosaic that is the Greek Orthodox Church. See p. 140.

❷ The Land Walls/Edirnekapı ⚜⚜

In A.D. 412, Theodosius began construction on a system of defensive battlements destined to protect the city for the next 1,000 years. Among the 188 towers spaced along a total length of 6,670m (4 miles) is the Edirne Gate, or Edirnekapı. This was the main point of entry into the city of Constantinople for Byzantine emperors and Ottoman sultans alike, the latter having also made their first triumphal entrance into the conquered city in 1453. The juxtaposition of the battlements against a series of quiet and traditional neighborhoods makes a visit here especially rewarding. See p. 154.

> **❸ PIERRE LOTI**
> This nostalgic outpost recalls the time spent in Istanbul by literary giant Julien Viaud, a French national and protagonist of one of Istanbul's heart-rending legends. The cafe, which uses Viaud's pseudonym, is a simple and sparse tearoom and terrace offering romanticized views of the storied Golden Horn. See p. 146.

❹ Eyüp

The neighborhood of Eyüp commemorates the fall of Halid bin Zeyd Ebu Eyyûb (known as Eyüp Sultan), companion of Mohammad, in the Arab raids of the mid–7th century A.D. As Turkey's holiest Islamic site, the Eyüp Sultan mosque drew Ottoman sultans, paşas, and gentlemen here for official ceremonies, in pilgrimage, and as a prestigious final resting place. The cemetery along the lush path down from Pierre Loti serves as the latter, as does the grander *türbe,* or monumental mausoleums, closer to the mosque. The main plaza bustles with the comings and goings of the faithful, some of whom arrive from great distances, to honor their saint. On Sundays, chances are that you'll see some costumed little boys accompanied by their families visiting here prior to the boys' circumcision rite. See p. 144.

❺ Mısır Çarşışı (Egyptian Spice Bazaar) ⚜⚜

Constructed as part of the Yeni Valide Mosque complex, the adjacent market is named for the exotic spices and essential grains brought into the city from Egypt. Inside is an irresistible and almost theatrical display of sights, sounds, and smells, but the best fun is in jostling your way through the streets behind the building. You will encounter vendors proffering morsels of soft cheese, spoonfuls of spicy *ezme,* and samples of succulent strawberries. See p. 195.

❻ Galata Bridge ⚜⚜

Next, a walk across the Galata Bridge will reward you with one of the best, all-encompassing views of the hills, minarets, and domes of the Old City behind you.

You can either walk the upper deck, among fishermen and their catch, or stroll past the seafood restaurants and tea-houses on the lower deck. Better still, switch between the two utilizing the stair-ways halfway, and don't forget to admire the churning juncture of the Golden Horn and the Bosphorus. See p. 5.

🐟 GRILLED FISH ON THE QUAY
This is the most authentic of daytime snacks, provided by a chain of fishing boats repurposed as Istanbul's version of fast food. The Tarıhı Eminönü Balıkçısı is the original; just walk right up to the water's edge and order a freshly grilled fish on a roll. See p. 97.

---

❽ Mehter Band ⚜⚜⚜ in the Military Museum ⚜⚜
As an empire of conquest, the Ottomans bequeathed a wealth of military memora-bilia that tells the story of the empire's rise and fall. The Ottoman Mehter Band played advance guard to the Ottoman army of foot soldiers on military cam-paigns. The band's cacophonous, disso-nant, and tympanic sounds are both terrifying and exciting. Its re-creation—in full Ottoman regalia—is not to be missed. See p. 145.

❾ Taksim Square
The pulse of the city, if not the country, Taksim Square is a vibrant and vital center analogous to Times Square or Piccadilly Circus. Except that here, centuries-old domes rise above Burger King billboards, and head-scarved girls on cellphones share the sidewalk with Istanbul's growing pop-ulation of punk rockers. See p. 169.

❿ Istiklal Caddesi
If Taksim is the heart of Istanbul, Istiklal Caddesi is the coronary artery. This, now an emerging open-air shopping mall flanked on both sides by ornately con-structed former foreign embassies, recalls its earlier incarnation as the 19th-century Grand Rue de Pera. The evening crowd gets crushing, as laborers rush to arrive home for dinner and revelers seek out the trendiest nightspots. Continue down along Istiklal Caddesi or take the nostal-gic trolley.

⓫ Çiçek Pasajı
Halfway down Istiklal is a rococo arcade dressed in beer halls, fish restaurants, and hanging gardens of flowers. It's one of Istanbul's most touristed attractions, and rightfully so. See p. 166.

⓬ Balıkpazarı
The adjacent arcades and alleys that make up the Galatasaray Fish Market are pic-turesque, historic, and alluring. In the main avenue, displays of fresh fish vie for the attention of potential diners, until the street-side dining action begins on the narrow and cobbled offshoot of Nevişade Sokağı. Poke among the souvenirs, antiques, and luxuriant textiles for sale in the European, or Avrupa Pasajı, before calling it a day well spent and relaxing over a meal at one of the classic *meyhanes* (taverns) or restaurants recommended in the Beyoğlu section of the dining chapter. See p. 165.

---

3 The Best of Istanbul in 3 Days

With 3 days at your disposal (having spent your first 2 days following the 2-day itin-erary), you have the luxury on day 3 of stopping to smell the roses, figuratively speak-ing. After 2 days of manic exploration, it's time to poke your nose into the lesser-visited nooks and crannies that make Istanbul as complex and captivating as it is. *Start: Ecumenical Patriarchate, Fener.*

❶ Balat & Fener

The contiguous neighborhoods of Balat and Fener encompass authentic and timeless streets whose time is fast running out. The entirety of these two neighborhoods—a skeletal landscape of the former Jewish, Greek, Armenian, and Ottoman communities that resided here—has been identified as a restoration zone, and a patchwork of projects is either completed or under way. Dotting the streets are Byzantine-era basilicas interspersed between crumbling ancient ruins, stately merchant-class town houses, and the odd goat. I recommend that, for an abbreviated tour, you follow walking tour 2 in reverse from the Ecumenical Patriarchate until you arrive at the Balat Market. See p. 162.

❷ Istanbul Modern 𝒦

After 2 days chock-full of antiquity, the very contemporary Istanbul Modern provides a gentle reminder that this city is an international player. Fascinating portraits, landscapes, and multimedia exhibits are illustrative interpretations of a culture in transition between traditional Ottoman and Republican Turkey. See p. 156.

❹ Dolmabahçe Palace 𝒦

Lavish in its ornamental European architecture and sumptuous interior decor, Dolmabahçe Palace represents the later Ottoman sultans' desire to replicate all things modern and Western. The palace proper sits on 25 hectares (62 acres) of landfill and is made up of 285 rooms, 46 salons, 1,427 windows, and 68 toilets. See p. 150.

❺ Ortaköy 𝒦

The modern and trendy seaside village of Ortaköy is Istanbul's uptown location with the downtown feel. Its labyrinth of cobbled alleys converge on a picturesque waterside quay, where you'll find restaurants, cafes, boutiques, and sidewalk vendors hawking everything from accessories to scarves to a hefty assortment of wigs—the compromise of choice for headscarf-wearing female students who aspire to attend state-run universities. See p. 47.

☕³ ISTANBUL MODERN RESTAURANT AND CAFÉ

Although not individually listed in this guide as a destination restaurant, the museum restaurant, which gets fantastic views of Topkapı Palace, serves a sophisticated selection of Turkish and international dishes at reasonable prices. It's open Monday to Saturday 10am to midnight and Sunday 10am to 6pm.

4

Getting to Know Istanbul

In many ways, time seems to have stood still in Istanbul, especially in the neighborhoods of the Old City. Yet, at the same time, progress in the form of transportation, technology, academics, and global engagement have set Istanbul and Turkey on a forward-moving course that makes your head spin. Still, in the contradictory spirit of this city bridging continents and cultures, many feel a reverse tug in the political and religious swing of the pendulum. One might visit Istanbul a dozen times over a lifetime, and at each visit be greeted both by an old friend and by an altogether unexpected paradigm.

1 Orientation

VISITOR INFORMATION
In addition to offices at the airport (© 0212/663-0798) and in Sirkeci train station (© 0212/511-5888), you may stumble upon an official tourist office *(Turizm Ofisi)* in one of the many tourist hubs around town. The location at the northeast corner of Sultanahmet Meydanı near Divanyolu (© 0212/518-1802) is pretty handy, as are the ones in the Hilton Hotel Arcade (© 0212/233-0592), in Beyazit Meydanı (near the tramway exit outside of the Grand Bazaar; © 0212/522-4902), and at the Karaköy Seaport (© 0212/249-5776). If you're out and about and encounter trouble (pickpockets, scams, muggings), stop in to the passably multilingual **Tourism Police** at Yerebatan Cad. 6, in Sultanahmet (© 0212/527-4503 or 528-5369).

CITY LAYOUT
Istanbul is split down the middle by the mighty Bosphorus Straits, making it the only city in the world on two continents. To the east of the waterway is the **Asian side,** a predominantly residential retreat with little of the chaos of its European counterpart on the west. The modern business district of Taksim and the historic peninsula of the Old City occupy the **European side** of the Bosphorus, separated by the picturesque **Golden Horn** estuary and connected by a number of bridges and ferries. While the major sightseeing draw is over in the south in the **Old City** (aka the **Historic Peninsula** or **Old Istanbul**), you should plan to give at least equal time to the modern heart of Istanbul on the northern side, essential in gaining a balanced picture of the many facets of the city, and of Turkey.

HOW TO FIND AN ADDRESS Addresses in Turkey name the major thoroughfare followed by a logical walk-through of the smaller avenues until you get to the actual street address. Of course, in villages, where there are no major thoroughfares, you'll see a lot of the word *mahalle(si),* which means, roughly, neighborhood. For example, if you're trying to find the Hotel Avicenna, located at Mimar Mehmet Ağa Caddesi, Amiral Tafdil Sok. 31–33, Sultanahmet/Istanbul, isolate the Sultanahmet neighborhood on the map of Istanbul and look for Mimar Mehmet Ağa Caddesi, one of the main arteries. Next, look for a cross street by the name of Amiral Tafdil Sokağı and you will find the hotel at numbers 31–33. (In this case, the hotel takes up two old Ottoman houses.) In many cases, another number comes after the street address following a slash (/) and it specifies the floor on which a place is located—usually in the case of apartments, Internet cafes, offices, and other entities not located on the ground floor. Another handy word is *karşısı*, which means *across from*, as in *Isabey Camii karşısı Serin Sokak, Selçuk* (across from the Isabey Mosque on Serin St., in Selçuk). Where the less-orientating *mahalle* is in operation, just ask. Really.

In Istanbul, particularly on the repaved Istiklal Caddesi, two types of number plates are used for addresses: the old blue ones and the new red ones. The address of an establishment will, where applicable, be listed as 51r or 33b, for example.

Free maps are available at any tourist information office (until they run out). Also available for purchase in bookstores are maps with clear and easily identifiable main attractions, but the smaller streets are left nameless, if included at all. None of these maps are 100% accurate, but you may not even notice because signs are posted everywhere for museums, hotels, and restaurants, and there will be plenty of people on the street offering to give you a hand. Asking directions is part of the local culture and a great way to get local tips.

ISTANBUL'S NEIGHBORHOODS IN BRIEF

The sprawling muddle that is Istanbul-the-city comprises nearly 260 sq. km (100 sq. miles) of layered history spread over two continents. The city of Istanbul is part of the province of Istanbul—think New York City, inside New York State—allowing for a bit of confusion. But seeing as how this is a city guide, we will mainly concern ourselves with the four central districts of **Beyoğlu, Beşiktaş, Eminönü,** and **Fatih,** plus throw in the highlights of the Bosphorus (both European and Asian sides).

The European and Asian sides of the city are bisected by the churning north-south artery that is the Bosphorus Straits. Strategic waterway and stuff of legends, the Bosphorus is the conduit for nations of the Black Sea into the coveted trade routes of the Mediterranean and beyond.

The European side of Istanbul is itself separated by the estuary known in English as the Golden Horn and in Turkish as **the Haliç.** Bordering the south of the Golden Horn are the districts of Eminönü and Fatih, neatly cinctured by what remains of the Byzantine-era defensive walls. These two districts make up the **Historic Peninsula** (aka Old Stamboul, Old Istanbul, and Rome of the East). To the north of the Golden Horn are Beyoğlu and Beşiktaş, a hodgepodge of ancient and modern, of historic and progressive.

So as not to confuse you with a short description of every corner of Istanbul, it's important to know that neighborhoods generally bear the name of a major landmark, such as the mosque that serves the quarter, and that neighborhood delineations are anything but clear-cut. Below is a liberal selection of areas ranging from the "must see" to "off the beaten track," but this list is by no means exhaustive.

European Side: Old Istanbul

The Historic Peninsula, home to the remnants of Classical, Roman, Byzantine, and Ottoman eras, is now known as the modern-day district of **Eminönü.** The neighborhoods that live within the

Istanbul at a Glance

boundaries of the ancient city walls are oriented around the famed seven hills in a nearly 22 sq. km (8.5 sq. miles) area. Eminönü also refers to the neighborhood and transportation hub at the base of the Galata Bridge (a decided lack of creativity in naming ports, neighborhoods, districts, cities, and provinces is a running theme throughout Turkish geography and a source of consternation for visitors). This transport hub is where you'll find ferries to just about

everywhere, a metropolitan bus and *dolmuş* hub, the Egyptian Spice Bazaar, the Yeni Valide Camii (New Queen Mother's Mosque), and Rustem Paşa Mosque, as well as a frenetic warren of passageways and back streets that wind their way uphill through local shops to the Grand Bazaar. Just steps to the east of Eminönü's transport hub is the Sirkeci train station (final stop of the legendary Orient Express), a bustling and utilitarian hub of people with

Istanbul

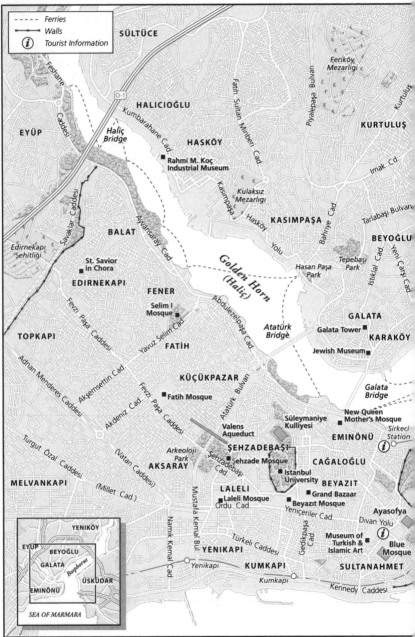

Ferries

Walls

(i) Tourist Information

SÜLTÜCE

FERİKÖY Mezarlığı

HALICIOĞLU

KURTULUŞ

Feshane Caddesi

EYÜP

Haliç Bridge

Kumbarahane Cad.

HASKÖY

Rahmi M. Koç Industrial Museum

Fatih Sultan Minderi Cad.

Piyalepaşa Bulvarı

İmak Cd.

Kulaksız Mezarlığı

Kasımpaşa

Sakaklar Caddesi

BALAT

Ayvansaray Cad.

KASIMPAŞA

Haskoy Yolu

Bahriye Cad.

Tarlabaşı Bulvarı

BEYOĞLU

Edirnekapı Şehitliği

St. Savior in Chora

Golden Horn (Haliç)

Hasan Paşa Park

Tepebaşı Park

İstiklal Cad.

Yeni Çarşı Cad.

EDİRNEKAPI

FENER

Selim I Mosque

Abdülezelpaşa Cad.

Atatürk Bridge

GALATA

Galata Tower

KARAKÖY

Fevzi Paşa Caddesi

Yavuz Selim Cad.

TOPKAPI

FATİH

Jewish Museum

Akşemsettin Cad.

KÜÇÜKPAZAR

Galata Bridge

Adnan Menderes Caddesi

Akdeniz Cad.

Fevzi Paşa Caddesi

Fatih Mosque

Atatürk Bulvarı

Süleymaniye Külliyesi

New Queen Mother's Mosque

Turgut Özal Caddesi

(Vatan Caddesi)

Valens Aqueduct

ŞEHZADEBAŞI

EMİNÖNÜ

Sirkeci Station

(i)

MELVANKAPI

(Millet Cad.)

Arkeoloji Park

Şehzadebaşı Cad.

Şehzade Mosque

İstanbul University

CAĞALOĞLU

AKSARAY

İstanbul University

BEYAZIT

Mustafa Kemal Bul.

LALELİ

Laleli Mosque

Ordu Cad.

Grand Bazaar

Beyazıt Mosque

Yeniçeriler Cad.

Ayasofya

Divan Yolu

(i)

Namık Kemal Cad.

Türkeli Caddesi

YENİKAPI

Gedikpaşa Cad.

Museum of Turkish & Islamic Art

Blue Mosque

Yenikapı

KUMKAPI

SULTANAHMET

Kumkapı

Kennedy Caddesi

YENİKÖY

EYÜP

BEYOĞLU

GALATA

Boğhorus

ÜSKÜDAR

EMİNÖNÜ

SEA OF MARMARA

O-1

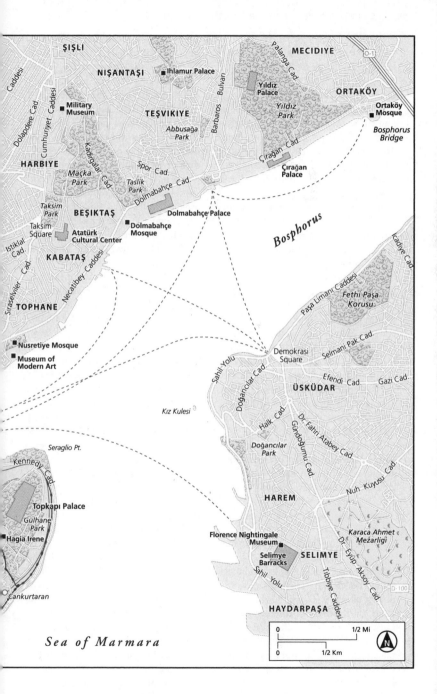

43

places to go. As expected, it's easy to find comparatively affordable food and lodging around this neighborhood as opposed to the more popular and adjacent neighborhood of Sultanahmet. The easternmost tip of the peninsula known as **Sarayburnu** or Seraglio Point (literally, palace point) is where Topkapı Palace presides over the strategic convergence of the Marmara Sea, the mouth of the Bosphorus, and the Golden Horn.

At the heart of the district of Eminönü is the neighborhood of **Sultanahmet,** centered around the Hippodrome—ancient racetrack, political arena, and present-day commons. Anchoring the historic center of the city are the Blue Mosque and the Ayasofya, two massive and magnificent edifices challenging each other from opposite ends of Sultanahmet Park. Bordering Sultanahmet to the southeast is the as-of-yet still characteristically residential quarter of **Cankurtaran,** named for the train station stop at Ahırkapi Gate and, for all intents and purposes, absorbed under the umbrella heading of Sultanahmet.

To the southwest of Sultanahmet along the Marmara Sea and along the ancient Sea Walls is **Kumkapı,** destination of the daily catch by local fishermen, location of the city's fish market, and home to a dense cluster of touristy fish restaurants.

Eminönü is divided by the main avenue of **Divanyolu** (whose name changes to Yeniçeriler Caddesi and then Ordu Caddesi as it runs westward to the district of Fatih). Paving what was formerly the ceremonial entrance to the Great Palace, Divanyolu begins (or ends, if you were the emperor) at Sultanahmet Park, running westward through the neighborhoods of **Çemberlitaş,** former site of the Forum of Constantine and close to the Nuruosmaniye

entrance to the Grand Bazaar; **Beyazit,** built on the ruins of the Forum of Theodosius and named for the Beyazit Mosque Complex; and **Laleli.** North and west of Beyazit is the neighborhood of **Süleymaniye,** named after the mosque complex of the same name.

Back at Divanyolu (now Ordu Caddesi), the road splits just as it enters the district of Fatih at **Aksaray.** The tramway, which follows Divanyolu, continues along the southernmost avenue (Millet Caddesi, aka Türgüt Özal Caddesi), while the northern fork becomes the major thoroughfare of Vatan Caddesi (aka Adnan Menderes Bulvarı).

The district of **Fatih** is named after the Fatih Mosque and complex built by and for Mehmet the Conqueror immediately after the conquest. It was constructed on the site of the Havariyun, the second-most revered Byzantine church after the Ayasofya, which was the victim of earthquakes and fire. The prominence of the district in both the Byzantine and Ottoman eras can be credited with the great number of monuments that dot this now bustling working-class conglomeration of diverse and authentic (and yes, some fundamentalist) neighborhoods.

From north to south beginning at the Golden Horn are the twin quarters of **Balat** and **Fener,** Ottoman-era enclaves where Armenian, Greek, and Jewish immigrants first settled. This combined quarter is thick with the crumbling remains of monumental Byzantine palaces, synagogues, schools, and mosques and is even the home of the Eastern Orthodox Patriarchate.

Several of the defunct Byzantine defensive gates continue to exert their influence on the surrounding neighborhoods that now bear these names: **Edirnekapı,** which is the gateway to the Church of Saint Savior in Chora or

Kariye Camii; and **Ayvansaray,** which sits at the base of the Old Galata Bridge near the remains of the Blachernae Palace and sections of the land walls.

Fatih's southeastern-most point is the busy port of **Yenikapı,** departure point for seabuses to Bursa, the Marmara Islands, and the southern shores of the Marmara Sea. Yenikapı is the site of the construction of one of the metro stations for the in-progress Marmaray project, made famous for the extraordinary archaeological discoveries being made there.

Following the southern Marmara Sea shoreline is the **Sahil Yolu** (or the coastal road); this main thoroughfare connects the Old City with the airport and suburbs. The last neighborhood of interest as the road heads out of Fatih is **Yedikule** (literally, seven towers), the fortress constructed by Fatih Mehmet the Conqueror incorporating the earlier Theodosian land and sea walls. Almost no one goes to this neighborhood or museum, which is why you should go. Fewer and fewer places like this can be found in Istanbul these days.

While not within the district boundaries laid out above, I need to mention one more neighborhood on the southern banks of the Golden Horn. Located just northwest of the Haliç Bridge (above Fener and Balat) is the quarter of **Eyüp,** named for the Prophet Mohammad's warrior companion and standard-bearer, and one of the holiest figures in Islam, Eyüp Sultan. Tradition holds that Eyüp was slain in battle on this hill, and the site, marked by a mosque complex and tomb, is now a point of pilgrimage for Muslims.

European Side: Beyoğlu, Beşiktaş & the Bosphorus Villages of Europe

If the Old City is the jewel of Empires, then the landmass on the opposite side of the Golden Horn is its crown.

The fairly unwieldy district of **Beyoğlu,** which also straddles the centuries, is subdivided, at least colloquially, into a mosaic of characteristic quarters, with slightly more modern layers of historic, cultural, religious, and political reference than those on the other side of the Golden Horn. This triangle of Istanbul is connected to the Old City by the Galata Bridge (at Eminönü and the opposite port of Karaköy) and via the Atatürk Bridge.

The fortified area between the Atatürk and Galata bridges and extending up from the shoreline to the Galata Tower encloses one of Istanbul's more characteristic (and now gentrified) neighborhoods—known as **Galata.** Istanbul's earliest (pre-classical) settlements were found in and around Galata, today a hodgepodge of steeply sloping streets radiating from the Galata Tower. Where Karaköy and Galata merge, you'll find a wealth of architectural monuments left by the European communities that thrived here during the Ottoman period, as well as a small community of street urchins and—on the fringes—at least one brothel.

At the bottom of Galata Hill (and technically absorbing it) is **Karaköy,** a functionally messy and exhilarating transport hub worth a visit for its local eateries along with a number of significant monumental Ottoman constructions. Recent additions include the Istanbul Modern, as well as the leafy tea gardens and waterpipe cafes of **Tophane.**

At the summit of Galata Hill is **Tünel,** which also refers to the very short and very old one-stop funicular called Tünel. To make matters worse, both the upper and lower entrances of the funicular are called Tünel; thus, to avoid confusion, I refer to the area around the upper entrance as **Upper**

Tünel and the lower as **Lower Tünel** or Karaköy.

Radiating around Upper Tünel (a part of Beyoğlu also referred to specifically as Beyoğlu) are the turn-of-the-century Belle Epoque buildings—including a high density of foreign consulates—of 19th-century **Pera.** Pera recalls a bygone era of wealth, entitlement, and gaiety. Today, strolls along the previous Grand Rue de Pera have evolved into a nightly crush of humanity walking up and down the same artery now known as Istiklal Caddesi.

Lining the slopes southeast of Istiklal Caddesi is the steep-stepped Renaissance quarter of **Cihangir.** Alternating antique and artistic shops can be found on and around **Çukurcuma.** These combined neighborhoods attract artists, diplomats, expat journalists, and just plain commuters to its streets full of gentrified cafes, restaurants, bars, and antique boutiques.

If Beyoğlu is the heart and soul of modern Istanbul, then **Istiklal Caddesi** is its lifeline. This hectic shopping street bisects the district north from Tünel to the modern, pulsating, chaotic nucleus of the city known as **Taksim Square,** Istanbul's equivalent to New York's Times Square. Standing at the center is a statue of Atatürk and the founding fathers of Turkey, representing on one side the War of Independence and on the other the Republic. The Atatürk Cultural Center (Atatürk Kültür Merkezi) houses the Istanbul State Opera and Ballet, and serves as a sometimes venue for the Biennale; there is talk of tearing the hideous but much-loved building down. The area is yet another commuter hub, city commons, business center, and open-air food court. A concentration of full-service, high-rise hotels targeting businesspeople makes

the area around Taksim a perfect place for bustle and convenience. The location is also connected to a transportation network that includes the metro, a recently restored cable car/tramway along Istiklal Caddesi, a plethora of municipal buses, and a daunting network of *dolmuşes* (minibuses).

As the city, even the country's, center, Taksim Square and the neighborhoods on its fringe are thickly dotted with nightclubs, seedy bars, and Internet cafes, attracting the indigents and pilferers of Istanbul. The pre-gentrified neighborhood of **Tarlabaşı,** located on the opposite side of Tarlabaşı Caddesi, is home to a high density of crumbling architectural gems, but it's also where you'll find Istanbul's subculture of transvestites, criminal indigents, and prostitutes, newly displaced from the now-hip neighborhood of Çukurcuma. Steer clear for now, but watch this space, as the Municipality (and real estate investors) have their sights eagerly set on this neighborhood.

The city gets increasingly more elite the farther north of Taksim you go. Immediately to the north (and inland) of the square is the business district of **Harbiye,** which sidles up to the fashionable shopping neighborhood of **Nişantaşı,** a pleasant cross between New York's SoHo and Madison Avenue (this is technically in the district of Şişli, but never mind). Boutiques along **Teşvikiye Caddesi** and the smaller side streets are stocked with high-quality merchandise in elegant settings, with major names like Mudo, Emporio Armani, Vakko, and Beyman.

Maçka can be considered Istanbul's Wall Street, while the neighborhoods become more residential the farther away from Taksim you go.

Beşiktaş-the-district refers to the Bosphorus-front real estate above Beyoğlu, made popular by a long

> **Fun Fact Did You Know?**
> Beşiktaş, meaning "cradle stone," is named after the crib in which Jesus was
> born, which was thought to have been brought here by early Christians.

string of sultans, paşas, and empresses who constructed European-style palaces all along the historic Straits, including the Dolmabahçe, Yıldız, and Çırağan palaces. The better hotels are scrambling for this real estate; the new Four Seasons will be open by the time this book hits the stands, while the stylish new Radisson SAS has already established itself as a favorite. Like Eminönü, **Beşiktaş** is also the neighborhood of a bustling shopping, port, and transport hub.

To the north is the uptown village with the downtown feel—**Ortaköy,** which sits at the base of the Bosphorus Bridge.

The waterfront northward becomes a picturesque chain of fishing coves transformed into bourgeois residential neighborhoods as far north as the Black Sea mouth of the Bosphorus. These include **Aravutköy, Bebek, Rumeli Hisarı, Emirgan, Istinye, Tarabya, Sarıyer,** and **Rumeli Kavağı.** You can visit these by hopping on a local bus or sightsee from the bow of a Bosphorus ferry.

The Asian Side

The Asian side is a quiet and predominantly upper-class residential area that, incredibly, has more European character than the layered exoticism predominant on the European side. The districts of **Kadiköy** and **Üsküdar,** interspersed with a smattering of architecturally outstanding mosques, monuments, and synagogues, cover a lot of territory worthy of a student of architecture, but nothing so remarkable that

you need to forfeit a day on the opposite shores. Many visitors include a midday stop at **Anadolu Kavağı** halfway through a Bosphorus cruise (see "Take a Quick Cruise," below) for lunch and perhaps a walk up to a panorama of both the Marmara and Black seas. Unfortunately, the charm of this characteristic fishermen's village has recently been compromised by summer tourists all descending with the same idea.

The tree-lined shopping section along **Bağdat Caddesi** is frequently touted as a destination, but frankly has nothing exceptional to offer a foreigner accustomed to a cosmopolitan shopping day out.

Still, visitors insist. **Beylerbeyı Sarayı,** the summer palace of the sultans, commands the right banks of Üsküdar above the Bosphorus Bridge. Combine a visit to Beylerbeyı with lunch at one of the most charming boat landings (**Çengelköy,** famous for its cucumbers and persimmons, or **Kanlıca,** where people flock for yogurt from heaven), or on Tuesdays spend a few hours wandering through the Salı Pazarı ("Tuesday Bazaar" near the Kadiköy landing), and you can tell everyone you spent the afternoon in Asia.

Because of the phenomenal views from the newer hotels (which also provide complementary boat shuttle service to the European side), Asia might actually be a reasonable place to hang your hat, particularly if it's a wedding veil.

2 Getting Around

BY PUBLIC TRANSPORTATION

Transportation in Istanbul is like the Internet: It's anonymous, indispensable, and completely decentralized. Implemented with little thought of how one service might be integrated with another, the network of buses, minibuses, funiculars, ferries, catamarans, subways, trains, trams, and trolley cars will certainly get you where you're going, but you may have to take all of them to get there. For a quick reference guide to transportation in central Istanbul, turn to the inside front cover of this book.

A one-way ride, without a transfer, on the bus, tramway, historic trolley, funicular to Taksim, metro, or Istanbul City Ferry costs 1.30YTL ($1.15/50p). Note that the *dolmuş,* the Tünel, and several of the ferry lines have their own prices. Each time you transfer lines or modes of transport, you have to pay again, although buying a transit pass will make it a bit easier (see "Transport Made Easy with the Akbil," below).

THE BUS Metropolitan buses in Istanbul are frequent, comprehensive, economical, and easy—*if you know your way around.* There is no bus map nor are the routes of any individual bus line depicted anywhere near the bus stops (usually your typical glass shelter with a metal bench). What you will find is a plaque at the bus stop with a list of the stops along the route. The bus's final destination is indicated above the front windshield, with a selection of major stops listed on the side of the bus next to the entrance (admittedly, not much help if you aren't familiar with the basic layout of the city). To help you navigate, we have provided a selection of the more useful bus routes on the inside front cover of this book. Still, always check with the driver before getting on to make sure the bus is going in the direction you need, and once boarded, frequently ask your neighbor when to get off. Some of the most useful major hubs are at Eminönü, Taksim, and Beşiktaş. Tickets are sold at the major hubs or on the bus— if your bus doesn't have a "cashier" on board, there's an informal system whereby you can pay the driver, who will in turn hand you his own personal Akbil to use (this earns the driver about .05YTL per cash-paying customer). Buses run, roughly, from 6 or 6:30am until around 11pm or midnight.

THE *DOLMUŞ* *Dolmuşes* are yellow minivans that operate like group taxis with set routes. A relatively informal system, *dolmuşes* run from early morning to early evening daily, including Sundays. A *dolmuş* will leave its terminus (marked with a blue "D") only when it fills up (the word *dolmuş* means "stuffed") and then pick up and drop off passengers along the route. The main *dolmuş* stands are located in Taksim, Sirkeci, and Aksaray, and connect to points all over the city. *Dolmuşes* are often more direct than metropolitan buses and cheaper than taxis, cutting down on time and leaving more money in your pocket. Look for a *dolumuş* with the name of your destination displayed in the window. When boarding, tell the driver your destination and ask how

---

Tips We'll Tell You Where to Go

Not sure how to get where you're going? The transport arm of the Istanbul municipality operates a great website, **www.iett.gov.tr**, where you can find all the routes for the whole range of transport options. You can also plug in your starting point to find out which public transport options stop there.

> ## ⟮Tips⟯ Transport Made Easy with the Akbil
>
> True to its name (Akbil means "smart ticket"), a refillable plastic contrap-
> tion hanging from the key chains of Istanbul's commuters offers both con-
> venience and savings for an initial deposit of 6YTL ($5.20/£2.30) plus the
> prepaid cost of travel. Keep your receipt so that you can get your deposit
> back before you leave. The buses, tramway, trolley, metro, and seabuses
> (not the ferries, which are privately owned) have been outfitted to accept
> the Akbil, available for purchase (and refills) at booths displaying the Akbil
> logo in Taksim Square, Eminönü, and Aksaray. In addition to the per-ride
> savings for trips requiring multiple transfers, the Akbil will get you a savings
> of around 10% per ride. And better still, one Akbil can be used by multiple
> travelers in a group. Pre-loaded Akbils can also be purchased daily (7.50YTL/
> $6.55/£2.85), weekly (40YTL/$35/£15), 15-day (60YTL/$52/£23), or monthly
> (100YTL/$87/£40).

much it will be *(ne kadar?)*. For shorter distances, 3YTL ($2.60/£1.15) should cover
it. The driver will drop you off at your destination, but if you want to get off sooner,
say *inecek var* (this is my stop) or *inmek istiyorum, lütfen,* the short version of "I want
to get off" with a "please" stuck on the end.

THE TRAMWAY   When the tram from Eminönü to Zeytinburnu was built and
inaugurated in 1991, the planners had overlooked one very important detail: money
collection. Passengers rode for free for 1 year while the system installed booths and
printed tickets. The system has grown up quite a bit since then; the City recently
extended the tramway from Eminönü all the way to Kabataş (just below Dolmabahçe
Palace) and added an underground funicular that hoists passengers up the hill to Taksim in just 110 seconds. This collective service cuts trips between Taksim and Sultanahmet down to around 15 minutes (with transfers), while destinations in-between
(Eminönü, for the Egyptian Spice Bazaar; Çemberlitaş or Beyazit for the Grand
Bazaar; Tophane for the Istanbul Modern) are just a token away. Token *(jeton)* booths
are located at the entrance to the turnstiles; Akbils can be purchased/refilled at selected
stops, including Sultanahmet, Eminönü, and Taksim. Hours of operation are from
6am until about midnight.

THE HISTORIC TROLLEY   Just when you feel your feet are ready to fall off, you
hear the jingle of the lifesaving streetcar. The trolley now plies fresh tracks on newly
laid cobblestones along Istiklal Caddesi. As with most public transportation options,
you can pay with cash or with the Akbil. The trolley runs daily from 7am to 11pm
and makes three intermediary stops at Hüseyn Ağa Camii, at Galatasaray High
School/Flower–Fish Market, and in Beyoğlu at Nutru Sokak (in front of the Turkiye
Iş Merkezi).

THE FUNICULAR   The subway known as Tünel connects the sea level neighborhood of Karaköy near the Galata Bridge with the lofty neighborhood of Beyoğlu at
the southern end of Istiklal Caddesi. Tünel trains run Monday through Saturday from
7am to 9pm and Sunday from 7:30am to 9pm. The cost is 90Ykr.

Tips   Take a Quick Cruise

Two years ago, a cheeky young entrepreneur set a crew of expert craftsmen to replicating a traditional sultan's imperial caïque, fake gild, velvet, and all. The result is a kitschy, and yes, delightfully touristy, ride up the Bosphorus the way the royals used to do it. **Sultan Kayıkları (© 0212/265-7802; www.sultankayiklari.com)** has expanded to three motorized boats (the oars are for show) and now operates three different tours. Instead of craning your neck over the side of a crowed clunker, a maximum of 30 passengers each get a front row seat to the turning of the Ottoman centuries, sea spray and all.

Two of the three tours on offer (the third is a "Palace Tour" for groups) are quick excursions of up to an hour, no stops allowed. Choose between the tour of the Straits from Dolmabahçe to the Bosphorus Bridge and back (58YTL/$50/£22) or of the Golden Horn (45YTL/$39/£17). Boats depart from different docks and have differing schedules; reservations are required.

For a do-it-yourself Bosphorus cruise, take the **Istanbul Deniz Otobüsleri** seabus departing from Eminönü Pier #3 (10:35am daily; and 1:35pm summers only) for the 2-hour, zigzagged excursion up to Anadolu Kavağı. The ferry makes stops at all of the main docks on both the European and Asian sides (10 each), giving passengers the option of dumping ship early. Many visitors stay on until the last stop at Anadolu Kavağı (which can now confidently be called a tourist trap) for lunch at one of the many fish restaurants. Avoid the crush and disembark at one of the lesser-visited (for now) villages such as Emirgan, Bebek, Kanlıca, and Çengelköy; then either catch a direct ferry back or wait for the return of the ferry you started on (departs Anadolu Kavağı at 3pm year-round and at 5pm in summer as well). A one-way ticket on the ferry costs 7YTL ($6.10/£2.70); a round-trip costs 13YTL ($11/£4.75). For updated information and schedules, log on to www.ido.com.tr.

A second funicular was completed in 2006, providing a much-needed lift to those down at the docks of Kabataş (near Dolmabahçe Palace) up the very steep hill to Taksim. The trip, which takes a fleeting 110 seconds, costs 1.30YTL ($1.15/50p). There's a ticket booth at the turnstile entrance dispensing *jetons* or refilling the Akbil.

THE METRO/UNDERGROUND   Istanbul's modern underground currently connects Taksim with Levent (the closest stop to the shopping mecca of Akmerkez, which is an additional, short cab ride away). On the way it makes stops in Osmanbey (walking distance to Nişantaşı), Şişli/Meçidiyeköy (commercial center), and Gayrettepe (even more commerce). The metro is open from around 6:30am until midnight. You can buy *jetons* at the ticket window outside the turnstile or, if you're using the Akbil, just plug it into the turnstile receptacle.

The metro extension connecting the airport to town is now complete, providing access at Yenikapı (just outside the airport) to Aksaray via a roundabout route by way of the *otogar* (bus station). If your destination is Sultanahmet, exit the metro at

Aksaray ground level, transfer to the tramway (by paying the fare again), which is but a short walk away, and hop on any train marked EMINÖNÜ.

THE FERRY & SEABUS **Istanbul City Ferry Lines**, Şehir Hatları Vapurları (© **0212/244-4233;** port offices: Bostancı © **0216/361-3087;** Kabataş © **0212/ 243-3756;** Kadıköy © **0212/336-2198**), runs commuter ferry service between Europe and Asia, and to the nearby Princes' Islands. Some of the more useful shuttles depart from Eminönü to Kabataş, Üsküdar, Karaköy, and Haydarpaşa; this last crossing is indispensable for transfers to the train and points east. A one-way fare to points within Greater Istanbul (not including the Princes' Islands, which is nominally higher) costs 1.30YTL ($1.15/50p), and you can pay with the Akbil.

The faster seabuses are run by the **Istanbul Deniz Otobüsleri** (IDO; national toll-free line © **0212/444-4436;** www.ido.com.tr) and provide convenient service to the Asian side plus the Marmara Islands, Bursa, and Yalova. A one-way fare, for example, from Kabataş to Bostancı is 4.50YTL ($3.90/£1.70). Contact the port offices directly: Bakırköy © **0212/560-7291;** Bostancı © **0216/410-6633;** and Kabataş © **0212/ 249-1558.**

The ferry that takes the time-honored cruise up the Bosphorus leaves from Eminönü, making stops at Beşiktaş (near Dolmabahçe Palace and the Çırağan Palace) on its crisscross pattern up the channel (7YTL/$6.10/£2.70 one-way; 12YTL/ $10/£4.55 round-trip). The ferry departs daily, year-round at 10:35am. An additional 1:35pm departure operates from mid-April through November or December (confirm times, as they may change). Hours are posted on or near the ticket window. See "Take a Quick Cruise," above.

Long-distance ferries or the faster seabuses provide transportation to the Princes' Islands (from Eminönü and Kabataş) and to points along the southern coast of the Marmara Sea. If you're interested in traveling by car to cities along the Marmara region (for example, Bursa, Çanakkale, Izmir, and points south), the easiest and quickest way is to take a car ferry or seabus from Yenikapı to Güzelyalı or Mudanya (for Bursa) or Bandırma (for Çanakkale and the Northern Aegean). The trip takes 75 minutes and 1 hour, 45 minutes respectively.

BY CAR

With traffic getting denser and more aggravating on an hourly basis, having a car in Istanbul is the surest method for going nowhere. In the rare event that traffic moves smoothly, do you really think you know where you're going? Can you read signs in Turkish? Do you know what a "Cevreyolu" is? And once you get there, where are you going to park? If you do decide to disregard better judgment and good counsel (and the fact that traffic-related enforcement in general in Turkey has become rather unforgiving, given the potential revenues), or if you're only planning to pick up the car and drive out, here's some basic information:

The major car-rental companies in Istanbul are **Avis** (www.avis.com), **Sixt** (www. e-sixt.com), **Hertz** (www.hertz.com), **National** (www.nationalcar.com), **Budget** (www.budget.com), and **Alamo** (www.alamo.com). All have desks at Atatürk International Airport, as well as at locations in town. Meanwhile, Hertz and **Decar** (www. decar.com.tr) have desks in the international terminal at Sabiha Gökcen Airport, while Avis has one in the domestic terminal. Check your national website (www. avis.co.uk) for deals; at press time, the price for a compact car was about $60/£30 per day.

Tips **Don't Let Taxi Drivers Take You for a Ride**

You give up a certain amount of control when entering a taxi in a strange city. Your safest bet is to have your hotel concierge phone for the taxi rather than you flagging it down. Under no circumstances should you hire a taxi off the street in front of the Ayasofya. Some hotels and taxi companies have agreements that award the company repeat business in exchange for honesty and accountability at no extra charge to the passenger. Still, the risk that absolute ignorance of a location will be rewarded with a circuitous route is fairly high. Knowing in advance that there's nothing you can do about it is usually enough to let you sit back and relax. But there still are a few things to look out for to avoid being scammed.

Check to see that the meter is running, and that the correct rate applies. The less expensive day rate (*gunduz* alternately flashes with the metered fare) applies from 7am to midnight, but crafty taxi drivers will push the night (*gece*) rate button to increase the fare. If you've caught a driver in the act, threaten to summon the police, or get out of the cab.

Beware of the "bait and switch" routine, whereby the driver takes your 10YTL bank note (worth about $8.70 or £3.80) and accuses you of having given him a 1YTL note. You can avoid this by holding on to the bank note until you've received your change. Also, note that 1YTL notes are blue-toned and 10YTL notes are orange.

For longer distances or drives outside of the city limits, taxis usually have a list of set rates. Be sure you've discussed these in advance, as you may be able to negotiate a discount (though it's doubtful). A final word: Don't get into a cab expecting bad things to happen. Just be a smart customer.

BY TAXI

Taxis are plentiful in Istanbul and are more likely to hail you than vice versa. **Avoid taxis that congregate around the main tourist spots** such as Topkapı Palace, Ayasofya, and at the cruise ship landing in Karaköy—these are the ones adept at performing a bait-and-switch with large bank notes or setting the meter to the higher nighttime rates. Better to have your hotel call a cab for you, the agreement being that the hotel will continue giving the taxi stand business only as long as the drivers remain aboveboard (granted, not a fool-proof system). Similarly, when out and about, pop into the nearest hotel and have the receptionist call a taxi for you. A taxi from Sultanahmet to Taksim will cost between 10YTL ($8.70/£3.80) and 14YTL ($12/£5.30), depending on traffic levels and distance, while nighttime rates (midnight to 6am) are 50% higher.

3 Etiquette & Customs

On the surface, similarities between the Turkish and Anglo cultures abound. Dig deeper, however, and you will uncover some unexpected, sometimes infuriating, and often charming differences. This section will help you navigate the complexities of the Turkish way of conducting affairs, be they social, societal, or informal.

For more on the arts, history, and culture of Istanbul, turn to "Appendix A: Istanbul in Depth;" for key Turkish words and phrases, turn to "Appendix B: Useful Turkish Terms & Phrases."

APPROPRIATE ATTIRE In Istanbul, especially in the more modern neighborhoods, female dress is modern, even racy, but when visiting the more traditional neighborhoods in and around the Old City, modesty will at least broadcast a different message to those likely to leer. Male visitors might want to be aware that Turkish men simply don't wear shorts, no matter how hot it gets, so wearing Bermudas or cutoffs will at the very least brand you as a foreigner. Meanwhile, coverage for men and women entering a mosque is naturally more conservative: for women, shoulders, legs, and head must be covered, and men should be sensitive to any exposed skin exposed by shorts or tank tops. It's a nice idea to carry around a scarf, but all mosques provide some type of head covering at the entrance. Also, remember that shoes must come off before entering the mosque.

CLEANLINESS Turks were among the first civilizations to provide water as a public service, illustrating at a basic level how clean this culture is. Even restaurants and hotels will boast of themselves and their kitchens as being *hijyenik* (hygienic). Public water fountains can be found around town as well as in the entry courtyards to mosques (these are the ablution fountains). Hand washing is a serial activity in Turkey, and where water is scarce, most carry moist towelettes. After meals, it is customary to proffer the open palms of your hands to your waiter when he passes by with a small dispenser of cologne.

GESTURES Turks are enthusiastic hand shakers, so be prepared for sometimes enthusiastic greetings. Remember to proffer the right hand only, as the left hand is considered unclean. Responses to certain questions take some getting used to: Instead of shaking their heads in our familiar "no" gesture, Turks tip their heads slightly backward, raise their eyebrows, and sometimes accompany this gesture with a "tsk" sound. When answering a question posed in the negative, as in, "The Grand Bazaar isn't open today?" the Turkish response will be "yes" in confirmation that you are correct. Certain hand gestures that would almost never occur by a non-Turk are considered rude. For example, two gestures have sexual connotations. The first is a closed fist with the thumb protruding between the pointer and middle fingers. The second is slapping a closed fist. Now, forget I told you this.

GIFTS Turks love giving and getting gifts. Who doesn't? If you've been invited as a guest to someone's home, it goes without saying that you mustn't show up empty handed. Some nice chocolates are a good option (choose ones that are alcohol free if you don't know how religiously observant the family is) or bring flowers. If you've been invited to a restaurant, it's always good form to offer to pay (although no matter how forcefully you try, you'll lose).

AVOIDING OFFENSE The old adage that "sticks and stones may break your bones, but names will never hurt you" has no parallel in Turkey, because in this culture, words *hurt*. Sarcasm can be easily misinterpreted, meaning that you could insult someone without even realizing it. Topics that are generally sensitive include human rights, the Kurdish issue, the Armenian question, and anything to do with the movie *Midnight Express*. At the same time, Turkish people are quite interested and open to discussing these things, so just be sure to find a balance. Also, when seated (usually on the floor), pointing the sole of your foot at another person is considered an insult. When bargaining for anything, once you've agreed on a final price and shaken hands, the deal is done. Changing your mind at the last minute or reneging on the deal is the surest way to piss off your carpet salesman (or other), but in my opinion, all's fair in love, war, and commerce, particularly in Istanbul.

PHOTOGRAPHY In some places, photographing state buildings or military and police installations is forbidden. Taking video or photographs in a museum is often prohibited (a picture of a camera with an "X" through it will be posted around the building); where photography is permitted in museums, there is customarily an additional fee to be paid when purchasing your admission ticket. Also, it is generally advisable to get a subject's permission before photographing them. As a rule, women in *chadors* (the head-to-toe black robe) do not wish to be photographed under any circumstances.

FAST FACTS: Istanbul

American Express **Türk Expres** is the official representative of Amex Travel Related Services in Turkey, at Cumhuriyet Cad. 47/1, 3rd floor, Taksim (© **0212/ 235-9500**). The worldwide customer assist service center number is © **00800/ 4491-4820**. Amex also provides a toll-free number within Turkey for Global Assist (© **0312/935-3601**).

Area Codes The three-digit area code for the European side of Istanbul is **212**; for the Asian side, dial **216**.

Babysitters Most of the larger hotels provide some type of child-care service for a fee, be it an on-site nanny or a babysitter referral.

Business Hours Banks are open Monday through Friday from 8:30am to noon and 1:30 to 5pm. Government offices are open Monday through Friday 8:30am to 12:30pm and 1:30 to 5:30pm. Official hours of operation for shops are Monday through Saturday 9:30am to 1pm and 2 to 7pm, but I've yet to find a store closed at lunchtime, or a shop outside of the Grand Bazaar or the Egyptian Spice Market closed on Sundays. Museums and palaces are generally open Tuesday through Sunday from 9:30am to 5 or 5:30pm, while the closing day for palaces is Tuesday, Thursday, or both. Museum opening hours are generally extended by an hour or two in summer; note that museums generally also stop selling tickets up to an hour prior to the official closing time. While most official offices close for bank and religious holidays, there is no hard and fast rule over shops closing for these holidays. During Ramadan, however, many shops and businesses close early, while many restaurants either close down completely or offer limited menus at lunchtime.

Courier Services The post office (PTT) offers an express mail service *(acele posta servisi),* although you may feel safer with old reliables such as DHL (© **0212/ 444-0040**), Federal Express (© **0212/444-0505**), TNT (© **0216/425-1700**) or UPS (© **0212/444-0033**). The latter has a convenient office location at Küçük Ayasofya Cad., Aksakal Cad. 14, Sultanahmet.

Dentist Istanbul seems to have developed its own dental tourism niche. If the city's new **Dentistanbul** franchise is any indication, you should have little worries in an oral emergency. If Dentistanbul (© **0212/444-0-DIS** or 0212/327-4020; www.dentistanbul.com) in Beşiktaş can't solve your oral problems, then the **Koç American Hospital** in Nişantaşı (© **0212/311-2000**) and the **International Hospital** in Yeşilyurt (© **0212/663-3000**) can provide emergency dental services in an English-speaking atmosphere. For a selected list of private practitioners, log onto http://turkey.usembassy.gov/docistanbul.html.

Drugstores Pharmacists in Turkey are qualified to provide some medical services beyond filling prescriptions, such as administering injections, bandaging minor injuries, and suggesting medication. Local pharmacies *(eczane)* operate on a rotating schedule so that one is always open; each posts the address of the one whose turn it is in the window *(Nöbetçi* or "on night duty").

Electricity The standard is 220 volts, and outlets are compatible with the round European two-prong plug. You may be able to leave your hair dryer at home, as most hotel rooms come equipped with at least a weak one. Visitors from America and Canada with electronics that need to be recharged will need an adapter, a transformer, or both, depending on the appliance.

Emergencies Local emergency numbers are fire © **110,** police © **155,** and ambulance © **112.** Emergencies may also warrant a call to **Medline** (© **0212/444-1212,** 24 hr. a day), a private company equipped to deal with any medical crisis, including ambulance transfers (cost varies according to distance), lab tests, and home treatment. The **International Hospital** (see "Hospitals" below) also provides ambulance services.

Hospitals For optimal local emergency care, put yourself in the hands of one of the reputed *private* hospital facilities: the new **Koç American Hospital,** Güzelbahçe Sok., Nişantaşı (© **0212/311-2000); Metropolitan Florence Nightingale Hospital,** Cemil Aslangüder Sok. 8, Gayrettepe (© **0212/288-3400);** the **International Hospital,** Istanbul Cad. 82, Yeşilköy (© **0212/663-3000);** the **German Hospital,** Sıraselviler Cad. 119, Taksim (© **0212/293-2150);** and the **Balat Jewish Hospital,** Hisarönü Cad. 46–48, Fatih (© **0212/635-9280)** are just a few of the establishments with reliable English-speaking staff. Don't forget that payment is required at the time of treatment.

Laundromats All hotels provide laundry and dry-cleaning services, seeing to it in the process that they make a huge profit on the transaction. Indeed, even in Sultanahmet, laundry is becoming big business. The Turkish word for a laundromat is *çamışırhane.* You can drop your soiled clothing at **Popup Internet and Laundry** (Divanyolu, Evkaf Sok., Yapı Hanı 5/2; © **0212/458-1997;** open Mon–Sat 10am–8pm). On the other side of the Golden Horn, a couple of laundry/dry cleaners are near the Pera Palas Hotel, but the prices don't warrant circumventing the hotel service.

Language English, French, and German are widespread, and increasingly so are Russian, Japanese, and even Korean. For the linguistically challenged, it may not be so unusual to encounter some minor language barrier (including, surprisingly enough, established restaurants), but the inherent willingness of the Turks to help combined with a little sign language and a lot of laughs will almost always do the trick. See appendix B for a glossary of useful Turkish words and phrases.

Legal Aid Foreigners and tourists get the benefit of the doubt in most every run-in with the law, but some things you just can't talk your way out of. For real trouble, contact your embassy or consulate for assistance and ask for their list of private law firms catering to English-speaking foreigners.

Liquor Laws For a predominantly Muslim country, it might be surprising that alcohol is even sold in Turkey. The truth is, drinking alcohol is not an issue: Some do, some don't, although the current government is certainly discouraging consumption by setting sky-high taxes on wine, beer, and spirits. In most restaurants (but not all) alcohol is readily available, and theoretically you have to be at least 18 to purchase or consume it.

Mail The PTT, hard to miss with its black and yellow signs, offers the usual postal services, in addition to selling tokens *(jeton)* and phone cards for the phone booths located in and around the post office and in most public places. Postcards cost 35Ykr to Europe and 70Ykr to all other continents. The PTT also has currency exchange and traveler's check services; in major tourist areas PTT kiosks are strategically located for emergency money needs. For express deliveries or shipping packages, the PTT operates an *acele posta servisi* (or APS), but for your own sense of security, you'd better stick with the old reliable UPS or DHL (see "Courier Services" above).

Newspapers & Magazines For local and national information, the *Turkish Daily News* gives a basic rundown of the day's headlines. If you have access to the Internet, log onto the website of Zaman, **www.zaman.com**, the bilingual website of the Turkish language national paper. For local listings, the *Guide Istanbul* and *Time Out Istanbul* contain essential listings for tourists. Both are available at newsstands; the former is provided free at some hotels.

Passports The websites listed provide downloadable passport applications as well as the current fees for processing applications. For an up-to-date, country-by-country listing of passport requirements around the world, go to the "International Travel" tab of the U.S. State Department at **http://travel.state.gov**.

For Residents of Australia: You can pick up an application from your local post office or any branch of Passports Australia, but you must schedule an interview at the passport office to present your application materials. Call the **Australian Passport Information Service** at © **131-232,** or visit the government website at www.passports.gov.au.

For Residents of Canada: Passport applications are available at travel agencies throughout Canada or from the central **Passport Office,** Department of Foreign Affairs and International Trade, Ottawa, ON K1A 0G3 (© **800/567-6868**; www.ppt.gc.ca). *Note:* Canadian children who travel must have their own passports. However, if you hold a valid Canadian passport issued before December 11, 2001, that bears the name of your child, the passport remains valid for you and your child until it expires.

For Residents of Ireland: You can apply for a 10-year passport at the **Passport Office,** Setanta Centre, Molesworth Street, Dublin 2 (© **01/671-1633**; www.irlgov.ie/iveagh). Those under age 18 and over 65 must apply for a 3-year passport. You can also apply at 1A South Mall, Cork (© **21/494-4700**) or at most main post offices.

For Residents of New Zealand: You can pick up a passport application at any New Zealand Passports Office or download it from their website. Contact the **Passports Office** at © **0800/225-050** in New Zealand or 04/474-8100, or log on to www.passports.govt.nz.

For Residents of the United Kingdom: To pick up an application for a standard 10-year passport (5-year passport for children under 16), visit your nearest passport office, major post office, or travel agency or contact the **United Kingdom Passport Service** at © **0870/521-0410,** or search its website at www.ukpa.gov.uk.

For Residents of the United States: Whether you're applying in person or by mail, you can download passport applications from the U.S. State Department website at **http://travel.state.gov**. To find your regional passport office, either check the U.S. State Department website or call the **National Passport Information Center** toll-free number (© **877/487-2778**) for automated information.

Police To reach the police, dial © **155.**

Restrooms Public restrooms (WC, or *tuvalet*) are located all around town, in addition to those in public buildings such as museums. "Toll money" in Istanbul costs about 25Ykr, which occasionally includes a bonus handful of toilet paper. Flushing the toilet paper can sometimes be hazardous to the plumbing; when this is the case, you will usually see a sign above the tank requesting that you dispose of it in the nearby wastebasket.

Smoking A local saying goes something like this: "Eat like a Turk, smoke like a Turk," which roughly translates to "don't expect anyone to comply with non-smoking laws." In theory, smoking is prohibited on public transportation, in movie theaters, and in airports, and discussions are under way for a national law banning smoking in all public places. Until that happens, this might be a good time to work on tolerance, and remember to pack Visine and to sit upwind at outdoor cafes.

Taxes A flat 18% VAT (value-added tax) is incorporated into the price of almost everything you buy, although news is that this will be lowered to 8% for tourist services. While generally included, note that some hotels charge this tax over and above room rates. Taxes for luxury goods are higher, as is the tax on alcoholic beverages (the current government frowns on such un-Islamic vices).

Time Zone All of Turkey adheres to **Eastern European Time** (EET), which is Greenwich Mean Time +2. To make it easier: When it is noon in New York, it is 7pm in Istanbul. Daylight saving time, when clocks are set 1 hour ahead of standard time, is in effect as **Eastern European Summer Time** (EEST), from 1am on the second Sunday in March to 1am on the first Sunday in November.

Tipping Gratuities are a way of life in Turkey and are often expected for even the most minor service. Try to keep coins or small notes handy and follow these guidelines: Give the **bellhop** 50Ykr to 1YTL per bag; leave at least an additional 10% of the restaurant bill for your **waiter;** reward your **tour guide** with 10€ to 20€ for a job well done; and give the **attendant** in the Turkish bath 3€ to 5€ *before* the rubdown. Shows of appreciation are also expected from your **chambermaid,** your **barber or hairdresser,** and an **usher** who has shown you to your seat.

Water Water is an integral part of Turkish culture; when the French were perfecting the art of camouflaging fermenting bodily odors with perfume, the sultans were basting in spring water in a sky-lit marble chamber and doted on by a handful of naked members of the harem. But the reality is that the water you bathe in is not necessarily the water you want to drink. It certainly won't kill you if you do. But take it from someone with an iron constitution—it will *definitely* slow you down. Do yourself a favor: Drink bottled water and wash fruits thoroughly before eating.

5

Where to Stay

In the 1980s and 1990s, and earlier this decade, visitors could choose among a sparsely populated category of hotels that included decrepit aging blocks, guesthouses with dubiously reliable electricity and plumbing, and the rare restored standout. Prices remained criminally low, as all but the most coveted rooms (such as those in the Four Seasons) sat vacant. But what a long way Istanbul has come lately. With tourism numbers soaring and room rates skyrocketing, hotels are popping up like mushrooms, while older properties are turning up again like shiny new pennies. Now you can expect solidly progressive and decidedly competitive amenities that more often than not include Wi-Fi, plasma TVs hooked up to satellite connections, and free airport transfers. It's also rare these days (but not altogether unheard of) that your morning shower runs cold or that the backup generator fails in a blackout.

1 Best Hotel Bets

For a quick overview of the city's best one-of-a-kind places to stay, see p. 6.

- **Best Place to Pretend You're a Sultan:** No expense was spared in creating the sumptuous retreat that is **Les Ottomans,** Muallim Naci Cad. 68, Kuruçeşme (© **0212/359-1500;** www.lesottomans.com). If Muhzinzade Mehmet Paşa himself were to step into his former residence today, he would feel like he had gotten a promotion. See p. 81.
- **Best Views from in Bed:** Honeymooners can make the most of the ample Bosphorus views at **A'jia,** Ahmet Rasim Paşa Yalısı, Çubuklu Cad. 27, Kanlıca (© **0216/413-9300;** www.ajiahotel.com), where plush beds face picture windows. The Mezzanine Suite throws in a panoramic bathtub as well. See p. 82.
- **Best Nostalgic Hotel:** Istanbul's leaders of the onward march toward cutting-edge modernity will stand up and take notice when the restoration and preservation of the **Pera Palas Hotel,** Meşrutiyet Cad. 98–100, Tepebaşı (© **0212/251-4560;** www.perapalas.com), is complete in 2009. The project promises to restore the luster to this 19th-century icon of Istanbul. See p. 76.
- **Best Trendy Hotel:** By the time this guide hits the newsstands, trendy hotels will be more numerous than grains of sand. For now, and tying for first place, are the **Mısafır Suites,** Gazeteci Erol Dernek Sok. 1, Beyoğlu (© **0212/249-8930;** www.misafirsuites.com), an oasis of style and guiltless indulgence, and the **Lush Hotel,** Sıraselviler Cad. 12, Taksim (© **0212/243-9595;** www.lushhotel.com), with rooms decked out like the downtown studio you wish you had. See p. 74 and 75, respectively.
- **Best Bang for Your Buck:** Both the **Cihangir Hotel,** Aslan Yatağı Sok. 17, Cihangir (© **0212/251-5317;** www.cihangirhotel.com) and the **Apricot Hotel,**

Amiral Tafdil Sok. 18, Sultanahmet (© **0212/638-1658;** www.apricothotel.com), tie for the best value. The former offers affordable Bosphorus views, while the latter provides the warmth and scale of a bed-and-breakfast in a quiet, historic corner of the Old City. See p. 75 and 69, respectively.

- **Best Hotel Restoration:** The architects and owners of the **Sumahan,** Kuleli Cad. 51, Çengelköy (© **0216/422-8000;** www.sumahan.com), whose very name recalls the property's original use (a grain alcohol distillery), swathed the former factory in marble, and updated it without sacrificing arched windows, the distinctive chimney, its industrial feel, or a sense of indulgence. See p. 82.

2 Istanbul Accommodations

Hotels in Turkey follow the international star–rating system and properties are classified according to amenities and services provided like fitness centers or conference space. Because the level and qualities of services can fluctuate wildly, a worn-out, old five-star with moldy bathroom tile might look better on paper than a brand-new, skylit gem with nothing to offer but basic clean rooms, stunning balconies, and a pool. In hotels rated three stars or lower, it is common for the bathroom to have a "Roman shower" rather than an enclosed bathtub or shower stall. This is usually a feature of budget level hotels and is essentially a showerhead on the wall and a drain in the floor. In some cases, you'll get a square, enamel stall basin and a shower curtain, in which case a practiced proficiency with the hand-held showerhead will eventually ensure the least amount of leakage on the bathroom floor. In the hotel listings below, the presence of the Roman shower setup is included in the listing.

The category of hotels in Turkey designated as "S" or Special Class provides an added layer of confusion. Special Class hotels are typically restored historic properties or new boutique hotels. In this category, room size and amenities such as TVs are anything but standard, and even the use of the word "boutique" can be a bit of a stretch. One way to assess sight unseen what you are getting is to look at the rates—higher prices often bring higher quality. The second and more effective approach is to follow the advice in this book. We've been to all of these and know what you're getting.

The earliest restorations of these "S" class hotels were completed by the state-owned Turkish Touring Club (the pseudo-equivalent of AAA). Now everyone has gotten in on the act. These small hotels can be owned by single men, single women, families, foreigners, high-rolling entrepreneurs, and carpet sellers with adjacent showrooms (how convenient for them).

The following are features and quirks that you can expect to encounter in hotels not affiliated with an international chain.

Most hotels in Turkey seem to have more rooms with twin beds than doubles, so unless you specify that you want a double, called a "French" bed, you and your partner will feel like a couple out of a 1950s sitcom. Fitted sheets seem to be an anomaly in Turkey, so if you're a restless sleeper, expect to get a view of the mattress in the morning, particularly if you're staying in a budget property (or in a twin bed). Ask for an extra sheet if there's nothing between you and the blanket, as bed-making habits vary from hotel to hotel, and some provide only the duvet (with clean cover). And not even the Four Seasons Hotel will spare you from the startling blare of the neighborhood's *muezzin* at sunrise. TVs are generally a standard feature in rooms, but even a TV with a satellite hookup will limit you to BBC World, CNN, and endless hours of cycling tournaments. Local programming is at least captivating, with reruns of *Guys and Dolls* or *The Terminator* in Turkish. Another interesting in-room feature that is regrettably being phased out is a built-in radio with centrally piped-in music. You will generally have a choice of up to three channels, and if you don't like the music, I discovered that calling down to the reception for special requests was effective.

Be aware, too, that an ongoing problem of not just the older hotels is the rapidity in which a clear drain will get clogged. I've kept recommendations of these hotels to the exceptional minimum. Many hotels rely exclusively on Mediterranean solar power, which sounds great until you get in a cold shower at sunrise. This is increasingly rare, however, as many establishments are installing backup generators for "24-hour hot water." Power outages are an unavoidable part of daily life in this growing city with an aging infrastructure, and because the water supply operates on an electric pumping system, there will be no water for the duration of the outage, usually only a couple of hours. As mentioned earlier, this is increasingly rare, but not unheard of. In the sweaty heat of the summer, this is where the neighborhood *hamam* comes in handy.

All hotels provide laundry and dry-cleaning services, seeing to it that they make a huge profit on the transaction. Depending on the establishment, expect to pay anywhere from 3€ to 7€ ($4.20–$9.80/£2.15–£5) per item for ordinary laundry. At around 15YTL ($13/£5.70) a load, depending on the weight, a local laundromat, called *çamışırhane,* is a cheap alternative, as long as you don't mind borrowing the hotel iron. One additional service offered by five-star hotels is babysitting, arranged by the hotel through reputable outside agencies.

PRICES & TAXES

Unless stated otherwise, the price of hotel rooms listed here includes breakfast and tax, although a few higher-priced hotels charge for these on top of the room rate. It is imperative to note that except in rare cases (such as full occupancy), the room rates provided below are "rack rates," fictional prices that are almost never quoted—not even to the most desperate last-minute walk-in. It is more likely than not that a rate will adjust itself anywhere from 10% to 50% (or more!) at the time of booking, depending on the season and how hungry the owner is. This doesn't mean that hoteliers have become market hagglers; it simply means that the prices listed for hotels are inextricably tied to the market. In addition, hotels in Turkey make rooms available at absurdly low rates to travel agents to receive business on a regular basis. Ironically, a recent, not yet pervasive, development has been for hotels to undercut these agents with their own web rates. Be sure to keep an eye out for these Internet deals. It's not uncommon, for example, for a room listed at 250€ ($350/£178) a night to sell for significantly less via the Internet. Therefore, it is up to the buyer to do the legwork. But buyer beware: Not all travel sites advertising cheap hotels on the Web are equally reputable, so I recommend that you stick to the local travel agencies listed in this guide (or those recommended to you by friends and relatives). If all else fails, ask nicely. For all these reasons, you may find fewer options under the "Inexpensive" or "Moderate" headings below.

In rare cases (and only once in this book), the currency of operation is not specified by the hotel on its website. This leaves the hotelier some wiggle room to take advantage of the stronger currencies. For example, say I contact the hotel for the price of a room. Before I get a response, I'll be asked where I'm calling from. If I say the U.S., the quote will be, say, $300 (345YTL). The price quote in euros by contrast would be 300€ or 536YTL. Get it? This can be quite a shock when you go to pay and you have no written confirmation of the rate quote. Always get it in writing, as this scam is becoming sadly more prevalent in the smaller hotels. *Note:* Sometimes the

---

Tips Surfing for Hotels

In addition to the online travel booking sites **Travelocity, Expedia, Orbitz, Price-line,** and **Hotwire,** you can book hotels through **Hotels.com, Quikbook** (www. quikbook.com), and **Travelaxe** (www.travelaxe.net). Two other great resources for locating affordable hotels are **www.venere.com** and **www.hostelworld. com,** which in addition to youth hostels, list a number of respectable pension options.

HotelChatter.com is a daily webzine offering smart coverage and critiques of hotels worldwide. Go to **TripAdvisor.com** or **HotelShark.com** for helpful independent consumer reviews of hotels and resort properties.

It's a good idea to **get a confirmation number** and **make a printout** of any online booking transaction.

---

hotel will simply ask you where you're calling from in order to quote the list price in a currency convenient to you. Again, best to do this type of business in writing.

Parents with kids will be pleased to learn that children 6 and under, and in some cases 12 and under, stay free. While this is almost universal, it is wise to double-check when you book.

3 Choosing a Neighborhood

For someone new to the sprawling mass that is Istanbul, one of the first questions to ask is "where's a good place to set up base camp?" I used to unreservedly direct my readers to the historic bulls-eye that is **Sultanahmet,** where old dilapidated homes converted into "Special Category" hotels created the perfect gateway to an authentic past. But three very important developments in the past few years have caused me to change my mind.

First, because of unrelenting demand, hotels—the majority of which are run by people with absolutely no experience in hospitality—formerly charging $20 (£10) for a room now charge 150€ ($203/£107) and up, for absolutely no added value. Let me put this into perspective: The luxury five-star Ceylan Inter-Continental (reviewed p. 71) has advance purchase Internet rates from 176€ ($238/£126) *with a Bosphorus view.* Second, given the enormous profit margins that a hotel can bring in, it seems as if everyone has gotten in on the act—transforming what was a market of family-run houses into a sea of mass-produced, soulless "boutique hotels." Finally, and most disappointingly, the hassling by carpet salesmen and their ilk has reached new levels; last time I stayed in town several hotel guests opted for the safety of the hotel lobby rather than brave the irritating and stressful storm of harassment by salesmen flooding the streets of the tourist areas. It is therefore with a heavy heart that I recommend this neighborhood only with the admonition to book through a reputable agent, stay vigilant (for formal and informal crime), or preferably, base yourself in **Beyoğlu,** where hotels are managed by people schooled in hotel management (and not carpet sales), and the food and nightlife are better anyway. Plus, with the new, efficient transport system connecting Taksim and Sultanahmet, you can spend the day wandering around the Old City, and in under 20 minutes, be back in time for a decent meal.

4 Where to Stay on the Historic Peninsula

IN & AROUND SULTANAHMET

VERY EXPENSIVE

Eresin Crown Hotel ✮✮ While excavating the foundation to build the Eresin, workers uncovered Byzantine floor mosaics, marble columns, and a cistern, artifacts later identified as belonging to the women's quarters of Justinian's Great Palace. Altogether, the hotel recovered, registered, and now exhibits 49 historically significant museum pieces dating to the Hellenistic and Byzantine times, giving this hotel a "boutique museum" quality. Rooms in this quality hotel are well appointed, with bonus touches like window seats, plaster friezes, and Jacuzzis. Its enormous rooftop terrace has one of the most magnificent panoramic views of Old City in Sultanahmet.

Küçük Ayasofya Cad. 40, 34400 Sultanahmet. ✆ 0212/638-4428. Fax 0212/638-0933. www.eresinsultanahmet. com.tr. 59 units. 275€–325€ ($385–$456/£195–£231) double; 400€–600€ ($560–$840/£284–£446) suite. AE, MC, V. **Amenities:** 2 restaurants; 2 bars; business center; 24-hr. room service; laundry service; dry cleaning; elevator. *In room:* A/C, satellite and cable TV, minibar, hair dryer, safe.

Four Seasons Hotel ✮✮✮ Voted by *Travel + Leisure* in 2007 as Europe's best hotel, this Turkish neoclassical building located in the heart of Sultanahmet was originally a dilapidated prison for political dissidents. Much of the original marble and tile were retained and recycled into the hotel's present-day, five-star interior design. Rooms have plush furniture purchased from local vendors; the architect even stayed true to tradition by applying paint as they did in the Ottoman palaces—with a spatula. The opulent and luxurious bathrooms, all with separate toilet cabin, present a formidable amount of competition for time spent sightseeing, and the king-size beds are amazingly comfy. Plus, almost all of the rooms have views of something fabulous. The Four Seasons Sultanahmet is also now reaping the rewards of its newly opened sister property, the **Four Seasons the Bosphorus.** Guests of this hotel may use the considerable amenities of the other, and it is even possible to divide your stay among the two—the staff will pack up your room and lay it out in the new space precisely where you left it.

Tevkifhane Sok. 1, 34110 Sultanahmet. ✆ 800/332-3442 in the U.S., or 0212/638-8200. Fax 0212/638-8210. www. fshr.com. 65 units. High season 395€–1,050€ ($553–$1,470/£280–£745) double and suites; B&B rates are higher; all rates lower Nov–Mar. AE, DC, MC, V. Complimentary valet parking. **Amenities:** Restaurant (p. 93); 2 bars; fitness room; Jacuzzi; sauna; shopping arcade; 24-hr. room service; laundry service; dry cleaning; nonsmoking rooms; elevator; high-speed Internet and Wi-Fi. *In room:* A/C, satellite TV w/pay movies, minibar, hair dryer.

EXPENSIVE

Arena Hotel This three-story hotel located in an unpolished corner of Sultanahmet just steps behind the Hippodrome occupies a restored Ottoman house that has remained in the same family for over 80 years. The owner has retained traditional touches such as family heirloom furnishings and "grandmother Gül's caftan" in the lobby's salon. Rooms feature charming Ottoman style decor, wood floors, and classic Turkish rugs, but the rickety stall showers (reminiscent of two-star pensions I've stayed at in Rome) indicate that the bathrooms need updating. There are two suites, each with a balcony, the only two tubs in the house, and flatscreen TVs. Better yet, the basement level has a little *hamam* (reservations required).

Küçük Ayasofya Cad., Şehit Mehmet Paşa Yokuşu Üçler Hamam Sok. 13–15, 34400 Sultanahmet. ✆ 0212/458-0364. Fax 0212/458-0366. www.arenahotel.com. 27 units. 150€–180€ ($210–$252/£106–£128) double; 200€ ($280/£142) suite. Special Internet rates according to availability. AE, DC, DISC, MC, V. Limited hotel parking on street. **Amenities:** Restaurant; *hamam* for 10€ ($14/£7) extra; 24-hr. room service; laundry service; dry cleaning; elevator. *In room:* A/C, satellite TV, minibar, hair dryer, safe.

Ayasofya Konakları   In the 1980s, the State-run Turkish Touring and Automobile Club set off a craze for historic preservation when it restored a handful of clapboard Ottoman mansions on the historic, cobblestoned Soğukçeşme Street. Back then, the collection of pension-style rooms saw a veritable stampede of illustrious visitors including Bernardo Bertolucci and Roman Polanski, and in 2000, Sofia, the Queen of Spain. After more than 20 years and commensurate wear and tear (plus a new manager), the pension has grown into its stately skin: Rooms have been restored, preserving the original character. The rooms are not deluxe, but many now benefit from a number of additional comforts (including air-conditioning and TV). The *konakları*, or collection of houses, also enjoys one of the city's most characteristic settings, sandwiched between the imperial outer wall of Topkapı Palace and the Ayasofya. The area also encompasses open-air garden and terrace cafes, and an expansive garden that surrounds a wonderful *orangerie*.

Soğukçeşme Sok., 34400 Sultanahmet. ℂ **0212/513-3660.** Fax 0212/514-0213. www.ayasofyapensions.com. 64 units. 150€–180€ ($210–$252/£106–£128) double; 280€ ($392/£199) suite. AE, MC, V. **Amenities:** Restaurant; 2 bars; 24-hr. room service; laundry service; dry cleaning. *In room:* A/C, TV.

Lady Diana Hotel   There was no need, really, for this hotel to bizarrely capitalize on the name recognition of Lady Di. We would have found it regardless. The hotel is a polished, medium-size, four-star property practically in the bulls-eye of Sultanahmet. The only potential downer is that if you get a northern facing room, your view is of the dismal concrete facade of the neighborhood's main post office. The neo-Ottoman carpeting and upholstery warm up rooms of varying size (although comparatively, all the rooms are bigger than those in other new hotels in town). Use of the sauna and Turkish bath are free for guests, and the hotel offers free airport transfers for Internet bookings of 3 nights or more.

Binbirdirek Mah., Terzihane Sok. 9, 34400 Sultanahmet. ℂ **0212/516-9642.** Fax 0212/516-9650. www.ladydiana hotel.com. 75 units. 200€ ($280/£143) double; 300€ ($420/£214) suite. MC, V. Limited street parking. **Amenities:** Terrace restaurant and bar; lobby bar; *hamam;* sauna; fitness center; massage; doctor; babysitter; 24-hr. room service; laundry. *In room:* Satellite TV, Wi-Fi, minibar, hair dryer, safe.

Mavi Ev (Blue House) ⓐ   If the Blue House weren't actually painted blue, one would think the name came from the fact that the hotel is practically attached at the hip to the Blue Mosque. This hotel is a fine example of modern Turkish elegance, with its tile floors, carpets, stained glass, and understated details. Most of the rooms have stall showers, while suites have Jacuzzis. The rooftop restaurant (and bar) is especially noteworthy, if not for the food, then for the backdoor viewing of the sound-and-light displays above the Blue Mosque (summer months only). The entire effect is enchanting, and you couldn't get a better view of the domes if you were standing right on top of them.

Dalbastı Sok. 14, 34400 Sultanahmet. ℂ **0212/638-9010.** Fax 0212/638-9017. www.bluehouse.com.tr. 27 units (25 with shower). 140€ ($196/£100) double; 220€ ($308/£156) suite. Rates lower in winter. MC, V. Public parking across the street. **Amenities:** Restaurant; bar; 24-hr. room service; laundry service; dry cleaning; elevator; Wi-Fi. *In room:* A/C, cable TV, minibar, hair dryer.

Sultanahmet Palace Hotel   Designed in the style of a garden villa, this hotel features Byzantine-style hand-carved moldings above Roman terra-cotta flooring, a grand marble central staircase below a half-cylinder stained-glass dome, courtyards and terrace fountains, and breathtaking views in summer of the Marmara Sea from the breakfast terrace. The Blue Mosque creates a fourth wall in the street-side rooms, a view so impressive that you won't mind the brutal awakening of the *muezzin*'s dawn

Where to Stay on the Historic Peninsula

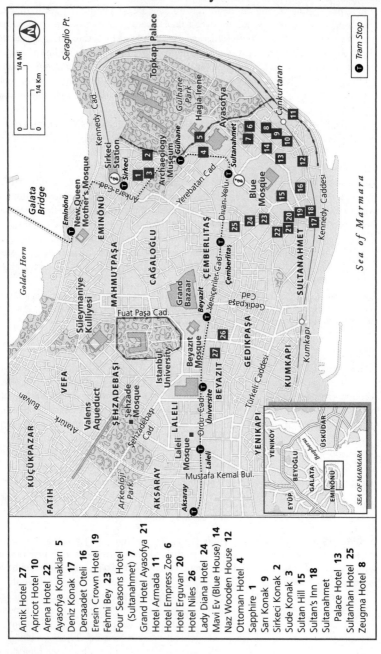

Antik Hotel **27**
Apricot Hotel **10**
Arena Hotel **22**
Ayasofya Konakları **5**
Deniz Konak **17**
Dersaadet Oteli **16**
Eresin Crown Hotel **19**
Fehmi Bey **23**
Four Seasons Hotel
(Sultanahmet) **7**
Grand Hotel Ayasofya **21**
Hotel Armada **11**
Hotel Empress Zoe **6**
Hotel Erguvan **20**
Hotel Niles **26**
Lady Diana Hotel **24**
Mavi Ev (Blue House) **14**
Naz Wooden House **12**
Ottoman Hotel **4**
Sapphire **1**
Sarı Konak **9**
Sirkeci Konak **2**
Sude Konak **3**
Sultan Hill **15**
Sultan's Inn **18**
Sultanahmet
Palace Hotel **13**
Sultanhan Hotel **25**
Zeugma Hotel **8**

call to prayer. Some rooms on the third (top) floor are disappointingly small, so when reserving, try to nab a second-floor (first floor) room or one of the two new deluxe top-floor rooms (#309 and #310) decked out with modern bathrooms and Jacuzzis. In all of the other rooms, each small bathroom doubles as a marble clad mini-*hamam* (no tubs; shower heads are provided for convenience); large-size visitors and creatures of habit used to enclosed showers or bathtubs might want to think twice before booking this hotel. Sadly, a glitch in the heating system prevents the *hamams* from producing any heat.

Torun Sok. 19, 34400 Sultanahmet. ℂ **0212/458-0460.** Fax 0212/518-6224. www.sultanahmetpalace.com. 36 units. Nov–Mar 143€ ($200/£102) double, 193€ ($270/£137) suite. AE, MC, V. Free parking next door. **Amenities:** Restaurant; 24-hr. room service; laundry service; dry cleaning; elevator. *In room:* A/C, satellite TV, minibar, hair dryer, *hamam.*

Sultanhan Hotel 🟆🟆   Muted echoes of guests' comings and goings bounce off the gracious marble walls of the lobby of this brand-new hotel located steps away from the Grand Bazaar and tramway. The elegance extends to the rooms, which are larger than what you might find at one of the many neighborhood "boutique hotels." All rooms have bathtubs, an oversize TV, and some even have sculpted entry archways. The hotel also has one of the most spectacular rooftop views in all of the historic peninsula, offering a completely unobstructed panorama of both the Blue Mosque and the Hagia Sofia *simultaneously.*

Piyer Loti Cad. 15, 34122 Çemberlitaş. ℂ **0212/516-3232.** Fax 0212/516-5995. www.sultanhanhotel.com. 40 units. 230€ ($322/£163) double. MC, V. **Amenities:** Rooftop restaurant; bar; *hamam* (50€/$70/£36); sauna; 24-hr. room service; laundry service; dry cleaning; nonsmoking rooms; elevator; Wi-Fi. *In room:* A/C, cable TV, dataport, minibar, hair dryer, safe.

MODERATE

Dersaadet Oteli 🟆   In Turkish, Dersaadet means "place of felicity and beauty"— an appropriate designation for this handsome hotel fashioned in the style of a 19th-century Ottoman house. The parquet floors and the deep wooden details lend a grace to the simplicity of the rooms, most of which have a view of the Marmara Sea and Asian side. A few of the bathrooms have showers and sinks jerry-rigged into the original small spaces, but all units are different, so ask ahead what to expect, or go for broke and simply opt for the recently renovated honeymoon-worthy Penthouse Suite. The rooftop terrace offers stunning views of the Blue Mosque and Marmara Sea.

Kapıağası Sok. 5, 34400 Sultanahmet. ℂ **0212/458-0760.** Fax 0212/518-4918. www.dersaadethotel.com. 16 units. 105€ ($142/£75) double; 115€ ($155/£82) sea-view double; 150€–220€ ($210–$308/£107–£156) suite. 10% discount for payment made in cash. MC, V. Free parking in adjacent lot. **Amenities:** Bar; 24-hr. room service; laundry service; dry cleaning; elevator; Wi-Fi. *In room:* A/C, satellite TV, minibar, hair dryer.

Fehmi Bey *(Kids)*   With so much "boutique hotel" competition in the neighborhood these days, it's only because Fehmi Bey recently renovated its rooms that I decided to give it a second look. Now, rooms are much better aesthetically, with upgraded bathrooms and polished original wooden floors. But except for a handful of extraordinarily large rooms, most are claustrophobic, making me question the value of this hotel in a season of high demand. I suggest booking one of the three deluxe corner rooms (nos. 103, 203, and 303), which have equally ample bathrooms. A "family room" is actually two rooms, one of which has a foldout sofa bed for kids. Otherwise, you can't beat the location (steps from everything), plus the hotel offers the added bonus of a sauna and business center. As almost all hotels in the neighborhood, this one also boasts an incredible rooftop terrace; there's also a nice little garden.

Ucler Sok. 15, 33340 Sultanahmet. ℂ 0212/638-9083. Fax 0212/518-1264. www.fehmibey.com. 34 units. 120€–
130€ ($168–$182/£86–£93) double; 170€ ($238/£121) suite; 200€ ($280/£143) family room. Rates lower off season. AE, MC, V. **Amenities:** Rooftop restaurant (summers only); bar; sauna; business center; secretarial services; 24-
hr. room service; laundry service; elevator; screening room. *In room:* A/C, satellite TV, safe.

Hotel Armada   Located on the outer edges of Sultanahmet in Cankurtaran near the
Ahırkapı Gate, the Hotel Armada is a true four-star hotel that makes a good choice for
groups. (Individuals who decide to stay here should realize that it's a short yet uphill
walk to all major sights.) It boasts an expansive lobby cafe, an atmospheric bar, and one
of the best rooftop terraces anywhere in the neighborhood. Rooms are decorated in
"Ottoman style" simplicity, with wooden chair rails, decorative painted flowers, and
subdued fabrics. The bathrooms are small but functional, with a negligible amount of
wear and tear around the edges. A buffet breakfast is served in a delightful penthouse
atrium adjacent to the terrace (the restaurant dining room), and the fish restaurants of
Kumkapı are within walking distance (as is **Balıkçı Sabahattin** restaurant; see p. 92).
Weekend guests may want to request a room away from the evening entertainment to
insulate themselves from the late-night echoes through the marble staircases.

Ahırkapı Sok. (just behind the Cankurtaran train station), 34400 Sultanahmet. ℂ 0212/638-1370. Fax 0212/518-
5060. www.armadahotel.com.tr. 110 units. 85€–100€ ($119–$140/£60–£71) double. Breakfast 9€ ($13/£6.40).
Rates do not include VAT. AE, DC, MC, V. Parking. **Amenities:** 2 restaurants; 2 bars; 24-hr. room service; laundry service; dry cleaning; elevator; Wi-Fi. *In room:* A/C, satellite TV, minibar, hair dryer, safe.

Hotel Empress Zoe ✪✪   Empress Zoe overlooks the crumbling remnants of the
oldest *hamam* in the city. Access to the rooms is via a narrow circular iron staircase—
good to know if traveling light wasn't on this trip's agenda. If you do hurt your back
on the way up, you'll be pleased to find extremely comfortable beds when you make
it to your room. The hotel combines five separate houses, and rooms range from
charming doubles with Byzantine or Anatolian style murals, to a variety of garden and
penthouse suites. Because of the configuration, secluded courtyards and panoramic
terraces unexpectedly appear around almost every corner. The rooftop bar is warmly
draped in deeply colored Turkish *kilims* and blankets, and there's a fireplace for those
crisp winter evenings. ***Note:*** Because of the construction of the Four Seasons annex,
all of the north-facing views to the Ayasofya are marred or completely obscured.

Akbıyık Cad., Adliye Sok. 10, 34400 Sultanahmet. ℂ 0212/518-2504. Fax 0212/518-5699. www.emzoe.com. 26
units. 105€ ($147/£75) double; 120€–225€ ($168–$315/£85–£160) suite. MC, V. **Amenities:** 3 bars; nonsmoking
rooms. *In room:* A/C, hair dryer, safe.

Hotel Erguvan ✪   This is one of those new boutique hotels I mentioned above.
The four-story building located just below the ancient retaining wall of the Hippodrome is fresh and welcoming. Rooms retain either the original parquet or laminate,
and an unobjectionable vanilla-pudding-colored paper covers the walls. Half of the
rooms have bathtubs, which is a rarity on this side of town, and every window in the
place is double-glazed, whether it needs it or not (it really doesn't, unless you haven't
gotten the hang of sleeping through that dawn call to prayer). The manager made a
point of mentioning that the building was reconstructed in compliance with Istanbul's
new earthquake code, a fact I'm not sure made me feel better or not. Pay an additional
15€ ($18/£11) and you'll get a sea-view room.

Aksakal Cad. 3, 34400 Sultanahmet. ℂ 0212/458-2784. Fax 0212/458-2788. www.erguvanhotelistanbul.com. 22
units. 145€ ($203/£103) double. Free airport pickup for stays of 3 days or longer. MC, V. **Amenities:** Rooftop restaurant
and bar (summer only); 24-hr. room service; laundry; dry cleaning; elevator; Internet point; Wi-Fi. *In room:* A/C, cable TV,
minibar, hair dryer, safe.

Naz Wooden House For anyone interested in sleeping in a room all wrapped up in the history of Byzantium, this is the place. The hotel is built directly into the ancient city walls, so chances are you'll be ducking under a Roman archway or sleeping under an expansive brick vault. Spaces are commensurately small and showers are of the closed sliding stall variety, but it's all very charming and historic. When Naz is booked up (there are only seven rooms, after all), the management encourages you to stay at one of their sister properties, the **Deniz Konak** (p. 69) or the **Sultan's Inn** (p. 69).

Akbiyik Degirmeni Sok. 7, 34400 Sultanahmet. © 0212/516-7130. Fax 0212/518-5453. 7 units. 70€–110€ ($98–$154/£50–£78) double. MC, V. **Amenities:** Rooftop bar; laundry service; dry cleaning. *In room:* A/C, cable TV.

Ottoman Hotel *(Value)* Originally connected to the adjacent Caferağa Medresi below (when it served as a dormitory for students there), the building was later converted to a hospital and then in 1972, a hostel. As of 2006, the hotel, which sits opposite the Ayasofya, joins the list of brand-new, Ottoman-influenced small hotels. Rooms are comparatively large, although the bathrooms, outfitted with albeit new European sit-in bathtubs, are a bit tight. Behind the hotel is an unexpected garden patio restaurant that sits above the undulating domes of Caferağa Medresi. During summer's eves, the hotel hosts a lone whirling derviş and hands-on ebru demonstrations.

Caferiye Sok. 6/1, 34400 Sultanahmet. © 0212/513-6150. Fax 0212/512-7628. www.ottomanhotelimperial.com. 50 units. 89€–129€ ($125–$181/£63–£92) double; 129€ ($181/£92) suite. AE, DC, MC, V. **Amenities:** 2 restaurants; bar; concierge; business services; 24-hr. room service; laundry service; dry cleaning; nonsmoking rooms; elevator; Wi-Fi. *In room:* A/C, satellite TV, dataport, minibar, coffee/tea station, hair dryer, safe.

Sarı Konak *(Finds)* It's easy to see why visitors choose to stay in this small family-run establishment. Bahattin and his son Umit roll out the red carpet for everyone. The rooms are simple but charming; the bathrooms are spotless and functional; and air-conditioning comes in half the rooms—the other half have ceiling fans. TVs were recently installed in the majority of the rooms, including the new suite, which also has high-speed Internet access and a Jacuzzi. The building next door was recently renovated into a multiroom, apartment-style annex (all suites), offering the opportunity for a real "local" experience. Breakfast is served to the soothing trickle of the garden fountain against the backdrop of an ancient Byzantine wall.

Mimar Mehmet Ağa Cad. 42–46, 34400 Sultanahmet. © 0212/638-6258. Fax 0212/517-8635. www.sarikonak.com. 17 units. 89€–129€ ($125–$181/£63–£92) double; 179€ ($251/£127) suite. Rates 30% lower off season. AE, MC, V. **Amenities:** 2 bars; 24-hr. room service; laundry service; dry cleaning; elevator. *In room:* A/C (in some).

Sultan Hill In 2006, this building was little more than a conglomerate of desiccated beams retaining, but for the grace of God, the shape of a house. Today, this brand-spanking new replacement of the 18th-century Ottoman house previously on the site is a small but gracious bed-and-breakfast located so centrally that you'll practically trip over the Blue Mosque, the Hippodrome, and the Küçük Ayasofya on your way out the hotel's door. Rooms, all of which have showers, are a bit tight but are set up to be as comfortable as possible. The ground floor breakfast room opens out onto a courtyard with an inviting traditional Turkish lounging corner. The hotel also makes best use of the requisite rooftop terrace.

Tavukhane Sok. 19, 34400 Sultanahmet. © 0212/518-3293. Fax 0212/518-3295. www.hotelsultanhill.com. 17 units. 50€ ($70/£36) single; 70€–75€ ($98–105/£50–£53) double; 100€–120€ ($140–$168/£71–£85) triple and family room. MC, V. **Amenities:** Rooftop bar; 24-hr. room service; laundry service; dry cleaning; Wi-Fi. *In room:* A/C, cable TV, minibar, hair dryer, safe.

Zeugma Hotel   The theme at this small, middle-end boutique hotel housed in a restored 19th-century Ottoman house is ancient Rome, with reproductions of mosaics discovered at the site of Zeugma decorating the walls. The best rooms are those on the top floor, as they get the sea views and Jacuzzis; otherwise, all the rooms are essentially the same—clean, bright, and functional, with cabin showers and parquet flooring. Windows are double-glazed to keep out the sounds of nighttime revelers across the street, but I'd play it safe and reserve a room in the back.

Akbıyık Cad. 35, 34400 Sultanahmet. ⓒ 0212/517-4040. Fax 0212/516-4333. www.zeugmahotel.com. 10 units. 70€–90€ ($98–$126/£50–£64). DC, MC, V. **Amenities:** 24-hr. room service; laundry service; dry cleaning; free Internet in lobby; free airport transfers. *In room:* A/C, cable TV, minibar, hair dryer.

INEXPENSIVE

Apricot Hotel ⭐ *(Finds (Value*   Because of a contract glitch, the Apricot was forced to move from its original location to an even more charming building on a parallel street. Although there are fewer rooms, they are prettier, larger, and better appointed. Indeed, the Apricot's owner, Hakan, has created the perfect example of why inexpensive doesn't have to mean cheap. The building provides an exclusive, stylish, and homey atmosphere at competitive (and fixed) prices with amenities such as Jacuzzis (in two rooms), *hamams* (two other rooms), and balconies (three rooms). With only six rooms, you'd better call now.

Amiral Tafdil Sok. 18, 34400 Sultanahmet. ⓒ/fax 0212/638-1658. www.apricothotel.com. 6 units. 59€–79€ ($83–$111/£42–£56). MC, V (add 5% for payment by credit card to the room rate). No traveler's checks. **Amenities:** Bar; Internet point; Wi-Fi. *In room:* A/C, cable TV, minibar.

Deniz Konak   This hotel at the fringes of Sultanahmet (near Küçük Ayasofya Camii and Kumkapı) is owned by the same people who run the Naz Wooden House (see above) and the Sultan's Inn (see below). All are small and charming, bed-and-breakfast-type places with various pros and cons. The main attraction of the Deniz Konak is the breathtaking views of the Marmara Sea. Alas, these very same sea-facing views come at a price: the commuter train just below (so much for the double-glazed windows). Each of the rooms facing the sea has a small bonus balcony, for 20€ ($28/£14) extra (no extra charge for the train). Guests have the option of taking breakfast at the Sultan's Inn across the street, which was actually a bit more ample than the one at the Deniz Konak when I visited. All of the major sites are in walking distance (mostly up gentle slopes), but perhaps just a bit farther than one might want.

Küçük Ayasofya Cad., Çayıroğlu Sok. 14, 34400 Sultanahmet. ⓒ 0212/518-9595. Fax 0212/638-3922. www.deniz konakhotel.com. 15 units. 40€–60€ ($56–$84/£28–£43) double. Add 20€ ($28/£14) for room with view. Rates reflect seasonal fluctuations. Rates spike over the New Year. MC, V. **Amenities:** Laundry service; dry cleaning. *In room:* A/C, cable TV, minibar.

Grand Hotel Ayasofya   This wouldn't make the top 10 list of hotels I'd recommend in Sultanahmet, but I include it here because the location is great (quiet, undiscovered back street), and after 27 years in business, it's iconic. Rooms are small and relatively clean, with bathrooms outfitted with old standing showers. Some of the rooms have carpeting, but I'd opt for one with wood floors, for hygiene's sake. I'd recommend this only as a budget option, and only if the price (preferably lower than quoted here) is right.

Küçük Ayasofya Cad., Demirci Reşit Sok. 28, 34400 Sultanahmet. ⓒ 0212/516-9446. Fax 0212/518-0700. 25 units. 60€ ($84/£43) double. MC, V. **Amenities:** Garden bar; airport transfer service; 24-hr. room service; laundry. *In room:* A/C, TV on request, minibar, hair dryer, safe.

Sultan's Inn   This little hotel, a sister property of the Deniz Konak and Naz Wooden House (both above), is basic without being dull. Sparely decorated rooms nevertheless have Turkish touches, and all rooms have modern bathrooms with showers. The rooftop terrace garden benefits from views of the Küçük Ayasofya Mosque, just a stone's throw away.

Küçük Ayasofya Sok., Mustafapaşa Sok. 50, 34400 Sultanahmet. ℗ **0212/638-2562.** Fax. 0212/518-5453. www. sultansinn.com. 17 units. 50€–100€ ($70–$140/£36–£71) double. MC, V. Rates reflect seasonal fluctuations. **Amenities:** Bar; 24-hr. room service. *In room:* A/C, cable TV, minibar, hair dryer, safe.

BEYAZIT & THE GRAND BAZAAR AREA
EXPENSIVE
Antik Hotel   If the idea of sleeping atop a 5th-century B.C. Roman cistern mere steps from the Grand Bazaar gets you going in the morning, then consider yourself at home here. The Antik is constructed over ruins connected to Theodosius' Forum; the neighborhood today still maintains the authentically quiet and untouristed streets of a working quarter. The entire hotel underwent a complete renovation in 2007, and each floor of this four-story hotel is designed around a pleasing color scheme of grape, lemon, cranberry, or olive. Ask for a high floor, because the spectacular basement cistern comes to life as a bar and restaurant at nights. The cistern, whose crumbling remains were restored but never thoroughly identified, was most likely associated with the Forum Tauri, Theodosius' grand forum that lies beneath nearby Beyazit Square. The actual "walk in" rate for a double when I visited was around 80€ ($112/£57).

Ordu Cad., Sekbanbaşı Sok. 10, 34130 Beyazit. ℗ **0212/638-5858.** Fax 0212/638-5865. www.antikhotel.com. 94 units. 250€ ($350/£179) double; 400€ ($560/£286) suite. MC, V. Limited street parking. **Amenities:** Restaurant; bar; sauna; concierge; 24-hr. room service; massage; laundry service; dry cleaning; nonsmoking rooms; elevator; meeting and event facilities; Wi-Fi. *In room:* A/C, satellite TV, minibar, hair dryer, safe.

INEXPENSIVE
Hotel Niles   This is the sister hotel to the **Dersaadet Oteli** (p. 66) and is located in a working neighborhood a 3-minute walk from the Beyazit transportation hub and the Grand Bazaar. The family that owns the two hotels runs them on the same principles of quality service and local knowledge. Though the two hotels are very different—Dersaadet is more of a historic inn, while the Hotel Niles is your standard tourist hotel—you get the same meticulous and friendly level of service. Hotel Niles provides the basics: a clean room, a clean shower, a knowledgeable staff, a roof terrace with a view of the Marmara Sea, and a generous breakfast spread. The rooms are big enough to fit their beds and not much else, but after hours of haggling in the Grand Bazaar, what more do you need? Considering that a double room is only 65€ ($57/£25) in the high season, and that you'll likely gorge yourself on homemade Turkish breads and *börek* for breakfast, this place is a bargain.

Ordu Cad., Dibekli Cami Sok. 19, Beyazit 34410. ℗ **212/517-3239.** Fax 212/517-0732. www.hotelniles.com. 29 units. High season 65€ ($57/£25) double; low season 60€ ($52/£23) double. MC, V. **Amenities:** Rooftop terrace; Wi-Fi. *In room:* A/C, TV, fridge, hair dryer, safe.

SIRKECI
MODERATE
Sapphire   This is not the newest or the most impressive hotel in the neighborhood. But if all one wants is a comfortable and clean room, with a great location and unpretentious, honest staff, that won't break the bank, then this is a reasonable choice. (The walk in rate when I last visited was about half the one listed here.)

Ibni Kemal Cad. 14–16, 34410 Sirkeci. ℂ **0212/520-5686.** Fax 0212/520-1009. www.hotelsapphire.com. 55 units. 140YTL ($122/£53) double. MC, V. **Amenities:** 2 restaurants; bar; concierge; 24-hr. room service; laundry service; dry cleaning; elevator. *In room:* A/C, satellite TV, minibar, hair dryer, safe.

Sirkeci Konak 🐵   One of the more charming additions to the neighborhood is the Sirkeci Konak, occupying a traditional clapboard reproduction around the corner from its older sister property, the **Orient Express Hotel** (ℂ **0212/520-7161;** www.orientexpresshotel.com). For years, the latter hotel has been a fallback for inexpensive, albeit charmless, rooms just steps from its namesake train station. Plus, it had a pool. It's still a reasonable option, but the Konak gets all A's for effort and implementation. The Ottoman interior decor goes well beyond the usual sateen bedspread (the ones here are textured in velvet). Cherry wood headboards frame the wall above the bed to lend a more oriental, and regal, sense to the decor. The Konak also has a pool (as well as a *hamam,* a sauna, and a fitness room); one thing you can do in the Konak that you can't in the Orient Express Hotel is make yourself a cup of coffee or tea in your room and sip it in the bathrobe freshly provided by housekeeping. As a bonus: two of the suites have balconies.

Sirkeci Konak, Taya Hatun Sok. 5, 34120 Sirkeci. ℂ **0212/528-4344.** Fax 0212/528-4455. www.sirkecikonak.com. 52 units. 135€–255€ ($189–$357/£96–£182) double; 230€–435€ ($322–$609/£164–£311) suite. AE, MC, V. **Amenities:** Rooftop restaurant; 2 bars; indoor pool; *hamam;* sauna; fitness room; concierge; 24-hr. room service; massage; laundry service; dry cleaning; nonsmoking rooms; elevator; meeting facilities; Internet cafe and free Wi-Fi. *In room:* A/C, satellite TV, dataport, Wi-Fi, minibar, hair dryer, safe.

INEXPENSIVE

Sude Konak   With prices going through the roof for rooms in Sultanahmet, it was really just a matter of time before the Sirkeci neighborhood became fashionable. As one of the newer and glossier additions to the neighborhood, the Sude offers fresh rooms and pristine bathrooms. The trade-off for all of this newness is that the building was obviously renovated with the goal of getting as many rooms on a floor as possible: Rooms are nice, but small. The hotel is conveniently located steps from the Gülhane stop on the tramway, but also an easy walk to Topkapı, the Aysafoya, and pretty much anywhere. This is a good option if the rates stay competitive.

Ebussud Cad. 24, 34410 Sirkeci. ℂ **0212/513-2100.** Fax 0212/513-2003. www.sudekonak.com. 40 units. 60€ ($84/£43) double; 85€ ($119/£61) suite. MC, V. **Amenities:** Restaurant; bar; concierge; meeting and business facilities; 24-hr. room service; babysitting; laundry service; dry cleaning; nonsmoking rooms; elevator; Wi-Fi. *In room:* A/C, satellite TV, dataport, minibar, hair dryer, safe.

5 Where to Stay in Beyoğlu
TAKSIM
VERY EXPENSIVE

Ceylan Inter-Continental 🐵🐵🐵   In 1996 the Istanbul Sheraton morphed into the Ceylan Inter-Continental, making way for yet another luxury five-star hotel. Unfortunately, the existing concrete-and-glass exterior didn't change its shape in the process. But structures like these are meant to please the eye from the inside, and that it does. The central glass-and-marble staircase sets the stage for just the right amount of pomp for the hotel's international clientele. The rooms are plush and elegant, with an armchair, desk, and love seat to create a homey feel. If you book online, you can get rates as low as 176€ ($246/£126). And it's all just a few steps away from the bustle of Taksim Square.

Asker Ocağı Cad. 1, 34435 Taksim. ℭ **0212/231-2121** or 800/327-0200 in the U.S., 0181/847-2277 in the U.K., 008/ 221-335 in Australia, or 0800/442-215 in New Zealand. Fax 0212/231-2180. www.interconti.com. 390 units. 450€ ($630/£320) double; 1,000€ ($1,400/£710) and up suite. Breakfast and tax not included. AE, MC, V. Garage parking. **Amenities:** 3 restaurants; 3 bars; patisserie; outdoor pool; state-of-the-art health club; *hamam;* Jacuzzi; sauna; tanning salon; shopping arcade; salon; 24-hr. room service; laundry service; dry cleaning; Wi-Fi, nonsmoking rooms; elevator. *In room:* A/C, satellite, cable TV and in-room movies, dataport, minibar, hair dryer, safe, bathtub.

The Marmara Istanbul 🏨🏨🏨   The Marmara is an excellent choice for those traveling for business or pleasure, particularly for its towering location above central and bustling Taksim Square. In fact, the hotel got so popular that they opened a second one, the **Marmara Pera,** down the street (p. 77). The Marmara Istanbul has everything necessary for an exclusive visit to Istanbul, including spacious bathrooms and spectacular views. The recently renovated Club Floor specifically pampers business travelers with 24-hour floor supervision, complimentary breakfast, and in-room fax and coffee service.

Taksim Sq., 34437 Taksim. ℭ **0212/251-4696.** Fax 0212/244-0509. www.themarmarahotels.com. 377 units. 166€– 196€ ($232–$274/£118–£139) double; 232€–275€ ($325–$385/£165–£195) Club Floor standard and suites; 490€–636€ ($686–$890/£348–£452) business and executive suites. Special weekend packages available. AE, MC, V. Ticketed parking lot. **Amenities:** 3 restaurants; 3 bars; cafe/patisserie; outdoor pool; health club; Jacuzzi; sauna; spa treatments; shopping arcade; salon; 24-hr. room service; laundry service; dry cleaning; nonsmoking rooms; executive floor; Wi-Fi; elevator. *In room:* A/C, satellite TV, dataport, minibar, hair dryer, safe, bathtub.

Ritz-Carlton Istanbul 🏨🏨🏨   The modern glass monolith that houses the Ritz-Carlton has marred the skyline above Dolmabahçe Palace for years, eliciting criticism at almost every turn. But the hotel's opulence and luxury make it forgivable. The hotel strives for a niche alongside that of the other multistarred hotels with exotic massage treatments, a premier health center, and fitness packages. Standard rooms are spacious, with large picture windows; the suites benefit from lovely parquet flooring and splendid views of the Bosphorus. Also, somewhere under all those pillows and bolsters, the beds are decadently high and plush. Bathrooms have bathtubs and separate showers, heated towel warmers, scales, handmade tiles, and designer soaps. The *hamam* is one of the most luxurious in town.

Elmadağ Askerocağı Cad. 15, 80200 Şişli. ℭ **0212/334-4444.** Fax 0212/334-4455. www.ritzcarlton.com. 244 units. 250€–425€ ($350–$595/£178–£302) double; 550€ ($770/£391) and up suite. AE, DC, MC, V. Indoor parking garage. **Amenities:** 2 restaurants; 3 bars; movie theater; indoor pool; health club; spa; *hamam;* Jacuzzi; sauna; concierge; tour desk; car-rental desk; shopping arcade; salon; 24-hr. room service; massage; babysitting; laundry service; dry cleaning; nonsmoking rooms; executive floor; elevator. *In room:* A/C, satellite TV, dataport w/high-speed Internet, minibar, hair dryer, safe, bathtubs.

EXPENSIVE

Germir Palas Hotel   Wooden wainscoting, faux Chippendale sofas, and Parisian-style cityscapes of Istanbul make stepping into the Germir Palas like stepping back in time to 19th-century Paris. The hotel's eye-catching and elegant style is a direct result of the Germir family's other enterprise: As owners of a textile business, they've coordinated warm floral wallpaper with leafy green and beige fabrics to create a warm and welcoming atmosphere. Rooms are comparatively small, so if possible, book one of the seven corner rooms, which are slightly bigger but sacrifice the view. Bathrooms are spacious and all come equipped with full bathtubs. The lobby-level brasserie-style bar is a great meeting place.

Cumhuriyet Cad. 17, 80090 Taksim. ℭ **0212/361-1110.** Fax 0212/361-1070. www.germirpalas.com. 49 units. 180€ ($252/£128) double. AE, MC, V. **Amenities:** Restaurant; bar; concierge; tour desk; car-rental desk; 24-hr. room service;

Where to Stay in Beyoğlu

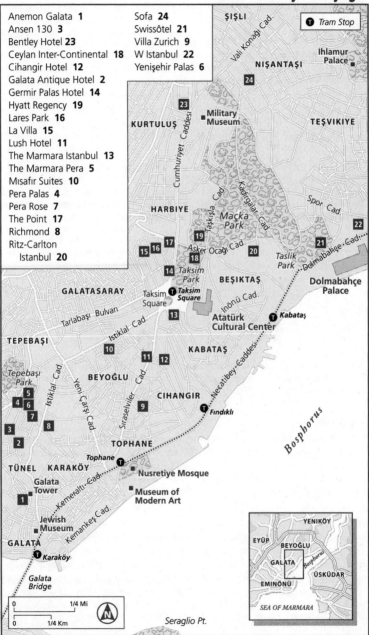

Anemon Galata **1**
Ansen 130 **3**
Bentley Hotel **23**
Ceylan Inter-Continental **18**
Cihangir Hotel **12**
Galata Antique Hotel **2**
Germir Palas Hotel **14**
Hyatt Regency **19**
Lares Park **16**
La Villa **15**
Lush Hotel **11**
The Marmara Istanbul **13**
The Marmara Pera **5**
Mısafır Suites **10**
Pera Palas **4**
Pera Rose **7**
The Point **17**
Richmond **8**
Ritz-Carlton
   Istanbul **20**

Sofa **24**
Swissôtel **21**
Villa Zurich **9**
W Istanbul **22**
Yenişehir Palas **6**

Tram Stop

ŞİŞLİ

Vali Konağı Cad.

Ihlamur
Palace

NİŞANTAŞI

Cumhuriyet Caddesi

KURTULUŞ

Military
Museum

TEŞVİKİYE

HARBİYE

Taşkışla Cad.

Kadırgalar Cad.

Maçka
Park

Spor Cad.

Asker Ocağı Cad.

Taslik
Park

Dolmabahçe Cad.

Taksim
Park

Taksim
Square

Taksim
Square

BEŞİKTAŞ

Dolmabahçe
Palace

GALATASARAY

Tarlabaşı Bulvarı

İstiklal Cad.

İnönü Cad.

Atatürk
Cultural Center

Kabataş

TEPEBAŞI

KABATAŞ

Necatibey Caddesi

Tepebaşı
Park

İstiklal Cad.

Yeni Çarşı Cad.

BEYOĞLU

Sıraselviler Cad.

CİHANGİR

Fındıklı

Bosphorus

TOPHANE

Tophane

TÜNEL KARAKÖY

Galata
Tower

Kemeraltı Cad.

Nusretiye Mosque

Museum of
Modern Art

Jewish
Museum

Kemankeş Cad.

GALATA

Karaköy

Galata
Bridge

0 ____ 1/4 Mi
0 ____ 1/4 Km

N

Seraglio Pt.

YENİKÖY

EYÜP

BEYOĞLU

GALATA

Bosphorus

ÜSKÜDAR

EMİNÖNÜ

SEA OF MARMARA

massage; babysitting; laundry service; dry cleaning; nonsmoking rooms; conference facilities; elevator. *In room:* A/C, satellite TV, minibar, hair dryer, safe, bathtub.

Hyatt Regency An Istanbul institution for decades, this is the Hyatt's first appearance in a Frommer's guide. The omission was deliberate: no point in sending visitors to a bland American-managed formula. With competition among visitors pushing prices sky high, the Hyatt now deserves a mention. Plus, it's got one of the best swimming pools in the center city and continues to lure expats to Spazio, its Italian restaurant. Even more tantalizing is the soon-to-open **Park Hyatt** just around the corner. Transformed into an Art Deco palace by New York-based architects Gerner Kronick and Valcarcel, the new property will cater to the world-weary business traveler by offering *spa rooms.*

Taskisla Cad., 34437 Taksim. Ⓒ **0212/368-1234.** Fax 0212/368-1000. http://istanbul.regency.hyatt.com. 360 units. 200€ ($280/£143) double; 400€–800€ ($560–$1,120/£286–£572) suite. AE, DC, MC, V. **Amenities:** 2 restaurants; 6 bars; outdoor pool; lit tennis court; Gaia fitness center and spa; *hamam;* Jacuzzi; sauna; salon; newsstand; concierge; business center; 24-hr. room service; babysitting; laundry service; dry cleaning; nonsmoking rooms; elevator; meeting facilities; Wi-Fi. *In room:* A/C, satellite TV, dataport, minibar, hair dryer, safe.

Mısafır Suites 🛝🛝🛝 Dutch-born Joost and his partners waited 4 years for the drug addicts and squatters to vacate the derelict building they purchased before razing it and starting from scratch. The facade, however, is original, while the inside is embellished with new basalt floors, marble bathrooms, and artistic textiles. Rooms are enormous (as are the bathrooms, which are stocked with complimentary L'Occitaine products), with king size beds, twin sofas flanking oversize circular ottomans, and long, conveniently placed upholstered benches. It's all very smart, very well planned out, and very, *very* delightful. The restaurant **Sekiz** (p. 100) has a hip vibe and top-notch creative cuisine. Airport pickup is included in the price.

Gazeteci Erol Dernek Sok. 1, 34430 Beyoğlu (from the Ağa Mosque on Istiklal, turn down Sadir Alışık Sok.). Ⓒ **0212/ 249-8930.** Fax 0212/249-8940. www.misafirsuites.com. 7 units. 200€–250€ ($270–$350/£140–£178) suites. AE, MC, V. **Amenities:** Restaurant; bar; concierge; limited room service; Wi-Fi; laundry; elevator. *In room:* A/C, satellite TV, DVD, minibar, coffeemaker, hair dryer, safe.

MODERATE
Lares Park Modern, luxurious, and architecturally appealing. Not what you'd expect from the fringe streets around Taksim (yet). A standard unit offers plenty of room to move around, while newer "deluxe" rooms are even bigger and recently redesigned. The Presidential suite, meanwhile, gets you a duplex with fridge, clothes washer, dishwasher, microwave, and CD/DVD player. The health club is a haven of relaxation, with patio-style lounge chairs set around a large indoor area with swimming pool, Jacuzzi, and juice bar. There's also a fitness center and tempting Turkish bath, and you don't have to pay a cent extra to use any of it (you do for the massage). The location right smack in the center of a vibrant commercial center is far enough away from the minarets of Sultanahmet to permit an uninterrupted night's sleep.

Topçu Cad. 23, 80090 Taksim. Ⓒ **0212/254-5100.** Fax 0212/256-9249. www.laresparkhotel.com. 179 units. 109€– 119€ ($153–$167/£77–£84) single; 130€ ($182/£92) double and deluxe; 200€–500€ ($270–$700/£140–£355) suite. Rates higher April–Oct, Christmas, and New Year's Day. AE, MC, V. **Amenities:** Restaurant; bar; cafe/patisserie; indoor pool; fitness room; *hamam;* Jacuzzi; sauna; business center; 24-hr. room service; laundry service; dry cleaning; elevator; Wi-Fi. *In room:* A/C, satellite TV w/pay movies, minibar, hair dryer, safe.

Lush Hotel 🛝 Doesn't the name say it all? It's lush and by the way it's hip. Previously, this hotel was actually the Lush Hip Hotel. Awaiting guests are down-filled duvets and pillows (regrettably, I had to avail myself of the non-allergic ones they keep on hand), 100% Turkish cotton sheets, complimentary l'Occitaine toiletries, and plump Turkish cotton bathrobes. And it's hip because it's got that certain *je ne sais quoi*. Maybe it's hip because it's a pioneer—Sıraselviler Avenue used to be a bit dicey, but it's now very close to having a clean bill of health. True to the building's 19th-century origins, details like exposed brick, parquet flooring, and decorative moldings are found throughout. The newest annoyance, however, among the truly hip hotels (like this one) is the placement of a digital scale in the bathroom. Perhaps this is to remind us of how good the food is in the brasserie downstairs?

Sıraselviler Cad. 12, 34433 Taksim. ℂ 0212/243-9595. Fax 0212/292-1566. www.lushhotel.com. 22 units. 125€–220€ ($109–$191/£48–£84) double. MC, V. **Amenities:** Restaurants; bar; fitness room; *hamam;* sauna; massage; concierge; business center; 24-hr. room service; laundry service; dry cleaning; nonsmoking rooms; elevator; Wi-Fi. *In room:* A/C, satellite TV, dataport, minibar, hair dryer, safe.

The Point The triangular, even Flatiron-like, Point Hotel is one of the earliest breed of "design hotels" offering something visually more appealing than the beige carpeting and innocuous floral bedspreads that pervade the hotel scene (but not this book!). Carpeting is checkerboard with Mondrian-esque stripes, and flatscreen TVs on the walls leave thick glass desktops sensibly uncluttered. I'm not sure this is even classified as superior design or just appealing decorating choices. The unmistakable advantage of this hotel, besides the spa and indoor swimming pool (also triangular), is the service, which is attentive, helpful, and friendly. The ground floor Japanese restaurant, Udonya, is extremely popular for the after-hours crowd.

Topçu Cad. 2, 80400 Taksim. ℂ 0212/313-5000. www.pointhotel.com. 194 units. 99€ ($139/£71) double; 144€–209€ ($202–$/293/£103–£149) suite. Breakfast 15€ ($21/£11) per person. AE, DC, MC, V. **Amenities:** 2 restaurants; cafe; indoor pool; spa; fitness room; *hamam;* sauna; concierge; 24-hr. room service; babysitting; laundry service; dry cleaning; nonsmoking rooms; elevator; 5 meeting rooms; Wi-Fi in public areas. *In room:* A/C, satellite TV, minibar, hair dryer, safe.

CIHANGIR
MODERATE
Cihangir Hotel *(Value)* *(Finds)* At first glance, the charm quotient is pretty low at best. Actually, the hotel is an eyesore from outside. But nowhere else in town will you pay 120€ ($168/£86) for a double room with a Bosphorus view. The hotel itself is pretty old, but rooms retain a newish patina even though they were last renovated in 2001. It's a short walk to Taksim Square, but remember that this neighborhood is very hilly.

Aslan Yatağı Sok. 17, 34433 Cihangir. ℂ 0212/251-5317. Fax 0212/251-5321. www.cihangirhotel.com. 90 units. 100€ ($140/£71) double; 120€ ($168/£86) Bosphorus view double. AE, DC, MC, V. **Amenities:** Restaurant; bar; 24-hr. room service; laundry service; dry cleaning; nonsmoking rooms; elevator; meeting facilities; Wi-Fi. *In room:* A/C, satellite and pay TV, minibar, hair dryer, safe.

Villa Zurich More people choosing to stay near Taksim Square are opting for the trendy neighborhood of Cihangir, the equivalent of the Village in New York or Soho in London. On the tourist map thanks to the excellent **Doğa Balık** rooftop restaurant (p. 102), the Villa Zurich is also a popular meeting point for neighborhood locals in the hotel's street level cafe. All rooms have Jacuzzis (except the singles, which have rain showers), and the one minuscule suite is little more than a standard room with a Bosphorus view. Still, you'd choose this hotel before you picked the Cihangir Hotel (unless you wanted the view at discount rates), and the rooms are comfortable and centrally located. Just book early for one of the more roomy units.

Akarsu Yokusu Cad. 44–46, Cihangir (follow Sıraselviler Cad. down from Taksim Square and turn left when you reach the mosque). ℂ 0212/293-0604. Fax 0212/249-0232. www.hotelvillazurich.com. 41 units. 95€ ($133/£68) double;

125€ ($175/£89) suite. AE, DC, MC, V. Free parking. **Amenities:** 2 restaurants; bar; car-rental desk; 24-hr. room service; laundry service; dry cleaning; elevator. *In room:* A/C, cable TV, dataport, minibar, hair dryer, safe.

TÜNEL & TEPEBAŞI
VERY EXPENSIVE

Ansen 130 ★★ *Finds*   It seems as though upgraded rooms in Istanbul are just flying off the shelves. Go figure. Ansen 130, inserted in a restored 19th-century architectural jewel, fills this need by offering 10 positively cavernous rooms that any bachelor looking for an apartment would kill for. Light wood and laminate dominate the decor, which is punctuated with more beige and a bit of black in the sofa, bedspread, and electronics. Bathrooms have pleasantly chunky hardware, and there's a kitchenette with everything you'll need for a long or short stay except the groceries. Ansen 130 has a ground-level bar that is popular even among nonguests, a cigar/wine bar next door, and a restaurant, **Saf** (p. 104), that's made Istanbul's top 15.

Meşrutiyet Cad., Ansen 130, 34430 Tepebaşı. ☎ 0212/245-8808. Fax 0212/245-7179. www.ansensuite.com. 10 units. 350€–500€ ($490–$700/£249–£355) suites. See website for weekly and monthly rates. MC, V. **Amenities:** Restaurant; 2 bars; 24-hr. room service; laundry; dry cleaning; meeting room; elevator. *In room:* A/C, satellite TV, Wi-Fi and Ethernet, kitchenette w/minibar, hair dryer, safe.

Pera Rose *Value*   When the reception quoted me a rate 30% below the listed rack rate in the fall of 2007, I started to smell a value. The Pera Rose is another renovated and restored business hotel on what used to be a dead end of Meşrutiyet Caddesi (most just passed by on the way to the Pera Palas or the Marmara Pera, both on nearby corners). I actually like this hotel more than the neighboring Yenişehir Palas, primarily because of the old-world feel imparted by the floral wallpaper and textured carpeting. All rooms are outfitted with scrumptious orthopedic mattresses. And as befitting a freshly renovated hotel, bathrooms are brightly tiled. Suites have Jacuzzis, and there are two pretty exciting duplexes.

Meşrutiyet Cad. 201, 34430 Tepebaşı. ☎ 0212/243-1500. Fax 0212/243-1501. www.perarose.com. 52 units. 232YTL ($202/£88) double; 318YTL ($277/£121) suite. MC, V. **Amenities:** 2 restaurants; bar; fitness room; *hamam;* sauna; concierge; business center; 24-hr. room service; massage; laundry service; dry cleaning; nonsmoking rooms; elevator; Wi-Fi. *In room:* A/C, satellite TV, dataport, minibar, hair dryer, safe.

Yenişehir Palas *Value*   Almost a half a century after opening its doors (and at least that long since the hotel has been screaming for a face-lift), the Yenişehir, or New City Palace, beckoned me with the fresh scent of recent renovations. As of 2008, the hotel

---

Pera Palas Hotel

In its heyday, the **Pera Palas** (Meşrutiyet Cad. 98–100, 80050 Tepebaşı; ☎ 0212/ 251-4560; www.perapalas.com) represented the Francophilia that had taken hold over the Ottoman Empire. It was built in 1892 as lodging befitting the exclusive passengers of the Orient Express, and accordingly the hotel's very own Orient Bar became a meeting place for drama and intrigue. The star-studded guest list includes Agatha Christie (who wrote *Murder on the Orient Express* in room no. 411), Atatürk (room no. 101, where he spent the days preceding the Gallipoli campaign, should remain intact), Jacqueline Kennedy Onassis, Greta Garbo, Edward VIII, Josephine Baker, and Mata Hari. This well-worn and beloved time capsule is currently under wraps as it undergoes what will be a 2-year process of renovation and restoration. Completion date is expected to be late 2009.

will have completed work on a full complement of rooms and common areas, allowing this formerly dreary hotel to latch on to the city's rising crest of tourism receipts. Rooms are now fresh—new carpeting and furniture and an overhaul of the bedclothes (ranging from sleek whites and beiges to Ottoman-style frilly)—and bathrooms are bright and modern. The hotel is ridiculously central: In 5 minute's walk you can be in Galata, Istiklal Caddesi, or Tünel, from which you can hook up with the transport system to Taksim Square or the historic center. I'm guessing that given enough competition, this hotel might become a great value.

Meşrutiyet Cad., Oteller Sok. 1–3, 34430 Tepebaşı. ℂ 0212/252-7160. Fax 0212/249-7507. www.yenisehirpalas. com. 171 units. 110€ ($154/£79) double; 125€ ($175/£89) suite. See website for special offers. MC, V. **Amenities:** Restaurant; bar; concierge; business center; 24-hr. room service; babysitting; laundry service; dry cleaning; nonsmoking rooms; elevator; meeting facilities; Wi-Fi. *In room:* A/C, satellite TV, minibar, hair dryer, safe.

MODERATE

Anemon Galata ⍟
The restoration of this 19th-century neighborhood gem was at the forefront of the revival of Galata. The building enjoys a front row seat to the neighborhood plaza at the base of the commanding Galata Tower. The hotel itself offers sophisticated old-world style and in-room architectural features such as original crown moldings and ceiling frescoes. Wall-to-wall carpeting (which I barely tolerate) and staid decor in the rooms do the building less than full justice, but the upside of all that sound-sucking upholstery is that you certainly won't hear the neighbors. For the best views, pick a room on the third floor or above.

Büyükhendek Cad. 11, 80020 Kuledibi. ℂ 0212/293-2343. Fax 0212/292-2340. www.anemongalata.com. 27 units. 125€–150€ ($175–$210/£89–£107) double. Rates include free airport transfers. AE, MC, V. **Amenities:** Rooftop restaurant; bar; concierge; 24-hr. room service; laundry service; dry cleaning; elevator. *In room:* A/C, satellite TV, minibar, hair dryer, safe.

Galata Antique Hotel
A clean, inexpensive option in this part of town is hard to find, but the Galata Antique, located just down the street from the British embassy and a few steps away from the entrance to Tünel and Istiklal Caddesi, provides a friendly and convenient one. The building was designed by the French architect Vallaury in 1881 and still retains some 19th-century charm in its caged elevator and carved wooden arches. The rooms are basic, tasteful, and elegant, and the bathrooms, although recently redone with fresh tile, are a bit disappointing due to the sparse sink and shower setups. The entrance to the hotel sits in the middle of a flight of exterior steps, so the Galata Antique may not be appropriate for everyone. However, the location is ideal.

Meşrutiyet Cad., Nergis Sok. 10, 80090 Beyoğlu. ℂ 0212/245-5944. Fax 0212/245-5947. www.galataantique hotel.com. 27 units. 110€ ($154/£78) double; 150€ ($210/£107) suite. MC, V. **Amenities:** Bar; concierge; 24-hr. room service; laundry service; dry cleaning; elevator. *In room:* A/C, satellite TV, minibar, hair dryer.

The Marmara Pera ⍟
The sister property of the Marmara Istanbul hit the ground running in 2005. It occupies a tower flanked by the Pera Palas Hotel and one of my favorite restaurants, **Lokanta** (p. 103), in the heart of the more vibrant section of Beyoğlu. And in spite of its 200 rooms, the hotel actually feels like a boutique property, as spaces are kept to manageable scale and the decor is understatedly trendy. The architect even saved the original tile paving where possible. Splurge the extra 50€ ($70/£36) or so for a sea-view room; it'll be worth it. There's a patisserie, bar, and restaurant on the ground floor, plus the independently-owned contemporary-style **Mikla** restaurant (p. 98) on the top floors commanding the best views.

> **(Fun Fact) A Mystery Worthy of Agatha Christie Herself**
>
> There has been much ado over **Agatha Christie's "mysterious" 11-day disappearance,** especially when it stands to substantiate the factual basis of a movie script *and* boost the profits of a historic hotel. The 1979 Warner Bros. movie *Agatha,* which makes reference to 11 missing days in the life of the author, was met with criticism by those who accused the movie studio of having fabricated the author's disappearance. In response, the movie studio hired a medium to get to the bottom of those 11 days. In a spiritual session, the medium, Tamara Rand, was "advised" by the late author that the answer to the mystery could be found in room no. 411 of the Pera Palas Hotel, where as a repeat guest between 1926 and 1932, Christie penned *Murder on the Orient Express.* In a much-hyped event, representatives of the film company and a group of reporters assembled in room no. 411 while a remote connection was established with Ms. Rand, who led them to a rusty old key hidden beneath the floorboards. Presumably, the key was to the author's diary and would reveal the answers to those 11 days. The key never left the premises, because the hotel and studio executives were unable to reach an agreement on compensation. (The hotel's chairman asked for $2 million plus 15% of the film's profits "for restoration of the hotel" in exchange for the key.) Rumors persisted about Christie's whereabouts, eventually putting her in a nearby hotel in the arms of Dashiell Hammett. That the author makes no mention of these 11 days in her autobiography has over the years only fueled the fire. In spite of the uproar caused by the recovery of her abandoned car and several cryptic notes she sent before her "disappearance," the truth may be less racy. It seems that she simply checked into a health spa in Yorkshire on December 4, 1926, under the surname of her husband's lover.

Meşrutiyet Cad., Derviş Sok. 1, 34430 Tepebaşı. © **0212/251-4646.** Fax 0212/249-8033. www.themarmarahotels. com. 200 units. 115€–190€ ($161–$266/£82–£135) double; 345€ ($483/£245) suite. Breakfast and tax not included. AE, MC, V. **Amenities:** Rooftop restaurant; bar; rooftop pool; fitness center; business center; laundry; dry-cleaning; elevator; four meeting rooms; Wi-Fi. *In room:* A/C, satellite TV, dataport, minibar, hair dryer, safe, bathtub.

INEXPENSIVE

Richmond (Value) The location of this Belle Epoque hotel couldn't be better. It's located close to the lively cafes and restaurants of Beyoğlu/Tünel, but remains accessible to Taksim, Galata, Karaköy, and the tramway to the Old City with a minimum of effort. It's a bit older than the snazzy new deluxe "boutique" hotels mushrooming around Taksim Square, but nevertheless a good value. Standard rooms have all of the necessary trappings above wall-to-wall carpeting. The newer rooms have parquet floors, sea views, and more space. The rooftop restaurant and bar is atmospheric and blessed with great views. Breakfast is served in the cozy brick cellar, but that's only in the unlikely event that you make it past the hotel's patisserie without stopping on your way down.

Istiklal Cad. 445, 80670 Tünel. © **212/252-5460.** Fax 212/252-9707. www.richmondhotels.com.tr. 206 units all with tub. 79€–120€ ($111–$168/£56–£85) double. AE, MC, V. **Amenities:** Bar; concierge; 24-hr. room service; laundry service; dry cleaning; elevator; Wi-Fi. *In room:* A/C, satellite TV, minibar, dataport, hair dryer, safe.

NORTH OF BEYOĞLU

Bentley Hotel ⚜ *Finds*   Off the tourist radar yet only a 10-minute walk to Taksim is this tribute to minimalist Milanese design. The Bentley has already fast become a favorite of the fashionista and publishing crowd, thanks to a combination of high-tech amenities, great aesthetics, and convenient proximity to the trendy SoHo-like section of Nişantaşı. The seven floors each contain two standard rooms, two ample singles, and two suites (one a corner), while the two penthouse suites enjoy the additional bonus of a private, semi-wraparound terrace. All rooms are decorated with a sleek and spare palette of white, beige, and black, offering top-quality electronics, Internet connections, and even an espresso machine.

Halaskargazi Cad. 75 (opposite the Military Museum), 80220 Harbiye. © 0212/291-7730. Fax 0212/291-7740. www.bentley-hotel.com. 14 units. 240€–280€ ($336–$392/£170–£199) double; 400€–800€ ($560–$1,120/£284–£568) suite. AE, DC, MC, V. **Amenities:** Restaurant; bar; fitness room; sauna; concierge; 24-hr. room service; laundry service; dry cleaning; meeting facilities; elevator. *In room:* A/C, satellite TV/VCR, CD player, fax, dataport, minibar, coffeemaker, hair dryer, safe.

Sofa ⚜⚜⚜ *Moments Finds*   Imagine standing in the middle of an artistic and elegant neighborhood, climbing the steps up from the cavernous entry level up to the clubby second-story reception desk (probably a Chippendale). Open your eyes and you could be in any of the cosmopolitan centers of the greatest cities of the world. The warm reception will remind you that you are indeed in Istanbul, in the city's toniest neighborhood. Since opening in 2006, the Sofa has been attracting fashion types, journalists, and the well-heeled in search of a high-end boutique experience. Although the hotel's "anything, anytime service" applies to guests of the suites only, the slogan is indicative of the personalized service the hotel strives to provide to all guests (think notepads with your name on them when you arrive). The management also recognizes how difficult it is to get out of a plush bed by keeping very liberal checkout policies (check in as early as noon; out as late as 3pm). Two of the hotel's children, the Taylife Spa and Tuus Restaurant, have already found their way into international magazines.

Tesvikiye Cad. 123, 34367 Nişantaşı. © 0212/368-1818. www.thesofahotel.com. 82 units. 280€–1,000€ ($392–$1,400/£200–£714) doubles and suites. Breakfast and tax not included. AE, MC, V. **Amenities:** Restaurant; 2 bars; indoor pool; fitness room; *hamam;* Jacuzzi; sauna; concierge; 24-hr. room service; babysitting; laundry service; dry cleaning; nonsmoking rooms; elevator; art gallery; conference and meeting facilities; computer rental; elevator; library; Wi-Fi. *In room:* A/C, satellite TV, dataport, minibar, hair dryer, safe.

Swissôtel ⚜⚜⚜   The Swissôtel is one of those brands that says quality, luxury, sophistication, and understated elegance, and the Istanbul location is no exception. The hotel sits on a wooded hill just opposite Dolmabahçe Palace on 26 hectares (64 acres) of grounds that were once part of the palace gardens. And with the tramway to Sultanahmet, the funicular up to Taksim, and buses up the Bosphorus just a stone's throw away, the location could not be better. Speaking of the Bosphorus, this hotel makes the most of views of the waterway by providing some sort of view from most of the hotel's 600 units. Levels of luxury vary from standard rooms to Executive and on to Panorama Suites, but everybody gets some.

Bayildim Cad. 2, 34357 Maçka. © 0212/326-1100. Fax 0212/326-1122. www.swissotel.com. 600 units. 160€–850€ ($252–$1,190/£129–£607) doubles and suites. AE, DC, MC, V. **Amenities:** 4 restaurants; 5 bars; indoor and outdoor pool; fitness room; *hamam;* Jacuzzi; sauna; concierge; shopping arcade; hairdresser; business center; 24-hr. room service; babysitting; 24-hr. laundry service; dry cleaning; florist; nonsmoking rooms; elevator; meeting facilities; 24-hr. medical service; Wi-Fi. *In room:* A/C, satellite TV, dataport, minibar, hair dryer, safe.

6 Where to Stay Along the Bosphorus

Those who choose to stay along the Bosphorus area are generally not the type of people concerned with price tags. These are the deluxe properties of Istanbul, offering staggering views, staggering meals, and staggering prices. Plus, the location isn't very central. Recognizing this, many of these properties offer shuttle boat service to the key points of the city (or anywhere you want to go, if you're willing to pay). If you can manage it and don't mind sitting in a little traffic (you can't go everywhere by boat, after all), the trade-off of convenience is more than balanced by the serene and spectacular experience of staying on the Bosphorus.

VERY EXPENSIVE

Çırağan Palace Hotel Kempinski Istanbul ★★★   Residence of the last Ottoman sultans, the hotel that you see today is actually two buildings: the faithfully restored stone-and-marble sultan's palace (housing the VIP suites) and the modern five-star deluxe hotel, both standing majestically on the shores of the Bosphorus and presiding over a magnificent collection of sculpted lawns, marble gates, a waterside swimming pool, and even a putting green. The guest list reads like a who's who of international royalty, all lining up for a Bosphorus-view room (not all get one). Standard rooms are nothing special really (except in the case of the ones with Bosphorus views, where you can forgive the room thanks to the scenery). Decor is sparse, and the full list of amenities is not enough to distinguish these rooms from, say, the Hilton. The suites in the modern wing add living space, upgraded decor, and views, but it's in the newly renovated palace section where things truly get interesting. These are salons that recall a statelier time: Sumptuous textiles swath elegant antiques, while high ceilings and gilded architectural features remind you that this was indeed once a working palace. Hard to believe that a little over a decade ago, the Çırağan was a burned-out shell of its current and former splendor.

Çırağan Cad. 84, 80700 Beşiktaş. 🕿 **800/426-3135** in the U.S., 800/363-0366 in Canada, 0800/868-588 in the U.K., 800/623-578 in Australia, 0800/446-368 in New Zealand, 0212/258-3377 in Istanbul. Fax 0212/259-6686. www. ciraganpalace.com. 316 units. $500–$765 (£250–£382) park-view double; $765–$1,015 (£382–£508) sea-view double; $1,058–$3,234 (£529–£1,617) hotel suite. Breakfast and tax not included. Double weekend rates available. AE, DC, MC, V. **Amenities:** 3 restaurants (Tuğra on p. 108); 4 bars; indoor and outdoor pool; putting green; health club; fitness room; *hamam;* Jacuzzi; sauna; concierge; car-rental desk; shopping arcade; salon; 24-hr. room service; babysitting; laundry service; dry cleaning; nonsmoking rooms; meeting facilities; elevator. *In room:* A/C, satellite TV w/pay movies, dataport, minibar, hair dryer, safe.

Four Seasons the Bosphorus   Eagerly anticipated for well on 4 years now, the new Four Seasons on the Bosphorus is going to keep us in suspense just a little bit longer. The latest scheduled opening was projected for November 2007, which came and went. Surely it will be up and running by the time this book hits the stores and in time for the 2008 summer season? As a result, I can only speak of this hotel in generalities: The hotel complex is composed of the restored and stately Ottoman Atik Paşa mansion, flanked by two regrettably practical modern blocks. (If the Çırağan can get away with it, then why not the Four Seasons?) Apart from that tiny criticism, the hotel aims to be—in the model of Four Seasons everywhere—a practically flawless center of hospitality and service. East-facing rooms in the paşa's mansion benefit from spectacular, head-on views of the Bosphorus. The (heated) outdoor pool sits seamlessly adjacent to the seafront, and a private dock provides convenient access, via the hotel's speedboat service (or one's private yacht) to key points around the city (or to nowhere, whichever is one's pleasure).

Çırağan Cad. 28, 34349 Beşiktaş. ℂ 0212/638-8200. Fax 0212/638-8210. www.fourseasons.com/bosphorus. 166 units. Contact hotel for rates. AE, MC, V. Valet parking. **Amenities:** 2 restaurants; 3 bars, indoor and outdoor pool; spa; *hamam;* sauna; massage; fitness room; concierge; business center w/translation services; 24-hr. room service; laundry service; dry cleaning; meeting facilities; banquet facilities; cinema; Wi-Fi and high-speed Internet; elevator. *In room:* A/C, satellite TV/VCR, CD/DVD player, fax, dataport, minibar, hair dryer, safe.

Les Ottomans ★★★ *(Moments)*   This lavish hotel is *the* talk of the town and only the most overused (but apt) superlatives will describe it. My apologies in advance. Let's start by saying that the powerhouse behind the hotel villa, Ahu Aysal, spared no expense (upwards of $60 million) in the reconstruction of the former Muhzinzade Mehmet Paşa, wooden mansion that stood on this site (the exterior is an exact replica). The result is a sumptuous, 10 room (plus one; Ahu lives on the top floor) . . . palace? abode? Shangri-la? In creating the hotel, Ms. Aysal employed the renowned Turkish interior designer, Zeynep Fadillioğlu, as well as the Feng Shui expert Yap Cheng Hai, to ensure the hotel conformed to principles of harmony. Feeling a bit underworthy upon my visit, I found that the hotel is opulent without being ostentatious; it's just what you'd imagine of a modern royal palace, gilded calligraphic friezes, (antique) ivory inlay, magnificent silk fabrics, and of course, let's not forget the plasma TVs (some suites have as many as three). And I haven't even gotten to the spa.

Muallim Naci Cad. 68, 34345 Kuruçeşme. ℂ 0212/359-1500. Fax 0212/359-1540. www.lesottomans.com. 10 units. 800€–3,500€ ($1,120–$4,900/£568–£2,485) suite single or double. Rates include breakfast and use of minibar but excludes taxes. AE, MC, V. Valet parking. Free parking. **Amenities:** 2 restaurants; bar; outdoor pool; Caudalie spa; *hamam;* sauna; fitness room; concierge; business center w/translation services; 24-hr. room service; massage; laundry service; dry cleaning; meeting facilities; banquet facilities; cinema; butler service; doctor; dietician; Wi-Fi; elevator; pet friendly. *In room:* A/C, satellite TV/VCR, CD player, fax, minibar, coffeemaker, hair dryer, safe.

W Istanbul ★★★   A few years back, my friend pointed to the Akaretler Row Houses from our perch at **Vogue** (p. 108) and said, "They're turning those into condos, and that's where I want to live." Except that instead of condos, the entire affair has been developed under the Starwood brand by the prominent Turkish businessman and former owner of the Beşiktaş football club. They allow pets (they offer "pet turndown service"), so now I want to live there too. The row houses were built in 1875 by Sultan Abdülaziz, either to provide income for the nearby Aziziye Mosque or to house the employees working at Dolmabahçe Palace. A more illustrious resident moved into No. 76 in 1918: Atatürk and his mother, Zübeyde Hanım. But even though they're not actually condos, the cavernous studios and duplex rooms, many with their own private gardens, feel like home. They're not actually on the Bosphorus either, but a mere 1 block away. The decor is both decadent and opulent, accomplished by marrying Ottoman sensibilities with modern desires they call "a harem of stylish luxuries." The in-room list of amenities includes ironing boards, sitting areas, bathrobes, the "W signature bed," and iPod docking stations. Bravo, W.

Süleyman Seba Cad. 27, 34357 Beşiktaş. ℂ 0212/327-9116. Fax 0212/327-5486. www.starwoodhotels.com/ whotels. 130 units. 345€–595€ ($583–$833/£246–£325). AE, MC, V. **Amenities:** Restaurant; bar; 24-hr. concierge; 24-hr. room service; babysitting; laundry service; dry cleaning; elevator; business and meeting facilities; Wi-Fi; non-smoking rooms. *In room:* A/C, satellite TV, dataport, minibar, hair dryer, safe.

EXPENSIVE

Radisson SAS Bosphorus Hotel ★   In January 2006, this piece of waterfront real estate adjacent to the artsy neighborhood of Ortaköy became one of the newer additions to the European Bosphorus. The target audience is business travelers, Turkish weekenders, and anyone else in the market for good design, seamless comfort, and a boutique experience. The hotel features a grassy "beach" and a spa offering a variety of treatments. There's a parking garage adjacent to the hotel, which is just steps away from the Ortaköy docks and some of the best nightlife the city has to offer.

Çırağan Cad. 46, 34349 Ortaköy. ℃ **0212/260-5757** or 0212/310-1500. (From the U.S. and Australia ℃ 800/333-3333; from the U.K. and New Zealand ℃ 800/3333-3333.) Fax 0212/260-6555. www.radissonsas.com. 120 units. 180€–450€ ($252–$630/£128–£320). Free parking. AE, MC, V. **Amenities:** Restaurant; 3 bars; wellness and beauty center; fitness room; *hamam;* Jacuzzi; sauna; concierge; car-rental desk; 24-hr. room service; laundry service; dry cleaning; nonsmoking rooms; rooms for those w/limited mobility, Wi-Fi; meeting rooms and business center; secretarial services; elevator. *In room:* A/C, satellite TV, dataport, minibar, hair dryer, safe.

7 Where to Stay on the Asian Side

Similar to staying in the hotels along the European side of the Bosphorus, by choosing this part of Istanbul as your base, you will be trading both convenience and cost savings. But if staying along the Bosphorus (on the European side) is serene and spectacular, the hotels of the Asian side are even more so, because they benefit from the slower pace of this primarily residential grouping of neighborhoods, and because from this side of the Bosphorus, the views include many of the first tier sights you came here for. All of the hotels listed also provide scheduled boat shuttle service to the European side.

A'jia ℞℞ The contemporary design of this sleek and stylish romantic getaway carries this traditional Ottoman *yalı* into the 21st century. The property was originally the stately mansion of the Turkish journalist and politician, Ahmet Rasim. In the 1970s, the house was converted into an elementary school (in fact, students still drop by to have a look). Accommodations range from sublime to otherworldly: ergonometric king-size beds, oversize goose feather pillows, oversize bathtubs, and picture windows for optimal Bosphorus views. The mezzanine suite (with the tub next to the bed) is host to many a romantic interlude; the management recently obliged by pasting rose petals on the glass to spell out "will you marry me?"

Ahmet Rasim Paşa Yalısı, Çubuklu Cad. 27, Kanlıca. ℃ **0216/413-9300.** Fax. 0216/413-9355. www.ajiahotel.com. 16 units. 250€–750€ ($350–$1,050/£178–£533) doubles and suites. AE, MC, V. Valet parking. **Amenities:** Restaurant; bar; 24-hr. room service; in-room Thai massage; private complimentary boat shuttle; waterfront sun deck; butler; meeting facilities; Wi-Fi; airport pickup upon request. *In room:* A/C, satellite TV, DVD player, hair dryer, minibar, safe.

Sumahan ℞℞℞ From an *ispirito fabrikası* for the production of *soma* (grain alcohol, today more benignly called ethanol) to an idyllic retreat, the Sumahan (note the apt name) is a prime example of functional architectural preservation. Mark and Nedret Butler met while studying architecture in America. When the Turkish State began proceedings to expropriate the land (owned by Nedret's family) in the 1970s, the Butlers, by then settled into their lives in Minneapolis, entered into a 30-year bureaucratic saga that ended in them relocating back to Istanbul. The rest is a story fit for *Architectural Digest,* with significant input from the Butler's interior designer daughter, Yaşa. Apart from the understated luxury, highlights include duplexes, bathrooms swathed in the same Marmar marble found in Topkapı and Dolmabahçe, and a studied forethought to even the placement of the soaps. The hotel provides three complimentary shuttles per day to the Kabataş docks. Commuter boats from the Çengelköy docks to Eminönü two times daily are a mere 200m (656 ft.) away.

Kuleli Cad. 51, 34684 Çengelköy. ℃ **0216/422-8000.** Fax 0216/422-8008. www.sumahan.com. 20 units. 280€–490€ ($392–$686/£199–£348) suites Apr–Nov; rates about 20% lower in winter. AE, MC, V. **Amenities:** 2 restaurants;

bar; *hamam;* 24-hr. room service; laundry service; dry cleaning; babysitting; library; Internet point; Wi-Fi and high-speed Internet; meeting facilities; elevator; rooms for those w/limited mobility. *In room:* A/C, satellite TV, CD/DVD player, minibar, hair dryer, safe.

8 Where to Stay near the Airport

Frankly, there's really no need to stay near the airport, no matter how early or late your flight is. The only potential exception might be if you're flying on a holiday, if it's snowing, or in the event of unexpected delays both on the road to the airport and at the gate. Road tie ups can drag a drive to the airport from Sultanahmet from 10 minutes to up to an hour. Traffic will be worse if you're staying around Taksim, along the Bosphorus, or on the Asian side.

Airport Hotel   Located on the grounds of Istanbul's Atatürk Airport, this is a sure-fire way to make sure you don't miss your flight. It's also a godsend on long layovers between international flights, because you never have to exit Customs to check in. Not surprisingly, the hotel attracts lots of business travelers—the business center and executive meeting rooms make sure of that—but even the most sun-kissed vagabond will enjoy breakfast views of the runway. Rooms are pleasingly bright, airy, and unusually spacious, and offer high-tech amenities like TVs that show flight details and Wi-Fi. The hotel also offers rooms at hourly rates (for naps on long layovers and such) and a well-appointed fitness room for those crack-of-dawn workouts.

Atatürk Havalimanı Dış Hatlar Terminali, Yeşilköy. ✆ **0212/465-4030.** Fax 0212/465-4730. www.airporthotel istanbul.com. 85 units. 140€–180€ ($196–$252/£100–£128) double runway side; 150€–220€ ($210–$308/£107–£156) land side. Hourly rates available. AE, MC, V. **Amenities:** Bar; fee-based fitness room; 24-hr. room service; laundry service; dry cleaning; elevator; Wi-Fi. *In room:* A/C, satellite TV w/pay movies, minibar, hair dryer, safe.

Sheraton Istanbul and Four Points by Sheraton   The Sheraton Istanbul is on the waterfront halfway between the airport (8km/5 miles) and the city center (10km/6 miles). It was closed down at the end of 2006 for renovations. Meanwhile, the Four Points will take over the old Holiday Inn and its 265 rooms right next door, and is expected to open its shiny new doors some time in 2008.

Ataköy. www.starwoodhotels.com. ✆ **888/625-5144** in the U.S. and Canada. 296 units. Contact hotel directly for details and opening dates.

WOW Convention Istanbul   The WOW (The World of Wonders) group of hotels never does anything halfway. Here, just a kilometer from the airport, in Istanbul's version of the World Trade Center, they've pulled together the four-star Airport Hotel (360 rooms), the five-star Istanbul Hotel (270 rooms), and the WOW Convention and Visitors center all under one (well, three) roofs. The complex targets the business traveler and convention goer by providing a complete biosphere of services in support of its niche as an event destination, including free shuttles to the airport and the city center. I'd opt for the Airport Hotel (see above) or even the Sheraton first, unless you lost your electric current converter somewhere, because this hotel has all the adaptors you will need.

Istanbul World Trade Center, Yeşilköy. ✆ **0212/444-0WOW.** www.wowconventionistanbul.com. 630 units. Doubles from 220 (currency not specified, so get it in writing). AE, DC, MC, V. Indoor parking garage. **Amenities:** 3 restaurants; 3 bars; indoor pool; fitness center; massage; spa; *hamam;* Jacuzzi; sauna; concierge; tour desk; car-rental desk; shopping arcade; barber/salon; business center; 24-hr. room service; massage; babysitting; laundry service; dry cleaning; nonsmoking rooms; executive floors; convention and meeting facilities; Wi-Fi (for a fee); elevator; movie theater. *In room:* A/C, satellite TV, dataport, minibar, hair dryer, safe, bathtubs.

6

Where to Dine

Turkish food has long been at the fore-front of international cuisine thanks to its use of the freshest produce and the incorporation of flavors from all of what was the Ottoman Empire. But just because an eatery bills itself as serving Ottoman cuisine doesn't mean your taste buds are going to explode. This is because many restaurants cater to tourists while keeping the menu lean and mean of anything really interesting. A week or two of grilled meat and you'll see what I mean. Lately,

though, Istanbul has regained its place as a culinary destination with celebrity chefs from the U.K., the U.S., Sweden, Japan, and, of course, Turkey. The progressive kitchens led by these chefs are located north of the Golden Horn, but even without a visit to one of these cover-story kitchens, the better meals will be had up in the neighborhoods of Beyoğlu, Beşiktaş, and along the Bosphorus, and will be shared alongside Istanbullus.

1 Best Dining Bets

For an overview of the city's best dining experiences, see p. 7.

- **Best Regional Cuisine:** There are newcomers, and old reliables, but not even the several outposts of **Develi,** Balıkpazarı (Samatya Fish Market), Gümüşyüzük Sok. 7, Samatya (© **0212/529-0833**), can compete with the quality of the food and of the setting of the branch in Samatya. See p. 98.
- **Best Chef:** Swedish-born chef **Mehmet Gürs** is his own Istanbul restaurant franchise. His innovative, studied, and seductive cuisine takes several forms: at **Lokanta** and **NuPera** (**NuTeras** in summers) Meşrutiyet Cad. 149, Tepebaşı (© **0212/245-6070**), the settings and the menu are casual and international. At **Mikla,** Mesrutiyet Cad. 167-185, Tepebaşı (© **0212/293-5656**), Gürs provides cutting edge art for the taste buds. See p. 98.
- **Best Ottoman Cuisine:** While Turkish and Ottoman cuisine seem to have merged into indistinguishable categories, **Asitane,** Kariye Camii Sok. 18, Edirnekapı (© **0212/534-8414**), looks to translations of Topkapı recipes. Çırağan Palace's venerated **Tuğra,** Çırağan Palace Hotel Kempinski Istanbul, Çırağan Cad., Beşiktaş (© **0212/258-3377**), takes these same historical recipes and reinterprets them for a modern audience. See p. 96 and 108 respectively.
- **Best Kebaps:** For years a favorite of the local and expat business crowd, **Borsa,** Lütfi Kırdar Convention Center, Harbiye (© **0212/232-4201**), continues to merit its crown with the expertly executed fundamentals of the Turkish kitchen. See p. 106.
- **Best Bistro Menu:** As Istanbul's palate becomes more sophisticated, new dining spots appear with modern, healthy, and even intriguing flavors. **House Café,** Asmali Mescit 9/1, Tünel (© **0212/245-9515**), Atiye Sok., Iskeçe Apt. 10/1,

Teşvikiye (© **0212/ 259-2377**), and Salhane Sok. 1, Ortaköy (© **0212/227-2699**), takes the freshest essential basics of the Turkish cupboard and turns them into modern and healthy dishes. **Sekiz,** Azeteci Erol Dernek Sok. 1 (© **0212/249-8930**), makes old Turkish recipes seem new again, and also offers spicy Asian and fusion alternatives. See p. 102 and 100, respectively.

- **Best Seafood:** As a city surrounded by bountiful seas, Istanbul suffers from an embarrassment of riches of seafood. Where do Istanbullus go for their grouper? Depends. **Gelik,** Kennedy Street/Sahilyolu (© **0212/444-7999**), is an institution located along the Marmara seafront and a favorite of middle-class local families. **Poseidon,** Çevdetpaşa Cad. 58, Bebek (© **0212/263-3823**), tends toward the card-carrying socialites, while **Doğa Balık,** Akarsu Yokusu Cad. 44–46, Cihangir (© **0212/293-9143**), capitalizes on masterful mezes and twinkling nighttime panoramas. See p. 96, 107, and 102, respectively.

2 Turkish Cuisine

FOOD

As nomads, the Turks were limited by what the land offered and by what could be prepared over an open fire, so it's not a stretch to understand how kebaps and *köfte* became the centerpieces of Turkish cooking. Turkish food today concentrates on simple combinations, few ingredients, and fresh produce. With access to vast cupboards stocked with ingredients from the four corners of the Ottoman Empire, the palace chefs developed a more complex cuisine. The majority of these recipes, recorded in Arabic script, were regrettably lost in the post–World War II language reforms. Some Ottoman favorites have made it to us nevertheless, like the *hünkar beğendi* ("the sultan was pleased": cubed beef or lamb on a bed of puréed eggplant or aubergine), *imam bayaldı* ("the priest fainted": eggplant or aubergine halves filled with a sort of ratatouille that Barbara Cartland might have visually likened to a woman's "flower"), and *hanım göbeği* ("lady's navel": a syrupy dessert with a thumbprint in the middle). These have become staples in many run-of-the-mill restaurants, but true Ottoman cuisine is difficult to come by. Several restaurants in Istanbul have researched the palace archives to restore some of those lost delicacies to the modern table, providing a rare opportunity to sample the artistry and intricate combinations of exotic flavors in the world's first fusion food.

A typical Turkish meal begins with a selection of **mezes,** or appetizers. These often become a meal in themselves, accompanied by an ample serving of *raki* (see "Drink," below), that when taken together, form a recipe for friendship, laughter, and song. The menu of mezes often includes several types of eggplant, called *patlican; ezme,* a fiery hot salad of red peppers; *sigara böregi,* fried cheese "cigars"; and *dolmalar,* anything from peppers or vine leaves stuffed with rice, pine nuts, cumin, and fresh mint.

The dilemma is whether or not to fill up on these delectables or save room for the **kebaps,** a national dish whose stature rivals that of pasta in Italy. While *izgara* means

You'll Never Count Sheep Again

Bus drivers in Turkey abide by an unwritten rule never to eat *cacık*—a salad of yogurt, cucumber, and garlic, often served as a soup—while on duty. The dish is believed to be a surefire, and natural, cure for insomnia.

"grilled," the catchall word kebap simply put, means "roasted," and denotes an entire class of meats cooked using various methods. Typical kebaps include lamb *şiş;* spicy *Adana kebap,* a spicy narrow sausage made of ground lamb; *döner kebap,* slices of lamb cooked on a vertical revolving spit; *patlican kebap,* slices of eggplant and lamb grilled on a skewer; and the artery-clogging *Iskender kebap,* layers of *pide* bread, tomatoes, yogurt, and thinly sliced lamb drenched in melted butter. Turks are equally nationalistic over their *köfte,* Turkey's answer to the hamburger: flat or round little meatballs served with slices of tomato and whole green chili peppers. But even though signs for kebap houses may mar the view, Turkish citizens are anything but carnivores, preferring instead to fill up on grains and vegetables. *Saç kavurma* represents a class of casseroles sautéed or roasted in an earthenware dish that, with the help of an ample amount of velvety Turkish olive oil, brings to life the flavors of ingredients like potatoes, zucchini, tomatoes, eggplant, and beef chunks. No self-respecting gourmand should leave Turkey without having had a plate of *mantı,* a meat-filled ravioli, or *kreplach* dumpling, adapted to the local palate by adding a garlic-and-yogurt sauce. *Pide* is yet another interpretation of pizza made up of fluffy oven-baked bread topped with a variety of ingredients and sliced in strips. *Lahmacun* is another version of the pizza, only this time the bread is as thin as a crepe and lightly covered with chopped onions, lamb, and tomatoes. Picking up some "street food" can be a great diversion, especially in the shelter of some roadside shack where the corn and *gözleme*—a freshly made cheese or potato (or whatever) crepe that is the providence of expert rolling pin–wielding village matrons—are hot off the grill.

> (**Fun Fact A Punishment Worse Than the Crime?**
>
> In Turkey, tripe soup, called *Işkembe Çorbaşı* or *Korkoreç,* is a widely accepted remedy for a hangover.

Desserts fall into two categories: baklava and milk-based. Baklava, made of thin layers of pastry dough soaked in syrup, is a sugary sweet bomb best enjoyed around teatime, although several varieties are made so light and fluffy that you'll be tempted to top off dinner with a sampling. The milk-based desserts have no eggs or butter and are a guilt-free pick-me-up in the late afternoon hours, although there's no bad time to treat yourself to some creamy *sütlaç* (rice pudding). The sprinkling of pistachio bits is a liberal addition to these and many a Turkish dessert. Comfort food includes the *irmik helva,* a delicious yet simple family tradition of modestly sweet semolina, pine nuts, milk, and butter (okay, I lied about the guilt-free part).

So what's the deal with Turkish delight? Otherwise known as *lokum,* this sweet candy is made of cornstarch, nuts, syrup, and an endless variety of flavorings to form a squishy tidbit whose appeal seems to be more in the gift giving than on its own merit.

DRINK

Rather than the question, "Would you like something to drink?" Turkish hospitality leaps immediately to the "What?" **Tea,** called *çay* (chai) in Turkish, is not so much a national drink as it is a ritual. Boil the water incorrectly and you're in for trouble. Let the tea steep without prior rinsing and you've committed an unforgivable transgression. What's amazing is that so many tea drinkers manage to maintain white teeth. As you'll see though, some don't. Tea is served extremely hot and strong in tiny tulip-shaped glasses, accompanied by exactly two sugar cubes. The size of the glass ensures that the tea gets consumed while hot, and before you slurp your final sip, a new glass

A Restaurant Primer

The idiosyncrasies of a foreign culture can create some frustrating experiences, especially when they get in the way of eating. In Turkey, dining out in often boisterous groups has traditionally been the province of men, and a smoke-filled room that reeks of macho may not be the most relaxing prospect for a meal. A woman dining alone will often be whisked away to an upstairs "family salon," called the *aile salonu,* where—what else—families, and particularly single women (but men also), can enjoy a meal in peace and quiet. Take advantage of it, and don't feel discriminated against; it's there for your comfort.

Restaurants are everywhere, and although the name *restoran* was a European import used for the best establishments, nowadays practically every type of place goes by that name. Cheap, simple, and often the best of Turkish home cooking *(ev yemekleri)* can be had at a family-run place called a *lokanta,* where the food is often prepared in advance (and ready to serve, called *hazır yemek,* or "ready food") and presented in a steam table. If you don't see any ready to eat food or aren't sure, ask if they have any on offer that day: *"hazır yemek var mı?"* A *meyhane* is a tavern full of those smokin' Turks I mentioned earlier, whereas a *birahane* is a potentially unruly beer hall. Both are said to be inappropriate for ladies; however, in the past few years, *meyhanes* have morphed into civilized places for a fun and sophisticated night out.

Now that you've picked the place, it's time to sit down and read the menu, right? Wrong. Not all restaurants automatically provide menus, instead offering whatever's seasonal or the specialty of the house. If you'd feel more comfortable with a menu, don't be shy about asking, and politely say, *"Menüyü var mı?"* This is also important if you would like to know what you're paying in advance.

The level of English proficiency may be a bit lower at restaurants (as is the pay and the staff longevity), but as long as you keep your requests simple, you should have little trouble making yourself understood. Regrettably, at the time of this writing, nothing you say will get you a table away from some heavy smoker (although the process is in place for a future smoking ban in bars and restaurants).

Mezes (appetizers) are often brought over on a platter, and the protocol is to simply point at the ones you want. Don't feel pressured into accepting every plate the waiter offers (none of it is free) or into ordering a main dish; Turks often make a meal out of an array of mezes alone. When ordering fresh fish, it's perfectly acceptable—actually, it's strongly advised—to visually inspect your fish and to have it weighed for cost; otherwise, you may wind up with not only the biggest fish in the kitchen, but also the biggest check at the register, since some catches go to auction at near 100YTL ($87/£38) per kilo. If the price is higher than you planned to pay, either choose a less expensive variety or ask the waiter if it's possible to buy only half. While we're on the subject of cost, many restaurants are now starting a new trend: charging a cover *(kuver)* of anywhere from 2YTL to 9YTL ($2.30–$10/76p–£3.40) per person.

When you're bursting at the seams and ready to go, ask for the check by either saying *"hesap, lütfen,"* or by making the universal gesture of writing in midair. Gratuities are rarely included in the price of the meal, and 10% is a customary amount to leave as a tip.

88 CHAPTER 6 · WHERE TO DINE

> **Fun Fact Caffeined Out**
>
> As a result of the Ottoman's second unsuccessful siege on Vienna, many of the army supplies were left behind in the retreat, including sacks and sacks of coffee beans. Believing them to be sacks of animal waste, the Viennese began to burn the sacks, until a more worldly citizen, aware of the market value of the bean, got a whiff and promptly saved the lot. He later opened up the first coffeehouse in Vienna.

will arrive. If you find the tea a bit strong, especially on an empty stomach, request that it be *"açik,"* or "opened," so that the ratio of water to steeped tea is increased.

The **coffee** culture (Turkish coffee, not the Starbucks version) is a little less prevalent but no less steeped in tradition. Ottoman clerics believed it to be an intoxicant and consequently had it banned. But the *kahvehane* (coffeehouse) refused to go away, and now the sharing of a cup of Turkish coffee is an excuse to prolong a discussion, plan, negotiate, or just plain relax. Turkish coffee is ground to a fine dust, boiled directly in the correct quantity of water, and served as is. Whether you wait for the grinds to settle or down the cup in one shot is entirely an individual choice, although if you leave the muddy residue at the bottom of the cup, you may be able to coax somebody to read your fortune.

There are two **national drinks:** *rakı* and *ayran. Rakı* is an alcoholic drink distilled from raisins and then redistilled with aniseed. Even when diluted with water, this "lion's milk" still packs a punch, so drink responsibly! *Rakı* is enjoyed everywhere, but is particularly complementary to a meal of mezes.

Ayran is a refreshing beverage made by diluting yogurt with water. Westerners more accustomed to a sweet-tasting yogurt drink may at first be put off by the saltiness of *ayran,* but when mentally prepared, it's impossible to dismiss the advantages of this concoction, especially after a dehydrating afternoon trudging through shadeless, dusty ruins.

3 Restaurants by Cuisine

ARMENIAN
Boncuk ★★ (Beyoğlu, $$$, p. 102)

BISTRO FARE
Enginar (Galata, $$, p. 105)
House Café (Tünel, $$$, p. 102)
Midpoint (Şişli, $$, p. 107)
Saf ★ (Tepebaşı, $$, p. 104)
Smyrna ★ (Cihangir, $$, p. 102)

BLACK SEA
Refik ★ (Tünel, $$$, p. 103)

FISH
Balıkçı Sabahattin ★★★ (Cankurtaran, $$$$, p. 92)
Degustasyon Lokantası (Beyoğlu, $$, p. 103)
Del Mare (Çengelköy, $$$$, p. 109)
Doğa Balık ★★ (Cihangir, $$, p. 102)
Gelik Balık (Sahilyolu, $$$, p. 96)
Körfez ★★★ (Kanlıca, $$$$, p. 109)
Malta Köşkü (Beşiktaş, $$, p. 108)
Poseidon ★★★ (Bebek, $$$$, p. 107)
Refik ★ (Tünel, $$$, p. 103)

Key to Abbreviations: $$$$ = Very Expensive $$$ = Expensive $$ = Moderate $ = Inexpensive

FRENCH
Café du Levant (Sütlüce, $$$, p. 107)
Sarnıç (Sultanahmet, $$$$, p. 93).
Yeşil Ev ✿ (Sultanahmet, $$$, p. 93)

FUSION
Banyan Seaside (Ortaköy, $$$, p. 108)

GEORGIAN
Galata House ✿ (Galata, $$, p. 105)

HEALTHY & VEGETARIAN
Deli-Bakkal (Tünel, $, p. 104)
Parsifal (Taksim, $, p. 101)
Saf ✿ (Tepebaşı, $$, p. 104)
Zencefil (Taksim, $, p. 101)

INDIAN
Dubb ✿ (Sultanahmet, $$, p. 94)

INTERNATIONAL
Lokanta at Nu Pera/Nu Teras ✿✿
  (Tepebaşı, $$, p. 103)
Sekiz ✿✿ (Taksim, $$, p. 100)
Vogue ✿✿ (Beşiktaş, $$$, p. 108)

ITALIAN
Beymen Brasserie (Nişantaşı, $$$,
  p. 106)
Da Mario ✿✿ (Etiler, $$$, p. 108)
Fes Café (Nuruosmaniye, $$, p. 95)
Flamm (Tünel, $$, p. 103)

KEBAPS & LOKANTA FARE
Adigüzel Restaurant (Galata, $,
  p. 105)
Beyti (Florya, $$, p. 98)
Buhara 93 (Sultanahmet, $, p. 94)
Eminönü Belediyesi Sosyal Tesisleri
  (Cankurtaran, $, p. 94)
Hamdi Et Lokantası (Eminönü, $$,
  p. 90)
Saray Muhallebiçileri (Beyoğlu and
  Eminönü, $, p. 101)
Şeker Mantı (Taksim, $, p. 101)
The Pudding Shop (Sultanahmet, $,
  p. 94)
Zinhan (Eminönü, $$, p. 92)

KOSHER
Carne (Şişli, $$, p. 106)

MEDITERRANEAN
A'jia (Kanlıca, $$$$, p. 109)
Carne (Şişli, $$, p. 106)
Divan Lokantası (Elmadağ, $$$,
  p. 100)
Mikla ✿✿✿ (Tepebaşı, $$$$, p. 98)
Seasons Restaurant ✿✿✿ (Sultanah-
  met, $$$, p. 93)
Tuus ✿✿ (Nişantaşı, $$$$, p. 105)

MEZES
Degustasyon Lokantası (Beyoğlu, $$,
  p. 103)
Doğa Balık ✿✿ (Cihangir, $$, p. 102)

MIDDLE EASTERN
Felafel House (Taksim, $, p. 101)

OTTOMAN
Asitane ✿✿✿ (Edirnekapı, $$$,
  p. 96)
Feriye Restaurant ✿✿ (Ortaköy,
  $$$$, p. 107)
Hacı Baba Restaurant (Beyoğlu, $$,
  p. 100)
Hünkar ✿✿ (Nişantaşı, $$, p. 106)
Konyalı Topkapı Sarayı Lokantası ✿
  (Sultanahmet, $$$, p. 93)
Orient Express Cafe (Sirkeci, $$,
  p. 92)
Tuğra ✿✿✿ (Beşiktaş, $$$, p. 108)
Zeyrekhane (Zeyrek, $$, p. 96)

PATISSERIE
Saray Muhallebiçileri (Beyoğlu and
  Eminönü, $, p. 101)

RUSSIAN
Rejans (Galatasaray, $$$, p. 103)

SUSHI
Vogue ✿✿ (Beşiktaş, $$$, p. 108)

THAI
Pera Thai (Beyoğlu, $$, p. 104)

TURKISH
Boncuk ✿✿ (Beyoğlu, $$$, p. 102)
Borsa ✿✿ (Harbiye, $$, p. 106)
Çiya Sofrası ✿✿✿ (Kadıköy, $,
  p. 109)

Darüzziyafe (Süleymaniye, $$, p. 95)
Develi Restaurant ★★★ (Samatya, $$, p. 98)
Divan Lokantası (Elmadağ, $$$, p. 100)
Hacı Abdullah (Beyoğlu, $$$, p. 100)
Konyalı Topkapı Sarayı Lokantası ★ (Sultanahmet, $$$, p. 93)
Malta Köşkü (Beşiktaş, $$, p. 108)
Marmara Terrace Restaurant (Sultanahmet, $$, p. 94)

Otantik (Beyoğlu, $, p. 104)
Pandeli Lokantası (Eminönü, $$, p. 92)
Sultanahmet Köfteçısı Selim Usta (Sultanahmet, $, p. 95)
Tamara ★ (Sultanahmet, $, p. 95)
Yakup 2 (Tepebaşı, $$, p. 104)
Ziya Şark Sofrası (Aksaray, $$, p. 96)

4 Where to Dine on the Historic Peninsula

For the most part, 90% of the restaurants and eateries in the Old City are sadly lacking, and although you can forgive an eatery a less than stellar meal at lunchtime, I for one can't forgive the extortion. Instead, I recommend you sample the honest home cooking at the various innocuous *lokantas* (dives with steam tables), particularly along Piyer Loti Caddesi, between the Hippodrome and Cağaloğlu and in the working streets around the Grand Bazaar, or grab a taxi to the restaurants I've starred below.

Another popular option is the neighborhood of **Kumkapı,** on the southern tip of the historic peninsula, a year-round carnival crammed with typical *tavernas,* which benefits directly from the fish market across the highway. Appropriately, Kumkapı translates to "sand gate." Pick the restaurant with the most people or the freshest looking fish, and hold on to your valuables, as the dimly-lit surrounding streets attract the worst petty thieves.

SIRKECI & EMINÖNÜ
MODERATE
Hamdi Et Lokantası KEBAPS Hamdi's southeastern kebaps will never come close to Develi Restaurant (p. 98), but this is a good alternative to the overpriced mediocrity of Pandeli Lokantası only steps from the entrance to the Egyptian Spice Market. The popular terrace views of Galata Tower and the Golden Horn add to the convenience of the location, and you can move to the cozy *şark* (Oriental-style seating area) for your after-dinner cup of coffee or tea. Specialties of the house include the *erikli kebap,* minced meat from a suckling lamb in which all of the fat has been cooked out, and the showcase *testi kebap,* a stew of diced meat, tomatoes, shallots, garlic, and green pepper cooked in a terra-cotta pot over an open fire and served tableside by breaking the pot (minimum 10 people, advance orders required). Hamdi caters to vegetarians with the vegetable kebap, spiced with parsley and garlic; don't pass up the *yuvarlama,* a flavorful yogurt soup with tiny rice balls served only at dinnertime.

Tips Dining with a View

Restaurant dining rooms resemble ghost town eateries in the summer, but if you just continue up the steps, you'll see why. Istanbul is a city of rooftop terraces, and summer dining is almost exclusively enjoyed high above the city accompanied by warm breezes and breathtaking panoramas.

Where to Dine on the Historic Peninsula

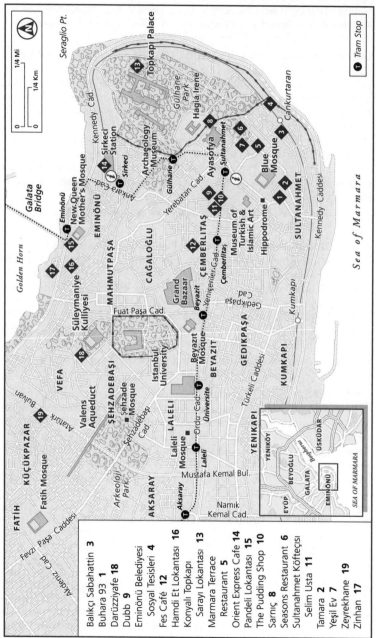

Seraglio Pt.

Topkapi Palace

Gülhane Park

Hagia Irene

Kennedy Cad.

Sirkeci Station

Archaeology Museum

Ayasofya

New Queen Mother's Mosque

Sirkeci

Ankara Cad.

Galata Bridge

Eminönü

Gülhane

Yerebatan Cad.

Sultanahmet

Blue Mosque

Çankurtaran

SULTANAHMET

Kennedy Caddesi

Golden Horn

EMİNÖNÜ

MAHMUTPAŞA

CAĞALOĞLU

Museum of Turkish & Islamic Art

Hippodrome

Grand Bazaar

Beyazit

Yeniçeriler Cad.

ÇEMBERLİTAŞ

Çemberlitaş

Gedikpaşa Cad.

GEDİKPAŞA

KUMKAPI

Süleymaniye Külliyesi

Fuat Paşa Cad.

Beyazit Mosque

BEYAZIT

Türkeli Caddesi

Kumkapı

Sea of Marmara

İstanbul University

VEFA

Valens Aqueduct

ŞEHZADEBAŞI

Şehzade Mosque

Şehzadebaşı Cad.

Beyazit Üniversite

LALELİ

Ordu Cad.

Laleli Mosque

Laleli

YENİKAPI

Mustafa Kemal Bul.

Atatürk Bulvarı

KÜÇÜKPAZAR

FATİH

Fatih Mosque

Arkeoloji Park

AKSARAY

Aksaray

Namık Kemal Cad.

Fevzi Paşa Cad.

Akdeniz Caddesi

ÜSKÜDAR

YENİKÖY

BEYOĞLU

GALATA

EYÜP

EMİNÖNÜ

SEA OF MARMARA

1/4 Mi

1/4 Km

Balıkçı Sabahattin **3**
Buhara 93 **1**
Darüzziyafe **18**
Dubb **9**
Eminönü Belediyesi
  Sosyal Tesisleri **4**
Fes Café **12**
Hamdi Et Lokantası **16**
Konyalı Topkapı
  Sarayi Lokantası **13**
Marmara Terrace
  Restaurant **5**
Orient Express Cafe **14**
Pandeli Lokantası **15**
The Pudding Shop **10**
Sarnıç **8**
Seasons Restaurant **6**
Sultanahmet Köfteçısı
  Selim Usta **11**
Tamara **2**
Yeşil Ev **7**
Zeyrekhane **19**
Zinhan **17**

🚋 Tram Stop

Tahmis Cad., Kalçin Sok. 17 (set back behind the bus depot), Eminönü. © 0212/528-0390. Reservations required for dinner. Dress smart. Appetizers and main courses 6YTL–18YTL ($7–$21/£2.30–£6.85). MC, V. Daily 11am–midnight. Closed 1st and last 3 days of Ramadan.

Orient Express Cafe *Finds* TURKISH/OTTOMAN   Located next to track no. 1 of Sirkeci station, the Orient Express Cafe—a real find—is proof that you don't have to pay an arm and a leg for white tablecloths, good food, and nostalgia. The elegant niches with their large stained-glass window insets and the handsome clapboard ceiling take you back at least a century, although the decorator would have done well to scrap the enormous *Shining Time Station* oil painting on the wall.

The limited but satisfying menu relies heavily on lamb, with a tender lamb shoulder as the chef's pride. If you're craving eggplant, order the *beğendili kebap*, cubes of flavorful beef atop a bed of eggplant purée (or was that ambrosia?). The crème caramel was a formidable substitute to an empty coffer of rice pudding, and the black-tie service was flawless.

Sirkeci Train Station, Sirkeci. © 0212/522-2280. Appetizers and main courses 5YTL–22YTL ($5.85–$25/£1.90–£8.40). MC, V. Daily noon–11pm.

Pandeli Lokantası *Overrated* TURKISH   Pandeli is one of those neighborhood traditions that lives on more for its location and longevity than for anything particularly outstanding about the food. Pandeli was opened in 1901 by a Greek of Turkish descent and has become a local institution ever since its arrival on the upper level of the Egyptian Spice Bazaar. It's a popular place among businessmen on expense accounts as well as for bazaar shoppers looking for a place to eat. If you nab a table in the main room facing the ancient blue Iznik tiles and windows overlooking the bazaar, you can watch the human traffic come and go.

Mısır Çarşısı 1, Eminönü (immediately inside the entrance to the Egyptian Bazaar). © 0212/527-3909. Main courses 9YTL–18YTL ($11–$21/£3.40–£6.85). MC, V. Mon–Sat 11am–4pm.

Zinhan KEBAPS   This 19th century *zindan han* ("dungeon" or prison) on the docks of Eminönü was restored by the Storks chain of jewelry shops, which has filled the lower five stories with high-end retailers and topped it all off with a panoramic restaurant on the sixth floor. And because the restaurant is set in a pentagon shaped pavilion with glass walls, the 360-degree panorama alone is giving the nearby Hamdi (see above) a run for its money. Zinhan specializes in kebaps typical of Southern Anatolia and is already a mandatory lunch stop on personalized day tours that have the Egyptian Spice Market on its itinerary.

Ragıpgümüşpala Cad. 2–5 (the tall building at Eminönü with the Storks sign on it). © 0212/512-4275. Appetizers and main courses 4YTL–23YTL ($3.50–$20/£1.50–£8.75). MC, V. Daily noon to midnight.

IN & AROUND SULTANAHMET
VERY EXPENSIVE

Balıkçı Sabahattin *Finds* FISH   One of the few consistently good, high-quality restaurants in a neighborhood of amateurs, Balıkçı Sabahattin is still cranking out top-quality treasures from the sea for eager fans. Meals are served alfresco on the cobbled streets in summer. When the air turns crisp, diners fill the many rooms of this restored 1927 house. Don't pass up the tahini ice cream, and what you can't finish you can feed to one of the hungry kittens milling about.

Seyit Hasan Koyu Sok. 1, Cankurtaran, Sultanahmet (behind Armada Hotel). © 0212/458-1824. Appetizers and main courses 2.50YTL–35YTL ($2.20–$30/95p–£13) and up for fish by weight. V. Daily noon–3pm and 7–10:30pm.

Sarnıç *(Moments* *(Overrated* FRENCH/TURKISH   The setting for this restaurant, an old Roman cistern tucked away behind the Ayasofya, is nothing less than dramatic. The flickering light of 500 candles bounces off the iron grillwork, the lofty brick domes, and the stone pillars, while the crackling of the fire in the massive stone chimney (an inauthentic but effective addition) supplies more romance than a girl can handle. Only a few years ago, before the Turkish Touring and Automobile Association bought and restored it, the cistern served as a greasy, old auto repair shop.

The menu marries traditional French entrees like beef bourguignon with standard Turkish grills. But while the service is good and the ambience is great, my experience there was (twice) reminiscent of a large institutional wedding (except for the marinated beef salad, which was truly memorable). Perhaps, then, it is a hit-or-miss thing.

Soğukçeşme Sok., Sultanahmet. ⓒ 0212/512-4291. Reservations required. Dress smart. Appetizers and main courses 10YTL–50YTL ($8.70–$44/£3.80–£19). AE, MC, V. Daily 6pm–midnight; lunch available for groups only.

Seasons Restaurant ⭐⭐⭐ MEDITERRANEAN   Rated no.1 in Zagat's "Best of Europe" since the book first came out, the Four Seasons' restaurant continues to be a favorite, not only for expats and foreign visitors, but for locals as well. The menus for breakfast, lunch, and dinner are each adapted to seasonal offerings approximately every 3 months. The *izgara levrek madalyon* (medallions of grilled sea bass) seems to be a recurrent theme, served with a ragout of vegetables, yellow tomatoes, a beet reduction, and chive essence; you can also find Oriental-leaning dishes such as seared scallops with shrimp rolls and ginger.

In the Four Seasons Hotel (p. 63), Tevkifhane Sok. 1, Sultanahmet. ⓒ 0212/638-8200. Reservations required. Dress smart. Appetizers and main courses 14YTL–38YTL ($12–$33/£5.30–£14). AE, DC, MC, V. Daily 6:30–11am, noon–3pm, and 7–11pm.

EXPENSIVE

Konyalı Topkapı Sarayı Lokantası ⭐ TURKISH/OTTOMAN   Diners at Topkapı are treated to a stunningly situated stopover on a short walk through history. Don't confuse the more casual cafeteria with the formal restaurant, the latter being where all the culinary action is. Konyalı has been serving celebrity royalty for more than 100 years, and its got the black-and-white photographs to prove it. Some of the specialties of the house are their *börek,* the slow-cooked *tandır* lamb, and orange baklava. Konyalı recently opened a second location at the Kanyon shopping center in Levent.

Topkapı Palace, Sultanahmet. ⓒ 0212/513-9696. A la carte main courses 9YTL–32YTL ($7.80–$28/£3.40–£12); does not include entrance fee to the palace. AE, MC, V. Wed–Mon 10am–4pm.

Yeşil Ev ⭐ FRENCH/TURKISH   Located in one of the first reconstructed replicas of an Ottoman mansion in Sultanahmet, the Yeşil Ev restaurant takes full advantage (in the summertime) of the luxurious setting provided by the enclosed garden and grand fountain. The Ottoman/French menu includes a decent duck *à l'orange,* the one-time selection of choice for the visit of France's prime minister. Although reputed as one of the top restaurants in Istanbul, meals here sometimes get mixed reviews. The elegant *orangerie* is open in good weather only (in winter for groups of eight or more), and on a balmy summer's eve.

Kabasakal Cad. 5, Sultanahmet. ⓒ 0212/517-6785. Dress smart. Appetizers and main courses 8YTL–28YTL ($7–$24/£3–£11); prawn and fish by weight. AE, MC, V. Daily noon–11pm.

MODERATE

Dubb ✸ INDIAN   The owner of this inventive restaurant grew to love the cuisine of India while based there for his carpet-exporting business. Returning to Istanbul, he discovered a way to combine the two unrelated activities in Dubb, an Indian restaurant housed in a beautifully restored Ottoman house doubling as a gallery for his most prized collection of Turkish carpets and *kilims*. The house is composed of four intimate levels, each painstakingly preserved and decorated, with a rooftop terrace view that makes you feel like the Ayasofya landed on your plate. Try the tandoori chicken and the spinach purée with feta cheese, and wash it all down with one of four types of flavored lassi (yogurt drink).

Incili Çavuş Sok. 10, Sultanahmet. ✆ 0212/513-7308. Main courses 11YTL–24YTL ($9.60–$21/£4.20–£9). MC, V. Daily noon–midnight.

Marmara Terrace Restaurant TURKISH   With massive domes of the Blue Mosque towering over the rooftop terrace restaurant, the chef doesn't really have to work too hard to draw a crowd. Regrettably, the terrace is only open evenings June through September; the rest of the time, there's a lovely enclosed street-side cafe or an indoor lobby-level dining area. The appetizer of mixed mezes is a tasty and innovative sampler consisting of carrot rolls with yogurt, seafood with smoked salmon and shrimp, cold vegetables, and Ottoman spring rolls with cheese and potatoes. Traditional main courses include lamb chops and the Ottoman-style *köfte*.

In the Mavi Ev (Blue House, p. 64), Dalbastı Sok. 14, Sultanahmet. ✆ 0212/638-9010. Reservations suggested. Appetizers and main courses 5YTL–25YTL ($4.40–$22/£1.90–£9.50). AE, MC, V. Daily noon–11pm.

INEXPENSIVE

Buhara 93 LOKANTA   For some pretty good, cheap, basic Turkish fare, Buhara is an old reliable. I tend to stick to the *ev yemekleri* (home cooking)—the stewed dishes displayed in the window. The menu narrows to serve only kebaps during Ramadan.

Nakilbent Sok. 15A, Sultanahmet. ✆ 0212/518-1511. Menu 3YTL–10YTL ($2.60–$8.70/£1.15–£3.80). MC, V. Daily 9am–10pm.

Eminönü Belediyesi Sosyal Tesisleri (Value) (Finds) TURKISH   The security guards sporadically stationed at the gated entrance aren't exactly an inviting presence, but this is indeed one of the neighborhood's finds. It's actually a combined tea garden and restaurant, placed strategically on an outdoor terrace that makes up part of the ancient Byzantine fortress wall. There's a small building situated at the back of the grounds, containing a dining room serving traditional Turkish meals. Because it's owned by the Municipality—presumably the reason for the guards—this destination is bone dry (no alcohol). I recommend this place regularly for anyone looking for an authentic, atmospheric, and hassle-free meal at the right price.

Ahırkapı Iskele Sok. 1, Cankurtaran (near the Armada Hotel, under the train tracks at the Dede Efendi entrance to the neighborhood from the sea road). ✆ 0212/458-5415. Appetizers and main courses 4YTL–14YTL ($3.50–$12/£1.50–£5.30). MC, V. Daily 11am–midnight.

The Pudding Shop (Overrated) KEBAPS/TURKISH   In its heyday, the Pudding Shop was an obligatory stop on the "hippie trail," a starting point for restless vagabonds from the West on their way through the exotic East. With its anti-establishment clientele, it wasn't long before it gained the reputation of ground zero for drug dealings and other unsavory business propositions—in Oliver Stone's *Midnight Express,* Billy Hayes gives up his cabdriver supplier here. Today, the Pudding Shop fades into history alongside the other fast-food restaurants on Divanyolu Caddesi, with fluorescent backlit menu displays and stacks of expat publications. Turkish and Ottoman staples are pre-prepared and displayed in steam tables behind a counter; just point at what looks good. The menu features stuffed grape leaves, lentil-stuffed eggplant/aubergine, as well as *köfte* and *şiş*, but you should get these last two things next door at the Sultanahmet Köfteçısı Selim Usta (see below), if that's what you plan on ordering.

Divanyolu Cad. 6 (across from the tram), Sultanahmet. ☏ 0212/522-2970. Appetizers and main courses 4YTL–13YTL ($3.50–$11/£1.50–£5). MC, V. Daily 8:30am–10pm or later.

Sultanahmet Köfteçısı Selim Usta ★★ *Kids Value* TURKISH   This little, quality dive on the main drag has been around longer than Turkey has been a republic, and after one bite it's easy to see why. It's hard to imagine a simple meatball as delectable as the ones made here, but if you're not in the mood, there's not much in the way of an alternative. They also serve lamb *şiş* for 9YTL ($7.83/£3.60), but here, it's beside the point. Side dishes are limited to white beans or a shepherd's salad (tomato, cucumber, onions, and chile). Top the meal off with the *irmik helvası*, a modestly sweet semolina comfort food beloved by Turks.

Divanyolu Cad. 12/A, Sultanahmet. ☏ 0212/513-1438. *Köfte* 7YTL ($6.10/£2.70). No credit cards. Daily noon–10pm.

Tamara ★ *Finds Value* TURKISH   The stars have so far aligned for this relatively new upstart. The menu features an unusually broad selection of kebaps, pides, and salads. Still, my advice is to order one of the stew-like regional dishes. One such delight is *keldoş*—a delicious concoction of lentils and beef à la Van from Eastern Turkey. Or the *orman* (forest) *kebap*—a stew of lamb, chick peas, potatoes, and carrots. The narrow entry and large steam pans conceal a clean and comfortable, open-air dining room at the rear (enclosed in winter).

Küçük Ayasofya Cad. 6, Sultanahmet. ☏ 0212/518-4666. Appetizers and main courses 2YTL–14YTL ($1.75–$12/76p–£5.30). MC, V. Daily 9am–11pm.

AROUND THE GRAND BAZAAR
MODERATE
Darüzziyafe TURKISH   Darüzziyafe is actually the banqueting hall built by Sinan on orders of the sultan in preparation for the 100-year anniversary of the conquest of the city. There are three large dining rooms plus an ornamental courtyard shaded in centuries-old trees. The kitchen serves an endless menu of traditional and regional dishes, including those that extended into the four corners of the empire, from the Balkan soup, to the Üzbek pilaf. The menu also features a daunting array of boiled, braized, and pickled vegetables.

Şifahane Sok. 6, Süleymaniye. ☏ 0212/511-8414. Appetizers and main courses 4YTL–22YTL ($3.50–$19/£1.50–£8.40). MC, V. Daily noon to 11pm.

Fes Café ITALIAN   The original Fez Café began as a tiny cafe serving much needed caffeine and sugar for the much-needed boost required by a grueling day wandering the Grand Bazaar. This second location, tucked just outside of the Nuruosmaniye Gate, sets the bar slightly higher with a sophisticated menu of Italian dishes and street-side dining. While the chef is boiling your pasta, you can step into the adjacent shop selling a selection of some of the most sumptuous bath sheets I've ever laid eyes on.

Ali Baba Türbesi Sok. 25–27, Nuruosmaniye. ☏ 0212/526-3070. Appetizers and main courses 7YTL–18YTL ($6.10–$16/£2.70–£6.80). MC, V. Mon–Sat 9am–11pm.

FATIH

Zeyrekhane OTTOMAN/TURKISH   Just a few short years ago, Zeyrekhane became the destination of choice for the few foreign visitors intrepid enough to seek out neighborhoods beyond the historic center. The neighborhood of Zeyrek, for centuries a major Byzantine religious hub, is now attracting the mainstream visitor, but Zeyrekhane still holds its own as a charismatic rest stop. The restaurant sits atop the Byzantine walls, opening up to a massive paved terrace just a few steps below with incredible views. The interior is all cool stone and enormous brick. The menu gets mixed reviews, so stick with the tried-and-true standards like the *saç böreği* (fried pastries with meat or cheese) and the *Zeyrek kebap* (diced and mince meat on pide covered in yogurt).

Sinanağa Mah., Ibadethane Arkası Sok. 10, Zeyrek/Fatih. ℂ 0212/532-2778. Appetizers and main courses 7YTL–18YTL ($6.10–$16/£2.70–£6.85). MC, V. Tues–Sun 11am–10pm.

Ziya Şark Sofrası TURKISH   Truth is, it's not really in anyone's interest to venture into the dubious neighborhood of Aksaray, a seedy commercial and transport hub that attracts the worst type of petty criminals. Still, I'd be committing a sin of omission if I didn't include this veritable emporium of Anatolian regional cuisine. The appetizers are anything but ordinary: Try the *cevizli muhammara* (walnuts and hot spice) or the stuffed mushrooms. A sampling of the kebaps includes pistachio, tomato, spicy, and eggplant. Ziya is very popular, so even with a reservation, there might be a bit of a wait.

Millet Cad. 1, Ender Mağazası yanı, Aksaray. ℂ 0212/632-8479. Reservations suggested. Appetizers and main courses 4YTL–17YTL ($3.50–$15/£1.50–£6.50). MC, V. Mon–Sat 11am–10pm.

EDIRNEKAPI
EXPENSIVE

Asitane ★★★ *(Value* OTTOMAN   Clearly, it was good to be the sultan, if he indeed ate at all like you do when you visit Asitane. From records of meals at Topkapı Palace (*sans* quantities), the chef of Asitane has succeeded in re-creating 200 palace recipes plus about 200 original Ottoman-style recipes. The *etli elma dolması* (apple stuffed with lean diced lamb, rice, currants, pistachio, and rosemary) still makes my mouth water—the only regrettable thing is that I'll probably never eat it again, because the menu changes each season. There's a menu in honor of Fatih Sultan Mehmet (the Conqueror) May through June, while vegetarian main-course selections are on the menu year-round.

In the Kariye Oteli, Kariye Camii Sok. 18 (adjacent to the St. Savior in Chora), Edirnekapı. ℂ 0212/534-8414. Reservations suggested. Dress smart. Appetizers and main courses 10YTL–30YTL ($8.70–$26/£3.80–£11). AE, DISC, MC, V. Daily noon–midnight.

FROM SAMATYA TO THE AIRPORT
EXPENSIVE

Gelik Balık FISH   Istanbul is full of crowd-pleasers, and Gelik is one (or should I say two: there's a Gelik for fish and one for meat on opposite sides of the highway). More of an empire, Gelik enjoys a loyal following of fans, offering something for everyone, including the little ones, with outdoor picnic areas and playgrounds. Indoors is an expansive and regal chalet-style restaurant. The freshest selections of fish are displayed at the entryway of Gelik Balık; choose your poison and tell the waiter how you want yours cooked. Most choose grilled, but they also do a mean fish *güveç*—a casserole prepared in a terra-cotta dish by the same name. Gelik offers a daunting

Tips   Eating Your Way Through the Streets of Istanbul

The fastest way to the heart of a culture is through its stomach, and often the culture of food begins on the street. While this book provides some council on what to avoid, I rarely take my own advice and simply can't think of anything I'd rather do in Istanbul than noshing through its bustling streets (if they're not bustling, it might be better not to eat there).

Morning rush hour in Turkey wouldn't be the same without the sound of the neighborhood *simitçi* hawking his wares. A *simit* is a savory sesame covered pastry much like a bagel, only thinner (the *simitçi* being the guy who sells *simit*). I've always frequented the guy who stakes out his spot daily on the small triangle of sidewalk located at the entrance to Bankalar Sok., in Karaköy. Ask for a packet of *peyner* (cheese), the equivalent of a do-it-yourself schmeer.

Down the street at the Karaköy Pier is the humble (and famous) **Güllüoğlu** sweet shop, where you'll find the best *su boreği*—a buttery cheese- or meat-filled flaky pastry that's feathery and delicious, and a frequent staple of the Turkish breakfast. Güllüoğlu also keeps their glass cases full of baklava. Grab a slab to go and munch on this buttery wonder outside on a bench by the cruise ship docks.

All day long, vendors cloaked in Ottoman dress man the helm of boats bobbing wharfside at Eminönü, greeting arriving commuters and locals with **grilled fish** on a roll. It's fresh, quick, authentic and at 3YTL ($2.60/ £1.15), cheap. The **Tarıhı Eminönü Balıkçısı** is the original.

On your stroll along Istiklal Caddesi or through the Balıkpazarı (Galatasaray Fish Market), you'll be hard-pressed not to be distracted by the odors coming from the few fast-food vendors displaying *döner kebap* (shwarma) on a vertical spit or oversize shallow pans full of cubed meat. The latter is *tantuni,* stir-fried beef cubes served in a wrap. Sounds pretty unspectacular, but it's anything but.

Up in Ortaköy, stands displaying heaps of diced meats and vegetables, condiments and spreads, and ready-made salads line the street leading from the main road to the pier. These goodies are actually filling for **potatoes** (called *kümpir*). All you have to do is point at the things you want (some of which may be a bit of a stretch for a potato topping). Just grab a plastic fork (provided) and stake out a seat on a waterfront bench. For those with culinary abandon or simply stomachs of steel, those stuffed mussels on offer opposite the potato stands are actually quite delicious. Admittedly, though, these require a great leap of faith.

The seasons also usher in or out some street-food staples. In summer, corn-on-the-cob corpses dot the Emonönü wharf; in winter, chestnuts roast on open fires around town.

selection of appetizers, including *balık öfte* (fish balls) and cured fish "pastrami." Fish is not cheap, so don't expect a bargain here.

Kennedy Cad./Sahilyolu. (© 0212/444-7999. Appetizers and main courses 8YTL–30YTL ($7–$26/£3–£11); fish by weight. AE, MC, V. Mon–Sat 11am–midnight.

MODERATE

Beyti KEBAPS   One of Istanbul's most revered "meat restaurants," Beyti began as a humble eatery of four tables in 1945 and has since grown to encompass 11 richly decorated "salons" and a garden patio. At its peak (which it has yet to come off of), Beyti served princes, kings, presidents, and movie stars. Beyti was even at one time the supplier for the now-defunct Pan Am Airlines in-flight meals, as well as Air Force One, when Nixon was the aircraft's primary client. The house specialty is the restaurant's namesake: lamb filets wrapped in lamb fat and grilled.

Orman Sok. 8, Florya. (© 0212/663-2992. Appetizers and main courses 6YTL–22YTL ($5.20–$19/£2.30–£8.40). AE, MC, V. Tues–Sun noon–midnight.

Develi Restaurant ✦✦✦ TURKISH   Develi's success may have translated into a blossoming of sister locations around the country, but no matter how good the others may be, this Develi maintains a level of consistency and fabulousness worthy of more than a simple star rating will allow. For their regional specialties, they follow outstanding recipes from the Gaziantep region of southeastern Turkey—this translates roughly as *blisteringly spicy*. Adventurous eaters should order the fiery *çig köfte*, beefy meatballs combined with every spice in the book, served raw in a soothing lettuce leaf. Other notable menu items include the *muhamara*, a delectable purée of bread, nuts, and chickpeas; the *findik lahmacun*, a thin-crust pizza made Turkish-style with chopped lamb; or the lamb sausage and pistachio kebap. Leave room for the *künefe*, a warm slab of baklava dough oozing cheese, dipped in syrup, and covered with crushed pistachio nuts. The rooftop terrace is stupendous in the summer, and there's a non-smoking room for indoor wintry evenings.

Balıkpazarı (Samatya Fish Bazaar), Gümüşyüzük Sok. 7, Samatya. (© 0212/529-0833 and Tepecik Yolu 22, Etiler (© 0212/263-2571. Reservations required. Dress smart. Appetizers and main courses 4YTL–20YTL ($3.50–$17/ £1.50–£7.60). MC, V. Daily noon–midnight.

5 Where to Dine in Beyoğlu

TAKSIM

VERY EXPENSIVE

Mikla ✦✦✦ MEDITERRANEAN   Located on the top two floors of the new Marmara Pera hotel (p. 77), Mikla is the newest hit of the Istanbul Yiyecek Icecek A.S. ("eat drink") ventures, which includes the very popular Lokanta (at Nu Pera in winter and at rooftop as Nu Teras in summer, p. 103). The Swedish born chef, Mehmet Gürs, is somewhat of an Istanbul celebrity by now; he settled in Istanbul in the 1990s and has made all of the kitchens he's touched turn to gold. Reservations are hard to come by and the wait for a table is long; the management makes it easy with the upstairs bar views of the lights of the Old City. Raw grouper makes an outstanding appetizer, followed by the whole roast beef tenderloin for two. Try to leave space for the memorable pistachio and tahini ice cream.

Mesrutyiyet Cad. 167–185, Tepebaşı. (© 0212/293-5656. Appetizers and main courses 17YTL–55YTL ($15–$48/£6.50–£21). AE, MC, V. Daily noon–3:30pm and 6–11:30pm.

Where to Dine in Beyoğlu

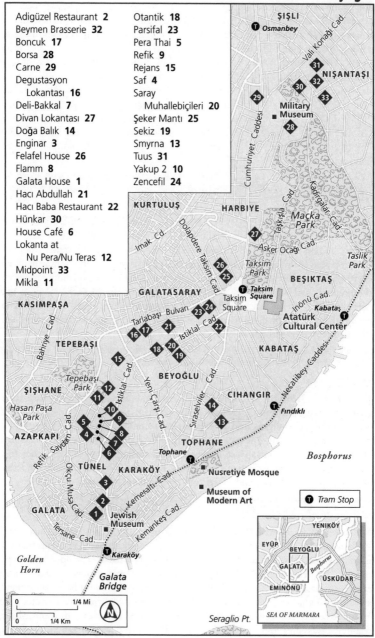

Adigüzel Restaurant **2**
Beymen Brasserie **32**
Boncuk **17**
Borsa **28**
Carne **29**
Degustasyon
  Lokantası **16**
Deli-Bakkal **7**
Divan Lokantası **27**
Doğa Balık **14**
Enginar **3**
Felafel House **26**
Flamm **8**
Galata House **1**
Hacı Abdullah **21**
Hacı Baba Restaurant **22**
Hünkar **30**
House Café **6**
Lokanta at
  Nu Pera/Nu Teras **12**
Midpoint **33**
Mikla **11**

Otantik **18**
Parsifal **23**
Pera Thai **5**
Refik **9**
Rejans **15**
Saf **4**
Saray
  Muhallebiçileri **20**
Şeker Mantı **25**
Sekiz **19**
Smyrna **13**
Tuus **31**
Yakup 2 **10**
Zencefil **24**

EXPENSIVE

Divan Lokantası TURKISH/MEDITERRANEAN   While tourists are inundating Tuğra (the Çırağan's five-star restaurant, p. 108) for authentic Ottoman cuisine, Divan Lokantası is considered by locals as one of the only restaurants in town where the food doesn't taste foreign. What Divan calls "World Cuisine" is just another way of saying that they're constantly updating traditional recipes with new innovations, creating a dining experience enriched by the sound of classical music in the background. Last I checked, you could delight in *balık pilakısı* (fish stew), *Çerkez tavuğu* (Circassian-style chicken), or the more Anatolian *analı kızlı* (poached lamb and veal patties with a bulgur and tomato *concasse*). Desserts feature goodies available in the adjacent Divan Patisserie, as well as a rich and decadent *künefe* (sweet, stringy pastry with melted cheese).

Divan Oteli, Cumhuriyet Cad. 2, Elmadağ. © 0212/231-4100. Reservations required. Dress smart. Appetizers and main courses 6YTL–29YTL ($5.20–$25/£2.30–£11). AE, DC, MC, V. Mon–Fri noon–3:30pm and 7–11:30pm; Sat 7pm–midnight.

Hacı Abdullah TURKISH   Politicians, businessmen, families, and out-of-towners have been coming to Istanbul's first licensed restaurant for over a century. The recipes reflect the best of traditional Turkish cuisine, serving substantial stews, whole artichokes baked with vegetables in olive oil, and their signature dish, lamb shank with eggplant. Lining the walls are enormous glass jars filled with fruit compotes made on the premises and incorporated into the chef's proud desserts, such as quince marinated in syrup or the sweetbread custard topped with figs, apricot, pistachio, and coconut. For those wishing to celebrate with a glass of wine, unfortunately, Hacı Abdullah serves no alcohol.

Sakizağacı Cad. 17, Beyoğlu. © 0212/293-8561. Reservations suggested. Appetizers and main courses 9YTL–33YTL ($7.85–$29/£3.40–£13). MC, V. Daily noon–10:30pm; later on weekends.

MODERATE

Hacı Baba Restaurant OTTOMAN   Many restaurants in Istanbul advertise themselves as serving Ottoman cuisine, but few of them actually do. This is one of the actual authentic kitchens, and in this simple second-floor dining room, the food makes up for the decor. The mezes and a variety of ready-to-grill kebaps are displayed at the entrance, but you can also request to see the baked goods in the kitchen to get an idea of what it is you're actually up against. Perhaps the enormous lamb tenderloins with rice spiced with liver and raisins, or crepes stuffed with lamb and cheese?

Istiklal Cad. 49, Beyoğlu (across from the French Embassy). © 212/244-1886. Main courses 8YTL–25YTL ($7–$22/£3–£10). MC, V. Noon–midnight.

Sekiz ★★ INTERNATIONAL   Joost, Sekiz' owner, apologized for the fact that the kitchen was working out a few kinks when I ate here, which basically means that Sekiz is destined for greatness, because I had some darn good meals. The open kitchen puts out delicious crispy spring rolls with a piquant dipping sauce; chicken satay; and vegetable samozas. But it's not all Asian; choose the marinated swordfish or lamb skewer, a grilled fish sandwich, or a hefty slab of steak. And Joost's wife Sercem makes a New York cheesecake that comes perilously close to the best I've ever had (Mom, yours is still #1); I was sorry to have offered to share. The bar/restaurant has a hip, cosmopolitan vibe; that it is hidden down a back street near Taksim Square in an unmarked building just makes it all the more fashionable.

In Mısafır Suites (p. 74), Gazeteci Erol Dernek Sok. 1 (from the Ağa Mosque on Istiklal, turn down Sadir Alışık Sok.). ℂ **0212/249-8930.** Appetizers and main courses 8YTL–21YTL ($7–$18/£3–£8). MC, V. Daily noon to 10:30pm (bar open until the wee hours).

INEXPENSIVE

Felafel House MIDDLE EASTERN   While not really a Turkish staple, felafel makes a nice change to the endless kebaps that are by now making you feel a bit top-heavy. This humble eatery also serves hummus and soup, and a number of mix-and-match menus for 12YTL ($10/£4.60) and under.

Şehit Mehtar Cad. 19A, Taksim. No phone. Soups, salads, and felafel 4YTL ($3.50/£1.50). MC, V. Daily 9am–10pm.

Parsifal *(Finds)* VEGETARIAN   The formerly derelict and now reclaimed Kurabiye Street is now home to an increasing number of tiny restaurants. This one, however, is a standout. The menu is entirely vegetarian—the type of vegetarian that keeps you coming back for more. Some of the creative dishes are broccoli *ograten* (sic), chard lasagna, black-eyed bean salad with walnut, and stuffed artichoke *dolma.* Zencefil (see below), across the street, may be healthy, but it's not veg like Parsifal.

Kurabiye Sok. 9A (the parallel street to Istiklal), Taksim. ℂ **0212/245-2588.** Lunch menu main courses 8.50YTL ($7.45/£3.20); dinner menu 20% higher. MC, V. Daily noon–11pm.

Saray Muhallebiçileri *(Value)* PATISSERIE/KEBAPS   People have been flocking to Saray Muhallebiçileri since its establishment in 1949, and a look in the window will tell you why. The colorful array of desserts lures you off the street and into this patisserie, although with such a huge choice and exceedingly low prices, it'll be difficult to rule out any one thing. Rice-pudding addicts should definitely not pass up this opportunity, although the chocolate pudding is irresistible as well. This is also a good place to try the *tavukgögsü,* a sweet, gummy pudding made with chicken that would be less difficult to avoid in another less-tempting establishment. There are now a number of franchises all over the city; the one in Eminönü has a cafeteria, prepared foods, and the expected wide array of sweets.

Istiklal Cad. 102–104, Beyoğlu. ℂ **0212/292-3434.** Appetizers and main courses 4YTL–9YTL ($3.50–$7.85/£1.50–£3.40). MC, V. Daily 6am–1:30am.

Şeker Mantı KEBAPS   When you get a craving for those little meat dumplings topped with buttery yogurt and chile, you just gotta have 'em. These are not the best I've ever had, but they'll do. This Taksim joint also serves a rare dish in fast-food (a term used very lightly here) establishments: *çiğ börek,* a lightly fried pastry that melts in your mouth. They've also got chicken wings.

Şehit Mehtar Cad. 11, Taksim. ℂ **0212/255-0297.** Nothing over 8 YTL ($7/£3). MC, V. Daily 9am–10pm.

Zencefil VEGETARIAN   Billed as a vegetarian cafe (in spite of the chicken with leeks on the menu), this spot serves up wholesome fare worthy of its healthy designation. Homemade bread with herb butter accompanies every meal, which might be a big healthy salad, an ample slice of quiche, or Indian stew with exotic spices and vegetables. Menus have been skillfully translated into English, which is useful, because pumpkin pie probably isn't in your basic Turkish dictionary, and it's too good to miss. Zencefil will be moving to a new location across the street at an undetermined date in the future; if it's not at the address below, turn around 180 degrees.

Kurabiye Sok. 3, Taksim. ℂ **0212/244-4082.** Main courses 6YTL–12YTL ($5.20–10/£2.30–£4.60). MC, V. Mon–Sat 9am–11pm.

CIHANGIR
MODERATE

Doğa Balık ☆☆ MEZES/FISH   People's eyes light up at the mention of this highly popular restaurant positioned on the rooftop (top floor in winter) of the Zurich Hotel in the newly arrived expat-heavy neighborhood of Cihangir. But the view is almost beside the point here. The very freshest fish of the season is served here: amply sized *palamut* (bonito) or *kalkan* (turbot) costing upwards of 30YTL ($26/£12) per kilo. However delectable the fish may be, the real attraction is the overwhelming selection of mezes. Some 30 varieties of wholesome forest greens are all guaranteed to delight: from nettles, to feverfew, to purslane, to "goat food." Don't miss the non-green mezes, in particular the *mercemek köfetsi* (lentil balls), and the monkfish salad. Indeed, load up on the appetizers and skip the main course.

Akarsu Yokusu Cad. 44–46, Cihangir (follow Siraselviler Cad. down from Taksim square and turn left when you reach the mosque). ℂ 0212/293-9143. Appetizers and main courses 5YTL–16YTL ($4.35–$14/£2–£6); fish by weight. MC, V. Daily noon–1:30am.

Smyrna ☆ BISTRO FARE   This diminutive space has a very "village-y" feel. No wonder: It used to be an antiques shop, which accounts for the living room atmosphere and the kitschy collection of antique cars and typewriters near the front entryway. There are two or three tiny bistro tables on the sidewalk in front of an extremely narrow and long storefront for those wishing to stop by for just a coffee break. Hanging out is encouraged (stacks of newspapers abound), and the service is friendly. Steak is a favorite at dinnertime: Try the filet with blue cheese or artichoke sauce.

Akarsu Cad. 29, Cihangir. ℂ 0212/244-2466. Appetizers and main courses 9YTL–25YTL ($7.85–$22/£3.40–£9.50). MC, V. Sun–Thurs 9am–11pm; Fri–Sat 9am–1am.

GALATASARAY, TEPEBAŞİ & TÜNEL
EXPENSIVE

Boncuk ☆☆ Ⓥalue TURKISH/ARMENIAN   Located on a side street off the Galatasaray Fish Market, this small rustic *meyhane* is the one restaurant on this saturated stretch of restaurants that is consistently full. Boncuk serves delicacies such as fried brains (mmm . . .) and stuffed spleen, but thankfully there's a variety of more recognizable hot and cold mezes like *kızır*, flavorful and spicy bulgur balls, and *topik*, an Armenian specialty made of chickpea paste around a nucleus of onions and currants. Because availability is seasonal, try not to be too disappointed when the waiter informs you that your choice is not on the menu that day.

Nevizade Sok. 19, Beyoğlu. ℂ 0212/243-1219. Appetizers and main courses 4YTL–20YTL ($3.50–$17/£1.50–£7.60); fish by weight. No credit cards. Daily noon–midnight.

House Café BISTRO FARE   In 2002, a little cafe opened in a house in Nişantaşı. But the creative (and enormous) soups, sandwiches, and salads gained a following until House Café burst at the seams. There are now three locations (the other two are in Teşvikiye and Ortaköy) along with a solid and successful Istanbul brand. I barely made a dent in my lentil salad with purslane and goat cheese in truffle oil, although I may have had I not sunk my fork into my companion's huge and unexpectedly authentic Italian (not the Turkish kind) pizza. A handful of tiny tables line the cobbled alley, while indoors is a well-styled, cozy space.

Asmali Mescit 9/1, Tünel. ℂ 0212/245-9515. Atiye Sok., Iskeçe Apt. 10/1, Teşvikiye. ℂ 0212/259-2377. Salhane Sok. 1, Ortaköy. ℂ 0212/227-2699. Appetizers and main courses 17YTL–30YTL ($15–$26/£6.50–£11). AE, MC, V. Mon–Thurs 8am–10:30pm; Fri–Sat 8am–11pm; Sun 8am–9:30pm (bar opened until 2am Mon–Sat and 11pm Sun).

Refik ⭐ BLACK SEA/FISH   Tucked into a back street in Beyoğlu, Refik is unassuming, even unimpressive, from the outside. But this little restaurant has been an institution in the neighborhood since its inception in 1954. Success lies equally with the unfailing quality of the ingredients and the pride that goes into the preparation. The earliest shifts arrive at 6am to start preparing for a menu distinct to the Black Sea region, and therefore heavy on dishes with black cabbage.

The *hamsibuğulama* (fish steamed in season) and the *arnavut ciğeri* (sautéed Albanian liver and onions) are house specialties, as is the *kara lahana dolması* (stuffed cabbage). Mezes change seasonally, and in the summer, tables spill onto the narrow street. Bonus: A ventilation system sucks the cigarette smoke up and away from diners.

Sofyalı Sok. 10–12, Tünel. ℭ **0212/243-2834.** Reservations required. Appetizers and main courses 6YTL–14YTL ($5.20–$12/£2.30–£5.30); fish by weight. AE, DC, MC, V. Daily noon–10:30pm.

Rejans RUSSIAN   The elegance and Old-World experience typical of the Rue de Pera is re-created at Rejans, a Beyoğlu institution since 1932. Treat yourself to the *blini,* or pull the stops out for one (or all) of the three types of caviar. The borscht is prepared both regular and vegetarian, and along with the familiar components of a traditional Turkish meze plate are Russian dishes such as smoked salmon rollade, chicken Kiev (deep-fried), or the *tandır* duck in an apple and orange sauce. End the meal with the dessert sampler and save yourself the agony of having to decide.

Emir Nevruz Sok. 17, Galatasaray. ℭ **0212/244-1610.** Appetizers and main courses 7YTL–48YTL ($6.10–$42/£2.70–£18). MC, V. Mon–Sat noon–3pm and 6pm–midnight.

MODERATE

Degustasyon Lokantası MEZES/FISH   In the midst of the confusion of the Balıkpazarı (the Galatasaray Fish Market in Beyoğlu), Degustasyon serves a huge selection of mezes, and not just the usual selection of eggplant purée (which is phenomenal) and *ezmel*pepper paste. Here you'll get some Armenian recipes, such as the fava loaf, thrown in with Turkish traditional dishes. It's just as full of life as the other nearby *meyhanes,* but slightly classier. And obviously, in deference to the location, the restaurant serves a good selection of fish.

Balıkpazarı, Sahne Sok. 41, Beyoğlu. ℭ **0212/292-0667.** Appetizers 4YTL–6YTL ($3.50–$5.20/£1.50–£2.30). Main courses 8YTL–16YTL ($7–$14/£3–£6); fish by weight. MC, V. Daily 11am–1am or later.

Flamm ITALIAN   Things don't really get started here until dinnertime, but the menu works great for a light lunch of clever salads and sandwiches. The short string of tables on Sofyalı Sokak offer some of the best people-watching in the area, while on cooler evenings, most diners opt for the intimate, mezzanine-level dining room. Dinner options are more substantial: choose from teasers like grilled rock grouper, bresaola with avocado, risottos, or the Flamm steak (the most expensive menu item) with rosemary, oyster mushrooms, and spinach in a cream sauce.

Sofyalı Sok. 16, Tünel. ℭ **0212/245-7604.** Appetizers and main courses 7YTL–42YTL ($6.10–$37/£2.70–£16). MC, V. Daily noon–2:30am (open until later on Sat).

Lokanta at Nu Pera/Nu Teras ⭐⭐ INTERNATIONAL   Nu Pera is actually the name of a renovated building in the neighborhood of Pera, now an utterly reborn neighborhood chock-full of cafes and restaurants. In summer the rooftop Lokanta Nu Teras Restaurant offers an elegant and upscale atmosphere and views of a twinkling city—one of my favorite dining spots, actually. The blackboard "tapas" menu at the rear bar is a favorite. In winter, the party moves to more cramped quarters on the ground-floor level.

Meşrutiyet Cad. 149, Tepebaşı. ⓒ 0212/245-6070. Appetizers and main courses 12YTL–38YTL ($10–$33/£4.60–£14). AE, MC, V. Daily noon–3pm and 7pm–12:30am (until 4am on weekends).

Pera Thai THAI   Back when Istanbul had no more than a handful of Asian eateries (only in 2001), Pera Thai occupied the number one spot. But although Asian fusion menus have caught on like wildfire and the growth of sushi joints seems to threaten the survival of local bluefin species, Pera Thai remains unique in holding to authenticity. Expect the expected like fresh herb and spiced salads, traditional Thai curries, and lip-burners like spicy-sour seafood soup. Yum.

Meşrutiyet Cad. 134, Beyoğlu. ⓒ 0212/245-2526. Appetizers and main courses 10YTL–25YTL ($8.70–$22/£3.80–£9.50). MC, V. Mon–Sat noon–midnight.

Saf ⭐ (Finds) HEALTHY/BISTRO FARE   You won't find meat, dairy, wheat, sugar, or anything refined on the menu of Saf, a new international chain of organic bistros with locations in Turkey, the U.K., and Germany. What you will find is a mouthwatering selection of innovative and healthy recipes like seared sage polenta with garlic and vegetables or beet ravioli with cashew-dill peppercorn and balsamic-fig compote. The restaurant, or more accurately, its celebrity-chef Chad Sarno, is attracting an entourage of celebrities and moguls from Turkey and beyond. Saf also has an organic wine and martini bar, a creation of Joe McCanta, another international organic superstar, stirring up dairy-free shakes, infused liqueurs, and creative cocktails. Saf, which translates as "pure," has locations in Beyoğlu, Kuruçeşme, and Beşiktaş. This one in the Ansen 130 is the most central.

In the Ansen 130 (p. 76), Meşrutiyet Cad. 130, Tepebaşı. ⓒ 0212/245-7870. Appetizers and main courses 12YTL–20YTL ($10–$17/£4.60–£7.60). MC, V. Mon–Thurs noon–11pm; Fri–Sat noon–midnight.

Yakup 2 TURKISH   The regular clientele keeps coming back to this Istanbul *meyhane* for the consistently good traditional Turkish mezes, kebaps, and fair prices. The decor is nothing to speak of, and the best you can say about the expansive outdoor terrace is that it's outside. But the quality of the food is first-rate.

Asmalı Mescit Mah. 35–37, Tepebaşı. ⓒ 0212/249-2925. Appetizers and main courses 6YTL–19YTL ($5.20–17/£2.30–£7.20); fish by weight. MC, V. Daily noon–2:30 and 6:30pm–1am.

INEXPENSIVE

Deli-Bakkal HEALTHY   A *bakkal* in Turkey is your little corner grocery. Here, the ingredients are transformed into grilled ciabatta sandwiches, muffins, brownies, and chocolate mousse (okay, maybe not so healthy, but it *is* organic). If the menu is a little light for your tastes, the super smoothie with banana, sesame paste, mixed nuts, milk, honey, wheat germ, and vanilla will certainly fill you up. The bonus? The place is nonsmoking.

Sofyalı Sok. 24, Tünel. ⓒ 0212/245-6845. Smoothies, sandwiches, and salads 9YTL–13YTL ($7.85–$11/£3.40–£5). Cash only. Tues–Fri 8am–8pm; Sat 9:30am–8pm; Sun 9:30am–6pm.

Otantik (Kids) TURKISH   For a special night out, Turks head to their favorite *et* or *balık* (meat or fish) restaurant, ready to splurge for dishes they themselves rarely cook at home. Finally, someone realized how delicious these "poor man" home-style recipes are, compiling a menu that includes *hıngal* (potato dumplings served with yogurt), *otantik yuvarlama çorba* (spicy lentil-based vegetable soup), and *keşkek* (a familiar-tasting dish of cream of wheat with pieces of chicken), along with various types of *gözleme* (filled pancake), *pilav,* and kebaps at extremely fair prices. The restaurant has four floors, each with its own traditional style, and the room in the fourth-floor annex sits right over the inner atrium of the Beaux Arts Çiçek Pasajı.

Istiklal Cad. 170 (next to the entrance to the Çiçek Pasajı). ℂ 0212/293-8451. Appetizers and main courses 5YTL–13YTL ($4.35–$11/£1.90/£4.95). No credit cards. Daily 8am–midnight.

AROUND THE GALATA TOWER

Adigüzel Restaurant LOKANTA   Serving the working men of the neighborhood, Adigüzel is a reliable *lokanta* with friendly staff and stick-to-your ribs cooking the way someone's Turkish grandmother makes it. Dishes revolve around the traditional green beans in tomato sauce, soups, and stews, a pleasant respite from the grilled kebaps that dominate menus around town. It's located in the basement level of a building just steps from the Galata Tower.

Galata Kulesi Sok. 31, Galata. ℂ 0212/245-0278. Appetizers and main courses 3YTL–6YTL ($2.60–$5.20/£1.15–£2.30). MC, V. Daily 11am–4pm.

Enginar BISTRO FARE   As with much of the history of Galata, no one knows for sure what the first building on this sight was, but turn the clock back 100 years and envision these bright "new" stones (additions to foundations that could date back 400 years) as an Italian bank, then later as a coffeehouse for the neighborhood Jewish community, and most recently as an Akbank. With its attractive lighting and interior resembling an old warehouse, Enginar is a comfortable and quiet place for a drink, and the food, seemingly simple by the looks of the menu, is quite good, too, although the portions are minuscule. Try their vegetable crepe for a lighter lunch, or go for broke with the ginger steak.

Şah Kapısı Sok. 4/A, Galata (straight down Istiklal Cad. to the Galata Tower, the cafe is on your right). ℂ 0212/293-9697. Appetizers and main courses 5YTL–20YTL ($4.35–17/£1.90–£7.60). MC, V. Daily 10:30am–12:30am.

Galata House 🍴 *Finds* GEORGIAN   Hidden along the steep slopes of Galata's historic streets, this little restaurant, the brainchild of an architect/city planner and his wife, occupies a row house that served as the British jail at the beginning of the 1900s. The coziness of the dining rooms—three small salons and an outdoor upper balcony—belie the building's earlier purpose, except for the few preserved squares of plaster etched by prisoners during periods of extreme boredom. At first, the menu selections appear Turkish, but they arrive with an unexpected twist of flavor: The menu reaches into Caucasian territory, with Georgian dumplings, blini, borscht, and chicken and pea salad with yogurt and dill. Potential visitors should take note, however, of the steep incline of the streets in this neighborhood (wear rubber soles!), and that this particular street is often unlit.

Galata Kulesi Sok. 61, Galata (follow Kuledibi Sok. from the Galata Tower). ℂ 0212/245-1861. Appetizers and main courses 8YTL–16YTL ($7–$14/£3–£6.10). MC, V. Tues–Sun noon–midnight.

NORTH OF BEYOĞLU
VERY EXPENSIVE

Tuus 🍴🍴 MEDITERRANEAN   The menu has changed since *Condé Nast Traveler* selected Tuus for its Hot List Tables 2007. Indeed, the restaurant got a new chef in the fall of 2007. But that didn't set them back one bit. The management imported an Italian chef from Beijing, where he worked for the past 10 years with his Turkish wife.

The result is a sophisticated and creative menu that relies heavily upon Mediterranean sensibilities, but doesn't get stuck following rigid traditional recipes. Think pizza alla Turca, with *pastırma*, quail eggs, and cheese; rigatoni with venison ragu or wood-oven roasted lobster. As for ambience, the stylish dining area wraps around a large and central bar on three sides; the fourth wall of glass opens onto a delightfully verdant, canopied garden patio. Mull it all over with a plate of fried fig ravioli accompanied by an 8YTL ($7/£3.25) cup of American coffee.

Tesvikiye Cad. 123, Nişantaşı. ⓒ 0212/368-8181. Appetizers and main courses 19YTL–85YTL ($17–$74/£7.20–£32). AE, MC, V. Mon–Sat noon–midnight.

EXPENSIVE
Beymen Brasserie ITALIAN   Simple, even nondescript, a seat at the brasserie's sidewalk cafe has been the hot ticket in the neighborhood since it opened in 2003. The Mediterranean menu leans to Italian, with top-notch pastas executed in a way even an Italian would approve of (and they do; a couple of expats were next to me last time I ate here). The salad Niçoise or carpaccio of *bonfile* and mozzarella served with olive pesto are examples of some of the lighter choices, while the menu even offers half portions (thankfully, given the high prices).

Abdi Ipekçi Cad. 23/1, Nişantaşı. ⓒ 0212/343-0443. Appetizers and main courses 16YTL–40YTL ($14–$35/£6.10–£15). AE, MC, V. Sun–Thurs 9am–11pm; Fri–Sat 9am–1:30am.

MODERATE
Borsa TURKISH   Reservations are vital at this culinary favorite of the elite and influential. Opened in 1927, it's named for the stock exchange that operated near the original when both were located by the Golden Horn. Now it shares space with the convention center and sits protected behind military guard. Borsa features the best of Anatolian cuisine, from the peasant *plakı* (slow-cooked beans) to the more celebratory lamb *şiş* prepared over an open fire.

Lütfi Kırdar Convention Center, Harbiye. ⓒ 0212/232-4201. Appetizers and main courses 8YTL–25YTL ($7–$22/£3–£9.50). AE, MC, V. Daily noon–midnight.

Carne *(Kids* KOSHER/MEDITERRANEAN   The menu is kosher at Carne, though it leans heavily on classic ingredients of the Mediterranean. Carne puts out mouthwatering dishes such as entrecote or grilled rack of lamb with smoked eggplant, bell pepper, rosemary, and lamb glaze. The tempting appetizers leave little room for the main course, as who can resist a plate of salmon tartar or falafel served with humus or tomato sauce? The menu also has plenty of vegetarian options.

Halaskargazı Cad., Uzay Apt. 53, Şişli. ⓒ 0212/241-8585. Reservations suggested for dinner. Appetizers and main courses 7YTL–34YTL ($6.10–$30/£2.70–£13). MC, V. Mon–Thurs and Sun noon–11pm; Fri noon–4pm; Sat 7:30–11pm.

Hünkar OTTOMAN   This Istanbul institution was founded in the neighborhood of Fatih in 1950. The Fatih location has since closed, but the restaurant's loyal following ensured its survival in Nişantaşı, with a second branch in Etiler. Istanbullus wax lyrical over the traditional Turkish and Ottoman cooking served here. Hünkar is famous for it's *beğendili kebap* and roast lamb. Their warm *irmik helvası* (semolina dessert) is the model for all others. The Nişantaşı location fills up with local professionals at lunchtime; the homey Etiler location has an outdoor trellised sidewalk cafe.

Mim Kemal Öke Cad. 21/1, Nişantaşı. ⓒ 0212/225-4665. Reservations suggested. Appetizers and main courses 7YTL–15YTL ($6.10–$13/£2.70–£5.70). AE, MC, V. Daily 11am–11:30pm.

Midpoint BISTRO FARE When the nearby offices empty out for the evening, Midpoint fills up with young, hip executive types in for a quick dinner or drink. The ground floor becomes loud and lively as the evening wears on; the second-floor mezzanine is for those wanting a little peace and quiet. Meanwhile, the menu is overwhelming in its abundance, offering an amazing variety of pastas, wraps, and a whopping 17 salads. Try the grilled sea bass with artichokes or dive into the 250g (9 oz.) New York steak. Finally, the *janduje* (Gianduia chocolate semifreddo with raspberry sauce) is a slab of paradise on a plate. Tell the waiter to bring just one fork.

Abdi Ipekçi Cad., Kızılkaya Apt. 59, Şişli. © **0212/219-9401**. Appetizers and main courses 7YTL–22YTL ($6.10–$19/£2.70–£8.40). AE, MC, V. Mon–Fri 9pm–midnight; Sat–Sun 9am–2pm.

GOLDEN HORN/HASKÖY

Café du Levant FRENCH This authentic Parisian bistro is unexpected on the main Hasköy road as part of the Rahmi M. Koç Museum complex. Appropriately, there is no hint of Turkey on the quintessentially French menu, which features the requisite duck *à l'orange*, potatoes *dauphinoise*, and chocolate mousse. Otherwise, choose from lighter selections such as fish en carte or a number of vegetarian items.

Rahmi M. Koç Museum (p. 174), Hasköy Cad. 27, Sütlüce. © **0212/235-6328**. Appetizers and main courses 12YTL–32YTL ($10–$28/£4.60–£12). AE, DC, MC, V. Tues–Sun noon–2:30pm and 7pm–midnight.

BEŞIKTAŞ & THE BOSPHORUS VILLAGES
VERY EXPENSIVE

Feriye Restaurant 🐠🐠 OTTOMAN Lesser princes and dignitaries were relegated to this stunning auxiliary palace, which has been renovated and converted into a luxurious restaurant and cultural center. Summertime is definitely the season for this spot, as the tables move out to the seaside terrace, creating a spectacular dining experience little more than an arm's length from scores of jellyfish. The seafood dishes are worth mentioning, if not only for the festivity of the occasion, than for the medallions of swordfish topped with a seafood ragout. Carnivores will not be disappointed by a menu reflecting the tastes of an empire that spanned the Middle East all the way to the Asiatic Sea; try the breast of chicken stuffed with pistachios and see what I mean. Twinkling Bosphorus views and nighttime sea breezes are romance at its best, although this restaurant is equally popular during its Sunday brunch service.

Feriye Sarayı, Çırağan Cad. 124, Ortaköy (above the Çırağan Palace on the right). © **0212/227-2216**. Reservations required. Appetizers and main courses 18YTL–65YTL ($16–$57/£7–£25). AE, MC, V. Daily 12:30–3pm and 7pm–midnight.

Poseidon 🐠🐠🐠 FISH Almost as soon as this Bebek Bosphorus-front restaurant got a face-lift back in 2003, the actors, politicians, expats, and sporting celebrities started to roll in. It's got quite a loyal following now, particularly among jet-setting local residents. The bay at Bebek is particularly scenic with the twin fez-like towers of the Egyptian consulate rising above Bebek marina. When you take your eyes off the view and take note of the menu, you'll see seasonal specialties from the sea such as sea bass, bluefish, and red mullet. The fish appetizers are dreamy, and I'm a sucker for a plate of seaweed (seriously). Try to resist the bread basket, or you'll fill up on corn bread and focaccia before your first course arrives.

Çevdetpaşa Cad. 58, Bebek. © **0212/263-3823**. Appetizers 4YTL–18YTL ($3.50–$16/£1.50–£6.85); 30YTL–120YTL ($26–$104/£11–£46) fish by weight. Cover 9YTL ($7.85/£3.40). AE, MC, V. Daily noon–midnight.

EXPENSIVE

Banyan Seaside ASIAN FUSION   This top floor hot spot takes full advantage of its position overlooking Ortaköy and the Bosphorus, with an amazing outdoor terrace that in the crisper months is heated by an open firepit and heat lamps. It also capitalizes on a hip menu that fuses Mediterranean staples with Asian accents. There's seafood with ginger sauce, octopus carpaccio with wasabi aioli, and sake-marinated chargrilled filet mignon in a ginger teriyake sauce. The noodle bar caters to lighter appetites, and you can choose from 20 different types of tea. Banyan has a second location in Nişantaşı at Abdi Ipekci Cad. 40/3 (© **0212/219-6011**).

Muallim Naci Cad., Salhane Sok 3 (near the ferry landing), Ortaköy. © **0212/259-9060**. Appetizers and main courses 12YTL–37YTL ($10–$32/£4.60–£14). AE, MC, V. Daily 5pm–midnight.

Da Mario 🐪🐪 ITALIAN   This is widely acclaimed as the most authentic Italian restaurant in Istanbul and is another spectacularly successful enterprise by Istanbul Doors. They make a mean spaghetti alle vongole, and the wood fire ensures their pizza and breads are finger-licking good. It's located on the ground floor of a multistory building; the three upper floors are dedicated to Anjelique (p. 214).

Dilhayat Sok. 7, Etiler. © **0212/265-1596**. Reservations suggested. Appetizers and main courses 11YTL–31YTL ($9.60–$27/£4.20–£12). AE, MC, V. Daily noon–midnight (11pm on Sun).

Tuğra 🐪🐪🐪 OTTOMAN   This place has created a legend for itself with its innovative synthesis of foods from the entire Ottoman Empire. Tuğra is the epitome of fusion food, so much so that its Turkish clientele comments that the traditional Ottoman dishes taste unfamiliar. Dishes include a delicious mackerel and red mullet *dolma* and a marinated lamb loin grilled with yogurt, tomato, and spicy butter sauce. It's possible to drop upwards of 200YTL ($174/£76) per person on dinner and a few gin and tonics, but if you don't drink and you order a la carte, you can at least expect an exceptional dining experience without the heart failure.

Çırağan Palace Hotel Kempinski Istanbul (p. 80), Çırağan Cad. 84, Beşiktaş. © **0212/258-3377**. Reservations required. Dress smart. Appetizers and main courses 18YTL–45YTL ($16–$39/£6.85–£17). AE, DC, MC, V. Daily 7–11pm.

Vogue 🐪🐪 INTERNATIONAL/SUSHI   Who would expect that a restaurant located in an office building would create the buzz that has surrounded Vogue for years? The success of this restaurant owes to a high-quality international menu that relies heavily on Mediterranean and international cuisine, plus an amazing and ample sushi bar that predates Istanbullus growing craze for Japanese food. Floor to ceiling windows provide panoramic views as far as Maiden's Tower (and including the monuments of the Historic Peninsula), while in summer, an outdoor terrace gets graceful sea breezes.

Spor Cad., BJK Plaza, A Block, 13th floor, Akaretler, Beşiktaş. © **0212/227-4404**. Appetizers and main courses 16YTL–36YTL ($14–$31/£6.10–£14). AE, MC, V. Daily noon–midnight.

MODERATE

Malta Köşkü FISH/TURKISH   Up through the wooded paths (there's also an asphalt road) overlooking the treetops of Yıldız is this palatial rococo mansion, an addition to the grounds during the reign of Abdülhamid II. The infamously paranoid sultan had his brother Murad V, together with their mother, imprisoned in this gilded cage. The mansion is now another one of the city's evocative dining destinations and a popular choice for breezy weekend lunches and evening interludes. The lighter cafe menu features sandwiches like steak or salmon and cheese, as well as crumpets and clotted cream for a decadent afternoon tea. For dinner, the menu becomes much more interesting. Drinks can seem a bit overpriced, but the view from under the wooden trellis overlooking the treetops toward Maiden's Tower and the boats crisscrossing the Bosphorus is included in the price.

Yıldız Park, Beşiktaş. 🅒 0212/248-9453. Appetizers and main courses 6YTL–18YTL ($5.20–$16/£2.30–£6.50). MC, V. Daily 9am–10pm.

6 Where to Dine on the Asian Side
VERY EXPENSIVE
A'jia MEDITERRANEAN   Part of the Istanbul Doors family of highly successful restaurants (Lokanta, Vogue, Angelique, Da Mario, Wan-na), A'jia is certainly blessed. The menu changes seasonally, except (by popular demand) the octopus carpaccio, sea bass filet with vegetables in olive oil, and a hazelnut soufflé. On a recent visit, the menu featured a cinnamon-flavored lamb and an intriguing baklava-rolled seafood with asparagus in a tartar sauce.

Ahmet Rasim Paşa Yalısı, Çubuklu Cad. 27, Kanlıca. 🅒 0216/413-9300. Appetizers and main courses 12YTL–48YTL ($10–$42/£4.60–£18). AE, MC, V. Daily noon–midnight.

Del Mare FISH   There isn't much about this waterfront restaurant that isn't spectacular. The old stone building was part of a string of factories that lined the shorefront at the turn of the century; inside is an expansive dining room that spills out onto a canopied outdoor terrace overlooking the Bosphorus waterway. Local fishing boats cruise beneath the twinkling lights of the Bosphorus Bridge—probably some of the same local fishermen that hauled in today's catch. Del Mare is known for its salt fish and grilled calamari, though the *ahtapot patlican* (eggplant purée and octopus) was an unexpected hit. The chef will prepare the fish or meat of your choice whatever way you want it.

Kuleli Cad. 53/4, Çengelköy. 🅒 0216/422-5762. Reservations suggested. The restaurant shuttle will pick you up from Kuruçeşme. Fish by weight (expect around 50€–70€/$70–$98/£36–£50 per person). AE, MC, V. Daily noon–11pm.

Körfez 🟌🟌🟌 FISH   This is one of those rare pioneers that dares to innovate in a place where culinary tradition is king. Some of Körfez's teasing dishes are the signature salt-baked fish, a more complex grouper in a spicy Asian sauce, bonito "sushi," mackerel burgers with raisins and pistachios, and *levrek buğlama* (sea bass in a broth with shiitake mushrooms, ginger, tomato, and thyme). Part of the romance is the setting, an intimate waterside summer patio tucked into a small cove on the Asian side of the Bosphorus, with unexpectedly tranquil views of the floodlit fortress of Rumeli and the Bosphorus Bridge. In winter, dinner is served in what could easily be mistaken for the Captain's private cabin. Guests with advance notice can get picked up at the docks near Rumeli Hisarı on the European side in the restaurant's private skiff.

Körfez Cad. 78, Kanlıca (on the Asian side across from Rumeli Hisarı). 🅒 0216/413-4314. Reservations required in summer, year-round for shuttle boat transfer. Appetizers 6YTL–25YTL ($5.20–$22/£2.30–£9.50); up to 120YTL ($104/£46) fish by weight. MC, V. Mon 7pm–midnight; Tues–Sun noon–midnight.

INEXPENSIVE
Çiya Sofrası 🟌🟌🟌 *Value* TURKISH   This humble eatery, whose kitchen is headed by Musa Dagdeviren, formerly of the California branch of the Culinary Institute of

America, has become an international phenomenon. It's located up a busy market street near the Kadiköy ferry stop (on the Asian side; take the ferry to Kadiköy from Eminönü) and serves delectable and rare regional creations. The chef was listed in *Saveur's* favorite 100 in the 2006 edition, while the restaurant has been featured in the *New York Times* and Zagat Survey's Europe's Best Restaurants. Çiya also has an annex up the street serving only kebaps.

Güneşli Bahçesi Sok. 43–44, Kadıköy. ℂ **0216/330-3190.** Appetizers and main courses 4YTL–15YTL ($3.50–$13/ £1.50–£5.70). DC, MC, V. Daily 11am–10pm.

7

Exploring Istanbul

Istanbul is a city that has successfully incorporated a rich past into a promising future—no small feat considering the sheer magnitude of history buried under those cobblestone streets. Three of the greatest empires in Western history each claimed Istanbul as their capital; as a result, the city overflows with extraordinary sites all vying for equal time. Conveniently, all of the top sights are located on or immediately around Sultanahmet Park, but that by no means is an indication that there's nothing worth seeing outside of that neighborhood. A dizzying number of restoration projects are under way in the Old City and the bustle of Taksim, Beyoğlu, Çukurcuma, Galata, and Tünel, where you can stroll past freshly restored turn-of-the-19th-century ambassadorial palaces and barracks, converted 16th-century waterhouses, and crisp, minimalist museums, all while shopping for an expensive pair of Levi's.

1 Sights & Attractions by Neighborhood

Çiçek Pasajı (Flower Passage; p. 166)
Galatasaray High School (Galatasaray
  Lisesi; p. 166)
Galerist (p. 155)
Gallery Apel (p. 156)
Platform Garanti Contemporary Art
  Center (p. 155)
Tarıhı Galatasaray Hamamı (p. 143)

HARBIYE
Military Museum (p. 167)

KABATAŞ
Dolmabahçe Palace (Dolmabahçe
  Sarayı; p. 150)
İnönü Stadium (p. 175)

KARAKÖY
Antrepo No. 3 (p. 155)
Arap Camii (Arab Mosque; p. 168)
Istanbul Museum of Modern Art
  (p. 156)
Jewish Museum of Turkey (p. 138)
Yeraltı Camii (Underground Mosque;
  p. 168)

LEVENT
Elgiz Museum Proje4L (p. 156)

SÜTLÜCE
Miniaturk (p. 174)
Rahmi M. Koç Museum (p. 174)

TAKSIM
Atatürk Kültür Merkezi (Atatürk Cul-
  tural Center; p. 169)
Aya Triada Ermeni Katolik Kilisesi
  (p. 169)
Cumhuriyet Anıtı/Republican
  Monument (p. 169)
St. Antoine Italyan Katolik Kilisesi
  (Italian Catholic Church; p. 169)
Taksim Maksemi (Water Distribution;
  p. 169)

TEPEBAŞI
Pera Museum (p. 167)

TÜNEL
Galata Mevlevihanesi (p. 166)
Tünel Pasajı (p. 168)

BEŞIKTAŞ & THE BOSPHORUS VILLAGES
ARNAVUTKÖY
American Research Institute in Turkey
  (p. 174)

BEŞIKTAŞ
The British Council (p. 174)
Galeri Nev (p. 156)
Naval Museum (Deniz Müzesi;
  p. 170)

ÇIRAĞAN
Çırağan Palace (p. 149)
Yıldız Palace and Park (Yıldız Sarayı
  ve Parkı; p. 151)

EMIRGAN
Sabancı Museum (p. 171)

SARIYER
Rumeli Fortress (Rumeli Hisarı;
  p. 171)
Sadberk Hanım (p. 170)

THE ASIAN SIDE
BEYLERBEYI
Beylerbeyi Palace (Beylerbeyi Sarayı;
  p. 149)

ÜSKÜDAR
Çinili Camii (p. 172)
Leander's Tower (Maiden's Tower/
  Kız Kulesi; p. 171)
Mihrimah Camii (Iskele
  Camii/Mihrimah Sultan Camii;
  p. 172)

KADIKÖY
Fenerbahçe Stadium (p. 175)

KANLICA
Tarıhı Kanlıca Yoğurdu (p. 173)

Tips **Hours & Admission Costs for Mosques & Churches**

Unless otherwise noted, **opening hours** for mosques and churches are daily, from dawn to dusk; unless otherwise noted, **admission** is free.

---

2 The Top Sights

Ayasofya ★★★   For almost a thousand years, the Ayasofya was a triumph of Christianity and the symbol of Byzantium, and until the 16th century, maintained its status as the largest Christian church in the world. The cathedral is so awesome that the Statue of Liberty's torch would barely graze the top. Erected over the ashes of two previous churches using dismantled and toppled columns and marble from some of the greatest temples around the empire, the Ayasofya (known in Greek as the Hagia Sophia and in English as St. Sophia, or Church of the Holy Wisdom) was designed to surpass in grandeur, glory, and majesty every other edifice ever constructed as a monument to God. Justinian began construction after his suppression of the Nika Revolt, indicating that combating unemployment was high on the list as well. He chose the two preeminent architects of the day: Anthemius of Tralles (Aydın) and Isidorus of Miletus. After 5 years and 4 months, when the construction of the Ayasofya was completed in A.D. 537, the emperor raised his hands to heaven and proclaimed, "Glory to God who has deigned to let me finish so great a work. O Solomon, I have outdone thee!" Enthusiasm for this feat of architecture was short-lived, because 2 years later, an earthquake caused the dome to collapse. The new dome was slightly smaller in diameter but higher than the original, supported by a series of massive towers to counter the effects of future earthquakes. Glass fittings in the walls were employed to monitor the weight distribution of the dome; the sound of crunching glass was an early warning system indicating that the weight of the dome had shifted. Several more earthquakes caused additional damage to the church, requiring repairs to the dome (among other sections), which was increased in height thanks to the support provided by the addition of flying buttresses (additional buttresses were added at two later dates).

In 1204 the Ayasofya was sacked and stripped down to the bare bones by the Crusaders, a desecration that robbed the church of precious relics and definitively divided the Greek Orthodox and Roman Catholic churches.

Fun Fact **I Wish I May, I Wish I Might**

According to legend, when construction of the Ayasofya reached the height of a man, the construction team set out to get a bite to eat, leaving their tools under the watch of a small boy. An angel appeared and urged the boy to fetch the men so that they could return to the work of building God's house. When the boy told the angel that he promised not to leave the tools unattended, the angel promised to keep an eye on everything until his return. After leaving the site and thus breaking his promise, the boy was never allowed to return, and the angel continues to wait for him. Go to the entrance of the basilica proper, to the left of the Imperial Door; legend has it that the angel grants a wish to all those who successfully complete a 360-degree circle with their thumb in the hole of this wish-worn column.

Ayasofya

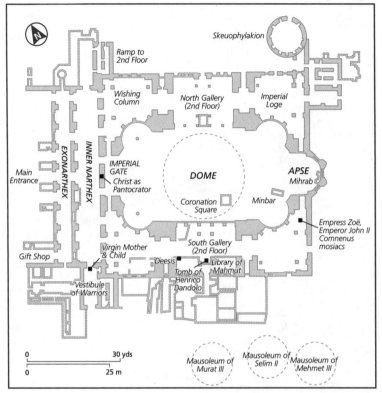

After Mehmet II penetrated the city in 1453, his first official stop was to this overwhelming symbol of an empire that he had conquered, and with his head to the ground, he invoked the name of Allah and declared the great house of worship a mosque.

In the years that followed, several adjustments were made to the building including the covering over of the frescoes and mosaics, due to the prohibition of Islam against the representation of figures. (The Iconoclastic movement of the 8th and 9th centuries A.D. had similarly disavowed the use of figural depictions and icons, during which many of the frescoes and mosaics were defaced, destroyed, or cemented over; any figural representations seen today date to after this period.) A single wooden minaret

> **Fun Fact Sizing up the Dome**
>
> At 46m (151 ft. and 1 in.) height, the Statue of Liberty (less the pedestal) could fit under the dome with 10.3m (32 ft., 11 in.) to spare.

was erected (and later replaced by Mimar Sinan during restorations in the 16th c.), and three additional minarets were added at a later date. The altar was shifted slightly to the right to accommodate a *mihrab* indicating the direction of Mecca, and an ablution fountain, along with a kitchen, was erected in the courtyard.

Exploring Istanbul

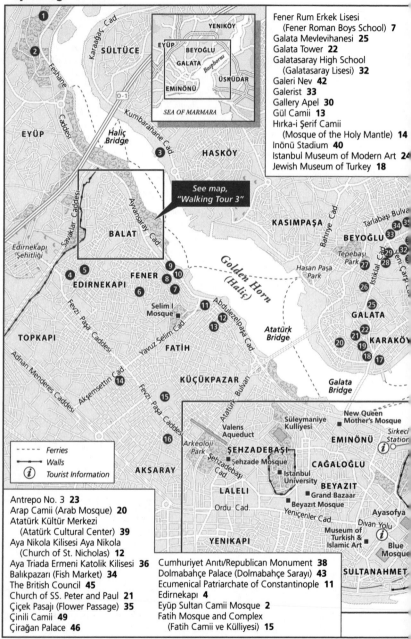

YENİKÖY

EYÜP BEYOĞLU

SÜLTÜCE

GALATA

Bosphorus

ÜSKÜDAR

EMİNÖNÜ

SEA OF MARMARA

Karadağç. Cad.

Teshane

EYÜP

Caddesi

Haliç
Bridge

Kumbarahane Cad.

HASKÖY

O-1

*See map,
"Walking Tour 3"*

Savaklar Caddesi

Ayvansaray Cad.

BALAT

Edirnekapı
Şehitliği

KASIMPAŞA

Tarlabaşı Bulva

BEYOĞLU

Bahriye Cad.

Tepebaşı
Park

Hasan Paşa
Park

İstiklal Cars

EDİRNEKAPI

FENER

Golden Horn
(Haliç)

Selim I
Mosque

Abdülezelpaşa Cad.

Atatürk
Bridge

GALATA

Fevzi Paşa Caddesi

Yavuz Selim Cad.

TOPKAPI

FATİH

KARAKÖ

Adnan Menderes Caddesi

Akşemsettin Cad.

KÜÇÜKPAZAR

Atatürk Bulvarı

Galata
Bridge

Fevzi Paşa Caddesi

New Queen
Mother's Mosque

Süleymaniye
Kulliyesi

Valens
Aqueduct

Sirkeci
Station

Arkeoloji
Park

Şehzadebaşı Cad.

ŞEHZADEBAŞI

EMİNÖNÜ

CAĞALOĞLU

- - - - - *Ferries*
▬▬▬ *Walls*
ⓘ *Tourist Information*

AKSARAY

Şehzade Mosque

İstanbul
University

BEYAZIT

Grand Bazaar

LALELİ

Ordu Cad.

Beyazıt Mosque

Yeniçeriler Cad.

Ayasofya

Divan Yolu

Museum of
Turkish &
Islamic Art ⓘ

YENİKAPI

Blue
Mosque

SULTANAHMET

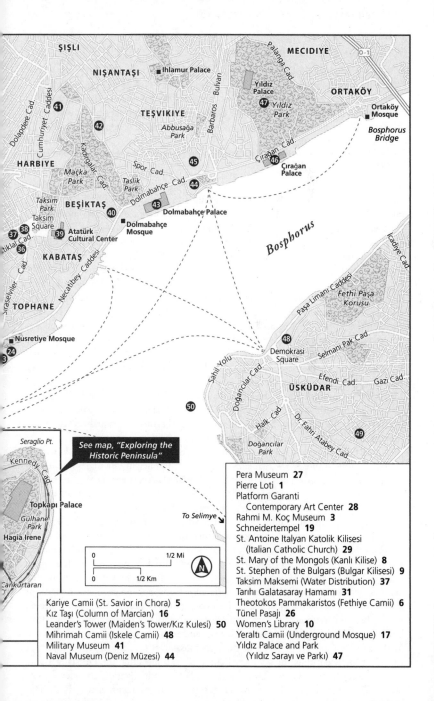

SİSLİ

NİSANTASI   ■ Ihlamur Palace

MECIDIYE   O-1

Palanga Cad.

Yıldız
Palace

ORTAKÖY

47 Yıldız
Park

Ortaköy
■ Mosque

TEŞVIKIYE

Abbusağa
Park

Bosphorus
Bridge

Barbaros Bulvarı

Dolapdere Cad.   41

Cumhuriyet Caddesi

42

Çırağan Cad.

HARBIYE

Kadırgalar Cad.

Maçka
Park

Spor Cad.   45

46

Çırağan
Palace

Taslik
Park

Dolmabahçe Cad.   44

Taksim
Park

BEŞİKTAŞ   40   43

Dolmabahçe Palace

Taksim
Square

■ Dolmabahçe
Mosque

37 38
Cad.   39 Atatürk
Cultural Center

Bosphorus

36
İstiklal Cad.

KABATAŞ

Necatibey Caddesi

İcadiye Cad.

Sıraselviler Cad.

TOPHANE

Paşa Limanı Caddesi

Fethi Paşa
Korusu

■ Nusretiye Mosque

24
3

48

Selmani Pak Cad.

Demokrasi
Square

Efendi Cad.   Gazi Cad.

Sahil Yolu

ÜSKÜDAR

Doğancılar Cad.

50

Halk Cad.

Dr. Fahri Atabey Cad.

49

Doğancılar
Park

Seraglio Pt.

See map, "Exploring the
Historic Peninsula"

Kennedy Cad.

Topkapı Palace

Gülhane
Park

To Selimye

Hagia Irene

0   1/2 Mi
0   1/2 Km

N

Çankurtaran

Kariye Camii (St. Savior in Chora) 5
Kız Taşı (Column of Marcian) 16
Leander's Tower (Maiden's Tower/Kız Kulesi) 50
Mihrimah Camii (Iskele Camii) 48
Military Museum 41
Naval Museum (Deniz Müzesi) 44

Pera Museum 27
Pierre Loti 1
Platform Garanti
    Contemporary Art Center 28
Rahmi M. Koç Museum 3
Schneidertempel 19
St. Antoine Italyan Katolik Kilisesi
    (Italian Catholic Church) 29
St. Mary of the Mongols (Kanlı Kilise) 8
St. Stephen of the Bulgars (Bulgar Kilisesi) 9
Taksim Maksemi (Water Distribution) 37
Tarıhı Galatasaray Hamamı 31
Theotokos Pammakaristos (Fethiye Camii) 6
Tünel Pasajı 26
Women's Library 10
Yeraltı Camii (Underground Mosque) 17
Yıldız Palace and Park
    (Yıldız Sarayı ve Parkı) 47

Fun Fact **Face-Off in the Corner**

Empress Zoë had a lot of clout in the early part of the second millennium. First she had this glorious golden mosaic, found at the end of the upper gallery, crafted in her honor, depicting Christ between herself and her first husband. When her husband died in 1034, she ordered the tiles of his face along with the inscription replaced to accommodate her second husband, repeating the procedure for the third.

Ayasofya was converted from a mosque into a museum by Atatürk in 1935, after a restoration led by Thomas Whitmore of the Byzantium Institute of America. Mosaics and icons that were previously defaced or whitewashed were rediscovered and restored. Excavations are continuing to reveal the foundations of the church built by Theodosius.

While this enduring symbol of Byzantium still has the power to instill awe after so many additions and reconstructions (including tombs, schools, and soup kitchens during its tour of duty as a mosque), the exterior's original architecture is marred by large and boxy buttresses; you'll get more of a representation of the intent of Justinian's original from the inside. On your way in, notice the stone cannonballs lining the gravel path of the outer courtyard. These are the actual cannonballs used by Mehmet the Conqueror in his victorious 1453 battle for the city. The main entrance to Ayasofya leads to the **exonarthex** 𝄐, a vaulted outer vestibule that was reserved for those not yet baptized. The **inner narthex** 𝄐𝄐, or vestibule, glistens with Justinian's original gold mosaics embellished with floral and geometric patterns. The most central of the nine doors leading into the nave of the church, called the **Imperial Gate** 𝄐, is topped by a **mosaic** 𝄐𝄐𝄐 of the Christ Pantocrator holding a book with the inscription "Peace be with you. I am the Light of the World." He is surrounded by roundels portraying the Virgin Mary, the angel Gabriel, and a bearded emperor, believed to represent Leo VI asking for forgiveness for his four marriages.

Through the Imperial Gate is a sight that brought both emperors and sultans to their knees: a soaring **dome** 𝄐𝄐𝄐 that rises 56m (184 ft.) in height (about 15 stories) and spans a width of approximately 31m (102 ft.). Light filters through a crown formed by 40 windows and ribs, glittering with the gold mosaic tiles that cover the entire interior of the dome. At its decorative peak, Ayasofya's interior mosaics covered more than 4 acres of space. Eight calligraphic discs, four of which are the largest examples of calligraphy in the Islamic world, ornament the interior and bear the names of Allah and Mohammed (above the apse); the four successive caliphs, Ali, Abu Bakr, Osman, and Omar (at each of the four corners of the dome); and Ali's sons Hassan and Huseyin (in the nave). The main nave, side aisles, apse, and semi-domes are covered with mosaics and frescoes, depicting religious and imperial motifs or floral and geometric designs. At the center of the space is a square of marble flooring called **Coronation Square,** believed to have been the location of the emperor's throne, the place of coronation and therefore, in the minds of the Byzantines (or at least the emperor), the center of the universe. Up in the southern gallery are some of the best mosaics in the church (restoration just recently completed; thus the additional entrance fee), including the **Deesis** 𝄐𝄐𝄐 (a composition depicting Christ, his mother, and St. John the Baptist), considered to be one of Byzantium's most striking mosaics, in spite of the missing lower two-thirds. This mosaic is one of the oldest, dating to the 14th century. Opposite the Deesis is **the tomb**

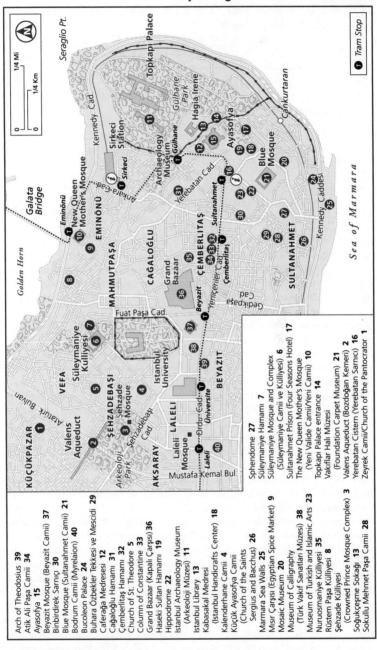

of Henrico Dandalo, the blind Venetian doge whose success in diverting the Fourth Crusade to Constantinople resulted in his capture of the city in 1204. Along the balcony railing near the deesis is the graffiti of a 9th-century-A.D. Viking—the equivalent to "Halvdan was here." At the far end of the gallery near the apse are two additional mosaics: one depicting **Empress Zoë** ✿✿ with her third husband, Constantine IX Monomachus (see "Face-Off in the Corner," above), separated by a figure of Christ, and a mosaic portrait of **Emperor John II Comnenus,** his wife, Empress Eirene, and their son, Prince Alexius (extended onto the panel on the wall to the right).

Exit the church through the small Vestibule of Warriors in the inner narthex opposite the ramp to the upper gallery. Previously used as an entrance, this is now an exit, so you're forced to turn around to view the mosaic lunette depicting an enthroned **Virgin Mother and Child** ✿✿✿, flanked by Constantine proffering a model of the city and Justinian offering a model (inaccurate) of the Ayasofya. (A mirror has been placed above the current exit to alert you to the mosaic behind you.)

Sultanahmet. ☎ 0212/522-1750. Admission 10YTL ($8.70/£3.80) to the grounds/museum; an additional 10YTL ($8.70/£3.80) for the second floor gallery. Tues–Sun 9am–4:30pm. Tram: Sultanahmet.

Blue Mosque (Sultan Ahmet Camii) ✿✿✿
This grand bubble of masonry, one of the great and defining features of Istanbul's skyline, was constructed between 1609 and 1617 by Sultan Ahmet I, who was not only driven by a desire to leave behind an imperial namesake mosque, but was also determined to build a monument to rival the Ayasofya. So great was the Sultan's ambition that he had one unfortunate architect executed before finally choosing Mehmet Ağa, probably a student of Sinan, who came up with a plan commonly accepted as impossible to build. The design is a scheme of successively descending smaller domes that addresses the problem of creating a large covered interior space. The overall effect is one of such great harmony, grace, and power that it's impossible to walk away from this building unaffected.

> **Fun Fact Did You Know?**
> Approximately 21,000 tiles were used to decorate the Blue Mosque.

There are several legends associated with the construction of the **six minarets.** One says that the sultan's desire for gold minarets—*altın* in Turkish—was understood as *altı,* or six. Whatever the reasoning, the construction challenged the preeminence of the mosque in Mecca, which at the time also had six minarets. The ensuing scandal, both in and out of Istanbul, resulted in the sultan's ordering the construction of a seventh minaret at the Kaa'ba.

The mosque was completed after just over 6½ years of work and to this day remains one of the finest examples of classical Ottoman architecture. The original complex included a soup kitchen, a *medrese* (Muslim theological school), a primary school, a hospital, and a market. A *türbe*, or mausoleum, stands at the corner of the grounds near the Hippodrome and Sultanahmet Park, and houses the remains of the Sultan Ahmet I, his wife, Kösem, and three of his sons. It also contains some fine examples of calligraphy on cobalt blue Iznik tile.

The main entrance (for worshipers; tourists must enter from a portal on the south side) is off the **Hippodrome,** beneath the symbolic chain that required even the sultan to bow his head when he arrived on horseback. Walk straight through the garden up to the main marbled courtyard of the mosque and you'll see an ablution fountain, no longer in use. The working ablution fountains are located at ground level of the

Grand Bazaar

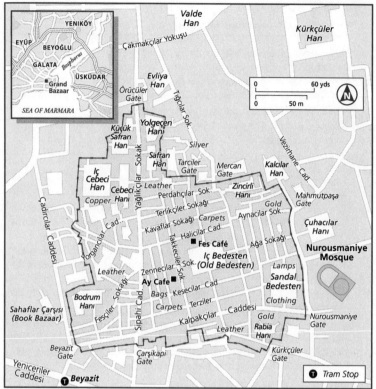

Valde Han
Kürkçüler Han
YENIKÖY
EYÜP
BEYOĞLU
GALATA
Bosphorus
ÜSKÜDAR
Grand Bazaar
SEA OF MARMARA
Çakmakçılar Yokuşu
Evliya Han
Örücüler Gate
Küçük Safran Han
Yolgeçen Hanı
Safran Han
Silver
Tarciler Gate
Mercan Gate
Kalcılar Han
Tığlcılar Sok.
Vezirhane Cad.
Mahmutpaşa Gate
İç Cebeci Han
Cebeci Hanı
Leather
Perdahçılar Sok.
Copper Hanı
Zincirli Hanı
Çuhacılar Hanı
Terlikçiler Sokağı
Gold
Kavaflar Sokağı   Carpets
Aynacılar Sok.
Halıcılar Cad.
Çadırcılar Caddesi
Yorgancılar Cad.
Yağlıkçılar Sokak
Takkeciler Sok.
Fes Café
İç Bedesten (Old Bedesten)
Ağa Sokağı
Nourousmaniye Mosque
Leather
Zennecilar Sok.
Ay Cafe
Lamps
Sandal Bedesten
Bags
Kesecilar Cad.
Carpets   Terziler
Clothing
Bodrum Hanı
Fesçiler Sokağı
Sipahi Cad.
Sahaflar Çarşısı (Book Bazaar)
Kalpakçılar   Caddesi
Gold
Rabia Hanı
Nourousmaniye Gate
Leather
Beyazıt Gate
Çarşıkapı Gate
Kürkçüler Gate
Yeniçeriler Caddesi
Beyazit
Tram Stop
0   60 yds
0   50 m

northern facade facing the Ayasofya. Visitors should enter from the opposite side (from the Hippodrome entrance, follow the garden path diagonally to your right to the south side of the mosque).

If you plan your visit during the morning hours when the sun is still angled from the east, the first effect once inside will be one of blindness as the light penetrates the stained glass, creating an illusion of false darkness. As your eyes adjust, the swirling blues, greens, reds, and yellows from the tile and stained glass increase the impression of immensity and grandeur. The abundant use of decorative tile represents the pinnacle of **Iznik tile** *★★★* craftsmanship, evident in the rich yet subtle blues and greens in traditional Ottoman patterns of lilies, tulips, and carnations. The overall dominance of blue prompted the mosque's early visitors to label it the Blue Mosque, a name that sticks to this day.

Lateral half **domes** resting on enormous elephantine **columns** *★★* (actually called elephant foot pillars) enhance the sense of open space, but critics contend that the pillars are too overbearing and cumbersome. The elegant **medallions** *★* facing the *mihrab* bear the names of Allah and Mohammed; the ones opposite are decorated with the names of the first four caliphs who ruled the Islamic world.

Sultanahmet. ℂ 0212/458-0776. Closed to visitors during prayer times. Tram: Sultanahmet.

Grand Bazaar (Kapalı Çarşısı) *★★★*   The mother of all tourist traps, the Grand or Covered Bazaar is a vivid illustration of all that's gone wrong with the free market.

The Imperial Ottoman Mosque

The majority of the mosques in Istanbul, and those highlighted in this book, are Ottoman Imperial structures. As their architecture is about the evolution of prayer space, there is no one floor plan per se, such as the cross plan of a Catholic church. However, you will notice several recurring elements:

- *avlu:* A monumental courtyard preceding the entryway to the mosque.
- *hünkar mahfili:* The sultan's loge, located in variable places and only in imperial mosques. This is where the sultan would (privately) attend services.
- *kürsü:* Generally located to the left of the *mihrab,* this is where the imam sits when reading from the Koran.
- *mihrab:* The niche indicating the *kıble,* or direction of Mecca.
- *mimbar* (or *minbar*): The "pulpit" from which the imam delivers his sermon.
- *minaret:* The more minarets, the more prestigious the building/builder/ namesake. The Blue Mosque, with its six minarets, is the only one in the world to match the number of minarets on the mosque in Mecca.
- *şadırvan:* An ornamental fountain, usually at the center of the courtyard, for ritual ablutions. In practice, these are decorative, and worshipers use faucets available on the side of the mosque.
- *şerefe:* The balcony of the minaret from which the *muezzin* calls the faithful to prayer.

Some Imperial and philanthropic mosques were the centerpiece of an entire complex, or *külliye,* serving the community. This complex would include some of the following: hospital, soup kitchen, primary school, public bath, public fountains, tombs/mausoleums, and a market.

The Grand Bazaar is actually the center of a commercial area within and around the covered section of the market that spreads all the way down the hill to Eminönü. The name "Grand Bazaar" refers to a vast collection of over 4,000 shops, 24 *hans* (privately owned inns or marketplaces), 65 streets, 22 gates, 2 *bedestens* (covered markets), restaurants, mosques, fountains, and teahouses within an area of 31 hectares (76 acres). Kapalı Çarşı refers specifically to the indoor and covered portion.

At the heart and soul of the bazaar are two *bedestens* (merchant centers), ordered built by Mehmet the Conqueror for the purpose of gaining revenue for the Ayasofya. These were the **İç, or Inner Bedesten** (more commonly known as the Old Bedesten), and the **Sandal Bedesten.** These two rectangular structures are typical *bedestens,* meaning that they are solid, significant, and capped by rows of vaults and domes covering a perimeter of cells surrounding an inner courtyard. Ottoman merchants gravitated to this center of commerce; it is estimated that by the end of Mehmet II's rule, the bazaar had already grown to a third of its current size. Artisans tended to congregate in one area, a legacy handed down through names of streets such as Fez Makers Street (Fesçiler Sok.), Street of the Washcloth Makers (Aynacilar Sok.), and Street of Fur Makers (Kürkçüler Sok.).

A number of characteristic *hans* that at one time (and now nominally) operated around a particular craft or trade are situated in and around the covered portion (or Kapalı Çarşı) of the Grand Bazaar. Of particular note inside the Kapalı Çarşı is the **Safran Han** (stuffing/sewing pillows and mattresses). Beyond the covered portion are the 17th-century **Valde Han** (weaving on looms), the **Çuhacılar Hanı** (antique silver and jewelry), and the 15th-century **Kürkçüler Han,** the oldest one still in use (yarns and knitting supplies; the furs are upstairs).

Over the centuries, the shops around the bazaar fell victim to a total of 10 fires and two earthquakes; the current configuration dates to 1894, when the Minister of Public Works under Abdülhamid II reorganized the bazaar following that year's earthquake.

Today, the main drag running from the Nuruosmaniye Gate to the Beyazit Gate is **Kalpakçilar Caddesi** ⊛, the glittering main thoroughfare lined on either side with shops of silver and gold, with anything and everything of your heart's desire elsewhere in the market.

For tips on shopping the Grand Bazaar, turn to chapter 9.

Beyazit. Free admission. Best entrances through the Beyazit Gate (across from the Beyazit stop on the tram along Divanyolu) and the Nuruosmaniye Gate (from the Çemberlitaş tram stop on Divanyolu; follow Vezirhanı Cad. to the arched entrance to the mosque grounds, which lead to the bazaar). Mon–Sat 8:30am–7pm. Closed Oct. 29. Shops close early during Ramadan. Tram: Sultanahmet.

Hippodrome ⊛ Watching the modestly clothed couples with their children strolling through the park on a Sunday afternoon, it's hard to imagine the centuries of rowdy chariot races, ostentatious royal celebrations, and bloody massacres that took place on these lawns. During the month of Ramadan, the trees above the park are strung with white lights, and temporary tents and imitation Ottoman houses full of fast food are set up along the perimeter, while a pink-and-blue fiberglass elephant ride for toddlers wipes away any remaining stains of the Hippodrome's complex past.

Polo games and horse races were popular sports in the day. The first track was built in A.D. 203 by Septimus Severus out of the ruins of the city he sacked. Modeled on the Circus Maximus in Rome, the Hippodrome was enlarged by Constantine in A.D. 324 through the help of supporting vaults and hefty stone walls on the southern portion of the tract. The lower areas (the **Spherion,** or retaining wall down the hill at the obelisk end of the park) were used as stables and quarters for the gladiators.

Forty rows of seats accommodated up to 100,000 agitated supporters divided into merchant guilds that over time degenerated into political rivalries. These factions were known as the Blues, Greens, Reds, and Whites. The Blues and Greens put aside their disagreements to demonstrate against the emperor in A.D. 532, which resulted in a riot with protesters screaming "Nika!" (Greek for victory). In what would become known as the Nika Revolt, much of the imperial palace and the original church of Ayasofya were destroyed. Justinian eventually regained control of his throne and ordered the massacre of some 30,000 to 40,000 people as punishment. With the arrival of the Fourth Crusade, the Hippodrome fell into disuse, eventually serving as a marble quarry for the Ottomans after their conquest of the city.

At the height of its splendor, the Hippodrome was crowned with a vast collection of trophies, statues, and monuments, either crafted by local artisans or lifted from the far corners of the empire.

Tips Two Cafes in the Grand Bazaar

Need a shot of caffeine? **Café Ist** (Tarakçılar Cad.; ℂ **0212/527-9353**), and **Fes Café** (Halıcılar Cad. 62; ℂ **0212/528-1613**), both located in the Grand Bazaar, are open Monday through Saturday 8:30am to 7pm, and offer sanctuary from endless cups of Nescafé with a wide selection of coffees, flavored teas, and fresh-squeezed juices. Fes also has a location just outside the Nuruosmaniye Mosque at Ali Baba Türbe Sok. 25/27 (ℂ **0212/526-3070**).

At the southern end of the park is the **Magnetic Column** 𝔊𝔊, also known as the Walled Obelisk, the Plaited Column, the Colossus, and the Column of Constantine. This column was erected in the 10th century under Constantine VII Porphyrogenitus and was faced with plaques of gilded bronze and brass plates. At one time this obelisk was used to support a pulley system for raising and lowering awnings to protect the spectators from the sun. In 1204 the bronze and brass plates were removed and smelted by the Crusaders to mint coins.

Farther along is the **Serpentine Column** 𝔊𝔊, a squat spiral standing 25% lower than its original 8m (26 ft.). The column was originally erected outside the Temple of Apollo at Delphi by the 31 Greek city-states to commemorate their victory over the Persians, and later brought to the city by Constantine. Made of melded bronze, the column represents three intertwining serpents and was crowned by three gold serpents' heads supporting a gold bowl, said to have been cast from the shields of the fallen Persian soldiers. The heads were lost until one resurfaced during the restoration of the Ayasofya, now in the Archaeology Museum. A second head was discovered and, like many ancient Turkish monuments, slithered its way to the British Museum in London.

The **Obelisk of Tutmosis III** 𝔊𝔊𝔊 is easily one of the most astounding feats of engineering in the city. This 13th-century-B.C. solid block of granite weighing over 60 tons was brought to Istanbul by Emperor Theodosius I from its place in front of the Temple of Luxor at Karnak, in Egypt. The four sides of granite are covered from top to bottom with hieroglyphics celebrating the glory of the pharaoh and the god Horus. The monument was placed in the square in A.D. 390, but *two-thirds* of the original was lost during transport. This portion, standing over 20m (65 ft.) high, was erected in under 30 days, on a Roman base depicting bas-reliefs of Theodosius's family, friends, and triumphs at the races.

At the northern end of the Hippodrome is the **Fountain of Wilhelm II (Alman Çeşmesi)** 𝔊𝔊, crafted in Germany and assembled in Istanbul to commemorate the emperor's visit to the city in 1895. Notice the initials of both the German monarch and Sultan Abdülhamid on the interior of the dome, inlaid with glittering golden mosaics.

The Hippodrome's crowning monument, long a distant memory of its original grandeur atop a disappeared imperial loggia, was a monumental **statue of four bronze horses.** In the Fourth Crusade's looting of the city in 1204, the monument was carried away to grace the facade of the Basilica of St. Marco in Venice. (Today, the ones on the facade are fake; the real ones are being protected from the elements in the Basilica of St. Marco's museum.)

Just to the north of the Hippodrome (on the corner where Divanyolu and Yerebatan Cad. converge) is the **Million (or Milion) Stone,** the point of departure for all roads leading out of the city and essentially ground zero for all measurements. The Milion Stone was modeled after the Milliarium Aureum, erected by Julius Caesar in the Forum in Rome. According to one tradition, the **True Cross** is said to have been brought from Jerusalem to Constantinople and placed by the Milion Stone during the reign of Constantine.

At Meydanı (Horse Plaza), Sultanahmet. Tram: Sultanahmet.

Istanbul Archaeology Museum (Arkeoloji Müzesi) 🏛️🏛️ The Istanbul Archaeology Museum is housed in three buildings just inside the first court of Topkapı Palace and includes the Museum of the Ancient Orient (first building on your left) and the Çinili Köşk (opposite the entrance to the main building). These museums, opened officially in 1891, owe their very existence to Osman Hamdi Bey, a 19th-century Turkish painter, archaeologist, curator, and diplomat, who fought for the Antiquities Conservation Act to combat the rampant smuggling of antiquities out of Turkey.

The Istanbul Archaeology Museum houses over one million objects, the most extraordinary of which are the sarcophagi that date back as far as the 4th century B.C. The museum excels, however, in its rich chronological collection of locally found artifacts that shed light on the origins and history of the city.

Near the entrance is a **statue of a lion** representing the only piece saved from the clutches of British archaeologists from the Mausoleum of Halicarnassus. In the halls to the left is a collection of sarcophagi found at Sidon (ancient Syria), representing various architectural styles influenced by outside cultures including Egypt, Phoenicia, and Lycia. The most famous is the **Alexander Sarcophagus** 🏛️🏛️🏛️, covered with astonishingly advanced carvings of battles and the life of Alexander the Great, discovered in 1887 and once believed to have been that of the emperor himself. The discovery that the occupant was in fact Sidonian King Abdalonymos may have initially been disappointing, but it hasn't diminished the impact of this great ancient work of art. Found in the same necropolis at Sidon is the stunningly preserved **Sarcophagus of the Crying Women** 🏛️🏛️🏛️, with 18 intricately carved panels showing figures of women in extreme states of mourning. Don't miss the monumental **Lycian tomb** 🏛️🏛️🏛️, carved in a style befitting a great king and just as impressive in this exhibit as on the hills of Lycia. Farther on is the recently inaugurated **Northern Wing** 🏛️🏛️, which rescues from storage a stunning collection of **monumental sarcophagi** 🏛️🏛️🏛️ and partially reconstructed **temple freizes** 🏛️🏛️🏛️.

Tips **Fishing for Customers: Local Shop "Commissioners"**

The dregs of Turkish society mill around the entrances to the major sites in Sultanahmet (Blue Mosque, Ayasofya, Topkapı, and the Hippodrome), lying in wait to pounce on you (and a percentage of anything you buy) with apparently harmless—even helpful—offers of assistance. It's called "fishing" in local jargon, and you're the fish. The point is to gain your confidence, so that you trust this person and the people/places/shops he recommends. If you don't mind the company, that's your choice. But in the event you buy, rest assured that after the transaction is completed, your new friend will find his way back to the shop (or hotel) for his cut. (Also, see "Important Tips for Women Travelers," in chapter 2.)

On the mezzanine level is the exhibit *Istanbul Through the Ages* ✿✿, a rich and well-presented exhibit that won the museum the Council of Europe Museum Award in 1993. To put the exhibit into perspective, the curators have provided maps, plans, and drawings to illustrate the archaeological findings, displayed thematically, which range from prehistoric artifacts found west of Istanbul to 15th-century Byzantine works of art. The recovered **snake's head** ✿ from the Serpentine Column in the Hippodrome is on display, as is the 14th-century bell from the Galata Tower. The upper two levels house the Troy exhibit and displays on the evolution of Anatolia over the centuries, as well as sculptures from Cyprus, Syria, and Palestine.

The newly renovated and reopened **Museum of the Ancient Orient** ✿✿✿ is an exceptionally rich collection of artifacts from the earliest civilizations of Anatolia, Mesopotamia, Egypt, and the Arab continent. The tour begins with pre-Islamic divinities and idols taken from the courtyard of the Al-Ula temple, along with artifacts showing ancient Aramaic inscriptions and a small collection of Egyptian antiquities. Although the individual exhibits are modest in size, the recent upgrade rivals Ankara's archaeological museum for organization and presentation.

Uncovered in the region of Mesopotamia and on display is an **obelisk of Adad-Nirari III** inscribed with cuneiform characters. Of particular significance is a series of colored **mosaic panels** ✿✿ showing animal reliefs of bulls and dragons with serpents' heads from the monumental Gate of Ishtar, built by Nebuchadnezzar, King of Babylonia. A pictorial representation on a **Sumerian devotional basin** of girls carrying pitchers of water whose contents are filling an underground source relates to the ancient Mesopotamian belief that the world was surrounded by water, a belief that has provoked questions over the origins of the biblical Great Flood.

With nothing dating more recent than the 1st century A.D., it's a real challenge to find something in this museum that is not of enormous significance. But two of the highlights are easily the fragments of the 13th-century-B.C. **sphinx** ✿ from the Yarkapı Gate at Hattuşaş (sadly underappreciated in its positioning against a passage wall) and one of the three known tablets of the **Treaty of Kadesh** ✿✿, the oldest recorded peace treaty signed between Ramses II and the Hittites in the 13th century B.C., inscribed in Akkadian, the international language of the era. (The Istanbul Archaeology Museum houses two; the third is in the Staatliche Museum in Berlin.)

Across from the Archaeology Museum is the **Çinili Köşk,** a wonderful pavilion of turquoise ceramic tiles whose facade displays eye-catching blue and white calligraphy. The mansion was originally built by Mehmet the Conqueror as a hunting pavilion, and now more appropriately houses the **Museum of Turkish Ceramics.** The museum, which is closed more often than not, contains a modest collection of Anatolian and Selçukian tiles, not the least of which is the 14th-century *mihrab* from the Ibrahim Bey mosque in Karaman in central Anatolia. Other highlights include some fine samples from Iznik and Kütahya, the two most important production centers for pottery, porcelain, and ceramics during the Ottoman period.

Entrance in the first court of Topkapı Palace (second portal on the left after St. Irene) and up hill at the back of Gülhane Park. ☏ **0212/520-7740.** Admission 5YTL ($4.35/£1.90); includes the Museum of the Ancient Orient and the Çinili Köşk. Archaeology Museum and Çinili Köşk: Tues–Sun 9am–5pm; Museum of the Ancient Orient: Tues–Sun 9am–1pm. Tram: Sultanahmet or Gülhane.

Museum of Turkish and Islamic Arts ✿ Ibrahim Paşa, swept into slavery by Turkish raids in Greece, became the beloved and trusted boyhood friend of Süleyman the Magnificent. Educated and converted to Islam and eventually appointed grand

---

Fun Fact **Did You Know?**

Whenever a sultan ordered the execution of someone abroad, he would require that the head be brought back to him as proof. Tradition has it that one such victim was none other than Vlad Tepes, a Wallachian nobleman and tyrant better known as Vlad the Impaler (and later as Dracula).

---

vizier, Ibrahim Paşa was the sultan's only companion at mealtime, earning him the favored title *serasker sultan* (commander in chief). He also earned the sultan's sister's hand in marriage.

The palace was a gift from the sultan and was built by Sinan. From this very special palace on the Hippodrome, the sultan's family and friends had front-row seats for festivities in the square. Roxelana, the sultan's wife, managed to dispose of her rival in one of her infamous intrigues by convincing the sultan that his grand vizier had become too big for his britches.

The palace now houses the changing exhibitions of the Museum of Turkish and Islamic Arts, a fine collection of calligraphy, peace treaties, several examples of the sultan's official seal or *tuğra,* and an insightful ethnographic section depicting the lifestyles of nomads and city-dwelling Ottomans.

Ibrahim Paşa Sarayı (on the Hippodrome), Sultanahmet. ② 0212/518-1805. Admission 5YTL ($4.35/£1.90). Tues–Sun 9am–5pm. Tram: Sultanahmet.

Topkapı Palace (Topkapı Sarayı) ⭐⭐⭐   Residence of the sultans, administrative seat of the Ottoman Empire for almost 400 years, and the source of legend on life in the harem, Topkapı Palace should be up at the top of the list for anyone interested in the vast and exotic world behind the seraglio walls. It's impossible to rush through the palace, so you should allot at least a half-day and be prepared to encounter a few bottlenecks throughout the enclosed exhibition halls, especially in the Holy Relics Room where the ardent faithful, in their religious fervor, tend to obstruct the display cases. Built by Mehmet the Conqueror over the ruins of Constantine's Imperial Palace, Topkapı Palace occupies one of the seven hills of the city at the tip of the historic peninsula overlooking the sea. Since it is easily the most valuable real estate in the city, it doesn't take a brain surgeon to see why this spot was preferable to the original palace situated on an inland tract where the university stands today. Mehmet II began construction of the palace 9 years after his conquest of the city, where the sultans reigned continually until 1855, when Abdülmecid moved the imperial residence up the Bosphorus to Dolmabahçe Palace.

Entrance to the grounds is through the Bab-ı Hümayün Gate at the end of the Babuhümayun Caddesi (also called the Gate of Augustus, for the square outside the gate that in Byzantine times was a busy crossroads called the Forum of Augustus). Serving as the entrance through which the public would access the grounds, the gate would often display the decapitated heads of uncooperative administrators or rebels as a warning to all who entered. Just outside the gate is the **Ahmet III Fountain** ⭐⭐, built by Mehmet Ağa in 1729 atop an ancient source of water as a gift to Sultan Ahmet. A poem by the sultan is inscribed in the stone, inviting passersby to "drink the water and pray from the House of Ahmet."

Topkapı Palace

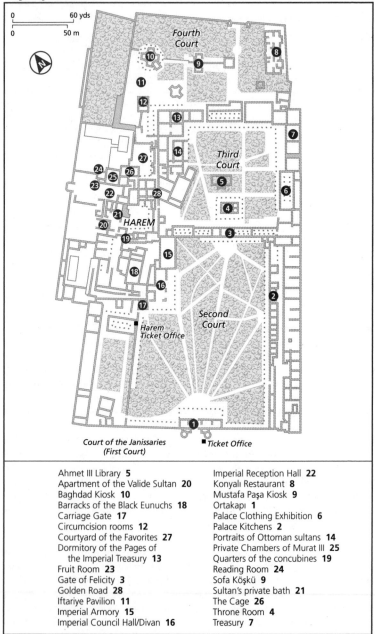

Ahmet III Library **5**
Apartment of the Valide Sultan **20**
Baghdad Kiosk **10**
Barracks of the Black Eunuchs **18**
Carriage Gate **17**
Circumcision rooms **12**
Courtyard of the Favorites **27**
Dormitory of the Pages of
  the Imperial Treasury **13**
Fruit Room **23**
Gate of Felicity **3**
Golden Road **28**
Iftariye Pavilion **11**
Imperial Armory **15**
Imperial Council Hall/Divan **16**

Imperial Reception Hall **22**
Konyalı Restaurant **8**
Mustafa Paşa Kiosk **9**
Ortakapı **1**
Palace Clothing Exhibition **6**
Palace Kitchens **2**
Portraits of Ottoman sultans **14**
Private Chambers of Murat III **25**
Quarters of the concubines **19**
Reading Room **24**
Sofa Köşkü **9**
Sultan's private bath **21**
The Cage **26**
Throne Room **4**
Treasury **7**

The first courtyard, known as the **Court of the Janissaries,** is a public park of gardens and trees, just as it was in earlier days. Along the center path are the remains of a 5th-century-A.D. Roman cistern. (You can save this for the way out.)

The diagonal path to the left leads to the stunning **Hagia Eirene (St. Irene)** ✸✸✸, the second-largest Byzantine church after Ayasofya, and a church that predates the arrival of Constantine's conquest of the city. The first temple on the site was dedicated to the goddess Aphrodite until it became the center of Christian activities between A.D. 272 and A.D. 398. During Constantine's pro-Christian reign, the emperor had the church enlarged, and then, following its near destruction in the Nika Revolt (along with that of the Ayasofya), Justinian had it reconstructed. Excavation between 1946 and 1950 indicates that a series of buildings existed connecting the church with the Ayasofya, and the fact that both churches were completed and rededicated at about the same time indicates that these houses of worship were in some way part of an ecclesiastical complex. The buildings were later demolished to make room for construction of the palace walls. Rumor has it that Mehmet the Conqueror's Italian consort convinced him to store the house porcelain there, where she could then secretly go and pray, but for the record, the Ottomans used the church as an arsenal. Hagia Eirene is closed to the public but is used as a venue for concerts and recitals during the **International Istanbul Music Festival** (p. 16) in the summertime. The church may be opened on special request (✆ **0212/520-6952**).

The ticket booths to the palace are located on the right side of the courtyard. Proceed to the Ortakapı (middle gate), known as the **Gate of Salutation** ✸, roughly translated from the Arabic (Turkish version) *Babüsselâm.*

Added by Süleyman the Magnificent in 1524, this gate signaled to all but the sultan to dismount before proceeding into the palace. On either side of the gate are two octagonal towers that essentially served as death row for those who fell out of favor; after a prisoner's execution, the body would be left outside the gate. To the right of the gate (facing), is a marble fountain where the executioner would wash the blood off his hands before reentering the palace.

Begin your visit with the **Palace Kitchens** ✸✸, a complex comprised of a string of lofty chambers topped by a series of chimney-domes, a narrow inner courtyard, and a smaller string of rooms. The largest in the world, the kitchens at one time employed over 1,000 servants working day and night to serve the 5,000 residents of the palace, a number that swelled to 15,000 during Ramadan. At the far end is the original wooden kitchen that survived a 16th-century fire; Sinan, who reconstructed the kitchens, added the massive conical chimneys and enlarged the original space. Suspended from the iron bars in the ceiling were the cauldrons, raised or lowered over the fire pits below according to the desired intensity of the flame. The kitchens are now used to exhibit the palace's rich collection of **porcelain** ✸ numbering close to 12,000 pieces, not all of which are displayed. Topkapı houses the third-most-important collection of porcelain in the world, after Beijing and Dresden, while the palace's collection of celadons surpasses that of Beijing because the Chinese destroyed all of theirs during the Cultural Revolution. Besides these 4th- and 5th-century-A.D. celadons are pieces from the Sung and Yuan dynasties (9th–13th c. A.D.), pieces from the Ming Dynasty (14th–17th c.), and porcelain from the Ching Dynasty (16th–20th c.). Many of these treasures found their way to Istanbul as gifts exchanged between the Ottomans, Chinese, and Persians as symbols of solidarity toward the maintenance and protection of the roads. There's also a rich collection of silver, particularly coffee services, candelabras, and mirrors

---

(Fun Fact **Better Safe Than Sorry**

Sultans preferred to eat off celadon china, because the pigments changed color when put in contact with poisons.

(ornamented on the backside because of the proscription requiring the reflective side to be lain facedown), and a display of Venetian glass and Bohemian crystal. The Ahmet III Fountain outside the main entrance is reproduced here in a stunning mass of silver, but there are examples of collectibles on a less grandiose scale as well.

Following a direct path along the length of the palace grounds, proceed to the **Gate of Felicity (Babüssaade)** ⚔, also known as the Gate of the White Eunuchs. For 400 years, enthronement ceremonies were held at the entrance to this gate, today used as a backdrop for the annual presentation of Mozart's *Abduction from the Seraglio* during the International Istanbul Music Festival. Decapitated heads found their way above this gate as well. Only the sultan and the grand vizier were allowed past this gate into the third courtyard (while the Valide Sultan used a back gate for entrances and exits), the private quarters of the palace. Immediately inside the Gate of Felicity and acting as a visual barrier to the private quarters beyond is the **Throne Room** ⚔, a pavilion used by the sultan as an audience chamber to receive (or affront) visiting ambassadors. Notice the interlocking marble used in the construction of the arched doorway; this design technique reinforced the archway and protected it against earthquakes.

Directly to the right is the Seferliler Quarters, now housing the **Palace Clothing Exhibition** or Imperial Wardrobe. Because the sultan's clothing was considered to be holy, a sultan's wardrobe would be wrapped up and preserved in the palace. This opulent display of silk, brocade, and gold-threaded clothing is only a small portion of the whole collection and includes enormously baggy costumes (to give the sultan the visual advantage of size), along with caftans and other garments showing influences from around the empire.

Past the Palace Clothing Exhibition is the Fatih Pavilion, containing a recently restored exhibition of the **Treasury** ⚔⚔⚔, one of the greatest collections of treasures in the world. In 400 years a sultan can amass a great quantity of wealth, supplied through spoils of war, gifts from neighboring kings and queens, and the odd impulse buy. The rooms were off-limits to everyone but the sultan, and in his absence, any visitor was required to be accompanied by at least 40 other men.

Room no. 1 of the Treasury is a collection of Ottoman objects and **ceremonial thrones** ⚔⚔⚔, including one in pure gold, weighing in at 250kg (550 lb.), presented to Murat III in 1585 by the Egyptian governor; an ebony throne crafted for Süleyman the Magnificent; and a jewel-encrusted throne, presented to Mahmut I by Nadir Shah of India.

The eye is immediately drawn to the jewel-studded mother-of-pearl and tortoiseshell throne of Sultan Ahmet I, crafted by the master of inlay, Mehmet Ağa, the same man commissioned by the sultan to build the Blue Mosque. (Rumor has it that during his 1995 visit, Michael Jackson requested permission to sit in one of the thrones; however, his request was denied.) Also of note in room no. 1 is the **sword** belonging to Süleyman the Magnificent, with his name and title inscribed on the blade.

Room no. 2 of the Treasury displays a collection of medals, and non-Ottoman objects and gifts (or plunder) received through the spoils of war. Highlights include figurines crafted in India from seed pearls, and in the same case, a miniature tree of life and a vessel presented as gifts to the tomb of Mohammed.

The focus of room no. 3 is a pair of shoulder-high **candlesticks** ✫ crafted of solid gold, caked with several thousand brilliants/diamonds, and weighing over 48kg (105 lb.) each. In a world absent of electricity, candlesticks like these would be placed on either side of the *mihrab* to provide light for the reading of the holy book. This pair was presented to the tomb of Mohammed in Medina and brought back to Istanbul after World War I. The rest of the exhibit in room no. 3, an overwhelming collection of jade, rock crystal, zinc, emeralds, and other precious gems, displays Ottoman objects made by artists and craftsmen for the sultans throughout the centuries.

Room no. 4 is the Treasury's *pièce de résistance*, a breathtaking view into the wealth of the Ottoman Empire. The famous **Topkapı Dagger** ✫ is here, weighted down by a row of emeralds and diamonds in the hilt and on the cover. This dagger was the protagonist in the 1964 film *Topkapı* (with Peter Ustinov), an amusing film about a plot to rob the Palace Museum. The actual dagger was intended as a gift from Sultan Mahmud I to Nadir Shah to warn him of an impending conspiracy on his life, but was returned by the couriers following a bloody revolution in which the shah was killed.

You'll notice a group of people hovering around a case at the far end of room no. 4, displaying the 86-caret **Spoonmaker's Diamond** ✫✫, or Kaşıkçı Diamond, the fifth-largest diamond in the world, glittering in a setting of 49 smaller diamonds. The diamond was actually discovered in the 17th century in a city dump by a local peddler who sold it to a jeweler for pennies.

The exhibit finishes with a stunning collection of "lesser" diamonds and gems, plus the **gold and jewel-encrusted chain mail** ✫✫ of Sultan Mustafa III. Also of note is the **ceremonial sword** ✫, attributed to either Caliph Osman (7th c. A.D.) or Osman Gazi (13th c.), and used in any sultan's inauguration, usually in front of Eyüp Sultan Mosque.

Another piece of note is the **golden cradle** ✫✫ in which newborn sons were presented to the sultans, as well as an **emerald pendant** ✫ with 48 strings of pearls originally sent by Sultan Abdülhamid I as a gift to the tomb of the Prophet Mohammed in Mecca. The pendant was returned to Istanbul after Mecca was no longer within the borders of the empire.

Exit the courtyard down the stairs to the right through a long passage. To the right and parallel to the sea is the second terrace, affording one of the best views in the city. Imagine the days of seaside attacks on the palace walls as you watch the maritime traffic go by. During Byzantine times, a chain, composed of links .8m (2½ ft.) long, was forged to span the Golden Horn and prevent enemy ships from accessing the waterway.

This fourth courtyard was the realm of the sultan, and a stroll around the gardens will reveal some lovely examples of Ottoman kiosk architecture. Near the center of the upper level of the courtyard is the **Mustafa Paşa Kiosk,** the oldest building in the complex, which served as the physician's quarters and as a wardrobe for the sultan

---

Tips **Topkapı Palace Lunch Break**

After touring the Treasury, you've reached the halfway point and a good place to stop for lunch or drinks. The expansive **Konyalı restaurant** (✆ 0212/513-9696; p. 93) includes indoor and outdoor dining rooms, as well as an outdoor cafeteria-style snack bar.

needing to effect swift changes during state functions. From the picture window over-looking the gardens, the sultan was known to observe wrestling matches, and even join in every now and again.

Perched on the upper terrace at the northernmost corner of the palace complex is the **Baghdad Kiosk** ⊕, magnificently sited to take best advantage of the views of the Golden Horn. The kiosk is decorated with priceless Iznik tiles, both inside and out. In addition to the tiles, the interior space is embellished with stained glass and crowned by a dome decorated with a traditional Ottoman motif in gold leaf. The kiosk served the sultan in colder weather; occupants of the kiosk were warmed by the central bra-zier. The **Sofa Köşkü** is the only surviving wooden pavilion in the palace. The golden roofed, **Iftariye Pavilion,** or "pavilion for breaking the fast," is the covered balcony on the northern edge of the courtyard), also called the *Mehtaplık,* or "Moon Place."

The **circumcision rooms,** rarely opened to the public, are also located in the fourth courtyard.

Backtrack through the passage and up the steps into the third courtyard. To the right past the Museum Directorate is the **Dormitory of the Pages of the Imperial Treasury,** formerly used to display decorative calligraphy from the Koran as well as jeweled Koran sets. At the far corner of the third courtyard is the **Holy Relic Section** ⊕⊕⊕, the largest collection in the world of this type, containing the personal belongings of the Prophet Mohammed, the caliphs, and even the unexpected **staff of Moses** ⊕. Also on display is a piece of St. John the Baptist's skull and a section of his forearm, enclosed within a solid gold model. The items on display were brought back to Istanbul by Selim the Grim in 1517, following his conquest of the holy cities of Mecca and Medina, and after declaring himself caliph. Since the Kaa'ba was restored annually, pieces of the mosque were regularly kept as ornamentation for mosques. This collection was off-lim-its to anyone but the most favored members of the sultan's family and was only open to public viewing in 1962. The domed space is ornamented with Iznik tiles and quotations from the Koran along with a priceless set of rain gutters, an intricately carved door, and an old set of keys taken from the Kaa'ba. Directly opposite the entrance are the **four sabers** belonging to the first four caliphs, and the first-ever copy of the **Koran** ⊕, doc-umented on deerskin.

To the right is the **Mohammed Chamber** ⊕⊕⊕, fronted by a booth in which an *imam* (religious guide) has been reciting passages from the Koran continually for the past 500 years. This tradition was started by Mehmet II and sets the stage for the col-lection of holy relics within. The **golden cloth** ⊕ that once covered the black stone in the central courtyard of the Kaa'ba in Mecca now hangs in this exhibit, as a new one is richly prepared each year. Considered a gift falling from the heavens, the stone prompted Abraham to build a temple on the spot, now the Kaa'ba, attracting wor-shipers from all faiths for several hundred years. The display cases here are almost always hidden behind fervent religious visitors communing with the spirit of the prophet through **relics** ⊕⊕ of his hair, a tooth, his footprints, and even soil from his grave. The **Holy Mantle,** the most sacred item in the collection, is contained in a **gold coffer** ⊕⊕ and sequestered behind a grilled door.

Turkish and Iranian miniatures as well as portraits of Ottoman sultans are exhibited in the rooms next to the one containing the Holy Relics. While the original collection amounts to a total of 13,000 specimens, this exhibit comes nowhere near this number. The main draw is the collection of portraits (both copies and originals) modeled after those painted by some of the Renaissance's most celebrated artists (Veronese, Bellini).

Fun Fact **The Forbidden City**

The word *harem,* Arabic for "forbidden," conjures up images of bellybuttons, grapes, and palm trees, and of limitless pleasure, unless you're the one fanning the sultan. The reality was closer to a deluxe prison, a stifling hierarchy of slaves, concubines, and wives from which only a few ever emerged. It was even common practice for a new sultan to drown the concubines of his predecessor, to eliminate the possibility that one might be carrying a child with designs on the throne. The mystery enshrouding these enclosed walls was never truly lifted, and even concubines who survived kept silent.

The institution of the harem was established by Süleyman the Magnificent in 1587 following a fire in the palace in Beyazit, when the cunning Roxelana convinced him to transfer his residence over to Topkapı. Muslims are exceedingly private people, and these enclosed and restricted quarters served to maintain the "curtain" over the feminine members of his extended family.

Lacking any record of the physiological characteristics of the first 12 sultans, the Ottomans had the ones painted by the Venetians brought back to Istanbul in 1579.

In the center of the courtyard is the **Ahmet III Library,** constructed in the 16th century of white marble and recently restored and opened to the public. The bookcases are inlaid with ivory and contain about 6,000 volumes of Arab and Greek manuscripts. The stained glass is from the early 17th century; the platform divan seating is typically Ottoman, and the carpets are over 500 years old.

Return to the second courtyard, where along the right side you will come upon the **Imperial Armory,** a collection of arms and objects acquired during the various military campaigns. Mehmet the Conqueror's sword is here, as is Süleyman the Magnificent's, but it's the unattributed 2.5m (8-ft.) one that really impresses.

Before entering the Harem, take a peek into the **Imperial Council Hall,** or **Divan** ⊛, constructed during the reign of Süleyman the Magnificent. State affairs were conducted here while the sultan eavesdropped from the grate above, which leads directly to the Harem. From this concealed position, the sultan could interrupt proceedings with a motion to his grand vizier and call for a private conference whenever the need arose. His wife, Roxelana, would often secretly attend these sessions, a privilege that ended in several unfortunate fatalities.

To visit the **Harem** ⊛⊛ you must purchase a ticket for one of the tours near the Carriage Gate entrance next to the Divan; your tour time will be indicated on your ticket. Tours depart on the half-hour and last about 30 minutes. Buy your ticket to the Harem at the beginning of your visit to the palace because when the tour buses arrive, the wait on both the ticket and entry lines can be very long. Of the 400 rooms, only around 20 are on the tour, with explanations that are not always audible or, for that matter, intelligible. Nonetheless, the tour is worth taking.

The Harem has three main sections: the outer quarters of the Black Eunuchs charged with guarding the Harem; the inner stone courtyard for the concubines; and the apartments facing the sea reserved for the sultan, his mother, favorite concubines, and future heirs to the throne. The tour begins at the Carriage Gate, where the sultan's mother and wives would be whisked away unseen by outsiders during exits and entrances. Past the first Guard Room is a long courtyard lined with cells that served as the Barracks of the Black Eunuchs. The upper levels were reserved for the younger eunuchs, with the lower cells housing the older ones. Winding through the maze of additions, the tour comes to the quarters of the concubines, unheated and often unsanitary rooms around a claustrophobic stone courtyard. The only way out was to be one of the very lucky few chosen by the mother for the sultan; the others were servants to the sultan, or to the girls higher up on the hierarchy. At its most crowded, the Harem housed over 800 concubines. Even if the sultan rotated every night, the numbers were against those girls, and although some were given to the harems of state officials or grand viziers, many died virgins (but who knows what really went on in there . . .).

In contrast, the **Apartment of the Valide Sultan** 🍂🍂, sultan's mother's room, sandwiched between the girls' quarters and the sultan's, is a domed wonder of mother-of-pearl, ivory, tortoise shell, gold leaf, porcelain tiles, and frosted glass. The apartment consisted of a bedroom, a dining room, a chamber for prayer, and an office around a courtyard.

The **sultan's private bath** 🍂, furnished with the usual *hamam* gear but infinitely more lush, has a guarded mesh gate so that the sultan could relax without the fear of being disturbed or assassinated. The sultan's apartments are close by, and the visit continues with the **Imperial Reception Hall** 🍂🍂, where celebrations or evenings of entertainment took place while musicians played discreetly from the mezzanine. While the sultan presided from his throne, the women adhered to a strict hierarchy, with the most important women seated at the center of the platform.

One of the few rooms preserving the luster of its creator is the grand domed **Private Chambers of Murat III** 🍂🍂, built by Sinan in 1578. The walls are covered with a classic blue Iznik tile with red highlights, a prototype that was never duplicated. A frieze of calligraphy runs the perimeter of the room, and elegant panels of flowers and plums surround a bronze fireplace. The room is also called the Fountain Room because of the marble fountain that was kept running to mask conversations not intended for prying ears.

The **Reading Room** used by Ahmet I is a small but well-positioned library that affords distracting views of the convergence of the three waterways: the Golden Horn, the Marmara Sea, and the Bosphorus.

The **Fruit Room** is more of a breakfast nook added by Sultan Ahmet III to his private chambers. One look and it's not hard to figure out how this room got its name. The room is enveloped in fruit and floral overkill, but evidently the sultan's attentions were focused on the Harem pool out the window.

The next stop on the Harem tour is at the twin apartments of the crown prince, better known as **The Cage** 🍂. In the early years of the empire, a crowned prince was well prepared to fulfill his destiny as a leader, beginning his studies in these rooms and later moving on to actual field experience in one of the provinces. When the practice of fratricide was abandoned, brothers of the sultan were sequestered in these rooms, where they either went crazy or languished in the lap of luxury—or both. The opulence of the stained glass and the tile work and the mother-of-pearl inlaid cabinets belie the chambers' primary function as a jail cell, which supports a recent discovery that the actual cage was located in another part of

> **(Fun Fact Historic House Calls**
>
> Maimonides, the Spanish philosopher and writer, was the personal physician to Sultan Saladdin.

the Harem. The tour guides continue to perpetuate the myth by billing these two rooms as the bona fide cage.

The Harem tour comes to an end at the **Courtyard of the Favorites** *⟨k⟨k*, surrounded by a charming building recalling the medieval residences of Florence. The apartments on the upper floors were reserved for the members of the Harem the sultan liked best, enjoying open space and sea views as far as the Princes' Islands. The circular spot in the center of the courtyard was covered with a tent for shaded outings, and the grooves served as water channels for cooling.

The exit to the second courtyard is through the **Golden Road,** a narrow stone corridor that was the crown prince's first taste of the world beyond the stifling confines of the Harem.

Sultanahmet, entrance at the end of Babuhümayun Cad., behind the Ayasofya. ⓒ 0212/512-0480. Admission to the palace 10YTL ($8.70/£3.80); separate admission for both the Treasury and the Harem 10YTL ($8.70/£3.80) each. Wed–Mon 9am–5pm (Harem closes at 4pm). Tram: Sultanahmet or Gülhane.

3 Byzantine Sights (or Byzantium Wasn't Built in a Day)

Church of Theotokos Pammakaristos (Joyous Mother of God Church, now the Fethiye Camii)   This church was built in 1292 by John Comnenus, probably related to the royal family, and his wife Anna Doukaina. Later additions and renovations were made, including the construction of a side chapel in 1315 to house the remains of Michael Glabas, a former general, and his family. In 1456 the Orthodox Patriarchate moved here from the Havariyun (see the Fatih Mosque/Fatih Camii, p. 145) and remained here until 1586. Five years later, Murat III converted the church into a mosque and renamed it in honor of his conquest over Georgia and Azerbaijan. To accommodate a larger inner space for prayer, most of the interior walls were removed.

The interior of the church/mosque contains the restored remains of a number of mosaic panels, which, while not as varied as those at the Kariye Camii, serve as another resource for understanding 14th-century Byzantine art. In the dome is a representation of the Pantocrator surrounded by prophets (Moses, Jeremiah, Zephaniah, Micah, Joel, Zechariah, Obadiah, Habakkuk, Jonah, Malachi, Ezekiel, and Isaia). In the apse Christ Hyperagathos is shown with the Virgin and St. John the Baptist. The Baptism of Christ survives intact to the right of the dome.

From the Kariye Camii, follow Draman Cad. (which becomes Fethiye Cad.); turn left onto Fethiyekapısı Sok. (just before the road bends sharply to the right), Fener. Ayasofya Museum Directorate at ⓒ 0212/635-1273. Admission 2YTL ($1.75/76p). Thurs–Tues 9am–5pm. Bus: 90 from Eminönü or 90B from Beyazit.

Ecumenical Patriarchate of Constantinople *⟨k*   The Ecumenical Patriarchate of Constantinople is the surviving legacy of a religious empire that dominated the affairs of Christians worldwide for more than 1,100 years. After the fall of Rome in A.D. 476, Constantinople inherited unrivaled leadership of the Christian world under the name "Rome of the East" and "New Rome." The Greeks, Bulgarians, Serbians, Romanians, Albanians, and Georgians who adhered to the Eastern Orthodox creed were referred to as "Romans" (thus the reason why many an Istanbul church include the word "Rum" in its title). While the pope continued to reject the primacy of the Bishop of Constantinople (soon after given the title of Archbishop), the influence of the Patriarch of Constantinople nevertheless grew under the patronage of the emperor. The initial seat of the Patriarchate was pre-Constantine Hagia Irene, now in the first court of Topkapı Palace. Upon Justinian's completion of the Ayasofya, the Church was rooted here for the next 916 years (with a brief respite when the Byzantine Court was forced to flee to Nicaea after the Fourth Crusade in 1204). The Ottoman conquest displaced the Patriarchate to the Havariyun (or Church of the 12 Apostles, now lost under Fatih Camii), before it moved to the Church of the Pammakaristos (Fethiye Camii) in 1456. In 1587, the Eastern Orthodox Church moved to the Church of the Virgin Mary in Vlah Palace, and then to St. Demetrios in Balat. The Patriarchate settled into its current spot in The Church of St. George (Ayios Yeoryios) in 1601. In the 19th century, assertions of national independence and religious autonomy whittled the influence of the Patriarchate, until its reach was constricted to the borders of the Turkish Republic and a mere handful of semi-autonomous communities abroad. Still, the Orthodox community considers the Ecumenical Patriarchate one of the two most prominent Christian institutions in the world, the other being the Holy See in Rome. Today, the Patriarch and Archbishop of Constantinople is *primus inter pares* or "first among equals," among the 14 autonomous and semi-autonomous Patriarchates-in-communion that make up the Eastern Orthodox Church.

The present church was built in 1720 on a traditional basilica plan. It seems to lack the grandeur one would expect of its station, but the building was constructed under the Ottoman prohibition against non-Muslim use of domes or masonry roofs on their places of worship. Instead, it is topped by a timber roof. The gilded iconostasis provides some insight into the opulence one imagines of Byzantium. The Patriarchal Throne is believed to date to St. John Chrysostom Patriarchate in the 5th century A.D. His relics and those of St. Gregory the Theologian, which were hijacked after the 1204 Crusader sacking of the city, were brought back from Rome by Patriarch Bartholomew in 2004. In the aisle opposite these relics are the remains of the female saints, St. Euphemia, St. Theophano, and St. Solomone. There are also three invaluable gold mosaic icons including one of the Virgin, as well as the Column of Flagellation. The small complex is comprised of the modest Cathedral, the Patriarchate Library, administrative offices, and the Ayios Harambalos spring.

Sadrazam Ali Paşa Cad. 35/3, Fener. ℭ **0212/531-9670.** Daily 8:30am–6pm. Bus: 36CE, 399B, 399C, 399D, 44B, 99, 99A from Eminönü, 35D from Balat, or 55T from Taksim.

Galata Tower and the Galata Neighborhood ⍟
The neighborhood of Galata, located on a steep hump of land north of the Golden Horn and historic peninsula, actually sits on the earliest foundations of the city, dating, as far as present-day archaeologists can tell, to Greek and Roman times. At one time, it was covered in gardens and vineyards; indeed the ancient Greeks called the district "Sykai," meaning "place of fig gardens," and later, the hilly expanse became known as "peran en Skai," or "fig gardens on the other shore." Or just plain Pera. There is also speculation that the name Galata comes from the Italian word for descent *(calata)*, an appropriate description of the steep and staired streets that slope down the hill from Beyoğlu to the Golden Horn. The district developed into its present form in the 13th century, when Eastern Roman Emperor Michael VIII Palaeologus granted the Genoese permission to settle here. The district became a magnet for merchants from all over Europe: Italians, Germans, Armenians, Jews, and Austrians, all re-creating their own micro-universe. The Genoese remained neutral during the Ottoman siege, so when Mehmet the Conqueror took over the city, although he installed his own Ottoman administration and assumed control of all commercial affairs, the Sultan granted them, along with the other minority communities, substantial commercial privileges. The ensuing commercial prosperity of the district fed trade throughout the Mediterranean and acted as a magnet for foreigners and ethnic minorities who established the district as centers of

---

Fun Fact **First in Flight**

Ahmet Çelebi, later nicknamed Hazarfen (a thousand sciences), wins the prize for first in flight, in 1638. Strapped to a pair of artificial wings, Çelebi launched himself off of the Galata Tower and glided across the Bosphorus to Üsküdar on the Asian shore, where he landed safely.

---

business, shipping, and banking. Serving the center of the financial district was a row of stately financial institutions lining both sides of what is now alternately called Bankalar Sokağı (Bank Street) and Voyvoda Caddesi. Bankers wishing to settle near their places of business constructed dignified residences for themselves and their families, and serving the community was a full complement of schools, churches, and synagogues. As Galata prospered, the population burst its boundaries to incorporate the neighborhoods northward (and eventually up to and along the Grand Rue de Pera or Istiklal Caddesi). A stroll up and down the steep cobbled streets will reveal schools, private residences, churches, synagogues, and Ottoman-era warehouses. (There are also the ruins of a *mikva* or Jewish bathhouse in dire need of restoration opposite the former private mansion of the Camondo banking family, now the Galata Residence. See p. 180.)

The decline of Galata and its subsequent revitalization are both relatively recent phenomena. With the turn-of-the-20th-century flight of the wealthy merchant class to Istanbul's tonier neighborhoods, Galata deteriorated into a magnet for poor rural migrant families and a location of no fewer than three thriving brothels. In the 1990s, the nation's trend for historic preservation arrived in Galata with an ambitious architectural revitalization project that created an inviting public square and a couple of charming and characteristic outdoor tea gardens at the base of the Galata Tower. In the past 4 or 5 years, the trend has caught fire, as local real estate gets snapped up by artists, expat journalists, and private developers and turned into galleries, cafes, hotels, and private homes. At last look, the plaza surrounding the tower and the storied Galip Dede Caddesi had been repaved and a restoration project was under way at the north corner opposite the tower. But the streets leading down to the Golden Horn, while hosting the odd new tea shop or guesthouse, maintain the grit that has settled on the district since its heyday. For a do-it-yourself walking tour, pick up a copy of John Freely's *Galata,* available at the Galata House (restaurant, p. 105) and the bookstores listed in chapter 9. Otherwise, turn to p. 176.

The origins of **Galata Tower** date back to the 5th or 6th century A.D., but the tower that stands today is a 14th-century reconstruction by the Genoese, built in appreciation of Michael VIII Palaeologus, who granted special permission to allow them to settle the area of Galata. One condition of the agreement was that the Genoese were prohibited from putting up any defensive walls, a ban that they unceremoniously ignored.

The Galata Tower has been used as a jail, a dormitory, a site for rappelling competitions, and a launching pad in the 17th century when Hezarfen Ahmet Çelebi attached wings to his arms and glided all the way to Üsküdar. The tower rises 135m (450 ft.) above sea level and stands 60m (200 ft.) high, with walls that are more than 3.5m (12 ft.) thick. From the summit of the tower, you can see the Golden Horn, the Bosphorus, and the Marmara Sea, a view infinitely more splendid in the evenings when the city takes on a spectacularly romantic glow. But frankly, you can get equally

700 Years of Turkish Jews

Jews visiting Turkey inevitably ask for a tour of a local synagogue, and as the default working temple in the heart of Galata, **Neve Shalom** is usually the first and only stop. While interesting to see (particularly after sustaining recurring terrorist attacks), a visit to Neve Shalom is far from the Holy Grail of Jewish sites in Istanbul. It's also not necessarily guaranteed, since a pre-visit request accompanied by a faxed copy of your passport is the *minimum* requirement for entry. I'd recommend instead the **Jewish Museum of Turkey,** located in the restored 19th-century Zulfaris Synagogue. The museum represents the vision of the Quincentennial Foundation (named for the 500-year anniversary of the Jewish expulsion from Spain) and showcases the peaceful coexistence of Jews and Turks in Turkey. The foundation's vision came to fruition in 2001 with this anthology of Jewish presence in Turkey beginning with the Ottoman conquest of Bursa, through Sultan Beyazit's invitation to those expelled from Spain, to the present day. The museum/synagogue is located at Karaköy Meydanı, Perçemli Sokak (facing the lower entrance to the Tünel funicular, Perçemli Sok. is the first alley to your right; the museum is at the end of the street on your right; ✆ **0212/292-6333;** www.muze500.com), and is open Monday through Thursday 10am to 4pm, and Friday and Sunday from 10am to 2pm. There is no admission fee but donations are encouraged.

spectacular views from restaurant terraces all over the city, so although the tower is used as a restaurant and nightclub for a traditional **Turkish folkloric** show (✆ **0212/293-8180**), at 100YTL ($87/£38) a pop, I'd pass (and indeed I have).

Şişane. ✆ **0212/293-8180.** Historic gate daily 9am–1am (no access during the folklore show). Elevator to the top of Galata Tower 8YTL ($7/£3). Daily 8:30am–8pm. Tram: Karaköy; Bus: 28 from Upper and Lower Tünel, 28T from Beşiktaş.

Küçük Ayasofya Camii (Church of the Saints Sergius and Bacchus) ℛ *Finds*
Started in A.D. 527 by Justinian in the first year of his reign, this former church represents an important stage in the process of Byzantine architecture, particularly in the support of the dome atop an octagonal base. The church took its name from two martyred Roman soldiers later elevated to the status of patron saints; the edifice later assumed the name of "Little Ayasofya" due to its resemblance to the Ayasofya in Sultanahmet Park, which was started in A.D. 532. The church was converted into a mosque in the 16th century by the chief eunuch under Beyazit II, who is buried in the garden. We know from the ancient historian Procopius that the interior of the church was covered in marble and mosaics; however, none of this remains. Opposite the entrance to the mosque is a *medrese* that encloses an uncharacteristically serene and leafy garden. An on-site eatery as well as teahouses share the arcade with a number of bookshops and **calligraphy boutiques,** and genuine finds offering samples at some of the most competitive prices in the city.

Lower end of Küçük Ayasofya Cad. No phone. Tram: Sultanahmet.

Mosaic Museum   In 1933 excavators discovered a mosaic pavement below what is now the Arasta Bazaar, identified as a section of **Peristyle Courtyard** (open court with porticos) of Constantine's Great Palace. As a decorative work of the palace, it is safe to assume (as scholars have) that the creation of the mosaic flooring employed the most gifted craftsmen of the era, collected from around the empire. Because of the exceptional nature of the mosaics, there are no comparable existing Byzantine era mosaics from which to date these. The current assumption is that they were crafted during either the reign of Constantine or of Justinian.

Archaeologists estimate that the size of the courtyard was 1,872 sq. m (20,150 sq. ft.), requiring a total of 80,000,000 *tesserae* of lime, glass, and terra cotta. Typical of Roman mosaics, the subjects depicted on the panels are representative of an earlier, pre-Christian artistic era absent of religious motifs, showing instead hunting scenes and scenes from mythology.

Entrance at Torun Sok., across from the entrance to the Sultanahmet Sarayı Hotel; accessible through Arasta Bazaar to the southeast of the Blue Mosque. (0212/518-1205. Admission 5YTL ($4.35/£1.90). Tues–Sun 9am–6:30pm (4:30pm in winter). Tram: Sultanahmet.

Sultanahmet's Streets Paved with Gold: The Great Palace

The Great Palace complex was the primary residence and administrative center of Byzantine (and Roman) emperors from A.D. 330, when it was begun by Constantine, to 1081, when the Comnenus Dynasty moved to Blachernae. In 1204, the palace became the home of the Latin Crusaders-in-Residence, but through their neglect, the palace slowly fell into decline. It was eventually picked over for parts for use in new construction projects. Tradition has it that when Mehmet the Conqueror took the city (by which time the Byzantine dynasty had returned and installed itself into Blachernae and the Great Palace), the sultan's reaction to the state of the palace was to quote a phrase of the Persian poet, Ferdowsi: "the spider spins his web in the Palace of the Caesars . . ."

Constantine's earliest construction was based on Diocletian's palace on the Dalmatian Coast and covered an area of 10 hectares (almost 25 acres) from the Hippodrome to the Marmara Sea. At its peak, the palace was comprised of a complex that included state buildings, throne rooms, gardens, libraries, thermal baths, and fountains (among which were the 5th century A.D. Chalke monumental gate and the Magnaura or Senate building). The Bucoleon (built by Theophilius in A.D. 842) and Justinian's Hormisdas (6th century A.D.; located to the West of the Bucoleon) were later additions. A few places around the neighborhood provide a peak of these remains. A section of the loggia from the Bucoleon that survived the construction of the commuter train can be seen on the southern edge of the peninsula outside the remains of the sea walls, to the east of Aksakal Caddesi. A mosaic floor of one of the peristyle courtyards of the Great Palace is now the **Mosaic Museum** (p. 139). Some remains were uncovered in the construction of the Eresin Crown hotel in Sultanahmet, while the Four Seasons project (they're adding a rear annex building) sits right atop the Magnaura.

St. Savior in Chora (Kariye Müzesi; formerly the Kariye Camii) 𝒜𝒜𝒜   Much of what remained in the coffers of the Byzantine Empire was invested in the embellishment of this church, one of the finest preserved galleries of **Byzantine mosaics** as well as a detailed account of early Christian history. The original church was built in the 4th century A.D. as part of a monastery complex outside the city walls (*chora zonton* means "in the country" in Greek), but the present structure dates to the 11th century. The interior restoration and decoration were the result of the patronage of Theodore Metochites, Grand Logothete of the Treasury during the reign of Andronicus II Paleologos, and date to the first quarter of the 14th century. His benevolence is depicted in a dedicatory panel in the inner narthex over the door to the nave, which shows Metochites presenting the Chora to Jesus.

When the church was converted into a mosque in the 16th century, the mosaics were plastered over. A 19th-century architect uncovered the mosaics but was ordered by the government to re-cover those in the section of the prayer hall. American archaeologists Whittemore and Underwood finally uncovered these masterpieces during World War II, and although the Chora became a museum in 1947, it is still often referred to as the Kariye Camii.

In total there are about 50 mosaic panels, but because some of them are only partially discernible, there seems to be disagreement on the exact count. Beginning in the exonarthex, the subjects of the mosaic panels fall into one of four themes, presented more or less in chronological order after the New Testament. Broadly, the themes relate to the cycle of the life of Christ and his miracles, stories of the life of Mary, scenes from the infancy of Christ, and stories of Christ's ministry. The panels not included in these themes are the devotional panels in the exonarthex and the narthex, and the three panels in the nave: *The Dormition of the Virgin, Christ,* and the *Virgin Hodegetria.*

The **Paracclesion** (burial section) is decorated with a series of masterful frescoes completed sometime after the completion of the mosaics and were presumably executed by the same artist. The frescoes reflect the purpose of the burial chamber with scenes of Heaven and Hell, the Resurrection and the Life, and a stirring **Last Judgment** with a scroll representing infinity above a River of Fire, and a detail of Jesus saving Adam's and Eve's souls from the devil.

Camii Sok., Kariye Meydanı, Edirnekapı. ℂ **0212/631-9241.** Admission 10YTL ($8.70/£3.80). Thurs–Tues 9:30am–6:30pm. Bus: 90B from Beyazit or 90 from Eminönü direct to the museum, or 91 from Eminönü to Edirnekapı.

Sphendome   The ancient retaining wall of the closed end of the Hippodrome joins the Obelisks and Spina as the only remaining relics of the early Byzantine period. Today, this enduring infrastructure supports the buildings of Marmara Technical University. The structure is best viewed from below (access down the hill along Şifa Hamamı Sok. to Nakilbent Sok.); notice the 2-meter-high niches that used to contain

---

Take a Break in the Retaining Wall of the Hippodrome

Arranged around a mushrooming fountain with choice seating tucked into the arches of the Sphendome, the **Havusbaşı Çay Bahcesi,** or Pond Head Tea Garden (Nakilbent Sok.; ℂ **0212/638-8819**), couldn't get more atmospheric. Nestle in for fresh squeezed fruit juice, tea, or light fare well into the evening hours. In the summer, the management mounts a tiny derviş show nightly.

Fun Fact **A Punishment Fit for the Crime?**

While coed baths are common in Turkey, under the Ottomans, the penalty imposed on a man found in the woman's section of a *hamam* was death.

---

statues (now evocative seating for an outdoor tea garden and restaurant). The high arched section served as the stables.

Southeastern end of the Hippodrome. Tram: Sultanahmet.

Valens Aqueduct (Bozdoğan Kemeri)   Now nothing more than a scenic overpass for cars traveling down Atatürk Bulvarı, the Valens Aqueduct or "Arcade of the Gray Falcon" was started by Constantine and completed in the 4th century A.D. by Valens. Justinian II had the second tier added; even Mehmet the Conqueror and Sinan had a hand in its restoration and enlargement. The aqueduct connects the third and fourth hills of Istanbul and had an original length of about .8km (½ mile). Water was transported under various rulers to the Byzantine palaces, city cisterns, and then to Topkapı Palace, and the aqueduct served in supplying water to the city for a total of 1,500 years.

Bridging Atatürk Bulv. between Aksaray and the Golden Horn. Bus: 36A, 36CV, 36D, 36V, 37C, 37Y, 38B, 39B, 39Y, 77A, or 86V.

Yerebatan Cistern (Yerebatan Sarnıcı) ☆☆   Classical music echoing off the still water and the seductive lighting make your descent into the "Sunken Palace" seem like a scene out of *Phantom of the Opera*. The only thing missing is a rowboat, which was an actual means of transportation before the boardwalk was installed in what is now essentially a great underground fishpond and stunning historical artifact. The cistern was first constructed by Constantine and enlarged to its present form by Justinian after the Nika Revolt using 336 marble columns recycled from the Hellenistic ruins in and around the Bosphorus. The water supply, routed from reservoirs around the Black Sea and transported via the Aqueduct of Valens, served as a backup for periods of drought or siege. It was left largely untouched by the Ottomans, who preferred running, not stagnant, water, and eventually used the source to water the Topkapı Gardens. The cistern was later left to collect silt and mud until it was cleaned by the Municipality and opened to the public in 1987. The water is clean and aerated thanks to a supply of overgrown goldfish that are replaced every 4 years or so.

Follow the wooden catwalk and notice the "column of tears," a pillar etched with symbols resembling tears. (An identical pattern is visible on the columns scattered along the tramway near the Üniversite stop, where the old Byzantine palace was once located.) At the far end of the walkway are two **Medusa heads,** one inverted and the other on its side; according to mythology, placing her this way caused her to turn herself into stone. Another superstition is that turning her upside down neutralizes her powers. Possibly, the stones were just the right size as pedestals.

Yerebatan Cad. (diagonal from Ayasofya), Sultanahmet. ℰ **0212/522-1259.** Admission 10YTL ($8.70/£3.80). Daily 9am–5:30pm. Tram: Sultanahmet.

---

4 Historic *Hamams* (Turkish Baths)

The number of *hamams* in Istanbul mushroomed in the 18th century when the realization hit that they were big business. Mahmut I had the Cağaloğlu Hamamı built to

Steam Heat: Taking the *Hamam*

In characteristic socially conscious fashion, the Selçuks were the ones to adopt the Roman and Byzantine tradition of public bathing and treat it like a public work. Lacking baths or running water at home, society embraced the *hamam,* which evolved into not only a place to cleanse body and soul, but a social destination as well. Even the accouterments of the *hamam* took on symbols of status: wooden clogs inlaid with mother of pearl, towels embroidered with gold thread, and so on. Men gathered to talk about politics, sports, and women, while the ladies kept an eagle eye out for suitable wives for their sons.

The utility of the *hamam* evolved and fell out of daily use, probably because the neighborhood ones have a reputation for being dirty, and the historic ones come with a hefty admission charge. But when experienced properly, a visit to a *hamam* can be a cleansing one—for both mind and body. And as the spa trend takes hold in Istanbul and as new, private (hotel or club) *hamams* materialize, Turks are once again embracing the pampered pleasure of this tradition.

What to expect? The main entrance of a Turkish bath opens up to a *camekan,* a central courtyard lined with changing cubicles surrounding an ornamental marble fountain. Visitors are presented with the traditional *pestamal,* a checkered cloth worn like a sarong (up higher for women). Valuables are secured in a private locker, provided for each customer, although it's a good idea to leave the best of it at home.

The experience begins past the cooling section (and often the toilets), into the steam room, or *hararet.* For centuries architects worked to perfect the design of the *hararet:* a domed, octagonal (or square) room, often with marvelous oculi to provide entry for sunlight, and with intricate basins at various intervals and a heated marble platform, known as the **naval stone,** in the center. Often the *hamam* is covered with elaborately crafted and ornately designed tiles.

finance the construction of his library near the Ayasofya, but new constructions were limited later that century because the *hamams* were using up the city's resources of water and wood. Only about 20 *hamams* have survived.

The most visited *hamams* today are the palatial **Çemberlitaş Hamamı,** Vezirhan Cad. 8 (off Divanyolu at the Column of Constantine; ⓒ **0212/522-7974;** 40YTL/$35/£15 for the traditional bath, massage, and *kese,* a scrubbing using an abrasive mitt; 28YTL/$24/£11 bath only; daily 6am–midnight with separate sections; Master-Card and Visa accepted), which was based on a design by Sinan, and the 18th-century **Cağaloğlu Hamamı,** Yerebatan Cad. at Ankara Cad. (ⓒ **0212/522-2424;** 36YTL/$31/£14 bath and *kese;* 68YTL/$59/£26 if you opt for the "Oriental luxury" treatment; daily 7am–10pm for men, 8am–8pm for women), which allegedly saw the bare bottoms of Franz Liszt, Edward VIII, Kaiser Wilhelm, and Florence Nightingale, and even had a part as an extra in *Indiana Jones and the Temple of Doom.*

Hamam protocol goes like this: You will be asked to lie on the naval stone by an attendant (who may be male or female). Many first-time visitors have questions about how much clothing to take off; in segregated *hamams* it's customary and acceptable to strip (this is a bath, after all), although I personally would reschedule if confronted with a male attendant. Step one is the scrubbing using an abrasive mitt *(kese)* aimed at removing the outer layer of dead skin and other organic detritus. The actual bath is next; the substantial and slippery soap bubbles create the perfect canvas for the accompanying massage. This is primarily where you will notice the difference between a private *hamam* (where you are the only "client") and one of the more commercial ones. In the commercial ones (listed above, all of which I have nevertheless frequented repeatedly), don't be surprised if your massage feels more like a cursory pummeling. After all, how many clients complain? (Not me.) The private hotel *hamans* have more of a long-term stake and therefore provide high quality service. The difference is like night and day.

The final act of the ritual is the rinsing (you may even get a relaxing facial massage), followed by a definitive tap on the shoulder followed by "You like?"—an indication that your session is over. At this point you are most likely dehydrated and sleepy, which is when the purpose of that **cold room** with the lounge chairs becomes evident. Refreshments are available and the price list is usually displayed nearby. (Refreshments are usually included in the price of a hotel *hamam*.) In the commercial *hamams* you can go back into the *hararet* as often as you like, whereas in a hotel *hamam* a session lasts 45 minutes to an hour.

Whether you opt for the $30 version or the $75 hotel service, definitely sign up for "the works" at least once in your life and you'll forever comprehend why it was indeed good to be the sultan.

The recently restored **Süleymaniye Hamamı** ⟨✿⟩, Mimar Sinan Cad. 20 (✆ **0212/ 519-5569;** daily 7am–midnight), part of the Süleymaniye mosque complex, is another architectural and social welfare wonder of Sinan and Süleyman the Magnificent. Pickup and drop-off from hotel is included in the price of admission, which includes the massage and *kese* (30€–35€/$42–$49/£21–£25 depending on the pickup location). One caveat: This *hamam* is coed.

In Beyoğlu, the **Tarıhı Galatasaray Hamamı,** Sütterazı Sok. 24 (from Istiklal Cad. in front of the Galatasaray High School, it's the second street to the left of the gate; ✆ **0212/249-4342;** 40YTL/$35/£15 admission plus 5YTL/$4.35/£1.90 if you want the massage and *kese;* daily 7am–10pm for men, 8am–8pm for women), was built by Beyazit II as part of the Galata Sarayı school complex. The men's section is generally accepted as gay.

Probably the most spectacular *hamam* is the decommissioned **Haseki Sultan Hamamı,** in Sultanahmet Park. Built by Sinan in 1557 on a symmetrical plan that provided two separate sections of identical domed halls, the *hamam* was decommissioned when it was found that the elongated layout resulted in too much heat loss. The Haseki Sultan Hamamı is now a beautifully restored exhibition center for Dösim (see chapter 9) and is used for textile and carpet displays.

If you're looking for luxury and personal attention, more in the lines of a modern day spa treatment, you'll want to visit a *hamam* at a hotel instead. My personal favorites are **Les Ottomans** (p. 81), **Sumahan** (p. 82), the **Ritz-Carlton** (p. 72), and the **Çırağan Palace** (p. 80).

5 Monumental Mosques & Tombs

Beyazit Mosque (Beyazit Camii)   Beyazit II, son of the Conqueror, is remembered kindly by history as one of the more benevolent of sovereigns, and indeed, in Turkey, he has been elevated to a saint. The mosque and complex bearing his name is the oldest surviving imperial mosque in the city (its predecessor, the Fatih Camii, succumbed to an earthquake and was reconstructed in 1766). The complex was built between 1501 and 1506 using materials taken from Theodosius's Forum of Tauri, on which it is built.

Again, the architect of Beyazit Camii looked to the Ayasofya, employing a central dome buttressed by semi-domes and a long nave with double arcades, although the mosque is half the size of the church. The Beyazit Mosque also borrows elements from the Fatih Mosque, imitating the system of buttressing and the use of great columns alongside the dome. Thanks to Sultan Beyazit II's patronage, the Ottomans found a style of their own, which served as a bridge to later classical Ottoman architecture. The sultan, who died in 1512, is buried in a simple tomb, decorated in mother of pearl and stained glass, at the back of the gardens.

Yeniçeriler Cad., across from the Beyazit tram stop. No phone. Tram: Beyazit; bus: 36A, 36CV, 36D, 36V, 37C, 37Y, 38B, 39B, 39Y, 77A, or 86V.

Eyüp Sultan Mosque (Eyüp Sultan Camii)   The holiest site in Istanbul as well as one of the most sacred places in the Islamic world, the Eyüp Sultan Mosque was erected by Mehmet the Conqueror over the tomb of Halid bin Zeyd Ebu Eyyûb (known as Eyüp Sultan), the standard-bearer for the Prophet Mohammed as well as the last survivor of his inner circle of trusted companions. It is popularly accepted that while serving as commander of the Arab forces during the siege of A.D. 668 to 669, Eyüp was killed and buried on the outskirts of the city. One of the conditions of peace after the Arab siege was that the tomb of Eyüp be preserved.

The burial site was "discovered" during Mehmet the Conqueror's siege on the city, although the tomb is mentioned in written accounts as early as the 12th century.

A little village of tombs mushroomed on the spot by those seeking Eyüp Sultan's intervention in the hereafter, and it's still considered a privilege to be buried in the nearby cemeteries. The Girding of the Sword ceremony was traditionally held here. In this Ottoman enthronement rite, Osman Gazi's sword was passed on, maintaining continuity within the dynasty as well as creating a connection with the Turk's early ideal of Holy War.

Eyüp is a popular spot animated by the small bazaar nearby, crowds relaxing by the spray of the fountains, and little boys in blue-and-white satin celebrating their

> ## Tips Etiquette for Entering the House of the Lord
>
> Respect for places of worship does not only apply to mosques. The legacy of the Byzantine and Ottoman eras appears in dozens and dozens of churches and synagogues as well. These faiths are no less expectant of proper, respectful, and conservative behavior under their roofs. For women, exposed shoulders and thighs are a no-no in all three, and heads should be covered both in mosques, and for married women only, in synagogues. Men get a bit more latitude, but should also be respectful in their choice of attire when visiting a house of worship. For visits to the mosque, remember to take your shoes off outside the entrance and *before* stepping on to the carpets. Depending on the size of the mosque, you will either leave your shoes outside or carry them in with you (there are little wooden shelves at the back of the interior for storage during prayer/visitation). In general, visitors are told that mosques are closed to visitors during prayer time, but I have yet to be turned away and find this to be one of the more solemn and telling moments to experience. If you do enter during services, remain respectful and near the perimeter of the mosque, and refrain from wandering around.

impending circumcisions. Unfortunately, it's a natural magnet for beggars as well. The baroque mosque replaces the original that was destroyed in the earthquake of 1766, but the real attraction here is the *türbe,* a sacred burial site that draws masses of pilgrims waiting in line to stand in the presence of the contents of the solid silver sarcophagus or meditate in prayer. Dress appropriately if you're planning to go in: no shorts, and heads covered for women. The line moves quickly in spite of the bottleneck inside the tomb; take a few moments to sense the power of the site. On Friday's at noon, there's an outdoor performance of the **Mehter Band** ♔ in the large square outside the mosque, and on Sundays, the plaza is filled with families parading around their little boys dressed like sultans (a pre-circumcision tradition).

Eyüp. Meydanı, off of Camii Kebir Cad. and north of the Golden Horn Bridge. No phone. Bus: 37C, 39, 39B, 39Ç, 39D, 39O, 39Y, or 48A.

Fatih Mosque and Complex (Fatih Camii ve Külliyesi)
Fatih Sultan Mehmet II had his namesake built on the ruins of the Havariyun, or the Church of Holy Apostles, which served as the seat of Christianity after the conquest, from 1453 to 1456. At that time, the church was second only to the Ayasofya in importance and therefore served as the burial place of every emperor from Constantine I to Constantius VIII (from A.D. 337 to 1028!). Alexius III Angelius looted the graves to fill his imperial coffers; the graves were again looted during the Fourth Crusade. In addition to the commanding mosque, the eight *medreses* (schools) founded by the sultan are the only surviving sections of a complex that included a caravansary, a hospital, several *hamams,* kitchens, and a market, which combined to form a university that instructed up to 1,000 students at any given time. Wanting a monument more spectacular than that of Ayasofya, the sultan cut off the hands of the architect, Atık Sinan (not Süleyman's Sinan), when the Fatih Mosque failed to surpass the height of the church, despite its position atop the fourth of the seven hills of Istanbul. The tombs of Fatih Mehmet II and his wife (mother of Beyazit II) are located outside of the *mihrab* wall.

Moments **A Cafe near the Eyüp Sultan Mosque**

If you've made it all the way to Eyüp to visit the mosque, take a short detour to **Pierre Loti,** Gümüşsuyu Balmumcu Sok. 1 (© **0212/581-2696**), a cafe of legend and a spectacular spot for serene views of the Golden Horn. The legend goes that French naval officer Julien Viaud fell in love with Aziyade, a married Turkish woman, during his first visit to Istanbul around 1876. The young woman would sneak out of her husband's harem when he was away for the chance to spend a few fleeting moments in the arms of her lover at his house in the hills of Eyüp. After an absence from Turkey of 10 years, Viaud returned to find Aziyade had died soon after his departure. Viaud gained fame during his lifetime, and his stories are romantic accounts much like the one of legend. This cafe, on the hill of Eyüp, was a favorite of his, and for reasons unknown, became known as Pierre Loti Kahvesi. Eyüp's historic cemetery is on the hill next to the cafe. The cafe is open daily 8am to midnight; no food or alcohol is served here; avoid weekends, when nary an empty table will be your reward for the ride up. A cable car from near the Eyüp Mosque makes the trip up to the top of the hill a little bit easier than walking up, although you may want to walk down through the old Ottoman cemetery.

Enter on Fevzipaşa Cad., Fatih. No phone. Bus: 28, 31E, 32, 336E, 336I, 36A, 36CV, 36D, 36KE, 36V, 37C, 37E, 37Y, 38B, 38E, 39B, 39Y, 86V, 87, 90, or 910.

The New Queen Mother's Mosque (Yeni Valide Camii or Yeni Camii)   Begun by Valide Safiye, mother of Mehmet III, in 1597, the foundations of this mosque were laid at the water's edge in a neighborhood slum whose inhabitants had to be paid to move out. Designed by the architect Da'ud Ağa, a pupil of Sinan, the Yeni Camii has become a defining feature of Istanbul's skyline.

The building of the mosque dragged on for over 40 years due to water seepage, funding problems, embezzlement, and the death of the sultan, which temporarily shut down operations completely. The mosque was completed by another queen mother, Valide Sultan Turhan Hattice, mother of Mehmet IV, who is buried in the valide sultan's tomb, or *türbe,* in the courtyard.

The mosque is part of a complex that included, at one time a hospital, primary school and public bath. The **Mısır Çarşışı** or **Egyptian Spice Market,** was actually constructed as part of the complex. In the open space formed by the inner "L" of the Spice Market and the northeastern facing side of the mosque are stalls selling garden and pet supplies, a busy and shaded tea garden, and some street vendors. At the far (northwestern) end of the mosque on the opposite corner is the *türbe,* housing, in addition to the Valide Sultan, the remains of sultans Mehmet IV, Mustafa II, Ahmet III, and Mahmut I.

Opposite the *türbe* is the house of the mosque's astronomer, or *muvakkithane,* from where the position of the sun would be monitored to establish the times of the five daily prayers. Just behind the *muvakkithane* is a ramp leading up to the entrance of the royal loge, or private prayer room. The loge is best viewed from inside the mosque; enjoying a view of the sea, it was richly decorated by tiles, a dome, a vaulted antechamber, and a private toilet.

Egyptian Spice Bazaar, Eminönü. No phone. Tram: Eminönü.

Şehzade Külliyesi (Crowned Prince Mosque Complex) ⚜ What was at the time considered a masterpiece of Ottoman architecture is now merely a footnote to Sinan's subsequent great works. In fact, Sinan was still an apprentice when he was ordered by Süleyman the Magnificent to build a monument to the memory of his beloved first-born son and intended heir, Şehzade (Prince) Mehmet, who died of smallpox in 1543 at the premature age of 21. The plan of the mosque is an important milestone in the evolution of his works, as it is a simple system of four semi-domes supported by four pillars that has been both criticized for being harsh and praised as harmonic. The use of four elephantine pillars is repeated in the Blue Mosque. The layout of the complex, consisting of the mosque, a *medrese,* a refectory, a double guesthouse, a caravansaray, and some tombs, follows no special plan, and indeed the primary school and public kitchens have been cut off from the rest of the complex by the main avenue. The prince's tomb is an octagonal masterpiece of arabesques, rare tiles, and stained glass housing a unique sarcophagus of wood lattice inlaid with ivory. The smaller octagonal tomb adjacent to that of the prince is that of Rüstem Paşa. For many years the Şehzade remained the largest building in Istanbul, but even before the mosque was completed, Süleyman had already ordered the construction of another, grander mosque as a monument to his reign.

Şehzadebası Cad., Vefa. No phone. Tram: Laleli; bus: 36A, 36CV, 36D, 36V, 37C, 37Y, 38B, 39B, 39Y, 77A, or 86V.

Sokullu Mehmet Paşa Camii This mosque is considered to be one of the "minor" works of Sinan, architect to the Sultans. But there are several reasons why this mosque is anything but minor. First, it represents a transition in the process of Sinan's experimentation with space: the return to a hexagonal formula (from one where the dome is supported on an octagonal base), resulting in a softening of the transitions from one feature to another and thus of greater spatial homogeneity. Second, it's one of the rare instances where the interior of a mosque is reveted in decorative tile. The Iznik tile motifs featured on the squinches supporting the dome, on the frieze below the galleries, and on the *qibla* (wall panel facing Mecca), depict chrysanthemums, carnations, and cornflowers. The calligraphic tiles proclaim the 99 Attributes of God. Third, and unique in Turkey, are the placement of three tiny black stones said to be from the *Kaaba* in Mecca embedded above the main portal, the *mihrab,* and the *mimbar.*

Şehit Çeşmesi Sok., Sultanahmet. No phone. Tram: Sultanahmet or Çemberlitaş.

Süleymaniye Mosque and Complex (Süleymaniye Camii ve Külliyesi) ⚜⚜ Perched on one of the seven hills of Istanbul and dominating the skyline, this complex is considered to be Sinan's masterpiece as much as the grand monument to Süleyman's reign. The complex covers an area of nearly 6 hectares (15 acres), and it is here

---

⎛Tips Catch the Ottoman Mehter Band Outdoors

That must-see **Ottoman Mehter Band** that I tout so much (p. 167) no longer requires that you head over to the Military Museum in the middle of your day. There's now a performance every Friday, an hour and a half prior to noon prayers, right in front of the Eyüp Sultan Mosque. After the music and a visit to the mosque complex, hop onto the brand-new **cable car** for the 2-minute ride up to the top of Pierre Loti Hill.

Tips **A Sweet Shop near Galata**

Wandering around the spice bazaar, you can really work up an appetite. Across the Galata Bridge at the Karaköy seaport is the humble (and famous) **Güllüoğlu** (℅ **0212/244-4567**) sweet shop, where you'll find the best *börek*—a cheese- or meat-filled pastry that's feathery and delicious. They also keep their glass cases full of baklava.

where Sinan achieves his goal of outdoing the dome of the Ayasofya. Here, the dome reaches a height of 49m (159 ft.) spanning a diameter of 27m (89 ft.; compared to the Ayasofya's 56m/184 ft.-high dome and 34m/112 ft. diameter). The mosque was completed in 7 years (1550–57); it is said that after the foundation was laid, Sinan stopped work completely for 3 years to ensure that the foundation had settled to his satisfaction.

Sinan returned to the Byzantine basilica model for the construction of the mosque with an eye to the Ayasofya. Critics have contended that this was an unsuccessful attempt to surpass the engineering feats of the church, but more than likely this was a conscious move on the part of the sultan to create continuity and a symbolic connection with the city's past. As the Ayasofya was analogous to the Temple of Solomon in Jerusalem, so was the Süleymaniye, as the name Süleyman is the Islamic version of Solomon. After the project was completed, Sinan recounts in his "biography of the Construction," how the sultan humbly handed the keys over to him and asked him to be the one to unlock the doors, acknowledging that the masterpiece was as much the architect's as his own.

The complex includes five schools, one *imaret* (kitchens and mess hall, now a restaurant for groups), a caravansary with stables, a hospital, *hamams,* and a cemetery. The construction of the mosque and complex mobilized the entire city, employing as many as 3,000 workers at any given time, and the 165 ledgers recording the expenses incurred in the building of the mosque are still around to prove it. The great sultan is buried in an elaborate tomb on the grounds, as is his wife Hürrem Sultan (Roxelana). In the courtyard outside the entry to the cemetery and tombs are a pair of slanted marble benches used as a stand for the sarcophagi before burial.

Süleyman carried the tradition of symbolism to his grave with a system of layered domes copied from the Dome of the Rock in Jerusalem. In the garden house next to the complex is the **tomb of Sinan;** the garden house is where he spent the last years of his life. The tomb was designed by the master architect himself and is inspiring in its modesty and simplicity.

Vefa. From the Grand Bazaar, cross the University park and follow the domes. ℅ **0212/522-0298**. Tram: Beyazit.

6 Palaces of the Sultans

While the power and prestige of a new and modern Europe were increasing, the Ottoman Empire was on its last leg. To create an image of prosperity and modernization, Sultan Abdülmecid had the Dolmabahçe Palace constructed, and abandoned Topkapı Palace along with what he considered to be the symbol of an old order. With the official, and Europeanized residence of the Ottoman Empire now on the northern shores of the Bosphorus, it wasn't long before members of the court and government officials began to build mansions in the area. More palaces sprang up, and the official shifting of power from south of the Golden Horn to the waterfront of Beşiktaş was complete. If the royal palaces fail to convince you of the Ottoman Empire's extravagance during its final economic decline, they will surely convince you of its opulence.

Beylerbeyi Palace (Beylerbeyi Sarayı)   Beylerbeyi, built under Sultan Abdülaziz by another member of the talented Balyan family of architects in the European style of Dolmabahçe, was the second palace to be built on the Bosphorus and served as a summer residence and guest quarters for visiting *bey* (dignitaries) during their visits to the city. The shah of Iran and the king of Montenegro were guests here as well as the French Empress Eugénie, who admired the palace so much that she had the design of the windows copied on the Tuilleries Palace in Paris. It's a bit dusty, and not as grand as Dolmabahçe, but worth a visit if you're on the Asian side and looking for a diversion.

Beylerbeyi, which replaced Abdülmecid's previous palace, was completed in 1865 on a less extravagant scale than the one on the European shores, employing only 5,000 men to build it. Although less grand and weathered by time, Beylerbeyi has some features worthy of a visit, not least of all the terraced garden of magnolias at the base of the Bosphorus Bridge. The monumental staircase to this marble palace is fronted by a pool and fountain which served as much to cool the air as to look pretty, and the floors are covered with reed mats from Egypt that act as insulation against dampness. The grounds contain sumptuous pavilions and kiosks, including the Stable Pavilion, where the imperial stud was kept.

Ironically, Abdülhamid II spent the last 6 years of his life admiring Dolmabahçe from the other side of the Bosphorus, having been deposed and kept under house arrest here until his death in 1918.

Take a ferry to Üsküdar and then a bus to Çayırbaşı. © **0216/321-9320.** Entrance/tour 5YTL ($4.35/£1.90), camera fee 10YTL ($8.70/£3.80). Daily 9am–4pm. Ferry: from Eminönü, ferry to Çengelköy or Üsküdar, and then bus 14M, 15, 15B, 15C, 15ÇK, 15F, 15H, 15KÇ, 15M, 15N, 15P, 15R, 15S, 15ŞN, 15U, or 15Y.

Çırağan Palace   From the first wooden summer mansion built on the spot in the 16th century to the grand waterfront palace that stands today, the Çırağan Palace was torn down and rebuilt no less than five times. Now a palace of sumptuous suites that make up part of the adjacent **Hotel Kempinski Istanbul** (p. 80), the palace takes its name from the hundreds of torches that lined these former royal gardens during the festivals of the Tulip Period in the latter part of the 18th century.

The foundations were laid in 1855 when Sultan Abdülaziz ordered the construction of a grand palace to be built as a monument to his reign. The architect, Nigogos Balyan, ventured as far as Spain and North Africa to find models in the Arab style called for by the sultan. The fickle Abdülaziz moved out after only a few months, condemning the palace as too damp to live in.

Murad V (who in 1876 deposed his uncle Abdülaziz), Abdülhamid II, and Mehmed V were all born in the palace. Murad V spent the final 27 years of his life imprisoned here, while his brother (who deposed him shortly after Murad V bumped his uncle) kept a watchful eye on him from the Yıldız Palace next door.

After Murad V's death, the Parliament took over the building but convened here for only 2 months because of a fire in the central heating vents that spread and reduced the palace to a stone shell in under 5 hours. (Some of the original doors were given as gifts by Abdülaziz to Kaiser Wilhelm and can now be seen in the Berlin Museum.) In 1946 the Parliament handed the property over to the Municipality, which for the next 40 years used it as a town dump as well as a soccer field. In 1986 the Kempinski Hotel Group saved the shell from yet another demise, using the palace

---

Fun Fact Bridge over Troubled Water

In 1501 Sultan Beyazit II invited Leonardo da Vinci to construct a bridge across the Golden Horn at the mouth of the Bosphorus—a technical feat deemed impossible until then. The master submitted a plan so revolutionary that it was deemed unbuildable. (Three years later, the sultan made the same proposal to Michelangelo, but Pope Julius II refused to let him go, and he politely declined.)

---

as a showcase of suites for its luxury hotel next door. Since its opening, the Çırağan has laundered the pillowcases of princes, kings, presidents, and rock stars, carrying on at least a modern version of a royal legacy of the original.

The palace grounds spread along 390m (1,300 ft.) of coastline and can only be visited as part of a stop-off at the main hotel, preferably from the seaside garden terrace, which provides ample views of the Palace Sea Gate, the Palace Garden Gate, and the main building itself. A cluster of secondary palaces that now serve mainly as schools are located outside the hotel's perimeter, while the one called **Feriye** has been restored as an elegant restaurant and cinema complex (p. 107).

Çırağan Cad., Beşiktaş. ✆ **0212/258-3377.** Free admission. Hotel common areas open 24 hr.; the bar and restaurant have individual hours. Bus: 22, 22RE, 25E, 30D, 40, 40T, 42, 57UL, DT1, DT2, or U1.

Dolmabahçe Palace (Dolmabahçe Sarayı) ☆ Extending for almost .8km (½ mile) on a tract of landfill on the shores of the Bosphorus is Dolmabahçe Palace (appropriately translated as "filled garden"), an imperial structure that for the first time looked to Western models rather than to the more traditional Ottoman style of building. The architect of Dolmabahçe was Garabet Balyan, master of European forms and styles amid a long line of Balyan architects.

At a time of economic reform when the empire was still known as "The Sick Man of Europe," Sultan Abdülmecid II sank millions into a palace that would give the illusion of prosperity and progressiveness. The old wooden Beşiktaş Palace was torn down to make room for a more permanent structure, and the sultan spared no expense in creating a house to rival the most opulent palaces of France. While many of his subjects were living without the basics, the sultan was financing the most cutting-edge techniques, tastefully waiting until the end of the Crimean War to move in, even though the palace was completed much earlier than that.

The result is a sumptuous creation consisting of 285 rooms, four grand salons, six galleries, five main staircases, six *hamams* (of which the main one is pure alabaster), and 43 toilets. Fourteen tons of gold and 6 tons of silver were used to build the palace. The extensive use of glass, especially in the Camlı Köşk conservatory, provides a gallery of virtually every known application of glass technology of the day. The palace is a glittering collection of Baccarat, Bohemian, and English crystal as well as Venetian glass, which was used in the construction of walls, roofs, banisters, and even a crystal piano. The chandelier in the Throne Room is the largest one in Europe at 4.5 tons, a bulk that created an engineering challenge during installation but that has withstood repeated earthquake tests. The extravagant collection of objets d'art represents just a small percentage of items presented to the occupants of the palace over the years, and much of the collection is stored in the basement awaiting restoration.

Tours to the palace and harem accommodate 1,500 visitors per day per section, a stream of gaping onlookers shod in blue plastic hospital booties distributed at the entry to the palace to ensure that the carpets stay clean. Tours leave every 20 minutes and last 1 hour for the Selâmlik and around 45 minutes for the Harem. If you're short on time, choose the Selâmlik.

Dolmabahçe Cad., Beşiktaş. (𝄆 **0212/236-9000.** Admission and guided tour to the Selâmlik (Sultan's Quarters) 10YTL ($8.70/£3.80), admission and guided tour to the Harem 8YTL ($7/£3). Tues–Wed and Fri–Sun 9am–5pm (last tour leaves at 4pm). Tram: Kabataş; Funicular: Kabataş; bus: 22, 22E, 22RE, 25E, 26, 26A, 26B, 27SE, 28, 28T, 29C, 29D, 30D, 325YK1, 41E, 43R, 46K, 52, 58A, 58N, 58S, 58UL, 62, 63, or 70KE.

Yıldız Palace and Park (Yıldız Sarayı ve Parkı)   Yıldız was one of the last residences of the Ottoman sultans, established by Selim III for his mother at the end of the 18th century. Over the years, the grounds sprouted a small colony of satellite buildings and kiosks, each one built by a different master. The result is a collection of different architectural styles sparsely scattered around the expansive grounds of Yıldız Park. In 1877, after two coup attempts, Abdülhamid II moved his residence up the hill to the more secure and secluded Yıldız from Dolmabahçe. He quickly set about opening the palace grounds to the Royal Garden, a small grove that was connected to the Çırağan Palace by a marble and stone bridge over the main road. He ordered the landscaping of the property, requesting rare flowers, plants, and trees from all over the world and having them set around fountains and pools to create a magical setting for the tulip festivities popular at the time. Today the collection of kiosks and pavilions spot the hillside landscape overlooking the Bosphorus, and the park has become a popular weekend getaway for city folk in pursuit of green surroundings. The wooded nooks and crannies also provide cover for what has infamously become known as (at

Swift Boated Through the Symplegades

According to mythology, Jason and his trusted band of Argonauts had one more hurdle to overcome before claiming the Golden Fleece for their own. At one point in their journey, the Argonauts had been warned by the blind seer, Phineus, that at the mouth of the Symplegades, described as a boiling caldron of black waves, was a sea of clashing rocks threatening to crush all who dared to enter. Indeed, the currents of the Bosphorus are so unforgivable that many a tanker has been grounded on the banks of Istanbul's straits.

According to lore, the first to navigate the treacherous waterway successfully was Jason and his mythical Argonauts (argo meaning "swift" in Greek) on their quest for the Golden Fleece. But Phineus's prophecy revealed how Jason and his crew could pass the smashing, grinding rocks called the Symplegades alive. Phineus told Jason to simply release a dove into the entrance to the straits and, as the rocks were reopening, to literally row for their lives. The Argonauts did as they were told, and with merely the loss of some dovetail feathers and the stern ornament, they managed to navigate the deathtrap alive. At that moment, the rocks froze in place and the Bosphorus was tamed forever (except for a few grounded oil tankers).

least by me) lover's lane: The park provides an unexpected and paradoxical picture of a conservative Islamic makeout session.

Probably the most beautiful structure on the property is the Şale Köşkü, a wood and masonry house (or chalet), with two additional wings constructed to accommodate two separate state visits by Wilhelm II, the Emperor of Germany. Later, the house was used by other foreign dignitaries, including Charles de Gaulle. The Şale Köşkü is one of the few buildings offering guided tours to the public which leave as often (or as infrequently) as necessary, as the guides are loathe to walk singles through the old and empty hallways. Although Yıldız Palace is in need of some TLC (a new coat of paint, a good dusting, and maybe some carpet cleaner), there are a couple of noteworthy highlights. Probably the most impressive of the interior private spaces is the Grand Ceremonial Hall, once lit by three enormous French crystal chandeliers and six towering red-tinted Bohemian crystal floor lamps. A single, custom-made Hereke carpet covers an area of 406 sq. m (4,370 sq. ft.) and weighs a total of 7,500kg (16,535 lb.). Also worth looking out for are the stunning pieces of handiwork that are the numerous china and porcelain floor-to-ceiling wood-burning stoves, and a dining set hand carved and inlaid with mother of pearl by Abdülhamid himself. Abdülhamid was passionate over his hobby of woodworking and had a carpentry workshop built close to the palace.

The Malta Köşkü, perched atop a steep hill, is where Murad V and his mother, as well as Midhat Paşa were imprisoned, the latter being tortured in the basement of the nearby Çadır Köşkü. When it wasn't serving as a penitentiary, the Malta Köşkü hosted state receptions. It is now a restaurant with trellised terrace overlooking the park toward the Bosphorus (see **Malta Köşkü**, p. 108).

If you're arriving by taxi, have the driver drop you off at the Şale Köşkü or the Malta Köşkü to save yourself the long hike uphill through the park.

Yıldız Park (entrance via Barbaros Bulv., Beşiktaş or opposite the Çırağan Palace). ✆ **212/258-3080.** Admission 4YTL ($3.50/£1.50). Tues–Sun 10am–5pm in winter, 9am–5pm in summer. Bus: 22, 22RE, 25E, 30D, 40, 40T, 42, 57UL, DT1, DT2, or U1.

7 One If by Land; Two If by Sea: Constantinople's Defensive Walls

Even before the arrival of the great Roman emperors, the city on the hill (then called Megara) was a target for attack. Persian King Darius I took the city in 512 B.C.; then in 478 B.C., the Athenians squeezed out the Persians. Alexander the Great reinforced the city's Hellenistic bend, until in 146 B.C. the city came under Roman domination. For the next 350 years, the city basked in the glow of Pax Romana, notwithstanding Septimus Severus' massacre and destruction of the city when, having proclaimed himself emperor, he was met with resistance by the citizens loyal to his opponent, Pescennius Niger. When Severus rebuilt the city, he expanded the original boundaries to those enclosed by a defensive wall running roughly north-to-south from the Galata Bridge around the Hippodrome to the Marmara Sea. Constantine's walls again enlarged the city, forming a ceinture that expanded the city out into the middle of today's Fatih district. Nothing of either the Severus or Constantine walls survive.

Marmara Sea Walls While not as impressive a feat as the Theodosian defenses, the Sea Walls, originally built by order of Constantine and extended by Theodosius, are worth a mention. Sadly, there's very little left of the original section along the southern coastal road, because in 1870, railway engineers simply knocked it down to make

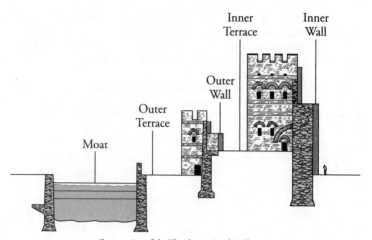

Cross-section of the Theodosian Land Walls

way for the commuter train. So walls that endured 1500 years of sieges, earthquakes, and even tsunamis fell to the onward march of urban "improvement."

The crumbling (albeit highly photogenic) decay of the sea walls greets you as you enter the Old City along the coastal road from the airport. The walls are predominantly to your left, leaving you to imagine the waves of the Marmara Sea lapping up over the road you're driving in on. Portions of the wall prop up houses constructed on the hill, and if you know what you're looking for, you can spot a handful of crumbling palatial arches remaining from the grand Bucoleon Palace. The wall was punctuated by eight gates designed to allow ships entry into the inner harbors. The Porta de Condoskali, or the Shallow Harbor Gate, now provides land access to the appropriately named neighborhood of **Kumkapı** (Sand Gate), now a lively area of fish restaurants recalling (barely) the fishermen's harbor that it once was. The **Ahırkapı,** or stable gate, served as the imperial port, but fell into disuse with the construction of the Bucoleon Palace to the west.

The best approach is either from the comfort of a car or on foot to one of the two gates mentioned above. It's also possible to walk along the walls all the way from Sirkeci around Sarayburnu to the southern face of Sultanahmet, but in spite of the views of the Marmara Sea, the traffic flow is too heavy and exhaust fumes too thick to make this a comfortable choice. A good compromise is to exit on foot either Aksakal Cad. (east of the Küçük Ayasofya Camii) or Ahırkapı and reenter the city via the other. You won't want to try this in the height of summer, as the sun's rays are just too strong.

The Theodosian Walls 𝕬𝕬 By the time Theodosius II arrived on the throne in A.D. 408, the city of Constantinople was bursting at the seams. As Septimus Severus and Constantine had done before him, Theodosius set about fortifying and enlarging the city, and the alternately towering and crumbling red brick and limestone monoliths you see running north from Yedikule (you'll see it at as you arrive into the city) all the way to Ayvansaray and the Golden Horn are what remain of Theodosius's Land Walls. Twenty-five years after their construction between A.D. 412 and 422, the walls all but collapsed in an earthquake, and with the Huns advancing from the east, the politically polarized factions of the city set aside their grievances and in a period of 2 months, not only fortified the wall, but built another, exterior wall plus a moat. (Constantinople nevertheless wound up paying Atilla the Hun protection money for 10 years after his attack.) Extensions to the wall, which under Theodosius ended at Blachernae, were added later by subsequent emperors. This latter section, from Ayvansaray down to the Golden Horn, was the weak link in the chain, and not surprisingly, the point at which Mehmet the Conqueror's army breached the city.

All together, the system of land defenses represents an impressive period in military architecture. The original, Theodosian wall consisted of a main (inner) wall 5m (16 ft.) thick and 11 to 14m (36–46 ft.) high, punctuated by 96 towers from 18 to 20m (59–66 ft.) in height. The refortification added an outer, crenelated wall reinforced with 92 towers placed at intervals of 50 to 70 or so meters (164–230 ft.), set in alternating position with the towers of the inner wall. Between the inner and outer wall was an inner terrace embankment (called a *peribolos*). Another wider embankment separated the outer wall from the moat, creating a vulnerable open space for those (un)lucky enough to get that far. The moat was the first line of defense, presenting invading armies with a formidable obstacle 20m (66 ft.) wide and 10m (33 ft.) deep. All told (including the additional sections north of Blachernae), the total length of the land walls is 6,670m (4 miles). Entrance and exit into and out of the city was via monumental gates constructed of stone, marble, and even, in the case of the Golden Gate at Yedikule, of gold. One of the most important gates of both the Byzantine and Ottoman periods was **Edirnekapı,** or the gate leading to Edirne. Edirnekapı, which is part of the original Theodosian wall, provided access to the main thoroughfare into the city center. Byzantine emperors used this gate when leaving for and returning from their campaigns abroad, and Fatih Mehmet (aka "the Conqueror") made his victorious entrance here. Later Ottoman sultans, after the official inauguration ceremonies at Eyüp, followed in Mehmet's footsteps and also entered via this gate.

Because of the derelict state of much of the structure and because there are no lights at night, the best approach to visiting the land walls is either to walk along them beginning at Edirnekapı (see chapter 8, "Istanbul Strolls") or view them up close and personal at Yedikule, where you can scramble to the top of the ramparts and get a good overview of the entire system heading north (see "Yedikule," below).

Yedikule (Seven Towers Fortress) ⟨★ ⟨Kids⟩   About a quarter of a mile inland from the Marmara Sea along the land walls is the Golden Gate entrance to the Byzantine city, a triumphal arch built by Theodosius. The arch predates the construction of the famed Theodosian walls and was used as a ceremonial entrance and exit to the city still for the most part confined to the boundaries set by Constantine's earlier defensive walls. From here, the main road, or Mese, led directly through the center of the city, to the Milion Stone and Ayasofya. Theodosius later incorporated the gate into the construction of his defensive walls. Nearly a thousand years (and several earthquakes later) in 1457, Mehmet the Conqueror took advantage of the two towers flanking the Golden Gate, added an additional five towers and enclosed them within a new defensive fortress. But the fort was never called to battle and served instead as the imperial treasury and a political prison for the likes of Mahmut Paşa, the Conqueror's Grand Vizier, and the deposed Mamluk caliph. Some unsavory incidents happened here too: When Sultan Osman II tried to reform the Janissaries in 1622, he was thrown in prison and then killed, and his head was tossed into what is now known as the "bloody well" in the center of the garden. Inside the Zindan Kulesi (Inscription Tower), some of the scrapings etched into the stone by the prisoners are still visible. The wooden scaffolding is what remains of the prisoners' cells. Steep and narrow stone stairways provide access to the top of the battlements, where you can breath deeply the salty sea air and contemplate some of the finest views of the city. The stairway on the eastern curtain wall (to the right of the entrance) has one lone banister; ascend and descend with care.

Imrahor Mah., Kule Meydanı 4, Yedikule/Fatih. © 0212/584-4012. Admission 5YTL ($4.35/£1.90). Thurs–Tues 9:30am–4:30pm. Bus: 80 or 81 from Eminönü; 80T from Taksim.

8 Istanbul's Contemporary Art Scene

Istanbul's **Biennale** (p. 211) may have put the city on the art-world map in 1987, but the city's fast-paced Europeanization and naturally creative and innovative vigor has captured international attention otherwise. If your trip to Istanbul fails to coincide with the installation of this biennial citywide celebration of art, not to worry, as these days, plenty of creative juices flow during in-between years, displayed in unique and sometimes historic environments and as part of noteworthy private collections.

The major talk of the town is the new, old **Santralistanbul** *✸✸* (Eski Silahtarağa Elektrik Santralı, Silahtar Mah., Kazım Karabekir Cad. 1, Eyüp; © 0212/444-0428; www.santralistanbul.org; free admission), the recently restored and repurposed Ottoman era Silahtarağa electric power plant. The industrial space, which also houses, appropriately, the Museum of Energy, also serves as a cultural and educational center. The Santralistanbul complex takes up 12 hectares (29 acres) of space on the Bilgi University campus on the northern shore of the Golden Horn. There are concert halls, a public library (in two of the former boiler rooms), an amphitheater, and living space for visiting artists. Santralistanbul is open Tuesday to Sunday, 10am to 10pm. A free shuttle departs from Atatürk Cultural Center in Taksim every half-hour.

Another gallery that has made a splash in Istanbul is **Antrepo No. 3** *✸✸* (Antrepo No. 3, Karaköy; © 0212/334-7300; www.antrepo.org; free admission), one of a cluster of Customs warehouses (among which is the Istanbul Museum of Modern Art next door, see below for review) lining the waterfront of the Bosphorus at Tophane. Designed as a warren of alternatively unexpected, chaotic, noisy, and thought-provoking exhibitions and installments, Antrepo intends to conceptually dissolve the barriers that separate art from urban life. It's a sort of micro-city teetering on the banks of one of the world's busiest maritime crossroads. The gallery is open Tuesday to Sunday, 10am to 7pm.

The cultural face of Garanti Bank, **Platform Garanti Contemporary Art Center** *✸* (Istiklal Cad. 115A, Beyoğlu; © 0212/293-2361; http://platformgaranti.blogspot. com; Tues–Thurs 1–8pm, Fri–Sat 1–10pm; free admission), has been one of Istanbul's most important art spaces since it arrived on the art scene in 2001. At the helm is Vasif Kortun, curator of past Istanbul Biennales, who has created an interactive space that includes the most comprehensive library of art publications in the city. In addition to showing contemporary exhibitions featuring art from Turkey and abroad, Platform acts as a national, regional, and international cultural portal, with residency programs available for artists from countries where artistic expression remains relatively untapped.

Galerist *✸* (Istiklal Cad., Mısır Apt 31¼, Beyoğlu; © 0212/244-8230; www. galerist.com.tr; free admission) is another one of Istanbul's and Turkey's more influential artistic spaces. Turkey's leading artists are showcased in this gallery, while one of Galerist's objectives is to expose the international artistic community to Turkish contemporary art through exhibitions abroad. Galerist is open Tuesday to Sunday, 11am to 7pm.

Since its founding in Ankara in 1984, **Galeri Nev** (Maçka Cad. 33, Maçka; © 0212/ 231-6763; www.galerinevistanbul.com; free admission) expanded to a second space in Istanbul and has mounted more than 300 exhibitions. The founding partners, architects by trade, concentrated the earliest exhibitions on Turkey's first modernists. The gallery has also hosted exhibitions of European modernists such as Bonnard, Dali, and Picasso. Nev has a private collection of original prints, more than a hundred limited edition reproductions, and 93 volumes of art books and catalogs. The Istanbul location is open Tuesday to Saturday, 11am to 6:30pm.

Also leading the charge to elevate the profile of progressive art in Turkey is the not-for-profit **Elgiz Museum Proje4L** (Harman Sok., Harmancı Giz Plaza Gültepe; metro to Levent; © 0212/281-5150; www.proje4L.org; free admission). In addition to housing the private collections of its founders Sevda and Can Elgiz—representing a range of media by both local and international artists—the museum organizes lectures and seminars and welcomes guest artists. The museum is open Wednesday to Friday, 10am to 6pm, and Saturday 10am to 4pm.

With all of this contemporary rebound to the antiquity of Istanbul, **Gallery Apel** (Hayriye Cad. 7, Galatasaray; © 0212/292-7236; www.galleryapel.com; free admission) offers some refreshing middle ground by featuring works created using traditional materials like felt, ceramic, wood, and glass. Exhibitions are constantly changing and feature modern sculptures, prints, and even full-size architectural mock-ups. The gallery is open Tuesday to Sunday, 11:30am to 6:30pm.

Istanbul Museum of Modern Art ✪   In a city of ancient empires, in a country whose political and economic supremacy is but a distant memory, Turkey, and in particular Istanbul, is carving itself a new niche. Only this time, it's looking forward, not back. The Istanbul Modern, opened in December 2004, occupies a crisp, utilitarian, and highly functional 7,990 sq. m (86,000 sq. ft.) in a former Customs warehouse just outside the cruise ship docks. The collection of paintings, portraits, sculptures, and photographs serve to tell us, in some sense, what was going on in the minds of the Turks in the 20th century. Some pieces simply make you tilt your head in wonder. That alone makes this museum worth a look.

Meclis-I Mebusan Cad., Liman İşletmeleri Sahası, Antrepo 4, Karaköy. © 0212/334-7300. www.istanbulmodern. org. Admission 7YTL ($6.10/£2.70), free for children under 12, free on Thurs. Tues–Sun 10am–6pm (Thurs until 8pm). Tram: Tophane.

9 Eminönü

SULTANAHMET

Binbirdirek Sarnıçı *(Moments*   The name means "Cistern of 1,001 Columns"—in spite of the actual presence of only 224. The cistern is thought to have been built by Philoxenus, a Roman senator and companion of Constantine the Great, as part of the Lavsus Palace. It is the oldest cistern in the city, and at 3,610 sq. m (38,858 sq. ft.), is the second-largest covered cistern (Yerebatan is the largest). The cistern was later used as a warehouse for the manufacture of silk yarn, but was then abandoned to the ignoble fate of garbage dump. As part of the process of recovery, 7,000 truckloads of detritus had to be removed. The current holders of the concession take advantage of the extremely atmospheric ambience as a background for a restaurant and waterpipe cafe, a wine bar, and patisserie as well as a venue for events.

Binbirdirek Mah., Imran Öktan Sok. 4 (opposite the Post Office), Sultanahmet. © 0212/518-1001. www.binbirdirek. com. Admission 5YTL ($4.35/£1.90). Daily 9am–9pm. Tram: Sultanahmet.

Bucoleon Palace   Imagine the lapping of the Marmara Sea onto the base of the palace ramparts, and visualize a continuous arcade of columned windows above a stepped portal flanked by twin lions allowing access to the palace by sea. These were the features of the Bucoleon Palace, the main living quarters of the Great Palace from the 9th to 11th centuries A.D., when the imperial family moved to Blachernae above the Golden Horn. The Bucoleon palace was mostly in ruins, and whatever remained was regrettably demolished to make way for the commuter railway. All that's left today is a bleak wall of arched windows, visible from the sea-facing side of Sultanahmet just outside of the entrance to Aksakal Caddesi. Those lions, by the way, are now in the Istanbul Archaeology Museum.

Kennedy Cad., Sultanahmet (Aksakal Cad. intersects with Küçük Ayasofya Cad. near the Küçük Ayasofya Camii). Tram: Sultanahmet or Çemberlitaş.

Buhara Özbekler Tekkesi ve Mescidi   This derviş lodge dates to 1692. Built by Ismail Bey, presumably to serve the minority Özbek community, it features a bi-level design due to the slope of the hill on which it is constructed. The lodge is currently undergoing restoration and should be open by the time you read this.

Özbekler Sok., Sultanahmet (exiting Sokullu Mehmet Paşa Mosque, turn right). No phone. Hours and admission to be established upon completion of restoration. Tram: Sultanahmet or Çemberlitaş.

Caferağa Medresesi   Built in 1559 by Sinan on the order of one of the eunuchs to the harem, this *medrese* hardly ever makes the guidebooks. It's actually one of those rare "living historical places," offering art and music exhibitions, as well as workshops and courses on a variety of traditional Ottoman art forms. Rooms are also designed to be exhibition spaces for the works created by the students within. The courtyard oasis is a perfect place for a break from pounding the hard pavement of Sultanahmet.

Caferiye Sok., Soğukkuyu Çıkmazı 1 (next to the Ottoman Hotel), Sultanahmet. © 0212/513-3601. Free admission. Daily 9am–6pm. Tram: Gülhane or Sultanahmet.

Column of Constantine   When Constantine established the city on the hill as the capital of the Roman Empire, one of his first projects was the construction of a forum, built just outside the then-city walls. The forum was circular with two monumental gates, and at its center Constantine erected a monumental column carved of red porphyry stone and topped by a Corinthian capital bearing his own likeness. A drawing by Melchior Lorick (1561) contains an illustration of the column showing a relief on the north, Senate-facing side of the base.

The Forum of Constantine is said to have been the inspiration for Bernini in his conception of St. Peter's Square in Rome. The column has been a victim of earthquakes and elements: In A.D. 418, part of the base cracked, prompting its reinforcement via the use of a ringed metal brace (additional braces were added later), and in 1106, the statue of Constantine was toppled by a hurricane. Manuel Komnenos presided over the first restoration of the monument, placing a simple cross atop the column in place of the destroyed statue of the emperor. Since then, periodic repairs have been done to cracks in the marble, and in 2003 a full-fledged, comprehensive restoration was begun.

Corner of Yeniçeriler Cad. (where the avenue changes its name from Divanyolu and behind the Çemberlitaş Tram stop) and Mahmut Paşa Yokuşu, Çemberlitaş. Tram: Çemberlitaş.

Kabasakal Medresi   No longer a school for Koranic studies, this restored 17th-century *medrese* nevertheless fulfils its earlier mission. Built by Şeyhülislam Mehmed

Efendi, the structure now serves as the Istanbul Handicrafts Center, where students and practitioners of traditional Ottoman arts can ply their trade. The small workshops ring a lovely rectangular porticoed courtyard.

Kabasakal Cad. 5, Istanbul Sanatlari Çarsisi (next to Yeşil Ev), Sultanahmet. ℂ **0212/517-6780**. Free admission. Daily 9:30am–6:30pm. Tram: Sultanahmet.

Soğukçeşme Sokagı   A cobbled mews of 12 wooden Ottoman houses and a roman cistern are sandwiched between the outer wall of Topkapı Palace and the imposing backside of the Ayasofya. The buildings were restored in the 1970s by the Turkish Touring Club and now comprise the **Ayasofya Konakları hotel** (p. 64). The **Istanbul Library** (see "Libraries & Cultural Centers," later in this chapter) and restaurant **Sarnıç** (p. 93) are also located here.

Access to the left of the entrance to Topkapı Palace, up the hill from the entrance to Gülhane Park, or along Caferiye Sok. from Ayasofya Meydanı. Tram: Gülhane or Sultanahmet.

Sultanamet Prison   When a prison in proximity to the nearby criminal courts was built in 1919, the local residents said "there goes the neighborhood." In fact, the then-occupants of the Şükrü Bey Mansion (now the Yeşil Ev hotel and restaurant, p. 93) constructed a high wall to enclose the garden for safekeeping. The prison, now the **Four Seasons Hotel** (p. 63), hosted such Turkish literary icons as Nazım Hikmet, Aziz Nesin, Rıfat Ilgaz, and Yaşar Kemal, all labeled as political dissidents. The prison was closed in the 1970s.

Tevkifhane Sok. 1, Sultanahmet. Hotel common areas open 24 hr.; the bar and restaurant have individual hours. Tram: Sultanahmet.

Vakıflar Halı Müzesi (Foundation Carpet Museum)   Some of Turkey's oldest textile treasures are housed in the private pavilion used by the sultan for prayers. The collection features primarily Usçak, Bergama, and Konya carpets, and *kilims* dating from the 16th to 19th century.

Blue Mosque Imperial Pavilion, Sultanahmet (facing the tourist entrance to the mosque, the pavilion and museum are to your left). ℂ **0212/518-1330**. Free admission. Tues–Sat 9am–noon and 1–4pm. Tram: Sultanahmet.

BEYAZIT & NEAR THE GRAND BAZAAR

Arch of Theodosius   There's very little left apart from the toppled Triumphal Arch scattered on either side of Ordu Caddesi, discovered during the construction of Beyazit Square in the 1950s. Nevertheless, there's something intangibly momentous wandering through such a thickly layered cultural metropolis and stumbling upon the main gate into the city ruled by the last sovereign of the Roman Empire. The arch was built adjacent to the Forum of Theodosius, which the emperor modeled on the Forum of Trajan in Rome. The forum, or what's left of it, remains buried several feet below Beyazit Square. It was also called the Forum Tauri, after the colossal bronze bull that greeted visitors at the center of the city.

From the remains, researchers were able to reconstruct (on paper, at least) the monument: The arch was composed of a high center arch flanked by two shorter lateral arches supported by eight sets of four columns topped by Corinthian capitals. Earthquakes and routine sieges on the city reduced much of the forum to rubble well before the arrival of the Ottoman Turks, and many of the buildings constructed later used the site as a marble quarry (some of the columns in the Basilica Cistern originated here, for example).

Ordu Cad. (opposite Istanbul University), Beyazit. Tram: Beyazit.

Atik Ali Paşa Camii   A smaller version of the Ulu Camii in Bursa and similar in style to the original Fatih Camii before it was destroyed in the 1766 earthquake, the Atik Ali Paşa represents a transition between Selçuk and traditional Ottoman architecture. The mosque was the center of a complex built in 1496 by the eunuch Grand Vizier of Beyazit II, Hadim Ali Paşa. The *tekke,* or derviş lodge, soup kitchens, and part of the *medrese* were razed for the widening of Divanyolu.

Divanyolu, next to the Column of Constantine. No phone. Tram: Beyazit.

Bodrum Camii or the Myrelaion   The story of this building is inextricably tied to the life of Romano Lakapenos, son of Armenian peasants whose father was an imperial guardsman. His biography is, as expected, tortuously long and convoluted, so suffice it to say that Lakapenos distinguished himself as a militarily and politically savvy individual who became the trusted friend, and then father-in-law, of the young Constantine VII Porphyrogenitus. In A.D. 920, a year after the wedding of his daughter to the under-aged emperor, Lakapenos was crowned co-emperor, and in later years bestowed the same honor upon his own sons Christopher, Stephen, and Constantine.

Around the time of his ascension to the throne, Lakapenos acquired a building, itself with a bit of history. Here we go again: The building once was an unfinished 5th-century-A.D. rotunda so huge that if completed would have been second in size only to the Pantheon in Rome. Later, it was surmounted—by the help of a raised platform—by a building reportedly used as a market and place of executions. When Lakapenos bought the building, he had it converted into a monastery and added the adjoining church, called the Myrelaion, or Place of Myrrh (finally, to the punch line). The oversize foundation of the church allowed it to sit at the same level of the palace. The church is built on a dome-in-cross plan, which makes it the first of its type of all of the churches of the same type in Constantinople. When converted to a mosque, the Ottomans called it Bodrum Camii, or mosque with a cellar. The adjoining palace has been replaced by concrete blocks.

Laleli Cad., Mesipaşa Cad., Laleli. No phone. Tram: Laleli.

Church of St. Theodore   We really know very little about the origins of this Byzantine church. Scholars are not even sure as to which St. Theodore the church was dedicated. Still, we can at least narrow down the construction of the building to a 200-year period between the 12th and 14th centuries. The church was predictably converted to a mosque immediately after the conquest and is alternatively known as the Kilise Camii (Church Mosque) and the Molla Gürani Camii, after the Kurdish scholar, tutor to Mehmet the Conqueror, and the first Mufti of Istanbul. Inside are what appear to be a number of recycled 6th-century-A.D. architectural elements (columns, capitals, supports). The building underwent a restoration in 1937, during which mosaics were revealed from under the whitewash. These are located primarily in the south dome of the exonarthex depicting the Virgin Mary surrounded by prophets.

Tirendaz Sok., Vefa (from Şifahane Sok., walk down Molla Şemsettin Camii Sok., and turn right. You'll see a seemingly out of place redbrick domed building). No phone. Tram: Beyazit.

Kalenderhane Camii &   The Kalenderhane Mosque was originally, and incorrectly, identified as the Church of Christ Akat28leptos. But when restorations in 1966 revealed two frescoes of the Mother of God Kyriotissa (Greek for enthroned), the jig was up. Actually, the first building on the site, taking advantage of the proximity of the aqueduct, was a Roman bath. The bath gave way to a small basilica, and then in the 7th century A.D., another portion was added to the south side. The Kalenderhane, built at the end of the 12th century, incorporates the main apse of the latter church (not the mosaic depicting the Presentation of the Temple). In 1204, the victorious Latin Crusaders embellished the church with a fresco cycle illustrating the life of St. Francis of Assisi, the earliest fresco cycle depicting the saint in the world. Another "first" is the Presentation of the Christ Child in the Temple, the only mosaic predating the iconoclastic period in the city. Also notable are two 13th- or 14th-century sculptural representations of The Throne of Justice and of Prayer, located in the right and left architraves.

16 Mart Şehitler Cad., Vefa. No phone. Tram: Üniversite.

Museum of Calligraphy (Türk Vakıf Sanatları Müzesi)   The fine art of calligraphy was the most important one in the Ottoman Empire. Sultans Beyazit II and Ahmet III were themselves masters in the art, and some of the more elaborate imperial seals (or *tuğra*) were set to paper by their hands. Dedicated entirely to this art, the Museum of Calligraphy is the only one of its kind, housed in what was originally the *medrese* of the Beyazit complex, and in the 20th century, a municipal library. The museum exhibits illuminate Korans from all over the empire, *tuğras,* official documents in elaborate script, and various tools of the trade, all displayed in the evocative workrooms set around a porticoed courtyard.

Beyazit Meydanı. ✆ 0212/527-5851. Admission 3YTL ($2.60/£1.15). Tues–Sat 8:30am–noon and 1–4:30pm. Tram: Beyazit.

Nuruosmaniye Külliyesi   The "Light of Osman" mosque was revolutionary when it was built in the middle of the 18th century. With the baroque style at its zenith in Europe, Sultan Mahmut I set to work, not without just a little resistance from the more traditional clergy. The architect, Simon Kalfa, found a "compromise" and incorporated the European baroque style to traditional Ottoman forms. The mosque was completed 8 years after it was begun by Mahmut's brother and successor, Osman II.

The irregular horse-shoe–shaped courtyard, shaded in plane trees and horse chestnuts, is alternatively a quiet oasis for contemplation or a bustling pathway leading to the frenzy of the Grand Bazaar. It all depends upon the time of day you visit (or day: the Grand Bazaar is closed on Sun), or whether or not it's high tourist season. At one time, the courtyard was an impromptu staging area for the Anatolian troubadours, called *aşıklar* (Turkish for lover, but more appropriate would be lovelorn).

Nuruosmaniye Cad. (from Divanyolu to Vezirhan Cad.). No phone. Tram: Çemberlitaş.

EMINÖNÜ & SIRKECI

Rüstem Paşa Külliyesi 🕸🕸   It is said that this Grand Vizier was a true Ali Baba, if you will. His nickname was Kehle-i-Ikbal, or the Louse of Fortune. How appropriate then that his namesake would be located amid one of the city's most commercial districts. The mosque and complex were built by Sinan in 1561. Primarily serving a blue-collar community of hardware merchants, the mosque is the most decorated one in the city, tiled top to bottom with dazzling Iznik tiles dancing with tulips, hyacinths, and spring flowers. It was commissioned by Süleyman's Prime Minister and son-in-law, Rüstem Paşa. The second-story prayer hall sits atop a street-level space designed to accommodate the commercial district below, and the prayer hall is accessed via a narrow quartet of staircases. Built on an octagonal plan, the Rüstem Paşa Camii is believed to be the precursor for Sinan's design of the Selimiye in Edirne.

Fun Fact **Locomotive Lore**

The construction of the original Orient Express was backed by King Leopold II, but the tracks fell short of the center city. Passengers were forced to complete the journey by bus and boat. In 1888, the Austrian Baron Hirsch completed the job. The meandering trajectory of the train tracks through the flatlands of Thrace owe their course to the fact that the Baron was paid per kilometer.

Uzun Çarşı Cad. at Hasır cılar/Kutucular Cads., Tahtakale-Eminönü, Eminönü (opposite the bus depot adjacent to the bazaar). No phone. Tram: Eminönü; bus: 35, 36CE, 44B, 74, 80, 81, or 90.

FATIH

Friends roll their eyes whenever I say I've been to Fatih; the entire district has been pigeon-holed as a place only fundamentalists could love. But the district is as diverse as the mosaic that makes up the rest of the city, and one cannot lump the "feel" of the more middle class Yenikapı or Samatya with the shadowy (chador-y) figures of Çarşamba. As citizens from the lowest economic rungs arrive in droves from the outer provinces, however, this stereotype may in fact prove all too apt.

ZEYREK

Church of the Pantocrator (Zeyrek Camii)

This former monastery church is one of the most important historic landmarks of the Byzantine period; however, because the structure is in a sad state of neglect, a detour here can only be recommended in tandem with a stroll through the narrow streets of the Zeyrek neighborhood. Dedicated to St. Saviour Pantocrator, the building is actually a composite of two churches and a chapel, making it the second-largest church in Istanbul after Ayasofya. The monastery was founded by Empress Eirene, wife of John II Comnenus, who completed the south church prior to her death in 1124. She was also the first to be buried here (her sarcophagus was moved in the 1960s to the Archaeological Museum, but now resides in the exonarthex of the Ayasofya). The northern church was added by the emperor (her husband) after Eirene's death and dedicated to Virgin Eleousa, the Merciful or Charitable. Nothing remains of its original ornamentation. The emperor also had the churches connected through the jerry-rigging of a chapel between the north and south church, which also required the demolition of part of the exterior walls of the two buildings. The *minbar* (pulpit), added when the church was converted into a mosque in the 15th century, is composed of recycled fragments of Byzantine sculpture. Although the building preserves some of its original decoration (marble pavement, door frames in the narthex, marble apse), it's almost impossible to get a sense of the interior, as each section has been blocked off by wooden partitions.

From Atatürk Bulv., follow İtfaiye Cad. and take the first street to the right. No phone. Open daily at prayer times only.

AKSARAY

Hırka-i Şerif Camii (Mosque of the Holy Mantle)

The cloak worn by the Profit Mohammad was under the care of the Veys family until Sultan Ahmet I had it brought to Istanbul in 1611. Sultan Abdülhamid I kept it in a small room he had built especially for the mantle. Then later, Sultan Abdülmecid cleared about 700 homes to build the mosque presently on this site (constructed 1847–51). The pew on the northern side of the mosque was exclusively for the use of the Sultan. Today the mantle is only displayed during the month of Ramadan.

Hırka-i Şerif (where it becomes Keçeciler Cad.), Karagümrük/Fatih. No phone. Tram: To Aksaray, change for train to Emniyet, then walk up Akdeniz Cad., and turn left onto Sarıgüzel Cad.

Kız Taşı or the Column of Marcian   The name of this 17m- (56-ft.) high monument translates to "maiden's stone." The Byzantine column erected for emperor Marcian was carved from a single block of granite. At one time, the column was crowned by a Corinthian capital bearing a statue of the Emperor. The Turkish name refers to the figure of Nike carved on its base.

Kız Taşı Cad. (at the plaza that intersects with Dolap Cad.). Tram: Aksaray.

ALONG THE GOLDEN HORN
AYVANSARAY, BALAT & FENER

When Fatih Mehmet the Conqueror proclaimed freedom to all despite race or religion, many of the Greeks who had fled the city under siege, plus others, settled in this neighborhood. These Greeks were known as "Phanariots" and were an integral part of Ottoman life. Many of the stately homes, schools, monasteries, and churches date to this period of prosperity. Built on one of the city's seven central hills, this neighborhood was called Petrion (rock) by the Byzantines, and it was primarily inhabited by Rum. To the north, bordering the Fener neighborhood, the community, predominantly Balat Jews, was represented by its share of influential politicians, physicians, and diplomats. But in spite of the relative prosperity of the neighborhood, Balat never quite rose to the level of neighboring Fener and still maintains the stigma of being Fener's poorer cousin.

Ayadimitri Kilisesi (St. Demetrios Kanavis Kilisesi)   This 13th-century Byzantine church housed the Greek Orthodox Patriarchate from 1597 until the Patriarchate moved to its current location in 1601. A church bearing this name has existed on the site since 1334, but the current church dates only to the first half of the 18th century.

Corner of Mustafapaşa Bostanı Sok. and Ağaclı Çeşme Sok., Balat. No phone. Ferry: Fener; bus 36CE, 399B, 399C, 399D, 44B, 55T, 99, or 99A from Eminönü.

Ahrida Sinagogue   The first synagogue in Istanbul was constructed by a group of Macedonian Jews emigrating from the town of Ohri, for which the synagogue is named. It dates to the first half of the 15th century, when Istanbul was still under Byzantine rule, but after Macedonia had already fallen to the Ottomans. Over the next 500 years, the congregation grew to include Jews from Spain, Germany, and Russia. The synagogue was restored in the 17th century. Much of the Jewish community in Balat has moved on to other of the city's neighborhoods, but the synagogue still operates for a much-reduced number of remaining congregants. The most striking feature is the *bima,* constructed in the form of a ship's bow. The recurring images of boats, seen etched above doorways and windows around the neighborhood, represent the lifeline provided to the expelled Jews of Spain in 1492 by Beyazit II.

Vodina Cad. 9 (extension of Kürkçüçeşme Sok.), Balat. ℂ 0212/523-4729. Visits by appointment only via the Balat Foundation. ℂ 0212/523-7407. Ferry: Fener; bus: 36CE, 399B, 399C, 399D, 44B, 55T, 99, or 99A from Eminönü.

Atik Mustafapasa Camii   There have been several theories as to the origins of this former Byzantine church, but none has emerged as the fitting piece to the puzzle. Some say that it was built by Leo I in A.D. 458 for SS. Peter and Mark. A second theory puts construction in the 9th or 10th century A.D. and suggests that if this were so, it would have been the earliest example of a dome-in-cross church in Constantinople and therefore the precursor for the type of church that spread all over Russia in the 11th century. The building lay abandoned after the Ottoman conquest until it was converted into a mosque several decades later; the dome dates to this period of reconstruction, and many of the early architectural features were lost.

Cember Sok. between Mustafa Paşa Bostanı Sok. and the Golden Horn highway. No phone. Ferry: Fener; bus: 36CE, 399B, 399C, 399D, 44B, 55T, 99, or 99A from Eminönü.

Ayazma and the Church of St. Mary of Blachernae   This unremarkable church sits atop the site of one of the most celebrated shrines to the Virgin Mary in Byzantium. But even before Constantine set foot inside the city walls, the spring located on this spot was considered sacred. Citizens of Constantinople made regular pilgrimages to the spring, and in the 5th century A.D., Empress Augusta Pulcheria, wife of Emperor Marcian, had a church built on the site. Sometime between A.D. 457 and 474, Emperor Leo I added a marble statue of Mary, from whose hands flowed the holy water of the spring, as well as a sacred pool. He later added a chapel to house the relics of the Virgin Mary, which included the holy robe stolen by citizens of Constantinople on pilgrimage to Jerusalem and a gold and silver icon of the Virgin. This icon was paraded along the battlements when the city was under siege by the Avars in A.D. 626 and is credited with saving the city. According to another tradition, the Holy Shroud (of Turin) was brought here in A.D. 944. The church succumbed to the wrath of the iconoclast period, and later, to fire. The church, and indeed the entire complex of buildings, was destroyed by fire in 1434. A replacement chapel was built in 1867, and later other sections were added on.

Mustafapaşa Bostanı Sok., Fener. No phone. Ferry: Fener; bus 36CE, 399B, 399C, 399D, 44B, 55T, 99, or 99A from Eminönü.

Fener Rum Erkek Lisesi (Fener Roman Boys School)   Housing the oldest surviving institution of learning in Istanbul, the crowning jewel of Fener is the principle school for the small Greek population. The building was erected in 1881 but served as the Patriarchate School during the Byzantine era. After the conquest, the Patriarchate was granted special rights and the school was allowed to reopen.

Under the sultanate, Greeks called the school the Megali Scholio (Great School), and some of the more prominent names of the Byzantine Empire were educated here, including Palaeologus, Cantacuzejnus, and Cantemir. The soaring dome sits on a thick drum whose upper floor houses an observatory for instruction in astronomy. The best view of the school is from down below (or halfway down the steeply sloping Sancaktar Yokuşu); you can't get in unless you're up for some aerobics, so just admire it from the base of the hill.

Sancaktar Yokuşu, Fener. No phone. Ferry: Fener; bus: 36CE, 399B, 399C, 399D, 44B, 55T, 99, or 99A from Eminönü.

Metochion of Mount Sinai   A metochion was essentially an ecclesiastical embassy church representing an autocephalous ("self-headed" or autonomous) branch of the Orthodox Church. It was also the parish of a monastery or patriarch. This is one of the more stately Feneriote mansions in the city, set on the edge of green wedged between the coastal highway and a narrow and deadly section of Mürselpaşa Caddesi. From 1686 to 1967, when the Turkish government confiscated the building, the metochion served as the residence and representative of the Monastery of St. Catherine on Mount Sinai. The untidy accouterments of a family of squatters litter the courtyard of the adjacent chapel and monastery of St. John the Baptist, but it may be a

relief to know that the present residents are only squatting on an 18th-century reconstruction of the chapel. With the frenzy of restoration projects being carried out in advance of Istanbul 2010, it is only a matter of time before the site is reclaimed and visitors are able to tour the complex.

Mürselpaşa Cad., near Hızır Çavuş Köprübaşı, on the green between the highway opposite the Balat Iskelesi/ferry docks. For information, contact the Patriarchate. ✆ 0212/531-9670. Ferry: Fener; bus 36CE, 399B, 399C, 399D, 44B, 55T, 99, or 99A from Eminönü.

St. Mary of the Mongols/Kanlı Kilise   This is the only Byzantine church to remain continuously in the hands of the its Greek congregation to this day. This unusual right of ownership was bestowed upon the Greek congregants by imperial decree under the sultanate of Fatih Mehmet. The *firman,* or sultan's imperial seal, is on display in the interior of the church.

According to tradition, this church was built (or rebuilt) around 1282 by Princess Maria Palaeologina, illegitimate daughter of Emperor Michael VIII Palaeologus. (Other sources suggest that the church was founded by Isaac Dukas, uncle of Michael VIII around 1261.) The princess was married off to a Mongols Khan by her father in 1265, but after the death of her husband 15 years later (assassination, actually), Maria returned to Constantinople, founded the church and a convent, and lived out the remainder of her life as a nun.

The building was originally constructed on a traditional quatrefoil plan, but the southern end of the church was completely destroyed, to be replaced by an incongruous square narthex that distorts the harmony of the original. The one major treasure remaining from its Byzantine period is a portative mosaic of Theotokos Pammakaristos, "the All-Joyous Mother of God."

Tevkii Cafer Mektebi Sok., Fener. ✆ 0212/521-7139. By appointment only. Ferry: Fener; bus: 36CE, 399B, 399C, 399D, 44B, 55T, 99, or 99A from Eminönü.

St. Stephen of the Bulgars (Bulgar Kilisesi) ✰   Although Bulgaria gained autocephalous recognition by Constantinople as early as A.D. 927, it wasn't until the nationalist movements of the 19th century when Istanbul's Bulgarian community was granted their own church. The first church was a small wooden one erected in 1849. As with all too many wooden structures in the city, it succumbed to a fire. The replacement had to be both fire resistant and appropriate for the weakness of the soil. In the end, plans for a cast iron cathedral were drawn, and the church was produced, piece by piece, in Vienna and shipped down the Danube and through the Black Sea in sections. The result is a stunning, 500-ton Neo-Gothic slab of iron affixed to a steel frame. A visit to the upper gallery will get you a close-up of the deceptively ornate workmanship—even at 6 inches of distance, the columns, pilasters, and frieze seem as if they were carved wood.

Mürselpaşa Cad. 85, Balat. No phone. Daily 9am–5pm. Ferry: Fener; bus: 36CE, 399B, 399C, 399D, 44B, 55T, 99, or 99A from Eminönü.

Tekfur Sarayı (Byzantine Palace)   Save for the crumbled stones of a handful of dungeons and towers, this is all that remains of the palace complex of Blachernae, and one of the few secular Byzantine buildings that remain, comparatively, intact. It is hard to imagine the opulence of the palace at its zenith; however, one could hazard a guess if it's true that the Stonemaker's Diamond—the one in the Topkapı Treasury—was found in the rubble here. The building is usually identified as the Palace of Constantine Porphyrogenitus and dated to the 13th century. Typical of Byzantine construction, the palace walls are made of alternating brick and marble.

Şişhane Cad., Ayvansaray (along the land walls). No phone. Closed for restoration, but you can wander around the exterior. Ferry: Fener; bus: 36CE, 399B, 399C, 399D, 44B, 55T, 99, or 99A from Eminönü.

AYAKAPI & CIBALI

Aya Nikola Kilisesi   The waterfront location of St. Nicholas is an appropriate one for a basilica dedicated to the patron saint of mariners and children. It dates at least to 1538, the year in which the Patriarch of Jerusalem makes mention of it. The current basilica, which was constructed in the courtyard of the ruins of the earlier church, dates only to 1837. It served as the metochion to the Vatopedi Monastery of Mt. Athos (Aynaroz in Turkish or Agion Ores in Greek). The feast of St. Nicholas is celebrated here every December 6.

Abdülezel Pasa Cad. 255, Ayakapı. (℃ 0212-521-2602. Ferry: Fener; bus: 36CE, 399B, 399C, 399D, 44B, 55T, 99, or 99A from Eminönü.

Gül Camii   According to tradition, this Byzantine church is a 9th-century-A.D. construction that housed the holy relics of St. Theodosia, an 8th-century-A.D. nun who was tortured and then martyred defending a sacred icon of Christ set into Constantinople's bronze gate. As the resting place for the saint's bones, the church became a point of pilgrimage, as the relics were believed to have healing powers.

In fact, the church is alternatively thought to be that of Saint Euphemia, Saint Theodosia, and Eurgetis Monastery, and indeed the entire affair dates only to the 12th century. To complicate the legend, Catholic sources question the entire validity of St. Theodosia's martyrdom.

The cellar of the church was used as a shipyard warehouse immediately after the conquest and was converted into a mosque in the 16th century. The interior is a bit whitewashed and dreary. There is a tomb to the right of the *mimbar* inscribed as "One of Jesus's Companions, the Apostle"; one tradition places the tomb of Constantine XI Dragases, last Emperor of Byzantium, here while locals believe that it is the tomb of "Gül Baba."

Ayakapı Mah., Vakıf Mektebi Sok., Ayakapı. No phone. The caretaker's quarters are to the left of the entrance; ring the doorbell for entry during typical business hours. Ferry: Fener; bus: 36CE, 399B, 399C, 399D, 44B, 55T, 99, or 99A from Eminönü.

10 Beyoğlu
GALATASARAY, TÜNEL & TEPEBAŞI

Balıkpazarı (Galatasaray Fish Market)   This fish market is a colorful cluster of much more than just fishmongers. Having just undergone a period of restoration (which in my opinion whitewashed some of the charm out), it also contains *dükkan* (small grocers), souvenir sellers, restaurants, tempting *tantuni* joints (fast-food sellers of fried spiced beef), and other must-try street food vendors. I'm a bit anxious that eventually it will homogenize into just another outdoor shopping mall, but let's just cross our fingers and not get ahead of ourselves.

Running perpendicular to Şahne Tiyatro Sokağı are three very picturesque alleys as well as an unobtrusive Armenian Church. The **Üc Horon Ermeni Kilisesi** (also called the Surp Yerrortuyan, both meaning Holy Trinity; Balıkpazarı 24Ab/6r) is a working church and the largest Armenian Church in Istanbul. It dates to 1838.

To the right of Şahne Tiyatro Sokağı is **Nevişade Street,** a narrow cobbled mews overflowing with traditional *meyhanes.* One can barely squeeze by on a summer's eve, which makes it half the fun. Try to nab a seat on the upper balconies (or roof terraces) if you can; these are often closed from October through April. From Şahne Tiyatro Sokağı branch off the quieter Duduodalar Street and the **Avrupa Pasajı.** The Avrupa, or European Passage, used to be reveted in mirrors designed to enhance the light emitted by the then-gas lamps, and thus was formerly called the Aynalı Pasajı or Mirrored Arcade. Here is a pleasing mixture of high-end antiques sellers, Anatolian textile boutiques, and down-market souvenir shops.

İstiklal Cad., opposite the Galatasaray Lisesi (near Mesrutiyet Cad.). No phone. Daily dawn to dusk. Restaurants open until late. Nostalgic tram; Tünel from Karaköy.

Çiçek Pasajı (Flower Passage) An icon of Beyoğlu's past and present, the Çiçek Pasajı occupies a stunning rococo arcade, the original of which dates to 1876. It was constructed as a bazaar and apartment building shortly after the 1870 Beyoğlu fire, when it soon became known as the Cité de Pera. After World War I, Russian aristocrats settled in alongside the cluster of florists and thus the building acquired its present name. This is also where the tradition of tables spilling out onto the street got started. The entire affair collapsed in 1978 due to neglect but was reconstructed a decade later. Today the soaring space teems with *meyhanes* and beer halls, staffed by a collection of eager, competing, and vociferous waitstaff. The arcade follows an "L" shape with the long portion running parallel to the adjacent Şahne Sokağı, better known by the name of the merchandise sold here: fish (see "Balıkpazarı," above).

İstiklal Cad., opposite the Galatasaray Lisesi (near Meşrutiyet Cad.). No phone. Daily dawn to dusk. Restaurants open until late. Nostalgic tram; Tünel from Karaköy.

Galata Mevlevihanesi This derviş lodge, now a museum, was once one of the most important derviş lodges in Istanbul. The lodge was built on the hunting farm of Iskender Paşa, governor of the province under Sultan Beyazit II, in 1491, but while it is the oldest surviving *tekke* in the city, the buildings on-site date to the period after the 1776 fire. The *tekke* is comprised of a *semahane* (ritual hall), derviş cells, library, *sebil* (fountain), kitchen, *türbe,* and cemetery.

The octagonal wooden *semahane,* built in the baroque style of the 18th century, is used as a museum for the display of musical instruments, manuscripts, and other items related to the culture of the sect. One of the more notable residents of the cemetery is Kumbaracı Ahmet Paşa, né Claude Alexandre Bonneval (later Count) in France under the reign of Louis IV. His military career, while distinguished, was punctuated by repeated upheaval; eventually, he offered his services to the Sultan, after which he changed his name to Ahmed and converted to Islam. He swiftly rose in the ranks to Paşa and served the sultan until he died in Istanbul in 1747.

Galip Dede Cad. 15, Tünel. (C) 0212/245-2121. Wed–Mon 9am–4pm. Nostalgic tram; Tünel from Karaköy.

Galatasaray High School (Galatasaray Lisesi) The school's origins date back to the 15th century, when on a hunting expedition in the area, then a thickly wooded forest, Sultan Beyazit II came upon an old man who had fought in the siege of Istanbul in 1453. At the end of this encounter, the man presented the sultan with one red and one yellow rose from his garden (the colors of the Galatasaray soccer team) and requested that a house of learning be built on the spot. The school was founded in 1481 as Galata Sarayı, the fourth of a network of existing palace schools. During the era of the Tanzimat, the school became a window onto the West, and much of Turkish-French relations have their origins here.

> ⌒ *Value* **See the Whirling Dervişes**
>
> The **Sufi Music Concert & Sema Ceremony** (ceremony of the Whirling Dervishes) ✦✦✦ is held on the second and last Sunday of the month at the historic Galata Mevlevihanesi, Divan Edebiyatı Müzesi, Galip Dede Caddesi, at the end of Istiklal Caddesi in Tünel (Ticket office: ℭ **0535/210-4565;** foundation office: ℭ **0542/422-1544;** www.emav.org). From October to April, the ceremony is at 3pm; from May to September it's at 5pm. Go early for a front-row seat in this finely decorated octagonal hall. If you miss this one, an alternative concert of Sufi Music and a Sema ceremony take place every Monday and Thursday at 7:30pm in the open hall off platform no. 1 in the Sirkeci train station (ℭ **0212/458-8834**). Tickets are 30YTL ($26/£11); both ceremonies last about an hour. (*Note:* Please call ahead to confirm showings, as schedules do change.)

For the past 500 years, Galatasaray High School has graduated grand viziers and palace administrators, and later, prime ministers, poets, artists, and journalists. Even today, the high school continues to set the standards of learning for all of Turkey.

Istiklal Cad., across from the Galatasaray Fish Market (Balıkpazarı). ℭ 0212/244-3666 or 0212/249-6698. Open with prior permission from the management. Nostalgic tram; Tünel from Karaköy.

Military Museum ✦✦ *Value*   Feared, respected, and loathed for 500 years, the Ottoman warrior was the brick on which the Ottoman dynasty was built. Indeed, it was the rising influence of industry and economics over combat and conquest that contributed to the ultimate downfall of the empire. Since war plays a pivotal role in the history and culture of Turkey, no visit to Turkey would be complete without a stopover at the Military Museum. Most people breeze through without a sideways glance, hurriedly following the arrows that direct visitors to the **Mehter Concert** ✦✦✦. This startlingly powerful musical performance re-creates the traditional military band of the Janissaries, the elite Ottoman corps abolished when their power became too great. The musical arrangement is an unexpectedly organized cacophony of sounds that, preceding the approaching army, also served to instill terror in the opposing army.

The exhibit, housed in the former military academy where Atatürk received his education (the building was converted into a museum in 1993), contains a chronological and functional assemblage of artifacts of warfare from the Ottoman era through World War II. The exhibit is anything but dull, showcasing chain mail and bronze armor for both cavalry and horses, leather and metalwork costumes, handsewn leather and arrow bags, swords engraved with fruit and flower motifs or Islamic inscriptions, and even a petroleum-driven rifle. Not to be missed is the hall of tents, an unanticipated display of *in situ* elaborately embroidered and silk encampment tents used on war expeditions.

Askeri Müse ve Kültür Sitesi Komutanlığı, Harbiye (about .8km/½ mile north of Taksim along Cumhuriyet Cad.). ℭ 0212/233-2720. Admission 1.50YTL ($1.30/76p). Wed–Sun 9am–5pm. *Mehter* concert 3pm (English) and 3:30pm (Turkish).

Pera Museum   Located on five floors in the heart of Old Pera, the Pera Museum houses a small but solid collection of Kütahya ceramics, Ottoman weights and measures, and Ottoman portraiture from the 18th to the 20th centuries rarely seen outside of Turkey. The portraits alone are worth the price of admission, and a quick lap around the museum can be accomplished in an hour, if you really try hard.

Meşrutiyet Cad. 141, Beyoğlu. ✆ 0212/334-9900. www.pm.org.tr. Admission 7YTL ($6.10/£2.70). Tues–Sat 10am–7pm; Sun 12–6pm. Nostalgic tram; Tünel from Karaköy; bus: 325YK2, 32T, 35C, 54E, 54HŞ, 54HT, 61B, 69A, 71T, 72T, 74, 74A, 76T, 77MT, 80T, 83, 87, 93T, 96T, E50, E51, or E52.

Tünel Pasajı   This highly evocative arcade is formed by the convergence of three separate buildings. The style is neoclassical, but the dates of construction are unknown. The antiques shops and ateliers occupying the spaces are slowly but surely giving way to modish cafés and restaurants (House Café is on the far corner), but some might say that this enhances the spaces utility.

Tünel, opposite the upper entrance to the Tünel Funicular. Nostalgic Tram; Tünel from Karaköy.

GALATA & KARAKÖY

Arap Camii (Arab Mosque)   Several stories compete in regards to the origins of this building. According to one source, the mosque dates to the Arab siege of A.D. 718, after which it was converted by Dominican Friars into a church. According to John Freely, author of the heavily researched *Strolling through Istanbul,* the building was constructed by the Dominicans between 1323 and 1337. The building has undergone quite a bit of repair and additions; it is now once again (if one believes the earlier version) a mosque topped by a belfry/minaret, with an interior courtyard and şadirvan (fountain).

Fütühat Sok., Karaköy. No phone. Open daily at prayer times only. Tram: Karaköy; Tünel to Karaköy; IDO Ferry from Kadıköy; bus: 28, 28T, 30D, 35, 74, 74A, 80, 910, or 99A.

Church of SS. Peter and Paul   Secreted behind an unobtrusive pink and purple gate is a Dominican church built in 1604 by the Genoese. The church was destroyed twice by fire then was rebuilt by the renowned Fossati brothers from 1841 to 1843. The exterior of the church—essentially a narrow alleyway enclosed by high walls—is covered in inscriptions. The main treasure of the church is the famous icon of Mary Odighitria (the guide). According to tradition, Luke himself painted the icon. Although its authenticity has never been proven, this seems unimportant to those who gaze upon it. At the back of the church is a well-preserved section of the original Genoese defensive walls.

Galata Kulesi Sok. (also written as Kuledibi) 44 (just down the steep hill from Galata House restaurant on the right where the street curves), Galata. ✆ 0212/249-2385. Mon–Sat 7am–5pm; Sun 10:30am–noon. Ring the doorbell. Tram: Karaköy; Tünel to Karaköy; IDO Ferry from Kadıköy; bus: 28, 28T, 30D, 35, 74, 74A, 80, 910, or 99A.

Yeraltı Camii (Underground Mosque)   This eerie underground mosque occupies the crypt of a former castle that was probably associated with the Castle of Galata. Tradition has it that the colossal chain used to blockade ships from entering the Golden Horn was anchored here. What remained of the ruins (the castle was destroyed during the Ottoman conquest) was converted into a mosque. The space is created by a low-ceilinged, vaulted maze supported by squat pillars. The columns are arranged in six rows of nine, forming little compartments for private prayer. Located in a side chapel are the tombs of two sainted Arab warriors killed in the first Arab siege. The location of these graves was revealed to a Nakşibendi derviş in a dream in 1640. It wasn't until later, in 1757, that the cellar space was converted into a mosque. It is also known as the Kursunlu Mahzen Camii (Gunpowder Warehouse Mosque).

Karantina Sok., Karaköy. No phone. Tram: Karaköy; Tünel to Karaköy; IDO Ferry from Kadıköy; bus: 28, 28T, 30D, 35, 74, 74A, 80, 910, or 99A.

TAKSIM

Atatürk Kültür Merkezi (Atatürk Cultural Center) There is talk of tearing this monstrosity down, but apparently the building has its defenders, if the level of dissent is any indication. The building dates to 1969 although a fire in 1970 required it to undergo significant repairs. The center houses the State Opera and Ballet, a theater company, and an exhibition gallery.

Taksim Square. ✆ 0212/251-5600. Tram: Kabataş; Funicular: Taksim; Nostalgic Tram: Taksim; Metro: Taksim; bus: 25T, 35C, 40, 54HT, 55T, 61B, 80T, 87, 93T, 96T, 559C, or E50.

Aya Triada Ermeni Katolik Kilisesi The striking presence above Taksim Square of the dome/semi-domes of this Armenian Catholic Church was quite revolutionary when the church was built in 1880. Under Ottoman rule, domes were prohibited for use in non-Muslim places of worship. But that all changed during the Tanzimat reforms. The church, which is still in use, is the largest Eastern Orthodox Church in Istanbul. The facade features two symmetrical clock towers, best admired from inside the expansive garden courtyard, where the space is shared with a number of domesticated farm animals and friendly feral cats.

Meşelik Sok., Kurabiye Sok. 2 (next to the side entrance to Hacı Baba Restaurant), Taksim. ✆ 0212/244-1358. Open for Sun mass. Off hours, knock and a caretaker may let you in. Tram: Kabataş; Funicular: Taksim; Nostalgic Tram: Taksim; Metro: Taksim; bus: 25T, 35C, 40, 54HT, 55T, 61B, 80T, 87, 93T, 96T, 559C, or E50.

Cumhuriyet Anıtı/Republican Monument Punctuating the entrance to Istiklal Caddesi (which means "Independence Street") is this monument to the republic. The sculpture, created by the Italian sculptor Pietro Canonica, symbolizes the War of Independence on one side. The opposite side is a representation of the Republic of Turkey. The monument was erected here in 1928 inside an arched foundation designed by Istanbul-born architect Gulio Mongeri.

Taksim Square. Tram: Kabataş; Funicular: Taksim; Nostalgic Tram: Taksim; Metro: Taksim; bus: 25T, 35C, 40, 54HT, 55T, 61B, 80T, 87, 93T, 96T, 559C, or E50.

St. Antoine Italyan Katolik Kilisesi (Italian Catholic Church) Also known as St. Anthony of Padua Franciscan Church, St. Antoine is a spectacular example of Italian neo-Gothic building, dating to 1913. The congregation was established in 1725 in Perşembe Pazarı, in Karaköy, and moved to this spot that same century. Giulio Mongeri, the Istanbul-born architect who created the foundation for the Republican Monument in Taksim Square, laid the foundations for the church in 1906. The church draws standing room only crowds at Christmastime.

Istiklal Cad. ✆ 0212/244-0935. Daily prayer times are posted outside (currently English Mass is held Sat 10am and weekdays 8am and 7pm). Tram: Kabataş; Funicular: Taksim; Nostalgic Tram; Metro: Taksim; bus: 25T, 35C, 40, 54HT, 55T, 61B, 80T, 87, 93T, 96T, 559C, or E50.

Taksim Maksemi (Water Distribution) As the first major building to grace Taksim Square, Istanbul's nucleus derives its very name from this octagonal building at the southwest corner of the square. Built by Sultan Mahmut I (1732–33) as a water collection and distribution center for water brought in from reservoirs in the Belgrade Forest, the building is being restored and transformed into the Republic Museum (to open, perhaps, on Republican Day, Oct 29, 2008) and will chronicle, in an area of about 1,000 sq. m (10,765 sq. ft.), Istanbul's contribution to the Republican period.

Taksim Square. For information, contact the Istanbul Greater Municipality. ✆ 0212/455-1300. Tram: Kabataş; Funicular: Taksim; Nostalgic Tram: Taksim; Metro: Taksim; bus: 25T, 35C, 40, 54HT, 55T, 61B, 80T, 87, 93T, 96T, 559C, or E50.

BEŞIKTAŞ

Naval Museum (Deniz Müzesi) *Kids*   Kids of all ages will be enchanted by this collection of original and model warships, navigational devices, and other tools particular to a naval culture. Keep an eye out for the VIP cabin of the Ertuğrul, used by Atatürk between 1925 and 1937, and a section of the iron chain used in the failed defense of the city, pre-Ottoman conquest. Barbarosa's standard is displayed in a case on the upper floor of the main building, embroidered with a trifecta of religious symbols (the Trinity, the Star of David, and the names of the first four Caliphs) to emphasize the Ottoman reign (or protection) over all three. A copy of Pirit Reis's map of North America, drawn in the first half of the 15th century, is also here, while the original is housed in Topkapı Palace. In the outbuilding at the back of the museum courtyard is a gallery housing a staggering collection of imperial caïques where you'll find original, and highly ornamental, wooden Sultans' caïques, including the *pièce de résistance:* a 40m (131-ft.) long, 5.7m (19-ft.) wide-beamed boat inlaid with nacre, tortoise shell, and ivory (so much for animal welfare)—the only original two-masted galley still in existence.

Hayrettin Iskelesi Sok. (at the Beşiktaş ferry landing), Beşiktaş. ℂ **0212/327-4346.** Wed–Sun 9am–12:30pm and 1:30–5pm. Admission 3YTL ($2.60/£1.10). IDO ferry: from Kadıköy or Üsküdar; bus: 22, 22RE, 25E, 25T, 27E, 28, 28O, 28T, 30A, 30D, 30M, 40, 40B, 40T, 43R, 559C, 57UL, 58N, 58UL, 62, 110, or 112.

SIGHTS ALONG THE BOSPHORUS

For over 2,500 years, kings and commanders have confronted the challenge of the Bosphorus, building rudimentary bridges out of boats and floating jetties to increase the size of their empires. Mandrokles of Samos crossed on huge connecting floats in 512 B.C. Persian Emperor Xerxes built a temporary bridge, as did Heraclius I of Byzantium, who crossed a chain of pontoons on horseback. Now that several bridges connect the shores of Europe and Asia, staying on the water has become more fashionable than actually crossing it. The shores are dotted with *yalıs,* or classic waterfront mansions, built as early as the 18th century: yellow, pink, and blue wooden palaces perched along the waterfront. The surrounding neighborhoods (best visited by land) retain much of their characteristic village feel, in stark contrast to the restored homes inhabited by the likes of ex-Prime Minister Tansu Çillar.

Cruising up the straits is a bit easier these days than when Jason and the Argonauts sailed through in search of the Golden Fleece. A number of local tour companies organize daylong or half-day boat cruises up the Bosphorus on private boats, often with a stop at the Rumeli Fortress and visits to Beylerbeyi Sarayı. Unless you've gotten a guarantee that the tour will *not* wind up on one of the public ferries, skip the tour and hop on one of the less-pristine (but serviceable) city ferries and go the route yourself.

A one-way ticket on the **Istanbul Deniz Otobüsleri** ferry (IDO; ℂ **0212/444-4436** toll-free in Istanbul; www.ido.com.tr) costs 7YTL ($6.10/£2.70). The last stop at **Sarıyer** is the most visited—and therefore most touristy, but the potential for a side trip to the **Sadberk Hanım Museum** (Büyükdere Cad. 27–29, Sarıyer; ℂ **0212/242-3813;** Thurs–Tues 10am–5pm; admission 6YTL/$8.10/£4.30) continues to make this disembarkation point one of the most popular. The museum, located in an old Ottoman house overlooking a section of the Bosphorus that was an old dockyard, houses a limited but excellent collection of artifacts representative of the progression of civilizations in Anatolia. If you're already up here, then it's worth a look; otherwise, you'll get a more comprehensive presentation of the same themes at the Museum of Anatolian Civilizations in Ankara.

A lesser appreciated alternative is to get off at **Anadolu Kavağı** instead, hike up the hill to the "Crusader's Castle"—named for a carved cross decoration dating to the crusader invasion but actually a Byzantine structure used as a Genoese Palace in the 14th century—and enjoy outstanding views of the European side.

The trip by sea from Eminönü (departures at 10:35am, winter only, and 1:35pm; the ferry makes a stop in Beşiktaş approximately 15 min. later) to the last stop at Anadolu Kavağı takes 2 hours (allow 6 hr. for the full round-trip excursion), with only two return departures leaving at 3 and 5pm. This schedule pretty much restricts the amount of jumping on and off you can realistically do in 1 day. Alternatively, you can take an IDO commuter ferry from any of a number of wharfs around the city to the destination on the Bosphorus of your choice for 1.30YTL/$1.15/50p.

Leander's Tower (the Maiden's Tower or Kız Kulesi)   Rising from a rock at the mouth of the Bosphorus is the Kız Kulesi, built by Ibrahim Paşa in 1719 over the remains of a fortress built by Mehmet the Conqueror and of the earliest original building constructed on the rock by Byzantine Emperor Manuel Comnenus I. The romance of the tower finds its root in an ancient myth along the lines of Romeo and Juliet: boy (Leander) falls in love with girl (the Aphrodite Priestess Hero); boy drowns swimming to meet girl; girl finds lover's corpse; girl commits suicide. The story originated around the Dardanelles, but was too juicy not to attach to this solitary tower. Legend also has it that the tower was connected to the mainland by way of an underwater tunnel, and that there used to be a wall between the tower and the shore—a rumor not altogether implausible considering that, according to a 19th-century historian, the remains of a wall could be seen in calm water.

Since as early as the 1600s, the tower has been used as a prison and a quarantine hospital. The tower is currently in service as a panoramic restaurant and tea lounge. Take advantage of the free shuttle over and get the chance both to visit the tower and enjoy a (pricey!) romantic meal, but be sure to book well ahead (© **0212/727-4095;** info@kizkulesi.com.tr).

Slightly offshore south of Üsküdar, on the Asian side. Ferry from Kabataş (7:15pm, 7:45pm, 8:30pm, 10pm; return at 11pm, midnight, 1am, 1:30am). Ferry service from Salacak Sat–Sun 9:30am–6pm; Mon–Fri 12:30–6pm (3.50€/$4.90/£2.15); ferries are less frequent at night (2.90€/$4.20/£2.10). Ferry from Ortaköy Mon–Fri every hour between 1pm and 4pm; Sat–Sun 10:30am and 11:30am. Ferry from Kabataş Sat–Sun 9:15am, 10am, and 10:45am (2.30€/$3/£1.60).

Rumeli Fortress (Rumeli Hisarı)   This citadel was built by Mehmet the Conqueror across from the Anatolia Fortress (Anadolu Hisarı) in preparation for what was to be the seventh and final Ottoman siege of the fortified Byzantine city. Constructed in only 4 months, the fortress served to cut off Black Sea traffic in and out of the city, together with the Anadolu Hisarı built by his great-grandfather across the Bosphorus on the Asian shores. The Ottoman army eventually penetrated the city by carrying the Turkish galleons over land by way of a sled and pulley system, and dropping them into the Golden Horn and behind the city's defenses.

Tarabya Yeniköy Cad. north of Sarıyer (some ferries make the stop at Rumeli Kavağı; otherwise, get off at Sarıyer and take a *dolmuş* the rest of the way). © **0212/263-5305.** 4YTL ($3.50/£1.50). Tues–Sun 9am–5pm. Bus: 25E or 40.

Sabancı Museum in Emirgan   A favorite of Istanbul's educated class is the private fine arts museum of Sabancı University. The building, which sits high above a sloping lawn on the upper Bosphorus, began its long journey into the 21st century as the private residence of Ismael Paşa, *Khedive,* or governor, of Egypt. Throughout the 19th century and into the early 20th, it served as the embassy of Karadağ until the khedive's grandson, Prince Mehmet Ali Hassan brought it back into his family in 1923. In 1951, the patriarch of the Sabancı dynasty, Hacı Ömer, acquired the property and added the bronze statue of a horse as an advance guard. (It is popularly known as the Atlı Kösk, or Horse Pavilion; I had no knowledge of this when I started calling it the Horse House several years ago.)

Although it opened in 2002, the hosting of three extremely high profile (and expertly marketed) exhibits put it squarely on the international map. These were exhibitions of works by Picasso and Rodin and an installation commemorating the 800-year anniversary of Genghis Khan. But the permanent collection of Ottoman and Turkish fine arts itself is enough to entice all but a casual, crunched-for-time visitor to Istanbul (it's about a 30-min. bus ride from Taksim). Priceless Chinese, French, and German porcelains, calligraphic items spanning 500 years of Ottoman art, paintings and portraiture (special attention to those by Osman Hamdi), and historical photographs fill the expanses. There's also a section on decorative arts and furniture, and one featuring ornamental marble and stone sculptures.

Sakıp Sabancı Cad. 22, Emirgan. ⓒ **0212/277-2200.** Tues–Fri 10am–6pm; Sat–Sun 11am–5pm. Admission 10YTL ($8.70/£3.80). Bus: 22, 22RE, 25E, 40, 40T, or 42T to Çinaraltı.

11 The Asian Side

ÜSKÜDAR

Chrysopolis (City of Gold) was a suburb of ancient Calcedonia (modern Kadıköy). Its history parallels that of Byzantium, but because it was geographically vulnerable to a long parade of armies with ambition, none of the monuments to this era remain.

Chrysopolis was the site of Constantine's final and victorious battle over Licinius in A.D. 324. The city fell to the Persians in A.D. 626, and in turn to the Arabs in A.D. 710 and 782, but none of these raiding armies succeeded in taking Constantinople, protected behind high defensive walls on the other side of the Bosphorus. Later, it was from here in 1204 that the Crusaders launched their successful attack on the city.

After retaking Constantinople, several Byzantine emperors were forced to hunker down here in the palace of Scutarion (from Scutarion, it's not a far journey until you get the name Üsküdar), the location of which remains unknown. Today, Üsküdar is a commercial and residential suburb of Istanbul, mostly populated by conservative-minded Turks drawn to the density of mosques located here. During Ottoman times, the main Square of the Falconers was the departure point for the imperial caravan as it set out on its annual pilgrimage to Mecca. The sights selected for inclusion here are the bare-bones highlights of the neighborhood and are all within easy reach of the Üsküdar ferry landing.

Çinili Camii   This mosque was built for the Valide Sultan Kösem, mother of Murat IV, in 1640. This simple square-planned mosque is entirely reveted, both inside and out, in precious Iznik tiles. The porch and minaret are baroque additions.

At the corner of Çinili Mescit Sok. and Çavuşdere Cad. IDO ferry: from Karaköy to Kadıköy or from Beşiktaş or Eminönü to Üsküdar, and then bus no. 110, 120, 127, 12A, 13, 13B, 14, 14D, 15F, or 500A.

Mihrimah Camii aka Iskele Camii or Mihrimah Sultan Camii   Sinan was around 40 years old when he built this mosque complex for Mihrimah Sultan, the daughter of Süleyman the Magnificent and wife of Rüstem Paşa. It was his second imperial commission after becoming Chief Architect, a post he earned thanks to the great civil engineering works he created while serving in the Ottoman army. In the design of the mosque, Sinan reinterpreted the theme of the square-based plan surmounted by a single dome by transferring the weight-bearing responsibilities from the four walls to an innovative system comprised of four arches and four pendatives. The central dome of the mosque is supported not by two or four semi-domes, but three. This transfer of weight freed the walls to sustain a lacework of rosette and arched windows, allowing a flood of light into the interior space. The baroque-style minaret dates to the 19th century. At the base of the mosque is another baroque work, the monumental Ahmet II Fountain, built in 1728 by Sultan Ahmet III for his mother, who is buried in Üsküdar. A calligraphic poem by the sultan is inscribed on the side facing the sea, with his signature below.

Üsküdar ferry landing. No phone. IDO ferry: from Beşiktaş or Eminönü.

Selimiye Barracks/Florence Nightingale Museum   Security is stiff at the First Army Command Post headquarters, so a visit to the building's main attraction, the Florence Nightingale Museum, won't be easy. The museum is located in the North Tower (although no one is certain which of the two towers actually housed her rooms) and commemorates the aid and comfort she and her nurses gave, in the face of demoralizing mortality rates, to the wounded and dying British soldiers of the Crimean War. The building itself is unremarkable although it has a strong presence—an elongated rectangle punctuated with two towers. It was constructed by Mahmut II to house the new troops he intended to take the place of the overly dominant and rebellious Janissary Corps. Adjacent to the barracks is a small mosque built by Selim III (an earlier wooden barracks preceded the one that Mahmut II built).

Selimiye Kislası Haydarpaşa. ℂ 0216/343-7310. Appointments must be made at least 48 hr. in advance for visits Mon–Fri 9am–4pm. Free admission. IDO ferry: from Karaköy to Kadıköy.

New Music Museum in Üsküdar *(Finds*   Watch this space for the inauguration of Turkey's first Music Museum, designed to chronicle the history and development of Turkish music, from classical, fold, sufi, *mehter,* symphonic, and contemporary. Instruments such as the *kanun, oud,* and *bağlama,* and other materials (including audio and video) were collected from places like Topkapı Palace and the Mevlana Museum in Konya, and will be on display here.

In the Tekel Deposu/Warehouse. Paşalimanı Cad., Üsküdar. Opening 2008. IDO ferry: from Beşiktaş or Eminönü.

Moments **Yogurt of the Gods**

It's a long way to go for a cup of yogurt, but I'm glad (after several years of pining) I did. The **Tarıhı Kanlıca Yoğurdu** has been churning out this creamy ambrosia since 1893. For 2.75YTL ($2.40/£1.30), you can get a 200-gram (a small) serving; sprinkle some confectionary sugar atop each bite for a decadent (or healthy, depending on how you look at it) treat. Open daily 8am to 11pm.

Hop on the Bosphorus cruise boat at Eminönü (departures at 10:35am and 1:35pm in summer) or at any stop along the route on its way up the Bosphоrus. (See p. 171 for departure times or www.ido.com.tr.) Or take a ferry from Eminönü, Karaköy, or Beşiktaş to Üsküdar and take bus no. 15 or 15P north along the Bosphorus road to Kanlıca.

12 Special-Interest Sights

LIBRARIES & CULTURAL CENTERS

The British Council, Posta Kutusu, Beşiktaş (© **0212/355-5657;** www.britishcouncil.
org.tr; Tues–Fri 10am–5pm, Sat 9:30am–2:30pm), is one of a global network of
British Councils working to connect people with learning opportunities and creative
ideas from the U.K. via courses in English, educational exchange, and special events.
The library is one of the best resources for multilingual information on antiquities in
Turkey, as well as a great reference center for translations of Turkish literary works.
They have a huge collection of English-language books, in addition to CDs, music,
and videos. The center is popular with students of the English language. Its American
counterpart is the **American Research Institute in Turkey** (Üvez Sok. 5, Arnavutköy;
© **0212/257-8111;** Mon–Fri 9:30am–6pm).

For books and historical documents on Istanbul, the Turkish Touring and Automobile Club runs the **Istanbul Library,** located in one of the old Ottoman houses it
restored on Soğukçeşme Sokagı in Sultanahmet (© **0212/512-5730;** Mon–Fri 9am–
noon; 1:30–5pm).

In a forgotten ancient building across from the Fener jetty on the Golden Horn is
the **Women's Library** (Kadın Eserleri Kütüphanesi; © **0212/534-9550;** Mon–Fri
10:30am–6:30pm; closed for religious holidays). Founded by Füsun Akatlı, a
renowned Turkish writer, the library has grown into a collection of materials—mostly
in Turkish—featuring female artists, photographers, directors, and artisans. There's
also a section on women in Istanbul and on women in Ottoman dress. (Entrance will
require you to show your passport.)

The **Istanbul Archaeology Museum** (p. 125) has a library of over 60,000 volumes
on archaeology and will be opened upon request. Two other archaeology centric
research centers are at the **Dutch History and Archaeology Institute Library** (Istiklal Cad. 393; © **0212/293-9283**) and the **German Archaeology Institute Library**
(Ayazpaşa Cami Sok. 48, Gümüşsuyu; © **0212/244-0714**).

ESPECIALLY FOR KIDS

Even though Turks are notorious pushovers for their children, Istanbul isn't really a
kid-friendly destination; even the most privileged and well-educated children will get
bored trudging around the recesses of ancient Byzantium. Istanbul does have a series
of kid-related cultural events, though, including the **Rahmi M. Koç Museum**
(Hasköy Cad. 27; © **0212/297-6639;** www.rmk-museum.org.tr/english), a hands-on
series of exhibitions a la the Smithsonian showcasing the history of human ingenuity
in the areas of transportation, industry, and communications. The transparent washing machines, carburetors, decommissioned submarine bridge, trains, and aircraft will
definitely push the buttons of any preteen boy (and then some) and are definitely
worth a visit. Admission is 8YTL ($7/£3) for adults, 4YTL ($3.50/£1.50) for students, plus an additional $4.50YTL ($3.95/£1.70), 3YTL ($2.60/£1.15) students, for
entry to the (formerly free and currently overpriced) submarine exhibit. The museum
is open Tuesday to Friday, 10am to 5pm, Saturday and Sunday, 10am to 7pm.

Miniaturk (Imrahor Cad. Sütlüce on the eastern banks of the Golden Horn opposite Eyüp; © **0212/222-2882;** www.miniaturk.com.tr), which opened in 2003, is an
open-air mini-museum sprouting models of Turkey's most-loved monuments reconstructed here at 1/25th of their actual size. The park is open from 9am to 5pm in winter, later in summer. Admission is 10YTL ($8.70/£3.80).

SPECTATOR SPORTS

To say that **soccer** is a popular national sport in Turkey is to miss the point entirely. Soccer is closer to a religious experience; club rivalries are waged with an intensity comparable to the holy wars.

The three main soccer clubs in Istanbul are **Fenerbahçe, Beşiktaş,** and **Galatasaray.** Main matches are played nights at 7pm from late August to May. (A few late summer matches are played at 8pm.) Home matches are played every other week at **Inönü Stadium,** above Dolmabahçe Palace, for Beşiktaş; at **Alisami Yen,** in Mecidiyeköy, for Galatasaray; and at **Fenerbahçe Stadium,** near Kadıköy on the Asian side, for Fenerbahçe. Tickets run from 50YTL to 350YTL ($44–$305/£19–£133) and are available at the stadium the day of a match, or through **Biletix** (www.biletix.com).

8

Istanbul Strolls

This chapter is designed to accommodate the traveling interests of first-time visitors with limited time as well as those with a bit more flexibility in their schedules, or repeat guests to Istanbul. You might consider the walking tour of Galata as the logical end to a stroll down Istiklal Caddesi, which is for all intents and purposes the outer fringes of the old neighborhood of Galata. As Ottoman Istanbul's original melting pot, Galata is a hybrid mosaic of the various components of Levantine commerce. The second walking tour is a whimsical walk through the streets of the Historic Peninsula. A mainstream walking tour of these neighborhoods seemed beside the point, given that you can't swing a cat without grazing a monumental open-air artifact. Instead, this tour weaves you through streets you may have overlooked, so that on your way to visiting the Byzantine cisterns, vaulted crypts, and ancient foundations of Istanbul underground, it will be possible to hone in on the main attractions as well. Finally, I've created a tour for those interested in going off the proverbial beaten path. While the neighborhoods of Balat and Fener, along the Golden Horn, were built by the Byzantines, traipsed over by the Crusaders, and reinvented by Greeks, Jews, and Ottomans, for decades these narrow streets crumbled into obscurity. Only in recent years has local government and even UNESCO taken interest in the significant cultural and historical sites that compose the walls, floors, markets, and backdrop of today's working-class Muslim neighborhood. On this tour you'll see all the extremes of Istanbul's historic sites: from exquisitely preserved gilded churches and tiled mosques, to restoration works in progress, to piles of rubble of a glorious past.

WALKING TOUR 1	GALATA

Start:	(Upper) Tünel Meydanı
Finish:	(Lower) Tünel Entrance
Time:	90 minutes (about 2km; about 1½ miles)
Best Time:	Any time in full daylight. To bask in the flurry of humanity, approach this tour during morning or evening rush hour. For those wishing to combine the tour with the performance of the Whirling Dervişes at the Galata Mevlevihanesi, you'll have to start the tour at the end and work your way backward, in order to enjoy this walk in full daylight. Although it's pretty safe, you don't really want to be wandering around here at night.
Worst Time:	Any day that it's raining (streets are slippery). Sunday will see Bankalar Sokağı (Voyvoda Caddesi) completely deserted.

A stroll through Galata will take you through one of Istanbul's historically most diverse neighborhoods. This hilly section was once the commercial hub of the Ottoman Empire, thanks to communities of enterprising immigrants from Europe and Armenia who had been granted permission to conduct business here in the 13th century. Although this neighborhood suffered decline and neglect throughout the 20th century, today it is enjoying a revitalization, as sidewalk cafes, art galleries, and small shops pull ever more foot traffic up and down these nostalgic streets.

To save those of you based in the Old City the effort of trekking up the steep streets that lead uphill to the Galata Tower, this walk begins at the entrance to Tünel at the end of Istiklal and works its way down to the Galata Bridge. For those holing up in Beyoğlu or along the Bosphorus, simply make your way down to the Tünel end of Istiklal Caddesi to begin this tour. (For those ready, willing, and even eager to trek uphill, this tour can also be followed from finish to start.)

Begin in the Tünel station.

❶ Metro Han

Our tour begins at the entrance to the world's third-oldest underground train (construction was completed in 1876; only New York's and London's are older). It's actually an underground funicular connecting "Upper Tünel" to the streets at the base of this steeply sloped hill surrounding "Lower Tünel." Locals just call them both Tünel, and you're left to work out which one they mean. With only one stop, this is the world's shortest line, facilitating the commute for more than a century's worth of daily commuters forced to haul themselves up and down the hill you are about to descend on foot.

Outside the entrance to Tünel is the terminus of the **Nostalgic Tramway.** Trolley cars replaced the horse-drawn carriage in Istanbul in 1869. Service connecting Tünel and Taksim was only added a few years later, as part of a much longer tramway line. All of Istanbul's tramways were decommissioned by the mid-1960s, but in 1990, the current system running the length of Istiklal Caddesi was inaugurated. It's practical, touristy, and truly charming: two cars spanning a distance of 1,640m (just over a mile) making 40 trips per day for a total of 23,944km (14,878 miles) per year.

Opposite the entrance to Tünel on the other side of the tramway tracks is the entrance to the Tünel Pasajı, a neoclassical-style arcade enclosed by three separate buildings. The passageway is one of the more atmospheric spots in Beyoğlu, even if the rare book and antiques dealers have ceded to the trendier (and higher grossing) cafes. Facing the entrance to Tünel, go right onto the continuation of Istiklal Cad., now named:

❷ Galip Dede Caddesi

At one time, this street, which goes by its original name of **Yüksek Kaldırım** south of the Galata Tower, wound its way down the slopes of Galata all the way to the Golden Horn. Yüksek Kaldırım, meaning "High Sidewalk," was originally the main bustling thoroughfare of neighborhood Greeks, Armenians, French, Jewish, and Ottoman merchants and a thriving center for publishing and booksellers. The street is (steeply) sloped rather than stepped as it was a hundred years ago—the characteristic cobblestones have been replaced with modern, evenly surfaced bricks, and hardware vendors are being replaced by smarter shops. Yet the essential nostalgia of the street can still be felt through the soul of now-soot-filled buildings standing vigil over a new guard of preoccupied pedestrians. **Librairie de Pera,** one of the oldest booksellers in Istanbul, is located at #22.

A few steps down Galip Dede Cad. on your left is the entrance to the 500-year-old:

❸ Galata Mevlevihanesi

This was the first and most important derviş lodge in Istanbul. If you time your walking tour right (see "See the Whirling Dervişes," in chapter 7), you can immerse yourself in the ritual *sema,* performed by the Lovers of Mevlana Foundation, in the extremely atmospheric octagonal wooden *semahane,* modestly embellished with calligraphy and exhibiting musical instruments, manuscripts, and other items related to the Mevlevi Order. For more on the lodge, turn to p. 166.

As you continue your descent, you will pass dusty shops, the occasional grocer, musical instrument stores, and a few newcomers, including an organic cosmetics store and a gag gift shop called Disturbed People. **Teutonia,** at #85, is the German Club founded in 1847, which served as a Nazi propaganda center during World War II. Today, Teutonia houses a German cultural center with events organized by, among others, the Goethe Institute and the nearby German School.

Continue down Galip Dede Cad. to the junction of Yüksek Kaldırım, and an open plaza.

❹ Galata Meydanı

Galıp Dede Caddesi spills out into the mouth of a small open plaza crowned by the medieval **Galata Tower** and encircled by an almost traffic-free street. The plaza is a brick and concrete living room to the neighborhood, where young boys kick around a football, old men contemplate life while seated on a park bench, stray dogs laze, and locals relax at the tea garden down the steps to the left of the tower.

The origins of Galata Tower date back to the 5th or 6th century A.D., but the tower that stands today is a 14th-century reconstruction by the Genoese, built in appreciation of Michael VIII Palaeologus, who granted special permission to allow them to settle the area of Galata. One condition of the agreement was that the Genoese were prohibited from putting up any defensive walls, a ban they unceremoniously ignored. A short set of partial wraparound steps provide access to the elevator to the top of the tower; admission costs 8YTL ($7/£3), but frankly, the city is so full of vantage points for stunning views that this one isn't a must-see.

TAKE A BREAK
You can stop here for a respite at the enclosed rooftop restaurant of the **Anemon Galata Hotel** (at the base of the tower at Büyükhendek Cad. 11; see p. 77), which has a full menu of Turkish cuisine and a decent wine list, all with a front and center view of the upper stories of the Tower—so close you can even see the imperfections in the tooling. Or, for a more relaxed experience, a further 5 minutes or so on you can also stop in at quirky new corner cafe/patisserie. Stay tuned, below.

Keeping the Anemon Galata Hotel on your left, follow Büyük Hendek Cad. until you approach, on your left:

❺ The Neve Shalom Synagogue

For some reason, Jews visiting Istanbul almost invariably want to see this site, though this is neither the most beautiful nor the only synagogue in town. Greater Istanbul is home to a total of 17 synagogues, many of them open to visitors willing to jump through advance notice security hoops, and Neve Shalom is no exception. To visit, you will have to call in advance and fax over a copy of your passport. Built on the former site of a primary school in the late 1930's to accommodate a growing population of Jews, Neve Shalom's claim to "fame" are three terrorist bombings, on September 6, 1986, March 1, 1992, and November 15, 2003, the latter attack coordinated with attacks on another synagogue, and 5 days later, on the British Consulate and the HSBC Bank. Of the 27 people killed in the attack all but six were congregants. Al Qaeda claimed responsibility soon after the bombings. By the way, Neve Shalom translates as "Oasis of Peace."

Backtrack to the Galata tower and through the plaza and continue straight into the little alley-like Camekan Sok., a characteristic cobbled lane flanked by one or two pre-gentrified bars. Follow Camekan Sok. around to the right and down the sloping street to the next intersection with Bereketzade Camii and Hacı Ali Soks.

1. Metro Han
2. Galip Dede Caddesi
3. Galata Mevlevihanesi
4. Galata Meydanı
   Anemon Galata Hotel
5. The Neve Shalom Synagogue
6. Beyoğlu Hospital
   Galata Konak Patisserie
7. The Camondo House
8. Schneidertempel
9. Camondo Staircase
10. Bereket Han
11. Church of SS. Peter and Paul
12. Voyvoda Caddesi
13. Arap Camii
14. Voyvoda Caddesi, #43-45
15. Ottoman Bank
16. Karaköy Square
17. Jewish Museum of Turkey
    (Zulfaris Museum)

F Funicular Stop

0   200 ft
0   100 m

❻ Beyoğlu Hospital

Founded during the Crimean War by the British Government to care for British seamen, this building was constructed in 1904 and designed by Percy Adams (the architect credited with the design of the Senate House at the University of London). The tower provided a clear sightline to incoming ships, allowing for hospital staff to get advance warning of any major illnesses on board. In 1924, just after the establishment of the Turkish Republic, the British handed the hospital over to the Red Crescent.

TAKE A BREAK
Across the street from the hospital is the **Galata Konak Patisserie** (Hacı Ali Sok.). This is the quirky destination of the style mentioned in the previous "Take A Break": a long and narrow corner shop with a tiny sitting room-cum-salon in the far corner. The bakery case displays a teasing array of fingerlike cookies and delectable pastries.

Exiting the patisserie, turn right. You are now following Hacı Ali Sok. around and down yet another one of Galata's treacherous inclines. About 76m (250 ft.), about ¾ of the way down the street and at the top of the brick staircase is a white building with red trim:

❼ The Camondo House

As a prominent 19th-century Jewish Galata banker, as well as a banker to the

Ottoman government, Avram Camondo, lived in this house. Camondo, who also held Venetian citizenship, was an exceptional philanthropist, and his gifts to Italian charities earned him the title of Count, bestowed upon him by King Victor Emanuel. In his own backyard (that is, in Constantinople), Camondo founded a school in the poorest section of the city. He also established a council to introduce reforms into the administration of the Jewish community, a move that provoked the conservative Jewish establishment to excommunicate him. He eventually died in Paris but was buried in the Camondo family plot in Hasköy (along the Golden Horn). His mansion is now the Galata Residence, a long-stay hotel. (I stayed in the annex above the outdoor staircase and purposely omitted it from this book.) The ruins in front of the building are what's left of the neighborhood *mikva,* the ritual bath serving the Jewish community. The ruins are in a terrible state; it's now a playground and haven for a family of neighborhood cats.

Continue along Felek Sok. with the Camondo House/Galata Residence on your right. Near the end of the street on your left is the:

8 Schneidertempel

When built in 1894 for a working-class and tradesmen community of Ashkenazi Jews, this synagogue was called the Tofre Begadim or Tailor's Synagogue. In 1998, the Ashkenazim Cultural Association converted it into the Schneidertempel Art Center, a gallery for contemporary art exhibits, including Biennial exhibitions. The gallery is open to the public during runs of these art shows.

Turn left and go down the steep Bereketzade Medresesi Sok. (the continuation of Camekan Sok.). The Gaudí-esque staircase at the base of this street is the:

9 Camondo Staircase

Another one of the many structures in the neighborhood built by Avram Camondo,

this staircase provided convenient passage for the banker as he made his way from his home to work on Bankalar Sokağı (Bank Street) at the base of the stairs.

Instead of going down the staircase (you'll return later in this tour), go to your right down Kart Çinar Sok. At the intersection with Galata Kulesi Sok. (also known as Kuledibi) is the back of:

10 Bereket Han

You are standing at the back entrance to probably the most historically significant building in all of Galata. Built in 1316 after the Great Fire of 1315, the Bereket Han occupies the site of the Podestà or Palazzo del Comune—essentially the town hall—of the Genoese community. In the 19th century, the building underwent numerous modifications, including removal of a grand marble entry staircase and portions of the building facing the street—to accommodate the Voyvoda Street (Bankalar Sokağı) tramway. Yet some of the building's earliest elements are still visible: The original rear walls and sections of the side walls are part of the 1316 construction. You can see a small Genoese coat of arms above the rear entrance. Inside is another, though it is thought to be a copy of a pre-existing emblem.

In the Genoese building across the street from Bereket Han is the **Galata Derneği,** a cultural center. If it's open, go up the stairs to the loft beneath a hidden treasure—a restored brick vaulted ceiling.

Back on the street, turn right and haul yourself up the steep incline. Just up the street on your left, in a little crook in the sidewalk, is the pink-and-purple doorway and entrance to the:

11 Church of SS. Peter and Paul

Knock on the door and the caretaker will let you in. See p. 168 for more on this Franciscan church. Up the hill a few steps on your right is the Old English Jail, expertly converted from a consular place of incarceration to the clubby **Galata House Restaurant** (p. 168).

Retrace your steps and follow the street until it ramps down to Bankalar Sok., today better known as:

⑫ Voyvoda Caddesi

It's impossible to overstate the centrality of this street in the financial and mercantile activities conducted during the Ottoman Empire. In the waning years of the empire, which was plagued by a hemorrhaging of economic influence, the sultan turned to many a bank on Bankalar Sokağı for credit—provided at crushing rates of interest. More on these banks and the buildings that housed them later.

Continue straight down Perşembe Pazarı Sok., and turn right onto narrow Galata Mahkemesi Sok., where you will soon see the tower of:

⑬ Arap Camii

This Gothic structure was most likely built as a Dominican church in the first half of the 14th century, incorporating (or including, no one is sure) a chapel dedicated to St. Paul. The church was taken over by a community of Moors who had been expelled from Spain in the 16th century. The building suffered from numerous fires; during the 1913–1919 restoration project, the original flooring was uncovered, revealing a number of Genoese tombstones (now in the Archaeology Museum).

Head back up Perşembe Sok., back to Bankalar Sok., and turn right, where you'll see the beginning of a long parade of stately bank buildings.

⑭ Voyvoda Caddesi 43–45

These two structures pre-date (and survive) the building boom of the 1890's. Their modest, four-story construction contrasted against the grandeur of the neighboring bank mansions, provide some insight into the early texture of the neighborhood.

Farther on along Voyvoda/Bankalar Sok. is the unmistakably grand:

⑮ Ottoman Bank

Built in 1890–1892 by architect Alexandre Vallauri, this is actually two buildings in one—twin structures occupied by the Ottoman Bank and later by the Central Bank of the Republic of Turkey. In 1896, a group of nationalist Armenians stormed the building with bombs and a list of grievances against the Ottoman state.

At this point, you see the Camondo Staircase. You can climb it, turn right, and then right again down the steps back down to Bankalar Sok., or you can simply continue straight along Bankalar Sok. toward:

⑯ Karaköy Square

Some impressive architectural jewels, like the Nordstern Han to your right and the neoclassical Ziraat Bank building opposite the square, command this open plaza, attesting to this section of the city as the center of commerce for not only an empire but for the entire Mediterranean. Turn right onto the square and meander passed the *simitçi* (a vendor selling bagel-like sesame rings), the plumbing vendors, and the crush of humanity; then turn right again onto the busy Tersane Caddesi.

Take a right onto the tiny Perçemli Sok., and follow it all the way to the end, where you will find the:

⑰ Jewish Museum of Turkey (Zulfaris Museum)

This museum chronicles 500 years of Turkish Jewry (p. 138). The elegant redbrick town house embellished by marble columns and an ornamental staircase dates to the early 19th century.

Head down to Tersane Cad., and at your right a few steps farther on you will arrive at the entrance to "Lower Tünel" (p. 177). This is the end of the tour, a convenient stop for those heading either back up to Tünel, or, via the tramway, to Taksim or the Old City.

Start:	Yerebatan Sarnıçı (Basilica Cistern), Sultanahmet
Finish:	Istiklal Caddesi, Beyoğlu
Time:	2–4 hours, depending on how much time you spend in the Mosaic Museum and in the Basilica Cistern
Best time:	Midafternoon Wednesday, Thursday, or Friday
Worst time:	Saturday, Sunday, Monday, Tuesday (when at least one of the destinations mentioned in this tour is closed)

Istanbul sits atop a mind-boggling wealth of significant ancient and Ottoman history. A few of the places featured here have been converted into restaurants, while others are preserved as museums. Some are both, while others are neither. This means that not all the sights on this tour will be open at the same time—museums are open during business hours while restaurants are only open after-hours. A visit to the sites under private ownership will require some warm personal interaction. It's best to approach this tour around midafternoon, but you can also choose to split the difference between the sites opened during and after business hours and do half during the daytime and the other by moonlight.

❶ Yerebatan Sarnıçı

Few would guess that beneath the institutional concrete facade on the corner of Yerebatan Caddesi and Divanyolu lies one of the last remaining, intact monuments to the Byzantine era in Istanbul, the **Yerebatan Cistern** (closed Tues; p. 141). After paying the admission fee, a flight of steps leads down to a humid subterranean underworld of imperial grandeur accentuated by modern spotlights and even a bit of artistry. The cavernous and palatial space glows with the reds and blues of theatrical mood lighting. You might recognize the space from a scene in the James Bond move, *From Russia with Love,* which was filmed here.

Upon exit, with Sultanahmet Park on your left, walk west along Divanyolu toward the Sultanahmet tramway stop. After the tramway stop, turn left onto Işık Sok. Down on your right is the main entrance to:

❷ Binbirdirek Sarnıçı (The Philoxenus Cistern)

In contrast to the celebrity of the Yerebatan Cistern, this underground space is generally ignored by the tour groups. Known colloquially as the Cistern of

1,001 Columns (p. 156), it was built during Constantine's time, but today the dry, cavernous, and vaulted space serves several purposes: In addition to a museum, the cistern is also a restaurant, cafe, and wine house that accommodates exhibits, cultural performances (like the *sema*), and weddings. The small cafe is on a platform to the back and serves fresh baked goods; in the evenings, the atmosphere, music, and a stock of waterpipes attract a young crowd.

If you're visiting between April and December, exit through the rear entrance to your right and turn left onto Klodferer Cad. Turn left onto Dostluk Yurdu Sok., and then cut through the little corner park on your right to Piyer Loti Cad. For visitors at other times of the year, retrace your steps to Divanyolu and turn left. Turn left again down Piyer Loti Cad. The entrance to the next attraction is in the blue Eminönü Municipality Building. Just inside the service entrance, to the right of the main entrance is:

❸ The Şerefiye or Theodosius Sarnıç

This cistern is still in a fairly raw state—no mood lighting and mirrors—but at least they've removed the debris that was scattered about the space. A tunnel in the

Walking Tour 2: Istanbul Underground

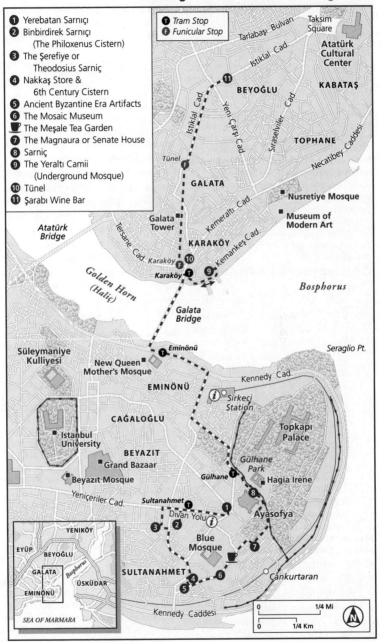

1 Yerebatan Sarnıçı
2 Binbirdirek Sarnıçı
   (The Philoxenus Cistern)
3 The Şerefiye or
   Theodosius Sarniç
4 Nakkaş Store &
   6th Century Cistern
5 Ancient Byzantine Era Artifacts
6 The Mosaic Museum
☕ The Meşale Tea Garden
7 The Magnaura or Senate House
8 Sarniç
9 The Yeraltı Camii
   (Underground Mosque)
10 Tünel
11 Şarabı Wine Bar

T Tram Stop
F Funicular Stop

Taksim Square
Atatürk Cultural Center
KABATAŞ
BEYOĞLU
Tarlabaşı Bulvarı
İstiklal Cad.
Yeni Çarşı Cad.
Sıraselviler Cad.
TOPHANE
Necatibey Caddesi
Tünel
GALATA
Nusretiye Mosque
Museum of Modern Art
Kemeraltı Cad.
Galata Tower
Tersane Cad.
KARAKÖY
Karaköy
Kemankeş Cad.
Atatürk Bridge
Golden Horn (Haliç)
Bosphorus
Galata Bridge
Eminönü
Seraglio Pt.
Süleymaniye Kulliyesi
New Queen Mother's Mosque
EMINÖNÜ
Kennedy Cad.
Sirkeci Station
CAĞALOĞLU
Topkapı Palace
Istanbul University
BEYAZIT
Grand Bazaar
Beyazıt Mosque
Gülhane Park
Hagia Irene
Gülhane
Yeniçeriler Cad.
Sultanahmet
Divan Yolu
Blue Mosque
Ayasofya
Cankurtaran
SULTANAHMET
Kennedy Caddesi

YENIKÖY
EYÜP
BEYOĞLU
GALATA
EMINÖNÜ
ÜSKÜDAR
Bosphorus
SEA OF MARMARA

0   1/4 Mi
0   1/4 Km
N

right wall is said to connect this cistern with the neighboring Binbirdirek cistern. This is a great place to practice your Turkish, because local security and service staff working in the municipal building hanging outside are eager to let visitors have a look. Closed Saturday and Sunday.

Retrace your steps back to Klodferer Cad. and turn right. Klodferer merges onto Üçler Sok., a narrow road with local shops, including a laundry, a grocer, and a neighborhood *pasthane* (mixed in with a creeping arrival of large restaurants and one or two carpet shops geared toward tourists). You will also pass a mosque with a tiny graveyard. Continue straight along the southwestern rim of the Hippodrome, veering right down the hill onto Nakılbent Sok. The road curves sharply to the left and opens up onto a raised tea garden on your right and, straight ahead, the:

❹ Nakkaş Store & 6th-Century-A.D. Cistern

The sleek operation of Nakkaş is a shopping complex that puts pretty much all of Istanbul's quality commercial ware under one roof. If you can get past the cases of diamond and gold jewelry (carpets, *kilims,* and ceramics are upstairs) without getting sucked into the glamour, ask a salesperson if they wouldn't mind your having a look at their art gallery, essentially a **6th-century-A.D. cistern** transformed into a space for exhibitions and concerts. Tell them I sent you. If you buy something then maybe I can get a free Iznik plate.

Turn left out of Nakkaş and stop at the next intersection. Notice on your right the Spherion, or retaining wall of the Hippodrome. Turn left. The next street is Küçük Ayasofya Cad.; turn right to see the bright Eresin Crown Hotel.

❺ Ancient Byzantine-era artifacts

A small section of another ancient cistern was uncovered during the construction of the **Eresin Crown Hotel** (p. 63). To the left of the lobby is a sitting area built on and around the cistern, and above an exposed (preserved) Byzantine mosaic detail. Off the lobby is the Column Bar,

where some of the 49 artifacts recovered during construction are on display, including upright columns, capitals, and funerary stelae.

Go up the incline of Küçük Ayasofya Cad. (taking the right fork at the top) and follow the road around to the right past the entrance to the Arasta Bazaar. Be careful, as there is little sidewalk to speak of. Just past where the road curves left and in front of the Sultanahmet Sarayı Restaurant and Hotel is the entrance to:

❻ The Mosaic Museum

For now, the **Mosaic Museum** (p. 139) is the best (and perhaps the only large-scale) example of the grandiose lost Great Palace. The museum preserves, partially *in situ,* a recovered portion of a peristyle courtyard that was completely tiled in mosaic patterns, in predominantly greens and ochers, of hunting and pastoral scenes. Amazingly, this portion of the "underground" tour was once the top layer of the city. Closed Monday.

The museum exit opens into the middle of the Arasta Bazaar. Continue up (to the left) and exit the bazaar, for a perfect place to:

> **TAKE A BREAK**
> The **Meşale Tea Garden** and cafe is a popular spot in Sultanahmet for people-watching. Carpet salesmen will be seen wooing their prey here, while locals sit back and toss back tulip glass after tulip glass of black tea. The cafe has a short menu of non-tea drinks as well.

Turn left onto Torün Sok. and go up the steep cobbled incline past the Blue House on your right and the domes of the Blue Mosque to your left. Straight ahead (the street changes names to Utangaç Sok.) are some of the more intrusive carpet salesmen in town; ignore them and turn right at the end onto Tevkifhane Sok. past the saffron-colored Four Seasons Hotel—converted in the 1970s from a political prison. Turn left onto Kutlugün Sok., and against my better judgment, turn right into the Asia Minor carpet shop and go into the garden courtyard at the back.

❼ The Magnaura or Senate House

A cement staircase in the courtyard leads down into the subterranean remains of the Senate House. The salesmen will be more than happy to let you have a look at the gray and dusty stones, and then give you a tour of their carpet collection in the adjacent shop.

This shop is just one of the hundreds of neighborhood structures built atop the ruins of the Great Palace. In fact, excavations and construction are ongoing next door behind the Four Seasons. After the lot behind the hotel was reclassified from an "archaeological park" to an "urban and archaeological site," the hotel obtained permission to build three new wings on the site. The additional wings will be supported by pylons, allowing excavations and eventually visits to continue to the remains of either the former Senate or Magnaura Palace below.

Continue along Kutlugün Sok. along the wall of the Four Seasons (on your left) and some dilapidated painted cement block houses on your right. At the end of the street is a restored Ottoman mansion, now a hotel; turn left here onto Işak Paşa Cad. and head up the hill along the outer wall of Topkapı Palace. Go around to the right of the grand Sultanahmet Fountain, past the entrance to Topkapı Palace, and enter into the cobbled and picturesque Soğukçeşme Sok. Down on your right, tucked against the palace walls, is:

❽ Sarniç

Believe it or not, this 1,600-year-old cistern used to house a mechanic's garage. The auto paraphernalia was removed only 25 years ago, and today the cistern is occupied by Sarniç, an atmospheric restaurant (p. 93). The "wow" quotient goes off the charts when the entryway and staircase down to the dining room/cistern glows under the light of hundreds of candles. Take a minute to survey this spectacular medieval re-creation. The only "modern" addition is the brick fireplace on the left wall.

Continue along the cobbled Soğukçeşme Sokağı past the rear gardens of the Ayasofya, full of archaeological pieces to the ancient puzzle strewn about the yard. If you happen to be back here when the bells go off, it'll be quite an audible shock. Soğukçeşme Sokağı descends sharply, past the open gardens of the Ayasofya Konakları containing a garden conservatory. The sharp descent spills out onto Alemdağ Caddesi, with the entrance to Gülhane Park on your right, enclosed behind the Topkapı Palace walls.

Here is the Gülhane tramway stop; hop on any tram heading toward Eminönü and get off at the third stop, Karaköy, just on the far side of the Galata Bridge. *Note:* If your train ends at Eminönü, just step out and wait for one heading to Kabataş. At Karaköy, exit the tram to the right and go down to the water and seaside promenade at the base of the Galata Bridge. Follow the promenade to the left (away from the bridge), passing seafood restaurants and fishermen along the way. Up on your left you will see a ramshackle but beautiful blue government building and a plaza. Directly behind the blue building is:

❾ The Yeraltı Camii (Underground Mosque)

This mosque (p. 168) is a somewhat ominous grid of isolated, individual spaces sectioned off by thick, squat columns supporting a low vaulted ceiling. The scattered prayerful, worshiping in the privacy of their little compartments, may either ignore you or gaze curiously upon you, as few visitors to Istanbul even know to venture here.

Exit the mosque and return to Karaköy Square, where you disembarked from the tramway. Cross Karaköy Square (via the underground pedestrian walkway) and head west to Tersane Cad. Almost immediately on your right is the entrance to the underground funicular.

❿ Tünel

Just as it always has from 1876 onward, Istanbul's one-stop subway, Tünel, will ease your passage up the very steep Galata Hill to the old neighborhood of Pera (now imaginatively called Tünel). In its early days, the public remained wary of this new system, so the city added an extra wagon and used it to transport animals as proof of its safety. Tünel consists of two cars cleverly designed to accommodate the heavy sloping of the landscape.

Exit Tünel to the right and follow the Nostalgic Tramway tracks up Istiklal Cad. (If you're tired or your feet hurt, take the Nostalgic Tramway and get off at Galatasaray Lisesi). Opposite the Galatasaray Lisesi (Galatasaray High School) is:

⓫ Şarabı Wine Bar

By now, the wine bar (p. 213) should be hosting enough guests to allow you to migrate to a table in the cellar, which is a brick vaulted cavern and a 19th-century aqueduct. According to the locals, this was part of a system that conducted water from the British Embassy around the corner all the way to Tophane, down the hill along the Bosphorus north of Karaköy. This is the end of the tour, and with a cellar representing around 100 labels, a perfect venue for sampling some of Turkey's outstanding wines.

WALKING TOUR 3 FROM THE LAND WALLS TO BALAT & FENER

Start:	St. Savior in Chora Byzantine Church (Kariye Muzesi)
Finish:	Golden Horn Road in Ayakapı, in front of the Aya Nikola Church
Time:	Two hours
Best Time:	Sunday, market day mornings, and during the Bayram, when you may actually get a glimpse of sheep being butchered for the Feast of the Sacrifice (or this could fall under "worst time"). Otherwise, any day during daylight.
Worst Time:	During the Feast of the Sacrifice (see "Best Time" above)

One could describe the combined and contiguous neighborhoods of Ayvansaray, Balat, and Fener as a miniature chronicle of the Byzantine, Ottoman, and modern times. These streets have hosted the most influential of empires along with their monuments; housed a mosaic of communities and their support systems; and sustained earthquakes, fire, and sieges. Until recently, the neighborhoods had been forgotten by all but the most destitute of modern Turkish society. In 1997, UNESCO took notice. Then, in January 2003, a program of restoration and rehabilitation of the adjacent neighborhoods began, underwritten by the European Union under the direction of the Municipality of Fatih. While dozens of restoration projects are underway, the streets on this tour remain, for the most part, a (faded) mirror of what they were a mere hundred, or hundreds of years, ago. In fact, this walking tour is sparse on the "take a break" feature, because as of the time of this writing, there simply was no place to take a break other than what's listed here. I suspect that will have changed by the time you get there.

---

❶ St. Savior in Chora

The heavy brick Byzantine structure that is the monastery of St. Savior "in the Country" (p. 140) was built in the 4th century A.D. on the main "Mese," or avenue, out toward Adrianople, today's Edirne, in Thrace. When Theodosius constructed his famous land walls in the 5th century A.D. (p. 153) to accommodate the growth of the city, the church was brought into the municipal fold, so to speak, and thus protected by the great line of defensive towers, walls, and moats that you will get a taste of just up the hill. But although the church

Walking Tour 3: From the Land Walls to Balat & Fener

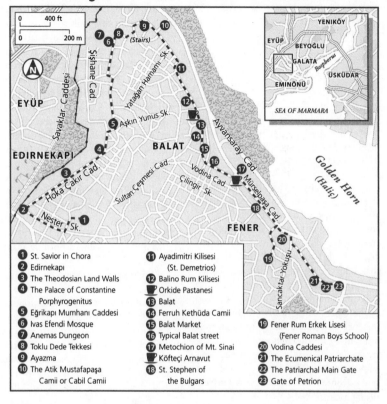

1 St. Savior in Chora
2 Edirnekapı
3 The Theodosian Land Walls
4 The Palace of Constantine
  Porphyrogenitus
5 Eğrikapı Mumhanı Caddesi
6 Ivas Efendi Mosque
7 Anemas Dungeon
8 Toklu Dede Tekkesi
9 Ayazma
10 The Atik Mustafapaşa
  Camii or Cabil Camii

11 Ayadimitri Kilisesi
  (St. Demetrios)
12 Balino Rum Kilisesi
🍵 Orkide Pastanesi
13 Balat
14 Ferruh Kethüda Camii
15 Balat Market
16 Typical Balat street
17 Metochion of Mt. Sinai
🍵 Köfteçi Arnavut
18 St. Stephen of
  the Bulgars

19 Fener Rum Erkek Lisesi
  (Fener Roman Boys School)
20 Vodina Caddesi
21 The Ecumenical Patriarchate
22 The Patriarchal Main Gate
23 Gate of Petrion

---

sits inside the walls, the Byzantine bustle that once grew up around it has long since ceded to the surrounding neighborhood of working-class rural transplants and their more traditional brand of conservatism. The church is flanked on one side by an open square now bustling with visitors lingering at the outdoor tea garden, or perusing among the various vendors selling scarves, ceramics tiles, and postcards (all made in China).

Follow Kariye Camii Sok. up away from the museum then turn right onto Neşter Sok., which you will follow up the hill. At the top of the hill you arrive at the land walls.

❷ Edirnekapı

Straight ahead you see the monumental **Gate of Charisius** (today known as Edirnekapı), the great portal into the

Eastern Roman (Byzantine) Empire and the entryway by which Mehmet the Conqueror victoriously arrived into a defeated Constantinople. A plaque next to the portal commemorates the sultan's arrival. In the words of Evliya Çelebi, the famous Turkish historian and traveler who was present during the procession:

"The Sultan then having the pontifical turban on his head and sky-blue boots on his feet, mounted on a mule and bearing the sword of Mohammed in his hand, marched in at the head of seventy or eighty thousand Muslim heroes, crying out 'Halt not conquerors! God be praised! Ye are the conquerors of Constantinople!'"

Look to the south along the walls to the **Mihrimah Sultan Camii,** her minarets rising in the distance (p. 172).

Walk along the walls, keeping them to your left. You are now walking the cobbled street running adjacent to a section of:

❸ The Theodosian Land Walls

This is Ayvansaray, one of the poorest—and most religiously conservative—neighborhoods along the Golden Horn. The next nine or so towers complete the original section of the Theodosian walls, while the section completing the defenses down to the waterway were added later by subsequent emperors. Although most of these secondary towers are gated off, one or two still serve as tradesmen workshops, and one contains a public fountain added during Ottoman times. You can still take a peek inside some of these towers to get a glimpse of the lower stories. You will also see a steep stone staircase that leads to the top of the walls for a sweeping view of the Golden Horn and Beyoğlu. The resident youth use the top of the walls as a pedestrian highway, and they will be surprised when you pop your head up. On the opposite side of the street are colorfully whitewashed and enchantingly dilapidated houses and shops fronted by the rare octogenarian sitting guard.

Along the road, you may pass a bundled housewife heading purposefully to her destination, but not so distracted that she won't cast a curious eye your way. Otherwise, your primary company will be the sound of your own shoes on the cobblestones.

About 600m (656 yards) farther on from Edirnekapı, the walls open up to a multitoned red brick and limestone monolith towering above a small park. This is all that remains of the imperial glory that was:

❹ The Palace of Constantine Porphyrogenitus

Known in Turkish as the Tekfur Sarayı, the palace is now under restoration. This palace is, or was, part of the Blachernae Imperial Complex, which began as a royal retreat in the middle of the 6th century A.D. under Emperor Anastasius, to accommodate visits to the nearby sacred *ayasma* (later in this walk).

The palace was enlarged and enriched over the next few centuries, particularly in the reign of Alexus I Comnenus. Under Manuele I (1143–80), the permanent residence of the imperial court was transferred from the Bucoleon Palace, along the Marmara Sea Walls, to this neighborhood, at that time known as Blachernae. After the fall of the city, the palace at Blachernae was abandoned and then used by the Ottomans as a stable for the elephants, giraffes, and other oversize and exotic animals that they corralled from Africa. Afterward, the building endured a further indignity as a brothel, and then later as a pottery plant, a bottling plant, and a poorhouse.

The perimeter is composed of the inner and outer rings of the defensive walls. In the park at the monolith's base there might be some old men tossing dice on a backgammon board, presumably one of them the patron of the goat chained nearby grazing on some blades of grass. There was also a chicken poking its head around the unkempt underbrush when last I visited.

If restoration work is completed by the time you arrive, climb up to the first story, where you can see the full and complex system that makes up the land walls stretching all the way south to the Sea of Marmara (open daily 9am–7pm; admission 2YTL/$1.75/80p).

Leaving the entrance of the Palace, turn left and follow Şişhane Sok. Take the 90-degree right at the mosque then the first left onto:

❺ Eğrikapı Mumhanı Caddesi

The street you are now on is presumed to be the trajectory of the later land walls, although except for some crumbling masses of stones, you're more apt to ogle the mixture of dilapidated houses and 70's style buildings swathed in funky exterior tiling. The road winds down and around through this quiet section of

Ayvansaray, departing from Eğrikapı Mumhanı Caddesi as it continues straight onto **Çedik Papuçlu Sokak.** At one of the bends in the road there is a dirt lot on your right, from which you can look out over the rooftops through to the Golden Horn. In the late afternoon, the schoolchildren may join you out of curiosity.

Continue down this street, through a zigzag to your left, and turn left at the "T" onto Mahkeme Külhane Sok. At the end of this short section of the street you will arrive at another "T." Directly opposite and slightly to the left is the:

❻ Ivas Efendi Mosque

This mosque is set in a small overgrown garden containing a tiny Ottoman graveyard. Inside, apart from the tiled *mihrab*, representing the height of Iznik ceramic craftsmanship, the most notable characteristic of this mosque is that it sits atop a section of the defensive walls attached to Blachernae Palace.

Walk around to the back of the grounds of the mosque and you will come upon the remains of the:

❼ Anemas Dungeon

It was from the **Tower of Isaac Angelus** that Emperor Alexius I Comnenus greeted the First Crusaders, and where the deposed Emperor Angelus was imprisoned. He was briefly released to share rule with his son Alexius IV, and then a year later, in 1214, both were locked up and then strangled. At least six Byzantine emperors shared similar fates, enduring either torture, mutilation, or the more traditional punishment for a deposed ruler, blinding. From the lone park bench you can admire the elevated view over the northern neighborhoods of the Golden Horn (and the highway) and contemplate the fate of emperors. The staircase leading down to the chambers is currently cordoned off. Imagine the neighborhood urchins who get to explore the caverns underneath their homes when nobody is looking. (Did you remember to bring your flashlight?)

Exiting the main gate to the mosque, turn left onto Dervişzade Sok. and stop at the next intersection, Ahmet Rufav Sok. On your right (there are some treacherous original marble stairs on the right side of Dervişzade Sok., but the easier, ground level entrance is on Ahmet Rufai Sok.) are the ruins of the:

❽ Toklu Dede Tekkesi

Though the site is currently undergoing restoration, if the workers see you hesitate at the entrance, they will most likely invite you in for a look. Sadly, there's not much of anything original here. At first, this was the site of a late Byzantine church of unknown origins. The church was converted to a derviş lodge and named after Toklu Ibrahim Dede who is said to have been a companion of Mohammad and present in the Arab siege of A.D. 673.

Ahmet Rufai Sok. narrows and ends at a wooden building that is also the Pembe Kösk Nargile Café. Take the meandering flight of stone steps straight down the hill to Albayrak Sok. Go left at the bottom of the steps and take the first right. At the next intersection, where the street meets with Mustafa Paşa Bostanı Sok., is a small church, housing the:

❾ Ayazma

The Ayazma or Sacred Spring, is the most celebrated shrine to the Virgin Mary in all of Constantinople (p. 163). Inside, is an altar swathed in marble above the spring and a lovely little garden.

Turning right from the church, continue down the main, albeit quiet, neighborhood street of Mustafa Paşa Bostanı Sok. and take the first left onto Çember Sok. The Byzantine-era church before you is now:

❿ The Atik Mustafapaşa Camii or Cabil Camii

The saint of this church has not been definitively identified; however, it is commonly understood, until proven otherwise, to be the Church of St. Thekla. What's special about the church—believed to date to the 9th or 10th century A.D.—is that it is the earliest example in Constantinople of a cross-in-square plan. It is also the first church constructed in the city after the period of Iconoclasm.

If scholars hold to the belief that the plan represents a transition in the construction of Byzantine churches (not a done deal, by any means), then Thekla would be the predecessor to the canonical churches that sprouted up all over Russia in the 11th century. If you're a fan of barrel vaults, it's worth a walk-through, while the garden courtyard will inevitably be occupied by a scant handful of neighborhood grandfathers.

Retrace your steps to Mustafa Paşa Bostanı Sok. and follow this street as it doglegs around to the right next to a high wall and empties into a triangular intersection. Turn left onto Ağaçlı Çeşme Sok., and then immediately to your left is the continuation of the wall and a solid metal gate.

⓫ Ayadimitri Kilisesi (St. Demetrios)

A church bearing this name has existed on this site as early as 1334, but the current church dates only to the first half of the 18th century. The church of St. Demetrius served as the Patriarchal See from 1597 to 1601; then briefly the Ecumenical Patriarchate operated out of the Virgin Paramythia until it found its final home at St. George, its current site (see below). You can take your chances and hope the caretaker answers the bell, or contact the Ecumenical Patriarchate in advance for an appointment to visit the church. The plain, timber-roofed exterior is adorned by a pretty landscaped garden, the simplicity of which belies the restrained opulence of the interior decor. There are scenes from the life of Christ in the gallery, and the gilded iconostasis is covered in icons.

Continue down Ağaçlı Çeşme Sok., a quiet street that runs parallel to and above the Golden Horn. By now, you've gotten the hang of identifying the Byzantine buildings by their construction of alternating red brick and limestone, often with a marble portal, so you should have no trouble now in locating the:

⓬ Balino Rum Kilisesi

Just a bit up on your right is the Balino Rum Kilisesi. This is the Church of the Mother of God Valinou. The church is in a terrible state of decay, both inside and out, so just admire the ruddy and ragged exterior and be on your way. Ağaçlı Çeşme Sokak begins to enliven a bit as you continue past where the street name changes to Mahkeme Altı Caddesi.

> ☕ **TAKE A BREAK**
> **Orkide Pastanesi,** Mahkeme Altı Cad. 34, with its pink exterior, is an unpretentious local cafe/bakery where you can sit down, get sweet or savory cookies and a cup of tea. (If you're hungering for more than just some pastries, an alternative "take a break" at a local eatery is below.)

Exiting the bakery, you are now in:

⓭ Balat

This is the point in the walking tour where the street life and people-watching gets more interesting. You are walking in the direction of the Balat Market, a local area of shops (many of which are being restored) formerly owned by local Jewish families. Today, they are a semi-collapsed grouping of stores hidden behind haphazard displays of household plumbing, hardware, and other daily necessities.

At the corner of Ferruh Kahya Sok. you see the portal to the:

⓮ Ferruh Kethüda Camii

This is a minor work of the architect Sinan. It was once used as a hall for performances of the whirling dervişes, as well as a lodge for the Sümbüli order of Dervişes. Some of the interior decoration, namely the marble *mihrab* and the wooden stalactite ornamentation on the capitals, is noteworthy, but I like this mosque for the intimacy of the courtyard. Park benches line the perimeter of the entry court, where on hot summer days the local men jockey for a spot on one of the benches out of the sun's rays. Have a seat here and soak up the vibe; these guys are not yet used to seeing visitors, so you can still enjoy a curious welcome and at the very least, a warm smile.

There is a narrow garden path that cuts through the mosque grounds to the left of the entrance; follow its diagonal trajectory back out to Mahkeme Altı Cad.

⓫ Balat Market

At its zenith in the 18th century, the labyrinth of streets that comprise the market was at the center of a flurry of activity, a bustling community revolving around these single-storied shops once owned by the Jewish merchants of the neighborhood. Most of the buildings have long since been scarred by metal shuttered doors or silenced behind layers of crumbling plaster, but if you look up, some of the buildings will reveal their faded glory. Look for the odd arched brick facade atop decorative friezes, hidden behind a thick mesh of ivy. Note the restoration in progress at nos. 1, 8, 12, 14, 16, and 17.

Straight ahead, the street splits in two by a crumbling island of burnished shops, many shaded by gloomy (albeit very photogenic) plastic or corrugated steel awnings. This cozy section of the market bustles with what seems to be mostly passersby, while a few hardware store owners and adolescent workers mill about the outsides of their shops. Take a minute to absorb this pseudo-square then take the left fork into the warren that is Lavanta Sokak.

After a few steps down this narrow stretch of sidewalk, you will arrive at a confusing intersection, with streets seemingly branching off into all directions. Turn left onto Hızır Çavuş Köprüsü Sok. Restoration work is scheduled for nos. 41, 49, 49A, 90A, 29 and 7, so I'm sending you down this way to show you a:

⓰ Typical Balat street

Here is an example of what a typical Balat street would have looked like in its heyday in the 17th to 19th centuries. Notice the architectural richness of the neighborhood, characterized by three and four storied narrow buildings with protruding enclosed balconies. This is a typical feature of the Jewish houses, with some bearing Hebrew inscriptions, displaying the star of David, or an engraved stone with the recurrent theme of a boat—the symbol said to represent the lifeline provided to the expelled Jews of Spain in 1492 by the Sultan.

At the end of Hızır Çavuş Köprüsü Sok. (before it changes names to Yıldırım Cad.), you will see the Golden Horn on your left and the manic Mürselpaşa Avenue. Carefully, and I mean carefully, cross the street. It's only two lanes, but they're wicked. You are now standing on a long strip of green parallel to the Golden Horn and sandwiched between two major roadways. This strip used to house some of Balat's statelier homes, but a project carried out in the 1980s by the mayor to "reclaim" what had deteriorated into an eyesore saw the demolition of entire paragraphs in Balat's and Istanbul's history. Look back at the crumbling wall of buildings from where you crossed, and you'll get an idea of what this neighborhood had come to. Immediately on your left, hiding in plain site, is the:

⓱ Metochion of Mt. Sinai

This building (p. 163) consists of a Feneriote mansion typical of the upper Ottoman Greek society. For now, it's boarded up, but you can walk around to the park side and see the surreal picture of an extended family of squatters spilling out onto the formerly grand marble terrace of the adjoining chapel. The house itself served for a time as a warehouse and factory.

TAKE A BREAK
Because of your proximity to one of the more renowned little meatball houses in the area, this might be a good time to stop for real sustenance. Back on the other side of Mürselpaşa Caddesi, at no. 155 (☎ 0212/531-6652), is **Köfteçi Arnavut.** Here you can order as authentic a working-man's meal as you can get: *köfte,* as the name implies, *piyaz* (bean salad), and *arnavut çiğeri* (fried liver the way the Armenians make it). The kitchen runs out of food by 2 or 3pm, and then shuts down for the day.

With the Golden Horn on your left, straight ahead at 12 o'clock is:

⑱ St. Stephen of the Bulgars

The Gothic exterior gives the impression that this church (p. 164) is an ornament on a wedding cake, and that you can almost eat it. As you approach, you'll notice a little hammock in the corner of the grounds where the caretaker takes refuge from the scorching heat of summer. He or his son will greet you at the gate, leaving you to your own devices in admiring the interior craftsmanship and the verdant and inviting garden. The son will likely follow you around, offering helpful hints in rudimentary English.

Past the church is the recently restored Eyüp Hüsrevpaşa Tekkesi, or derviş lodge, which has a nice little tea terrace if you care to take a load off. Right after that is the **Women's Library** (p. 174), a research resource on Turkish and Ottoman women's issues.

Cross back to the inland side of the street and turn right on the tiny street just before the lighted intersection. If you have it in you, continue up the steep cobbled hill, or you can just look up, as you can't actually go in the next building on our itinerary. What appears to be a château is the:

⑲ Fener Rum Erkek Lisesi (Fener Roman Boys School)

The sounds of childhood emanate from within both the school (p. 163) and its courtyard, but it's the unmistakable red steeple that dominates this corner of Istanbul.

Go back down the hill and turn right onto Vodina Cad. (or turn left if you did not go up the hill).

⑳ Vodina Caddesi

This street extends all the way back to the Ahrida Synagogue and was once the social stage of Balat, a promenade where families could stroll, socialize, gather, and hold events.

Just a short walk ahead, turn left where Vodina comes to an end, and then right onto Yıldırım Caddesi. At the next major

"opening" in the road, look to your left; this is where the **Fener (or Phanar) Gate,** one of the entryways through the defensive walls along the Golden Horn, used to be.

Continue straight on a few steps and you will come to an entryway; past a security check up some marble steps on your right is the:

㉑ The Ecumenical Patriarchate

Today enclosed within a high stone wall, the relocation of the Orthodox Patriarchate in 1601 to this spot gave the neighborhood of Fener a shot in the arm. For the next 2 centuries, the bourgeoisie of Greek Istanbul, wanting to be in proximity to this seat of power, descended on Fener, and built homes, mansions, and villas. You'll be sharing your visit mostly with the new class of wealthy Russian tourists and the odd Serbian couple here on pilgrimage. It's enough to see the wondrous reverence in their eyes to overcome your awe at the opulence of the interior. Admire the graceful mosaics of symmetrical angels over the interior portal of the nave, and try not to be blinded by the halo of lights reflected off of the iconostasis (the gold screen with icons).

Exit to the right and stop in front of the oversize steel gate in the section of the exterior wall of the grounds.

㉒ The Patriarchal Main Gate

On April 22, 1821, this gate was permanently welded shut as a symbol of the eternal grief caused by the death of Gregory V, then the Patriarch who was hanged at this very spot. Gregory was an unfortunate and innocent victim of the reprisals by the Ottomans after the Greek Revolt in Peloponnesus.

Continue along the cobbled Yıldırım Cad. which curves around to the left. Just before it empties out into the chaos of Istanbul, take note of the empty lot to your left. This is the former site of the:

㉓ Gate of Petrion

It was here that in 1204, Doge Dandalo breached the city's defenses and led the

Latin crusaders to victory (and why the bronze horses are at St. Mark's in Venice rather than at the Hippodrome, where they belong). The fateful precedent was set, for in 1453, although the Petrion Gate's defenses managed to withstand the onslaught by the Ottoman invaders, its defenders surrendered upon hearing that the city had fallen. Because of this admission of defeat, Fatih Mehmet spared the neighborhood from the general sacking permitted to his soldiers in the rest of the city. But, like the rest of Istanbul, this neighborhood was not spared the sacking that came in more modern times. The destruction of monuments like this one for municipal progress and development has been a sad, recurring theme throughout Istanbul, one that seems to be heading, thankfully, into decline.

This marks the end of the tour. You can either wander around (you are now in the extremely untouristy neighborhood of Ayakapı), or cross the highway to the banks of the Golden Horn and enjoy some sea breezes and Istanbul vistas. The ferry at the Fener docks can get you back to Haliç, near but not at Eminönü via Kasımpaşa, or hop on the 55T bus to Taksim or the 99A bus to Eminönü.

9

Shopping

Perhaps it was the renown of the Grand Bazaar that put Istanbul on the map of the world's great shopping destinations. But it's the hunting grounds of Old Istanbul, the elegant boutiques of Nişantaşı, and the revival in handicraft and artwork that have kept it there.

1 The Shopping Scene

WHAT SHOULD I BUY?

The first thing that comes to mind when plotting a plan of attack for acquisitions in Istanbul is a rug, be it a *kilim* or **tribal carpet.** Carpets, *kilims,* and a whole slew of related items that have lost their nomadic utility comprise an indescribably complex industry, but it is unlikely that you will get very far before being seduced by the irresistible excess of enticing keepsakes.

Most people are unaware that Turkey manufactures some of the best **leather items** in Europe, comparable in quality to those sold in Florence, Italy (and in some stores in Florence, the merchandise *is* Turkish). Because leather items are individually produced in-house, quality and fit may vary, but the advantage of this is that you can have a jacket, skirt, or trousers made to order, change the design of a collar, or exchange an unsightly zipper for buttons at prices far less than what you'd pay back home.

The entire length of Kalpakçılar Caddesi in the Grand Bazaar glitters with precious metals from the Nuruosmaniye Gate to the Beyazit Gate. But Turkish-bought **gold and silver** are no longer the bargains they used to be, as the cost of precious metals—particularly gold—continues to skyrocket. However, cheap labor in China and India might still keep Turkish jewelers from pricing themselves out of the market, so all hope is not lost.

Some of the world's best **meerschaum** comes from Turkey. This heat-resistant sea foam becomes soft when wet, allowing it to be carved into playful pipes that would make a collector out of the most die-hard nonsmoker. An afternoon in a historic *hamam* will expose you to some of the most beautiful traditional **white copper** objects, available as kitchen and bathing utensils, although keep in mind that you can't cook with this toxic stuff unless the inside has been coated with tin.

As far as **antiques** go, shopkeepers seem to be practiced in manufacturing bogus certificates of origin that will facilitate your trip through Customs, but beware: The certificate may not be the only counterfeit item in the shop. Collectors should keep in mind that it is prohibited by Turkish law to export anything dated prior to the 20th century.

Less traditional items can easily fill a suitcase, and with clever Turkish entrepreneurs coming up with new merchandise on a regular basis, you won't get bored on your second or third visit. **Pillowcases, embroidered tablecloths, ornamental tea services,** and **brass coffee grinders** are just some of the goodies that never seem to get old.

/ *Tips* **A Note About Bargaining**

That old measure by which you should offer the seller half of his initial price is old hat. They've caught on to our shopping savvy, and in fact they don't care. Plenty of stupendously wealthy Russians and groups of cruise ship passengers provide easy targets. Still I've heard that a good rule of thumb is to offer about 25% less than you're willing to pay. In my experience, you must hold off your counteroffer for as long as you can get away with it. This method will meet with counter offers and varying responses, and after a few times you might succeed in talking the price down. You'll get the hang of it.

Here's another bargaining tool: narrow down your choice to two pieces. Snub your first choice and put it down (with plans to come back to it later). Negotiate on your second choice—undoubtedly one of the finer samples in the shop, and therefore one of the pricier items on sale. Once you've established that it's out of your price range, turn to your first choice with a disappointed "and what about that one?"

COVERED BAZAARS & STREET MARKETS

Arasta Bazaar   Less overwhelming in scope than the Grand Bazaar is the picturesque shopping arcade attached to the southern edge of the Blue Mosque. It's a total tourist trap, but there are a few high-quality gems mixed in with the stacks of cheap ceramics and evil eyes made in China. Open daily from 9am to 7pm (closes earlier in winter and during Ramadan). Sultanahmet. Entrance on Topçu Cad. (across from the Blue House hotel) and on Küçük Ayasofya Çad.

Egyptian Spice Bazaar (Mısır Carsışı) 😋😋   At the center of the commercial hub of Eminönü, this is an indoor emporium of comestibles, rare (and counterfeit products), colorful elf slippers, and polyester scarves, among other interesting, if not dazzling things. To the left of the sea-facing entrance in the embrace of the "L" shape of the bazaar is an outdoor garden market; to the right of the entrance begins a string of vending stalls displaying countless varieties of olives, cheeses, fruits, and vegetables. The chaotic streets behind the bazaar deal in general necessities, from housewares, to long johns, to Viagra. Sometimes you really never know what you need until you stumble upon it. Open Monday to Saturday 8:30am to 6:30pm. Eminönü, opposite Galata Bridge. No phone.

The Grand Bazaar (Kapalıçarşı)   Perhaps it was the renown of the Grand Bazaar (aka the Kapalıçarşısı or Covered Market) that put Istanbul on the map of the world's great shopping destinations. It's certainly one of the world's major tourist traps. It's also a feast of color and texture, of glitter and glitz. It's also not to be missed. So take a deep breath, leave your valuables (and any cash you'd rather not spend) back in the hotel safe, and dive in. Open Monday through Saturday from 8:30am to 7pm (closes earlier during Ramadan). See also p. 121 for more suggestions on touring the historic shops in the Grand Bazaar. Beyazit, Eminönü. No phone. Best entrances through the Beyazit Gate (across from the Beyazit stop on the tramway along Divanyolu) and the Nuruosmaniye Gate (from the Çemberlitaş tramway stop on Divanyolu, follow Vezirhanı Cad. to the arched entrance to the mosque grounds, which leads to the bazaar).

Istiklal Caddesi   A bustling promenade of cafes, clothing stores, blaring record shops, and bookstores, Istiklal Caddesi from Tünel to Taksim Square may be starting to resemble an open-air mall, but it's still an essential activity for all who visit Istanbul. Be sure to pop in to the **Avrupa Pasajı** in the Balıkpazarı (near Meşrutiyet Cad. in Beyoğlu), a narrow gallery of artsy shops selling souvenirs from antique samovars to tiny harem outfits for 2-year-olds (plus merchandise like brass pepper mills at prices lower than in the Egyptian Spice Market). Istiklal Cad., Beyoğlu.

Ortaköy   The **arts-and-crafts fair** on Sundays (open year-round) in Ortaköy is Istanbul's equivalent of "downtown." Here you'll find a mixture of street-smart jewelry, tie-dyed textiles, and revolutionary Turkish ideas. The street food here is lots of fun. Around the Ortaköy boat landing, along the Bosphorus.

OUTDOOR MARKETS

Local markets offer a window into the vibrancy and color of the neighborhood, and provide a priceless experience in interaction with the locals. Istanbul has more than its fair share of outdoor markets, selling the usual assortment of fresh produce, household

Caveat Emptor! Carpet-Buying Tips

"Where are you from?" seems an innocuous enough question from a carpet dealer, but answer it, and you're on your way to being scalped. Questions like "Where are you staying" actually tell the salesperson about your economic status, as do "What do you do?" *(How much money do you earn?),* "Where do you live?" *(Hey what a coincidence! My cousin lives near you!),* "How much time will you be staying here?" *(How much time do you have before you have to make your final decision?),* "What are you looking for" *(Do you even have any idea about carpets?),* and "How long have you been here?" *(How much have you already learned about our sleazy ways?).*

First rule of thumb: Lie about where you're staying. Take note of the name of the humblest pension near to your actual hotel, and file it away for future use. Also, they know that Americans are among the biggest spenders of any other nationality visiting Turkey, and easily one of those with the least bargaining prowess. This is where fluency in a foreign language may come in handy. Above all, do your homework and know what you like before you arrive so you don't waste precious bargaining time overpaying for the "best sample in the shop."

Visitors traveling in groups inevitably wind up at a large roadside production center. Although these are interesting from an educational and cultural point of view, don't be had: Your tour guide, your tour company, and, hell, the bus driver, are each going to earn a hefty commission off of your sale. (Actually, the same commission system applies to almost everything you buy.)

Yes, buying a carpet in Turkey can be a very daunting task. But this is not meant to diminish your admiration of the pieces, only to arm you for the negotiations, which ultimately will get you an exceptional souvenir of a wonderful country and its wonderful crafts.

Fun Fact **Did You Know?**

The blue-and-white evil eye *(nazar boncuğu)* has its roots in Anatolian culture, although the symbol has its variants throughout the Middle East. Turks believe strongly in the power of the evil eye (if you could only see the tattoos beneath the *hijab* . . .) to ward off negative energy, especially against young children. But the evil eye transcends this culture—just check the pyramid on the backside of your U.S. 1-dollar bill. Oh, and by the way, all of the blue evil eyes are now made in China.

---

staples, sweatshirts, and maybe the odd antique. A walk through one of these provides yet another opportunity to witness another facet of this complex culture. The major markets are the **Çarşamba Pazarı** ("Wednesday" market), held next to the Fatih Mosque, and the **Salı Pazarı** ("Tuesday" market), Mahmut Baba Sokağı, Kadiköy on the Asian side. There is also a **flea market** between Sahaflar and the Grand Bazaar, and down at Eminönü every Sunday, and a daily **antiques market** in Horhor (Horhor Cad. Kırk Tulumba, Aksaray). With Feng Shui taking hold of the consciousness of Istanbul's upper crust, it's no surprise to see organic produce close behind. The **Ekolojik Pazarı,** a new organic market in Feriköy (in the car park on Bomonti Cad., Lala Şahin Sok.; take the metro from Taksim to Osmanbey), fills the niche. It's open every Saturday from 8am to 5pm.

2 Shopping A to Z

Shops in Istanbul are officially open Monday to Saturday, 9:30am to 7pm. In practice though, it is rare that a shop in Sultanahmet will be closed on Sundays. Shops along Istiklal Caddesi are open on Sundays; shops in the passageways along Istiklal Caddesi (the Galatasaray Fish Market, for example) share the same hours as shops along Istiklal Caddesi and are open on Sundays.

ANTIQUES & COLLECTIBLES

Objects dating to the Ottoman period make up a popular category for roving antiquers. As a rule, all items displayed can be legally purchased and exported to your home country (unless the piece is unique, in which case you need documentation from a museum director to buy it). Objects dated prior to the Ottoman period are considered fruit from the poisonous tree. Where carpets are concerned, the cutoff is 100 years—you'll need a certificate from the shopkeeper stating the age, origin, and authenticity of the carpet. (This is standard practice anyway.) So if you're serious, your first stop should be the neighborhood along Çukurcuma in the extremely hilly neighborhood below Beyoğlu and Taksim.

Artrium This shop is one of the last holdouts in the *pasaji*, or atrium, just outside the entrance to the Upper Tünel. The store stocks old-ish ceramics, textiles, costume jewelry, and printed matter. Tünel Geçidi 7, Beyoğlu. ✆ 0212/251-4362.

Atomik Saat Galerisi Vintage watches from Eastern Europe and the former Soviet Union clutter up the diminutive display case at the back of the İç Bedesten in the Grand Bazaar. If you're crazy about wristwatches and are hankering for something a bit exotic, this is the place. İç Bedesten 3-4, Grand Bazaar. ✆ 0212/520-7154.

Bedestan   This tiny storefront specializes in old watches and silver. At last peek, Bedestan had a 1940 model with only the Vacheron name, an 1886 with only the Constantin label, and a 1925 Art Deco Omega. If you see something interesting, call the mobile number provided in the window, as the shop is usually closed. Avrupa Pasajı 8, Galatasaray. ✆ 0212/249-9541 or mobile 0532/412-6873.

Galeri Alfa   This shop has limited-edition tin toy soldiers, inspired by several hundred years of the Ottoman Empire as well as by models from abroad. Galeri Alfa also deals in rare books and prints. Faikpaşa Yokuşu 47/2, Çukurcuma ✆ 0212/251-1672.

Horhor Bit Pazarı   One of the lesser-known and blissfully lesser touristed markets is where you'll find dusty Turkish memorabilia from the 20th century. Merchandise runs the gamut from tableware, lamps, and furniture, and on to oversize architectural remnants, spread out among the more than 200 shops on six floors. Horhor Cad., Kırk Tulumba, Aksaray.

Ottomania   Located in Beyoğlu just outside the Tünel atrium, Ottomania specializes in high-quality old maps and engravings. Sofyalı Sok. 30–32 (exit Tünel and walk straight through atrium), Tünel. ✆ 0212/243-2157.

Ottoman Miniatures & Calligraphy   Pointing is going to be your best means of communication at this shop if you're in the market for rare Ottoman and Islamic prints, or a superb original framed *tuğra*. İstiklal Cad. 6, Tünel. ✆ 0212/251-1966.

BOOKS

Galeri Kayseri   Anything you ever wanted to know about Istanbul or Turkey is somewhere inside this shop, or their branch across the street. Divanyolu 58 and across the street at no. 11, Sultanahmet. ✆ 0212/512-0456.

Homer Kitabevi   Down the street from the Galatasaray High School is this absolute superlative of a bookstore, stocking a rich selection of books on Turkish issues, including politics, history, architecture, photography, travel, and religion. If you can't find it here, it's either sold out or it doesn't exist. Yeni Çarşı Cad. 28/A, Galatasaray. ✆ 0212/249-5902.

Istanbul Kitapçısı   Owned and operated by the Istanbul Municipality, this bookstore stocks cassettes, videos, travel books, maps, and coffee-table books in a variety of languages. They also have a selection of prints and posters. İstiklal Cad. 191, Beyoğlu. ✆ 0212/292-7692.

Librairie de Pera   The last bookseller left on a street that was famed for its booksellers, Librairie de Pera is the little engine that could. The current owner, Ugur Güraca, presides over a multilingual collection of more than 40,000 rare books, some bound with goat skin, as well as prints, photographs, and etchings. Galip Dede Cad. 22 (opposite the Galatasaray Mevlevihanesi), Tünel. ✆ 0212/243-3991.

Nakkaş Books   Aykut, the laid-back owner of the now closed Aypa, opened a shop down the street in conjunction with the adjacent Nakkaş. He still carries a great selection of books on Turkish art, ceramics, history, religion, and the Ottoman Empire, some of which are rare or limited editions. The shop also carries a dizzying array of souvenirs like magnets, artistic cards, jewelry, copper, and textiles. Nakilbent Sok. 33, Sultanahmet. ✆ 0212/516-0100.

Sahaflar Çarşısı   The Book Bazaar is a wonder of the printed page. Vendors carry books on Turkish subjects ranging from art to architecture to music, both old and

---

Tips Carpet Buying

With consumer prices rising in Turkey, carpet vendors have been traveling far and wide to collect the less expensive Turkic carpets from Azerbaijan, Turkmenistan, Özbekistan, Afghanistan, and the other stans. Before you fork over thousands of dollars or pounds on one of these admittedly stunning pieces, compare prices at places like IKEA and at Worldstock, Overstock's site for global handicrafts (www.overstock.com).

---

new. Also, some of the finest examples of Ottoman art and calligraphy can be found in this book lover's mecca. Sahaflar Çarşısı, Grand Bazaar (enter from Çadırcılar Cad.).

Robinson Crusoe   Just before you head down to the coast for that weeklong Mediterranean vacation, stop off here to find something to read. Robinson Crusoe stocks a limited selection of English-language fiction, travel guides, and books on Istanbul and Turkey. İstiklal Cad. 389, Beyoğlu. © 0212/251-1735.

CARPETS

When in Istanbul, my days are filled with powwows with carpet dealers proud to show me the thank-you letters received from Washington, D.C., insiders, foreign dignitaries, and vacationing journalists. I could easily list a handful of stores where I go regularly for a cup of tea, but that wouldn't be fair to the shop owners that I have yet to meet. And just because I gave my business card to someone as a courtesy in passing doesn't mean that I endorse his (and in the rarest of cases, her) shop. In fact, just because I mention a shop in a previous edition of *Frommer's Turkey* doesn't necessarily mean I endorse them now.

Finding an honorable carpet seller is even more elusive than tracking down an honest car salesman. In a country where the minimum wage produces between 455YTL ($396/£173) *per month,* the business of selling carpets promises the equivalent of the American Dream, attracting the ambitious and sometimes immoral on the trail of easy money. This doesn't diminish the value of the carpets, nor does it mean that all carpet sellers are dishonest. In fact, Istanbul is full of carpet salesmen whose singular goal is to sell the finest quality, most beautiful specimens for the absolute highest price they can get. The challenge for the potential buyer is not so much about avoiding fakes and scams, it's about not getting scalped. This is, after all, a business. And it's *your* business to be an educated consumer.

My dilemma is that as soon as I recommend a carpet seller, you will automatically be at a disadvantage, because 1) you and many others will move heaven and earth to buy at this location, thus tipping the scales of demand in favor of the seller, and 2) the seller will therefore lose the incentive to compete. The result? You lose. So what's a shopper to do? Recognize that buying a carpet is an extremely labor- and time-intensive activity, and rest assured that these salesmen will find you. Your best, and only defense, is to go armed with the best information you can get, and to recognize in advance that no matter what you do, you're going to pay more than you should.

CERAMICS

Art House   Shop owner Fereç Zan sells a spectacular variety of urns and fireplace ornaments in his tiny shop in the Cebeci Han. Completed ceramic bowls are flown in

Deconstructing the Turkish Carpet

Turkish tribal rugs are divided into *kilims,* which are flat, woven rugs, and **carpets,** which are hand-knotted using a double or Gordian Knot, a technique unique to Anatolia that results in a denser, more durable product than the single-knotted carpets found abroad. *Kilims* are probably more recognizable, as they are inexpensive and sold abroad.

Four types of carpets are currently produced in Turkey. **Wool-on-wool** carpets represent the oldest tradition in tribal rugs and are representative of a wide range of Anatolian regions. The earliest examples display geometric designs using natural dyes that were reliant on local resources like plants, flowers, twigs, and even insects, so that the colors of the carpets reflected the colors of an individual region. Blues and reds are typical of designs originating around Bergama, which derive from the indigo root and local insects. Reds seem to be dominant in carpets made in Cappadocia. The oranges and beiges of the Üşak's are also becoming more popular among consumers.

Today the business of carpet weaving has been transformed into a mass industry. Weavers have for the most part switched over to chemical-based dyes, although the tradition of organic dyes is experiencing a rebirth.

The second type of carpet is the highly prized **silk-on-silk** samples, which developed in response to the Ottoman Palace's increasing desire for quality and splendor. Silk was a precious commodity imported from China that few could afford. In the 19th century the sultan established a royal carpet-weaving center at **Hereke** that catered exclusively to the palace. Today silk-on-silk rugs continue to outclass all others, using silk from Bursa woven into reproductions of traditional designs. (*Note:* Silk threads cannot hold natural dyes.) Silk rugs are also produced in **Kayseri,** but these have yet to attain the high standards set by the Herekes.

A more recent development in carpet production has been the **wool-on-cotton,** which, because of the lower density of the weft, accommodates a higher ratio of knots per inch, and therefore more detail in the design. Carpets of this type come from **Kayseri, Konya (Lakık),** and **Hereke. Cotton-on-cotton** is an even newer invention, duplicating the resolution and sheen of a silk rug without the expense.

Sales tactics include an emphasis on Anatolian carpet and *kilim* weaving as a high art. This certainly applies to rare and older pieces, which command hefty sums. But modern samples—albeit handmade copies of traditional designs—are created from computerized diagrams.

Finally, unless you're an expert, you should avoid buying antique rugs, which cost significantly more, and will present some challenges with Customs. The bottom line is that only antiques experts are equipped for a proper appraisal.

from Kutahya, and the copper is hand worked on-site in the workshop on the second level at the back of the adjacent Iç Cebeci Han. Modestly sized urns sell for around 75YTL ($65/£29; significantly less than the 220 *of whatever currency* they care to quote in the Arasta Bazaar). Yağlıçılar Cad., Cebeci Han 17, Grand Bazaar. ✆ **0212/526-5509.**

Istanbul Handicrafts Center   The street-front shop to the workshops in this restored 17th-century Ottoman *medrese* has a choice collection of precious ceramic and porcelain reproductions from Kütahya and Iznik. Kabasakal Cad., Istanbul Sanatları Çarşısı, next to the Hotel Yeşil Ev, Sultanahmet. ✆ **0212/517-6780.**

Iznik Foundation   Having revived the Ottoman-era craft of Iznik tilemaking, the Iznik Foundation is now selling its wares. The trick was identifying the chemical process for achieving the vibrant blues and green pigmentation of the originals. One of the criteria was that the ceramic "canvas" had to be composed of up to 80% quartz. This shop sells hand-painted tiles, platters, urns, and other household decorative items and tableware. Kuruçeşme Öksüz Çocuk Sok. 14, Kuruçeşme. ✆ **0212/287-3243.**

Kevser   Located on the main street that parallels the Bosphorus on its way through Ortaköy, Kevser is an eye-catching boutique carrying fine traditional and modern ceramic pieces as well as a variety of gift items. Muallim Naci Cad. 72, Ortaköy. ✆ **0212/327-0586.**

COPPER

Çadırcılar Caddesi   If you simply have to have a set of those white copper *hamam* bowls or a copper platter for a table *à la Turque,* root around the slightly disheveled stalls near the book bazaar. That is, if you aren't going to Ankara, where copper is king. Çadırcılar Cad. (past the entrance to the book bazaar near the Grand Bazaar), Grand Bazaar.

CRAFTS

Evihan   Handmade artistic pieces made using Turkish tiles and hand-blown glass beads are the main feature at this crafty boutique located in the up-and-coming neighborhood of Çukurcuma. Altıpatlar Sok. 8, Çukurcuma. ✆ **0212/244-0034.**

Istanbul Handicrafts Center (Istanbul Sanatları Çarşısı)   In another one of its commendable preservationist projects, the Touring and Automobile Club of Turkey has provided an outlet for the revival of Turkish and Ottoman crafts. Each room off the central courtyard of this restored 17th-century *medrese* serves as an atelier for a different craft. Here you can watch the creation of handmade treasures, including hand-painted silks, folk art dolls and puppets, gilded calligraphy and miniatures, fine porcelain reproductions, and modern examples of the art of *ebru,* or marbled paper. The center is open year-round, although you may have to knock on some doors to get a personal shopping tour during the off season. Better yet, their fixed pricing takes the guesswork out of buying. Kabasakal Cad. (the side street next to the Derviş Tea Garden and across from the Blue Mosque), Sultanahmet. ✆ **0212/517-6780.**

Paşabahçe   The nationwide chain has recently begun making a name overseas for its elegant ceramics, hand-cut glass, and typically Ottoman tableware. The more precious pieces are trimmed in silver or gold plate. The store also stocks everyday tableware, but that's not the stuff you're going to carry home. There are 15 locations in Istanbul, including in Beyoğlu, at the Kanyon shopping center and in Teşvikiye; the one on Istiklal Caddesi is the most convenient. Istiklal Cad. 314, Beyoğlu. ✆ **0212/244-5694.**

DEPARTMENT STORES & CHAINS

So you've packed for warmer weather and the winds from the Caucasus have arrived a bit early. Head for these chains, located along Istiklal Caddesi, though you'll find them in major shopping areas throughout the country.

Beyman   Beyman is Turkey's answer to Ralph Lauren, without the horsy patch. There's absolutely nothing cheesy about this store, which carries casual chic for men and women as well as housewares worthy of a museum. The Beymen Mega Store in Akmerkez (see "Malls & Shopping Centers," below) is more along the lines of an upscale department store, where you can find cosmetics, stationery, and even furniture. The small outlet store in Eminönü carries reduced-price men's shirts and ties. Abdi İpekçi Cad. 23/1, Nişantaşı. ✆ 0212/343-0404.

Mavi Jeans   These jeans started to make a showing in upscale stores in the U.S. Here, in Turkey, Mavi is more like a Turkish Gap, except that fabrics are *not* pre-washed, so you should *never* put items in the dryer. Look for their store also in the Akmerkez shopping center (see "Malls & Shopping Centers," below). İstiklal Cad. 117, Beyoğlu. ✆ 0212/249-3758.

Vakko   For the best designer men's and women's wear, check out Vakko, Turkey's answer to Barney's New York and worth a look if only for its dazzling silver embroidered scarves. There are a number of locations, including at the airport, in Kanyon Shopping Center, in Galleria Shopping Center, and in Nişantaşı. There's even a discount shop behind the Egyptian Spice Bazaar (at Sultanhamam Sok. 51; ✆ 0212/514-0545). Akmerkez Shopping Center. Nispetiye Cad., Etiler. ✆ 0212/282-0695.

FOOD

Galatasaray Fish Market (Balıkpazarı)   True, the Balıkpazarı is a great big tourist trap, but as a jumble of over 25 fish and fresh-produce vendors, as well as a handful of traditional *meyhanes* and the odd seller of dashboard ornaments, it's also an undeniable hoot. While in the Balıkpazarı, keep your eyes peeled in the various markets for vacuum-packed bunches of **sele olives**—soak them in hot water to dilute the saltiness, and then serve these precious little pieces of fruit with olive oil, lemon, and a sprinkle of oregano. İstiklal Cad., opposite Galatasaray High School (near intersection of Meşrutiyet Cad.), Beyoğlu.

Hacı Bekir   For the most extensive variety of Turkish delight, stop in to this legendary sweet shop with locations in Beyoğlu and Eminönü. İstiklal Cad. 129, Beyoğlu. ✆ 0212/244-2804. Hamidiye Cad. 81–83, Eminönü. ✆ 0212/522-0666.

Kurukahveci Mehmet   Turkish-coffee addicts should head to this corner behind the spice bazaar. A producer of the infamous precious brew, Kurukahveci Mehmet is also the best-known retail outlet. Tahmis Cad. 66, Eminönü. ✆ 0212/511-4262.

Tips Something Smells Fishy

Beware of anything labeled caviar. Turkey is notorious for its illegal trade in smuggled caviar, as well as for representing this lower-quality replacement fish roe as high-quality caviar using counterfeit labels copied from reputable brands.

Olive Oil: Anatolia's Black Gold

Turkey's **olive oil** really doesn't get the kind of respect it deserves—an absence of effective marketing has deprived the rest of the world of one of the country's most treasured resources. But that is changing, by the looks of the gourmet shop in the airport's duty-free area. If you've been bewitched by the flaxen temptress at the bottom of your meze bowl, pick up a bottle at any local convenience-type store. The grocery store chains carry some basic brands; opt for Komili.

Namlı Gurme Gida   Ferry passengers heading home and local workers and artisans crowd the cash register of Namlı, a specialty food purveyor stocking quality items such as olive oils, cheeses, helva, dried fruits, honey, and nuts, many of which are packaged and ready to go. Namlı is renowned for their *pastırma* and deli meats, as well as Kars cheese. They even carry items an extended visitor might not want to be without: HP sauce or Casa Fiesta salsa. The covered outdoor cafe is packed with lunchtime folk or commuters waiting for their ferries to board. It's open Monday to Saturday, 6:30am to 10:30pm. Rıhtım Cad. 1-1 (under the car park), Karaköy. (C) **0212/293-6880.**

Şutte   A delight for your eyes and your stomach, Şutte is a chain of charcuteries with outlets all over the city, but this is the most central. Şutte carries rare pork items like prosciutto and speck as well as hard-to-come-by wedges of *parmeggiano reggiano*. You can also take out one of the many prepared sandwiches or tempting mezes and eat them at the lone table in the Balıkpazarı. Duduodalar Sok. 21, in the Galatasaray Fish Market (Balıkpazarı). (C) **0212/293-9292.**

GIFTS & SOUVENIRS

Avrupa Pasajı   A couple of shops located down this passage in the Balıkpazarı reliably stock all of those little souvenirs you can't leave Turkey without: evil eyes, copper pepper mills, hookah pipes, and scarves, all at prices much, much lower than anywhere else in town. İstiklal Cad., Balıkpazarı, Avrupa Pasajı. No phone.

Disturbed People   They're calling it "shop'tertainment"—Turkish style. This whimsical new shop between Tünel and the Galata Tower sells art, books, maps, and items both decorative (candleholders) and functional (old 45's reshaped into ash trays), in addition to items that are just plain fun (a hanging terrier mobile, for example). Galipdede Cad. 34, Tünel. (C) **0212/252-4430.**

Dösim   This government-owned chain is a sort of collective operated by the Turkish Republic Ministry of Culture. Works by artists and craftspeople are commissioned independently and sold at fixed prices in a highly evocative setting near major museums and monuments. Lately, several of the stores are now stocking an array of high-quality baubles representative of Anatolian culture, in addition to their collection of regional carpets, *kilims,* and tribal pieces. Several outlets are in Sultanahmet alone; the Haseki Hürrem Sultan Hamamı displays carpets, *kilims,* and camel bags only. The gift shop in the entrance courtyard of Topkapı Palace and the one outside the main gate stock a good variety of items, including *meerschaum, kilims,* pottery, jewelry, and memorabilia. Haseki Hürrem Hamam (opposite the Ayasofya); left of entrance to Topkapı Palace; Topkapı Palace outer courtyard, Sultanahmet. For information, contact the office in Ankara (C) **0312/309-4953.**

Fine Art   As the distributor for Vakko in Japan, Fine Art carries their silk scarves, tablecloths, and other household textiles, as well as good-quality non-Vakko ceramics and silver jewelry. Divanyolu Cad. 13, Sultanahmet (next to McDonald's). ✆ 0212/638-9827.

Hava Spor   The soccer (sorry, football) craze being what it is, no closet would be complete without Galatasaray's yellow stripes or Fenerbahçe's blue and gold. Hava Spor has them both and more folded neatly on a handful of shelves, appropriately near the British Consulate. Meşrutiyet Cad. 76, Pera. ✆ 0212/249-3916.

HOME

Beymen Home   One could easily spend thousands of New Turkish Lira in this shop. Beymen is a candy store of contemporary home items à la Ralph Lauren or Calvin Klein. Here you'll find sleekly designed tableware, Ottoman-style copper serving platters, and sumptuously simple furniture. Boston Sok. 8, Nişantaşı. ✆ 0212/343-0404.

The Home Store   A veritable emporium of Turkish-made, stylish wear for both the home and for those who live in it, the Home Store deserves a reserved corner in your luggage. Come to think of it, bring a spare bag. Akmerkez Shopping Center, Nispetiye Cad., Etiler. ✆ 0212/291-6297.

Mudo   Mudo is a the anti-department store that carries things you never knew you needed. A sort of cross between Pottery Barn and Next, the stores carry stylish housewares and very wearable clothing for men and women. Mudo has branched out around the country (it has 32 locations in Istanbul), with some of the stores focusing on just one "department." A Mudo Outlet is now located in the Egyptian Spice Bazaar. Rumeli Cad. 58, Nişantaşı. ✆ 0212/231-3643. Also on Istiklal Cad., and in the Akmerkez Shopping Center, Nispetiye Cad., Etiler.

JEWELRY

Eller Art Gallery   Providing a more down-to-earth showcase for wearable art is this workshop (at the back) and gallery on a side street of Beyoğlu. These very Turkish designs are inspired by jewelry and other artifacts normally seen under protective glass at Ankara's Museum of Anatolian Civilizations. Istiklal Cad., Postacılar Sok. 12, Beyoğlu. ✆ 0212/249-2364.

Pegasus   For decorative (but not too much) silver pendants, rings, and earrings, this tiny storefront in Ortaköy is one of my favorites, and it's also gentle on the wallet. Muallim Naci Cad., Yelkovan Sok. 3/B, Ortaköy. ✆ 0212/258-7485.

Urart Ateliers   Urart is an upscale workshop complex of designers, artists, and craftspeople dedicated to re-creating the rich traditions of Anatolian civilizations in gold and silver. Urart's precious creations are available to the public in the label's exclusive boutique in Nişantaşı. Some of their pieces are also available in the small gift shop in Topkapı Palace, in the last courtyard. In the Swissôtel, Bayildim Cad. 2, Maçka. ✆ 0212/629-0478. And Abdi Ipekçi Cad. 18/1, Nişantaşı. ✆ 0212/246-7194.

TEXTILES

Abdulla Natural Products   Thou shall not covet these incredibly thick and plush towels. With two locations in and around the Grand Bazaar, Abdulla stocks goods like deliciously textured bath sheets, herbal olive-oil soaps, and all of the accouterments for a home-style *hamam* (silk pestamal, hand mitt, and so on). Halıcılar Cad. 62, Grand Bazaar. ✆ 0212/527-3684. And Ali Baba Turbe Sok. 25/27, Nuruosmaniye. ✆ 0212/526-3070.

Malls & Shopping Centers

You'd really have to have a lot of time on your hands in Istanbul to wind up at one of these shopping centers, but sometimes the lure of the fluorescent lighting and the chill of overtaxed air-conditioning is just too much to resist. The **Akmerkez Mall,** in Etiler, was actually voted the best shopping mall in Europe several years back. But clearly that wasn't enough: Last year saw the opening of **Istinye Park,** an urban re-creation of a village catering to those accustomed to the stratospheres of commerce. Even newer than Istinye Park is **City,** an indoor emporium of top brands (Gian Franco Ferre, Roberto Cavalli, D&G, Jean Paul Gaultier) in the tony neighborhood of Nişantaşı. The outdoor **Kanyon** is only a couple of years old, a Guggenheim-esque swirl of tasteful Turkish franchises and one-of-a kinders in the smart neighborhood of Levent. Other shopping malls include **Capitol Shopping Mall** in Üsküdar, **Carousel Shopping Mall** in Bakırköy, and **Galleria Shopping Mall** near the airport. **Olivium** is a newish outlet mall located halfway between the airport and Sultanahmet, where you can find various middle-of-the-range name brands at discounted prices.

Derviş   New ethnic fabrics created based on the traditional villages around Anatolia fill the shelves of this stall in the Grand Bazaar. Samples include a silk-on-silk embroidered man's shawl (700YTL/$609/£266)—the type worn by an Ottoman *zeybek* (parallel image of a Mafioso type); a raw silk waffle-texture bedsheet, a small collection of raw cotton *peştemels,* and handwoven linen towels. Keseçiler Cad. 33–35, and Halıcılar Cad. 5, Grand Bazaar (near the Iç Bedesten). ✆ **0212/514-4525** and 0212/528-7883.

Eğin Tekstil   This shop has been in the family for so long that Dr. Süleyman (a real medical doctor) proudly displays the *firman,* or order of Sultan Abdülhamid II—the equivalent to a license to operate. But that's not even his claim to fame: When a team with the film *Troy* was looking for period textiles, particularly woolens, they came here. Yağlıkçılar Cad. 1 (at the Örücüler Kapısı entrance), Grand Bazaar. ✆ **0212/528-2618.**

Ethnicon   You can't read an architectural magazine these days without bumping up into merchandise made here. Ethnicon puts a contemporary twist on a tribal art tradition by collecting bags, curtains, and other utilitarian objects made from sturdy wool textiles (even burlap) from around the southeast of Turkey, and then has the remnants arranged into a "quilted carpet" by a professional designer. The concept is very popular among local architects; you'll see Ethnicon products adorning places like the Sumahan Hotel, Conran's, and Restoration Hardware. Pieces are fixed and priced by the square meter (at $220/£110). Kapalıcarsı Takkeciler Sok. 58–60, Grand Bazaar. ✆ **0212/527-6841.**

LEATHER GOODS

Centilmen Han   If you're looking to score some first-quality leather at bargain basement prices, those days are long gone. Nevertheless, the fakes are pretty good these days (see below). For a good variety of leather bag and other manufacturers, poke around this han in the Grand Bazaar. Centilmen Han, to the right of the Çarşıkapı entrance to the Grand Bazaar. No phone.

Derimod   Locally crafted leather shoes, bags, and jackets for both men and women are sold under this Turkish national brand. Merchandise is made of fine quality hides and crafted into traditional forms. Akmerkez Shopping Center, Nispetiye Cad., Etiler. ✆ **0212/282-0668.**

Tips **Tax-Free Shopping**

There's an incentive for carrying that carpet home. Foreigners (and Turkish citizens with residence abroad) are entitled to a VAT (value-added tax) refund, worth 18% of the total amount of merchandise acquired during any one purchase. One word of caution though: There's an ongoing scam where a merchant will ask you to sign an invoice (written in Turkish) that actually states you have already received your VAT refund at the point of purchase. Imagine handing over your paperwork at the airport (including the receipt with your signature) only to learn that you have essentially waived your own right to the refund without even knowing it. Simply put: Don't sign anything you can't read.

To receive a refund, present the merchandise and receipt to the Customs inspectors on your way out of the country (but within 3 months of purchase). Refunds are issued in the form of either a Global Refund check, redeemable at the İş Bankası branch on the Arrivals level, or as a credit to a credit card account. The Customs Tax-Free office at the airport in Istanbul, located in the International Departure Terminal, is opened 24 hours a day.

Kıyıcı Genuine Fake Bags   Just because these are not the originals doesn't mean they're of inferior quality or you're not going to need a full wallet to walk out of here with a little morsel. GFB carries Prada (with bargaining that begins at $250/£125), Louis Vuitton, and other big names. Grand Bazaar. From Beyazit gate, to the right of the Kürkçüler han. © 212/526-5181.

THE NEW OTTOMAN CLOSET

Gonul Paksoy   Mass consumerism is desensitizing us to racks and racks of identical merchandise. At the Gonul Paksoy boutique, you'll find one-of-a-kind Ottoman-inspired purses, slippers, silk overcoats, and even tribal jewelry. Atiye Sok. 6A, Teşvikiye. © 0212/261-9081.

Ottomania   T-shirts with an Oriental twist to the modern graphic arts were an instant hit when they appeared on the torsos of Istanbul's cool crowd. Slogans that advertise logos like "Terrible Turk" or simple Ottoman silhouettes sell for 65YTL ($57/£25) and under. Kanyon Mall, Levent. © 0212/296-5619.

10

Istanbul After Dark

Primarily a destination for those seeking historical enrichment and a taste of the exotic, Istanbul presents itself to visitors in a number of unexpected ways. One of those ways is as a sophisticated citified, cosmopolitan denizen of the night. When the sun sets and the spotlights go on, Istanbul squeezes into a slinky black dress and invites its various and varied communities along for the ride. Dozens of rooftop lounges and exclusive Bosphorus-front restaurants are transformed into the living rooms of the smart set. Informal and sometimes raucous restaurants or tavernas teem with the pent-up energy of the long work-week. Students gyrate to the futuristic sounds of techno music while some of their classmates, with arms raised in the air, snap their fingers to the percussive rhythms of traditional Anatolian folk music. The energy is palpable, and as new and innovative nighttime destinations open up weekly, Istanbul is fast becoming a credible rival to Europe's other nightlife meccas.

1 Taking in Turkish Nightlife

Don't think that because 98% of Turks are Muslim that nobody's drinking wine with dinner. On the contrary, even in notoriously conservative Konya, bars outnumber mosques, figuratively speaking.

A typical evening on the town will involve large amounts of food accompanied by even greater amounts of *rakı*, that aniseed-flavored spirit known as "lion's milk"—traditionally consumed in a **meyhane,** a tavern or pub where patrons gather to eat and drink. Where *meyhanes* were once the realm of men only, today they are a hybrid of the lively taverna and sophisticated restaurant, the most popular ones found primarily in the back streets of Beyoğlu. On summer evenings, the main dining room moves to the rooftops (if it's not already there), where guests are treated to the twinkling lights of a timeless city.

The **şaraphane** or wine bar and the counterpart to the **birhane,** or beer hall, is a more recent nightlife trend in Istanbul thanks to the ever-improving quality of Turkey's wines.

Live music is a staple of Turkish nightlife, and Istanbul's cafes, clubs, and Turkish Houses (*Türkü Evleri*) all provide inroads to the niche of your choice. Bars, cafes, and nightclubs in Istanbul are generally not categorized according to the type of music they play, choosing to book instead groups with different styles from night to night. A good rule of thumb is, the earlier the hour, the softer the music. Rock and pop resounds onto Istiklal Caddesi, where bars, cafes, and clubs, a few of them seedy, are too numerous to cover. Another good rule is to avoid spots with neon lights and security guards and anything with the word "nightclub" or "club" in the name, as these have the reputation of being the seedy places where bad things happen to good visitors.

The Rhythm of the Night

A certain rhythm predicts the way things roll out after dark in this great metropolis. The choices run the gamut to bars, restaurants, live music venues, dance clubs, tea gardens, waterpipe cafes (serving a menu of fragrant tobacco for use in a *nargile* or hookah pipe), and a variety of publike locales. More often than not, there is significant overlap. For example, the popular Bosphorus nightclub, Reina, has three restaurants and a number of bars on several open-air levels. At the traditional *Türkü Evi,* live Turkish folk music can more often than not be appreciated while dining on mezes, grills, and sautés. Tea gardens are often also waterpipe cafes. And so on. See "Taking in Turkish Nightlife," p. 207, for a description of the different types of nightlife options.

As mentioned in the dining chapter, most restaurants move the dining upstairs to the rooftop in the warmer months. Some restaurants and nightclubs with locations "in town" (usually in Beyoğlu) move the action up to space along the Bosphorus in summer.

Cover charges are customary for admission to nightclubs, but usually only kick in after 11pm or midnight. The cover charge is generally waved for guests with reservations at one of the in-club restaurants, which start serving dinner around 7pm. The atmosphere at this earlier hour is usually romantic, candlelit, and seductive. As the evening wears on, the music becomes edgier and louder. Most of the musical venues or concert halls also charge an admission; tickets are generally sold at the box office or via **Biletix** (www.biletix.com), a sister company of Ticketmaster. As for closing hours, there rarely are any—although a club may advertise a closing time of 4am, the truth is that sometimes the party just lasts longer.

So now its 4am, your eardrums are busted and you're ready to go home. **Taxis** wait outside the entrance to the Bosphorus nightclubs, but you can also ask inside for the manager or maitre d' to call you one. In Beyoğlu, depending on the location and distance of your hotel, you can either walk or grab a taxi at one of the numerous taxi stands around the district. Taxi ranks in Beyoğlu include those in Taksim Square and on Meşrutiyet Caddesi near the Pera Palas Hotel; you can also walk over 2 short blocks to the busy Tarlabaşı Caddesi and hail one.

Nighttime in Sultanahmet is a bit more sober, although the restaurants, tea gardens, and waterpipe cafes provide more than an ample number of choices. By 10pm in the Old City, the streets have already gone quiet; it's pretty safe to walk around (or back to your hotel), preferably in pairs, but it's also best to stay in areas that are well lit. If "home" is in Beyoğlu, the tramway operates until midnight or 12:30. Unfortunately, the taxis waiting at taxi ranks, particularly in Sultanahmet, are predators, so best to have someone (a hotel receptionist, your waiter, your carpet salesman) call you one.

Tips **Safety for Single Men**

Scenario #1: You're wandering around Taksim and pop into a bar for a quick beer or two. Before you know it, you're surrounded by lovely women and even doted on by the owner. But 2 hours and two beers later, the check arrives: $500. I wish that were a typo. Refuse to pay, and the big boys come out of the woodwork; you may even find your life and limb threatened. It's startling how many times this scenario plays out in seemingly innocuous-looking "establishments" around Taksim. One way to counter, I suppose, is to dispute the charge with your credit card carrier once the bill comes in. But the best way to handle the situation is to avoid it altogether. Stay away from anything with neon and the word "night-club" or "club" in the sign. But sadly, there is no absolute guarantee. When in doubt, follow the advice of this guidebook, or stick to the hotel bars.

Scenario #2: You're taking an innocent evening stroll through the back streets of Sultanahmet. Suddenly, you are accosted by four young boys who identify themselves as police. Having done nothing wrong and always mindful that you are in a foreign country, you cooperate. They manhandle you (perhaps looking for ID, or even drugs) and then send you packing with a shove. It all happens so fast, except that now your wallet is empty. Unfortunately, with the migration of organized crime, nowhere is safe anymore. Don't walk anywhere alone, and avoid badly lit streets after dark.

Türkü Evleri are cozy little cafe/restaurants that book Turkish folk musicians performing typical Anatolian ballads to the accompaniment of the *saz* and drums. Clustered around Büyükparmakkapı Sokak in Beyoğlu, the cafes also serve basic Anatolian fare in a cozy setting, usually a narrow room with banquettes lining the two walls.

Meanwhile, no denizen of the night will be able to look him/herself in the mirror without having stood at the velvet ropes of one of Istanbul's **mega-clubs on the Bosphorus.** While different years find these multiplexes with ever-evolving names, the themes and even the locations, stay the same and invariably involve multiple candlelit restaurants, numerous bars, a dance floor, strobe lights, and fresh breezes off the Bosphorus, only inches away.

Clubs that book popular musical acts may sell tickets or impose a cover charge where normally there is none, but unless the headliner is very popular, tickets to most performing arts events and concerts can be purchased at the location the day of the performance. For tickets to the city's main events, contact Biletix (a Ticketmaster company; © **0216/556-9800; www.biletix.com**).

Hotel lounges or **rooftop bars** provide a mesmerizing alternative to wall-to-wall smoke-filled cafes. All over the city, splendidly romantic views present themselves from almost every rooftop, or you can succumb to the dubious appeal of one of the several **Turkish Night shows** around town.

The neighborhood of **Ortaköy** is particularly vibrant on summer evenings, when streets lined with outdoor vendors selling crafts, jewelry, and the like create a festival atmosphere. Hip waterside restaurants and coffeehouses are open until late, or you can graze through the stalls of food and gorge yourself on stuffed mussels.

GAY ISTANBUL

Although homosexuality can be traced back to Ottoman times, a stigma is still attached to it: The worst insult used among Turks (especially at soccer games) is *ibne,* a term referring to the receiving partner in a same-sex act. Practically speaking, homosexuality in Turkey is legal between consenting partners above the age of 18. Several *hamams* are generally accepted as gay (the men's side), including the **Tarıhı Galatasaray Hamamı** in Beyoğlu (for hours and fees, see p. 143); **Park Hamamı,** Divanyolu, Dr. Emin Paşa Sok., Sultanahmet (no phone); and **Aquarium,** Istiklal Cad., Sadri Alışik Sok. 29 (© 0212/251-8926). For more specific information, log onto **www.istanbulgay.com.**

2 The Performing Arts

Built originally as an opera house, **Atatürk Cultural Center (AKM)** in Taksim Square (© 0212/251-5600) houses the Istanbul State Opera and Ballet, the Symphony Orchestra, and the State Theatre Company. Tickets are absurdly low at 7YTL to 17YTL ($6.10–$15/£2.70–£6.50) and are usually available for purchase in the month of, as well as the day of, the performance. During the summer months, AKM hosts the **Istanbul Arts Festival,** but because of high demand, tickets may be hard to come by. For a schedule of performances, check out the government's website at **www. kultur.gov.tr** or log onto **www.mymerhaba.com** for upcoming events.

A new classical venue for the Istanbul State Opera and Ballet is the restored Süreyya Paşa building in Kadiköy, designed by parliamentarian Süreyya Ilmen between 1924 and 1927 as an opera house. No operas were ever staged here, however, as the incomplete building lacked a stage. The restoration took 2 years and was completed in December 2007, and now the **Kadiköy Municipality Süreyya Opera House** (Eski Süreyya Sineması Kadiköy; © 0212/251-1023) will host three performances a week of the Istanbul State Opera and Ballet. There is a box-office on-site, but tickets can also be purchased at the Atatürk Cultural Center. The 2008 season schedule features some of opera's best-loved works, plus a number of new Turkish ones. For more information, log onto **www.idobale.com.**

The annual **International Istanbul Festival** (© 0212/334-0700; www.iksv.org) is organized into four separate arts festivals averaging over 50 events yearly. The festival kicks off with the Film Festival in April, including two national and international competitions. The 2003 festival screened over 175 films in a variety of venues in Beyoğlu and Kadiköy. The theater section of the festival brings companies from all over Europe and takes place in May, with one or two offerings in English. At the end of October or in early November, selected international artists come together for the Biennale, but the big to-do takes place in June/July with the International Istanbul Music Festival, representing the worlds of opera, jazz, classical music, and ballet in evocative settings like the St. Irene, and featuring world-renowned performers like Wynton Marsalis or the traditional performance of *Der Entführung aus dem Serail* (Abduction from the Seraglio) appropriately staged in Topkapı Palace. A separate Jazz Festival, sponsored by Efes Pilsen, takes place in November in various venues around town, including local jazz clubs, cultural centers, and the open-air theater above Taksim. Tickets to all concerts and performances are available either at the box office or via **Biletix** (www.biletix.com).

TURKISH FOLKLORE

Galata Tower   In spite of mediocre food and high prices, visitors continue to insist on a "traditional" Turkish folkloric show. Inevitably there's a belly dancer and perhaps

Istanbul Biennale 2009

Istanbul has been celebrating a **Biennale** since 1987, but it wasn't until 2005, perhaps because of the anchorage of the new Istanbul Modern Museum, that the Biennale hit a home run. Artists were clustered around the revived neighborhood of Galata in venues that included an old apartment block, a tobacco depot, a Customs warehouse, and an office building. Previous exhibitions were housed in the Imperial Mint, in the Kız Kulesi (Maiden's Tower), in Santralistanbul (a former electric generating plant; p. 155) on the Bosphorus Bridge, and in Çemberlitaş Hamamı.

For information on venues, tickets, and artists, contact the **Istanbul Foundation for Culture and Art** (© 0212/334-0700; www.iksv.org).

---

a segment resembling a Cossack dance. The one at the Galata Tower at least comes with a fabulous view. The show runs Monday through Saturday. Dinner service begins at 8pm, followed by the folkloric show, which ends around midnight. Top floor of the Galata Tower. © 0212/293-8180. Admission 100YTL ($87/£38).

Orient Hotel   The belly dancers are always a crowd pleaser at the Orient Hotel, a one-stop nightlife venue featuring an evening of Anatolian song, wine, and average food. It's one of the more popular of the "Turkish Nights," and easily the most convenient. Dinner starts at 8pm and the show goes until midnight. Tiyatro Cad. 27, Beyazit (near the Grand Bazaar). © 0212/517-6163. Admission 30€ ($26/£11) per person.

Sound and Light Show   The floodlit domes and minarets of the Blue Mosque are the backdrop to a nightly (in summer) sound-and-light spectacle at the entrance to the Blue Mosque in Sultanahmet Park. The show has a charming spontaneous feel and accommodates visitors from round the globe by presenting shows on a schedule of rotating languages. For information, see the Tourist Information Office in Sultanahmet Park. Sultanahmet Meydanı. © 0212/518-1802. Free admission.

TRADITIONAL ANATOLIAN AFTER-HOURS

Türku Evi *(Finds*   Backgammon, hookah pipes, and popular local singers performing the traditional yearning nomadic melodies fill these "Turkish Houses." I confess that this listing does not refer to just one spot but instead covers the numerous cozy bars populating Hasnun Galıp Street in Beyoğlu that feature live performers singing traditional Anatolian folk songs. This is really the experience you've come all this way for. Generally, basic dinner items are served. The small space fills up with locals, who, having eaten, get up and dance in the narrow aisle between the musicians and the *kilim*-covered tables and banquettes. Istiklal Cad., Hasnun Galıp Sok. (perpendicular to Büyükparmakkapı Sok.) 18A, Beyoğlu.

Yeni Marmara *(Finds*   Inconspicuously located on a little-trod street of Sultanahmet, this sleepy little teahouse and *nargile* (waterpipe) cafe is one of the neighborhood's best-kept secrets. Locals relax on the back terrace jutting out above the old city walls to enjoy a game of backgammon and views of the Marmara islands. Walls and floors are covered in old rugs, and the whole space has an appealing worn vibe. Open daily 9am to 1am. Küçük Ayasofya Cad., Çayıroğlu Sok. 46, Sultanahmet. © 0212/516-9013.

3 The Local Bar & Club Scene

The destinations listed below include restaurants, pubs, bars, and waterpipe cafes. None of these charge a cover; but depending on the type of place you choose, it's perfectly acceptable to linger over mezes and *rakı,* a cup of tea, or as long as it takes for the tobacco in the waterpipe to burn down.

SULTANAHMET & EMINÖNÜ

Çorlulu Alipaşa Medrese   Not far from the Grand Bazaar is the outdoor living-room-cum-tea-gardens hidden in the courtyard of the old Çorlulu Alipaşa Medrese. The tree-filled garden is a perfect way to unwind, with a glass of apple tea and the essence of strawberry in your water pipe while you admire the display of carpets and souvenirs decorating the gardens of the bordering shops. The entrance to the tea gardens is on Yeniçeriler Caddesi near where the road changes names from Divanyolu Caddesi. Çorlulu Alipaşa Medrese, Çarşıkapı, Yeniçeriler Cad. No phone.

Galata Bridge   More central and ridiculously scenic is the cluster of bars, cafes, and fish restaurants newly occupying the upper and lower levels of the Galata Bridge. While there's nothing remarkable about the restaurants per se, a couple of the venues have leapfrogged over the dining experience straight to drinks and backgammon. The east-facing and always packed **Dersaadet** (© 0212/292-7002) is the hot ticket, as it faces the minarets of the Old City. Galata Bridge, between Eminönü and Karaköy.

Meşale Çay Bahçesi   Just at the entrance to the Arasta Bazaar is an outdoor collection of benches and tables perfectly placed for a balmy summer's eve or a midday tea break in the shadow of the Blue Mosque. In summer, a lone whirling derviş "performs" nightly at 8 and 10pm. Between Nakılbend and Turün Soks., at the entrance to the Arasta Bazaar. © 0212/518-9562.

Streets of Kumkapı   The narrow warren of streets in the neighborhood opposite the fisherman's wharf of Kumkapı are crowded with restaurants which have staked their claim to individual patches of cobblestone. The atmosphere combines food and fun in a lively villagelike setting, where celebration and sometimes dancing accompany all the seafood you care to eat. Pick your poison (so to speak) by choosing a restaurant, and dig in. Caparız Sok., Kumkapı.

TAKSIM, TÜNEL & BEYOĞLU

Taksim is undeniably the heart of this city's commerce, while the entire district of Beyoğlu brings to mind characteristic back-street cafes, atmospheric bars, and stylish restaurants. While the tourists are shuttling between Taksim Square and Sultanahmet, the residents of Istanbul are making reservations in Beyoğlu. Twenty years ago this was not so, when Istiklal Caddesi looked more like the pre-Disney 42nd Street than the open-air shopping mall it is today. But tucked inside this neighborhood of opulent 19th-century mansions and former consulates are some of the classiest bars in town. Beyoğlu is still a neighborhood in transition, and the closer you get to Taksim Square, the seedier it gets.

Beşinci Kat   Whimsical, even irreverent can best describe this funky, smoky and lavender-filled duplex restaurant-cum-nightclub with open-air rooftop terrace. Offering a playlist that runs the gamut "from Abba to Zappa," Beşinci Kat (which literally means "Fifth Floor"), bills itself as place for "anyone who's got style, taste and a free mind." Open daily 10am to 2am. Soğancı Sok. 7, fifth floor, Cihangir. © 0212/293-3774.

Babylon   This is a popular venue for music concerts full of hip and cosmopolitan chain-smoking Turks in black. There are frequent live concerts so it's a good idea to buy your ticket earlier in the day to avoid the long line. Previous artists included jazz performers Charlie Hunter, Leon Parker, and Harriet Tubman, but more often than not, the musicians are lesser-known imports playing an eclectic (even weird) fusion of music. For reservations and tickets, try to get somebody who can speak Turkish for you or log onto www.babylon.com.tr. Open Tuesday to Saturday 9pm to 4am. Closed July 20 through September 20. Şehbender Sok. 3, Beyoğlu (from Istiklal Cad. near Tünel, turn onto Asmalımecit Sok. and left onto Şehbender). ✆ 0212/292-7368. Cover 20YTL–30YTL ($17–$26/£7.60–£11).

Cezayir   The most popular locale among the new restaurants and cafes around the restored buildings of Francız Sokağı occupies an early-20th-century schoolhouse. There's a large garden shaded by enormous plane trees, and the food is creative without veering too far off the Turkish culinary map. Choose from an a la carte menu (appetizers and main courses 8YTL–28YTL/$7–$24/£3–£11) or from a selection of prix-fixe menus, including a "cocktail menu" for those not in the mood for a full meal. Open daily 9am to 2am. Hayriye Cad. 12 (follow Yeni Çarşı Cad. from Galatasaray High School and turn left on Hayriye Cad.). ✆ 0212/245-9980. Reservations suggested.

Leb-i-Derya   This candlelit rooftop is another one of Istanbul's exceptional panoramic locations and not surprisingly a popular magnet for the sophisticated night owls of Istanbul. In addition to the fab views, the bar is famous for its extensive cocktail menu, including things like Caipirovska and Balalaika, two drinks I've never even heard of. For those arriving with an appetite, the dinner menu offers some tantalizing options (slow-baked leerfish with tomatoes, capers, and olives; artichoke heart and Portobello salad with roasted red peppers and black-eyed peas). The festivities come indoors by the fireplace in winter. Open Monday to Thursday 11am to 2am, Friday 11am to 3am, Saturday 10am to 3am, and Sunday 10am to 2am. Kumbaracı Yokusu, Kumbaracı Han 115/7, Tünel. ✆ 0212/293-4989.

Nardis Jazz Club *Finds*   This joint is so small, so intimate, and so New Orleans that you may have to pinch yourself to see if you are indeed in Istanbul. Reservations are essential for seating next to the tiny stage, although an additional handful of tables is up on the mezzanine. Live acts cover the full range of jazz interpretations, from classical to modern, to fusion to popular. For program listings, log on to www.nardis jazz.com. Open Monday to Thursday 9:30pm to 12:30am; Friday and Saturday 10:30pm to 1:30am. Kuledibi Sok. 14, Galata. ✆ 0212/244-6327. Cover 20YTL ($17/£11).

Şarabı   This Istiklal wine bar looks like any other storefront cafe, but just a few steps down to the cellar—where those in-the-know head—is a late-19th-century underground aqueduct that is said to run from the British Embassy all the way to Tophane. The wine bar stocks more than 100 labels, including some of the better Turkish vintages. Try the Sarafin Cabernet, or the Karma Cabernet/Özküküzü blend. Open daily from 11am to 2am. Istiklal Cad. 80b, Beyoğlu. ✆ 0212/244-4609.

Taps   When asked for insider information on where the locals go, it is a rare response that includes an American-style brewery. But therein lies the paradox: They're certainly not going to the Turkish Night show in the Galata Tower. Taps dispenses seven or eight home-brews, along with a menu typical of this format (finger foods, pizza, salads, wraps, and pasta). The original outlet is in Nişantaşı (Teşvikiye Cad., Atiye Sok. 5; ✆ 0212/296-2020), but this is more central. Open daily 11:30am to 2am. Sofyalı Sok. 11, Asmalımescit, Upper Tünel. ✆ 0212/245-7610.

360 Istanbul ★★   With views as good as this, it's no wonder that Istanbul is sprouting restaurant and bar venues in what are traditionally apartment or office buildings. 360 Istanbul takes advantage of the belfry of St. Antoine and panoramic views of the Golden Horn; on a cool summer's eve, there's really no better place to be. The decor is an unexpectedly pleasing amalgam of brick, steel, glass, and velvet; tables, alfresco banquettes, and a lounge area ensure that everybody gets something he or she wants. The Thai and Turkish menu is rather beside the point, although, there are plenty of appetizers and finger foods to hold you over for the real meal. Go early for the best outdoor seating, or arrive late and mill about the wraparound terrace. Reservations are suggested for dinner (main courses 20YTL–34YTL/$17–$30/£7.60–£13). Open daily noon to 1am. Mısır Apartment Building, Istiklal Cad. 32/311, Beyoğlu. ✆ 0212/251-1042.

Viktor Levi Şarap Evi   A veritable institution in Beyoğlu, Viktor Levi is one of Istanbul's oldest wine houses. The *fer forgé* is the first indication of the 19th-century origins of the wine bar; it's a great spot to head to if you're looking to "go where the natives go" (if there is only one such place). Impress your date by ordering a bottle of the Viktor Levi special house wine. Open daily 11am to 2am. Hamalbaşi Cad. 12, Beyoğlu. ✆ 0212/249-6085.

V.S.O.P. Bar   Designed to re-create a traditional English library, V.S.O.P. is an elegant and definitely mature locale on the mezzanine level of the Marmara Istanbul hotel (p. 72). While I try to avoid hotel bars, this is actually an enjoyable spot for a drink and conversation. Open daily from noon to 11pm (later on weekends). Taksim Meydanı, Taksim. ✆ 0212/251-4696.

ALONG THE BOSPHORUS

Istanbul's nightlife succumbs to the lure of the Bosphorus in the summer months (generally Apr until the end of Oct), moving alfresco and up to the seafront venues of Ortaköy and Kuruçeşme. Names tend to change seasonally, but the locations and general theme stays the same. The most popularly frequented venues as of 2007 are listed here.

Anjelique   This is a sister operation to the majorly successful Vogue, Anna, A'jia, and Da Mario (not all listed here). The formula seems unable to fail. Anjelique takes up the top three floors above Da Mario (creating a dining dilemma, p. 108). Jazz and soul are played during dining hours, complementing a sensual decor backlit by the nighttime glow of the sea and sky. Dinner is served on the top two floors, while the lower floor is dedicated to the dynamic lounge. Open May through October. Restaurant is open 6pm to midnight, and the bar 7pm to 4am. Muallim Naci Cad., Salhane Sok. 10, Ortaköy. ✆ 0212/327-2844. No cover.

Q Jazz   Q Jazz Bar cut its teeth in the cellar of the Çırağan Palace hotel before coming up to the hotel's garden terrace in summers. True to its elite lineage, Q now draws the cream of Istanbul society to its new location on the waterfront of Les Ottomans (p. 81), where there's never an empty seat in the house. The bar and kitchen are open 7 nights a week, offering delectable appetizers such as lobster and caviar. Open daily 7pm until dawn. Live music begins at 11pm. Muallim Naci Cad. 68, Kuruçeşme. ✆ 0212/359-1500. Cover 30YTL ($26/£11) after 11pm.

Reina   As the grande dame of after-hours entertainment, Reina is a veritable multiplex of popular restaurants, a handful of waterfront dance floors, and bars, including the Zagat-rated Park Şamdan (reservations required for all restaurants). The music, and the crowd, is eclectic; pretty much anything goes. Open daily in the summer from 7pm to 4am. Muallim Naci Cad. 44, Ortaköy; ℭ **0212/259-5919**. Fri–Sat cover 30YTL ($26/£11).

Sunset Bar and Grill   A restaurant and bar overlook a particularly breathtaking stretch of the Bosphorus, sheltered by breezy stretches of sailcloth. When it opened in 1994, Sunset set a new standard for Istanbul nights, and as late as 2000, it was still the only game in town for sushi. The international menu takes advantage of the establishment's very own herb garden, and some would argue that Sunset still has the best sushi around. Take advantage of a rare vintage taken from probably the best wine cellar in Istanbul, or complement a glass of aged Bisquit cognac with a Cuban cigar. Open daily at noon until the last customer leaves. Kitchen closes at 11:30pm on Sunday through Thursday, and midnight Friday and Saturday. Adnan Saygun Cad., Yol Sok. 2, Ulus. ℭ **0212/287-0357**. No sushi at lunch on Sat–Sun.

Ulus 29   Istanbul's nightspots may come and go, but after 15 years, the popularity of this grand dame of a nightclub on the Bosphorus shows no signs of abating. An unbeatable location on the hilltop of Ulus, which translates into one of Istanbul's original unbeatable views of the Bosphorus, practically sealed its fate. One of the owners, Zeynep Fadıllıoğlu, who is an interior designer, likes to stay ahead of design trends and updates the decor annually. I can say, though, that each incarnation is even more plush, more rich, more lavish than the one before. The main event happens on the outdoor terrace—a collection of transparent netted tents enclose private dining or lounging areas. The international and Asian fusion menu gets mixed reviews, but gets an A+ for inventiveness. The restaurant is open daily noon to 4pm and 7pm to midnight. The bar is open until 4am in summer. Kirechane Sok. 1, Adnan Saygün Cad. Ulus Parkı, Ulus. ℭ **0212/358-2929**.

11

Side Trips from Istanbul

The emergence of domestic airline carriers puts Istanbul within an hour or two of almost everywhere in the country. This makes short hops both easy and cheap (cheaper than driving, with petrol prices at about $100/£50 per tank full, compared to fares as low as $50/£25). For the purposes of this book, short hops here will include only those select popular or significant spots reachable by land or ferry in less than 2 hours. You'll be able to return to your Istanbul hotel at night with enough time for a big night out or a relaxing night in.

1 Bursa: Gateway to an Empire

Bursa established itself as an important center as far back as pre-Roman times, attracting emperors and rulers for its rich, fertile soil and healing thermal waters. The arrival of the Ottomans in 1326 ensured the city's prosperity as a cultural and economic center that now represents one of the richest legacies of early Ottoman art and architecture. As the first capital of the Ottoman Empire, Bursa became the beneficiary of the finest mosques, theological schools *(medreses)*, humanitarian centers *(imarets)*, and social services *(hans, hamams, and public fountains)*. The density of arched portals, undulating domes, artfully tiled minarets, and magnificently carved *minbars* (pulpits) could easily provide the coursework for extensive study of the Ottomans, and without a doubt, fill multiple daylong walking tours.

Today Bursa is a thriving industrial and agricultural center, renowned for its fine silk and cotton textiles, and the center of Turkey's automobile industry. The nearby ski resorts at Mount Uludağ provide city dwellers with an easy weekend getaway, while others just make a special trip here to stock up on cotton towels. Still, many flock here for the same reasons the Romans, Byzantines, and Ottomans did: the indulgence afforded by the density of rich, hot mineral springs bubbling up all over the region.

If you plan on just a quick architectural and historical pilgrimage, you could reasonably make Bursa a day trip from Istanbul. An overnight excursion is more realistic if you want to make it a short spa getaway and leave time to wander through the exquisite *hans* (privately owned inns or marketplaces) of the early Ottoman era.

A LOOK AT THE PAST

It was common practice for a conquering king to attach his name to the cities that he founded, so the consensus is that King Prusia of Bithynia established a kingdom on the remains of a preexisting civilization here. Prusia (say it 10 times fast and it starts to sound like Bursa) of Olympus, distinguishing it from King Prusia's other conquests, was later leagued with Rome, a colonization that is attributed to the time of Eumenes II, leader of Pergamum. Bursa thrived, thanks to Rome's influence and the introduction of Christianity by the apostle Andrew. In the 6th century A.D., Emperor Justinian constructed baths and a lavish palace in the area, taking full advantage of the

Bursa

ACCOMMODATIONS ■
Çelik Palas Hotel **5**
Kervansaray Termal Hotel **4**
Safran Hotel **9**

DINING ◆
Çiçek Izgara **18**
Uludağ Kebapçısı **3**

ATTRACTIONS ●
Archaeology Museum (Arkeoloji Müzesi) **6**
Atatürk Museum (Atatürk Müzesi) **7**
Bursa Museum of Turkish and Islamic Arts
(Türk Islam Eser. Müzesi) **21**
Covered Bazaar (Bedesten) **13**
Emir Han **14**
Fidan Han **17**
Green Mosque (Yeşil Camii) **20**
Green Tomb (Yeşil Türbesi) **20**
Kara Mustafa Paşa Thermal Bath **2**
Karagöz Hacivat Memorial **1**
Kaynarca **2**
Koza Hani **16**
Muradiye Complex (Muradiye Külliye) **8**
Orhan Gazi Mosque (Orhan Camii) **19**
Pirinç Han **12**
Ipek Han **11**
The Great Mosque (Ulu Camii) **15**
Tombs of Osman and Orhan **10**
Uluumay Ottoman Museum **8**
Yeni Kaplica **2**
Yildirim Beyazit Mosque
(Yıldırım Beyazit Camii) **22**

See inset (left)

Map labels
BULGARIA   Black Sea
Istanbul
Bursa
TURKEY

Kükürtlü Cad.
Çekirge Cad.
Pinar Cad.
NILÜFER
CIRIŞHANE
Demiryolu Cad.
Mudanya-Bulvarı
Kültür Park
Çekirge Cad.
Stadyum Cad.
HAMZABEY
ESENTEPE
SELIMYE
INTIZAM
AHMET PAŞA
DOĞANBEY
KURUÇEŞME
Altıparmak Cad.
Tophane Park
OZMANGAZI
ŞEHREKÜSTÜ
Cumhuriyet Cad.
Haşim Işcan Cad.
REYHAN
TAHTAKALE
Inönü Cad.
Kemal Bengü Cad.
Beyazıt Cad.
MEYDANCIK
YEŞIL

1/2 Mi
1/2 Km

Bursa Center
REYHAN
TUZPAZARI
ŞEHREKÜSTÜ
Haşim Işcan Cad.
Cumhuriyet Cad.
Uzunçarşı Cad.
Atatürk Cad.
Cemal Nadir Cad.
Tophane Park

region's economic and thermal resources. From 1080 to 1326, Bursa bore the brunt of more than its fair share of invasions, with Selçuks, Turks, raiding Arabs, Byzantines, and Crusaders all trying to get a hold on this prosperous center. One of the Turkic tribes broke the chain when the Osmanlı tribe of Turks, led by Osman and later his son Orhan, entered Bursa in 1326 after a 10-year-long siege. Orhan established Bursa as the first permanent Ottoman capital, building a mosque and *medrese* on the site of a Byzantine monastery in what is now the Hisar District. The city expanded and thrived under Sultans Murat I, Yıldırım Beyazit, Mehmet I, and Murad II. Bursa's importance began to wane when the Ottoman capital was transferred to Adrianople (present-day Edirne).

ESSENTIALS

GETTING THERE   From Istanbul's Yenikapı docks are two ferry options for excursions to Bursa. The first is IDO's new service to the Güzelyalı port at Güzelyalı (© 0212/444-4436; www.ido.com.tr). The ferry takes 75 minutes and costs 20YTL ($17/£7.60 per person) with five departures daily (six on Fri and Sun). From Güzelyalı to Bursa, take the local bus to the metro which you will take to the last stop, arriving in the city center. Total time (including ferry, bus, and metro) from Istanbul to Bursa is about 2½ hours.

The other option from the Yenikapı docks in Istanbul is the 70-minute ferry ride (12YTL/$10/£4.60) to Yalova, north of Bursa. Ferries run every 2 hours in either direction beginning at 7:30am (last ferry: 9:30pm). From the ferry landing, hop on one of the many buses lined up outside the gates; the ride to Bursa's *otogar* (bus station) takes about 50 minutes and costs 7YTL ($6.10/£2.70). Bursa's *otogar* is located more than 10km (6 miles) out of town, so it will be necessary to either get on a municipal bus (no. 38 to Heykel or no. 96 to Çekirge) or take a taxi into town. The bus takes about half an hour and costs 1.50YTL ($1.30/60p). With luggage, this is a major stretch. Instead, a taxi is direct, quick, and cheap (expect to pay around 20YTL/$17/£7.60 for the 20-min. ride).

Both the ferry to Yalova and to Güzelyalı accept cars, so if you're not overly excited about the hoops you have to jump through to get there, you can shuttle yourself from the ferry docks straight into Bursa. IDO charges 60YTL ($52/£23) and 75YTL ($65/£29), respectively, for cars plus 15YTL ($13/£5.70) and 10YTL ($8.70/£3.80) for each *additional* passenger in the vehicle.

If you prefer to do the entire journey by land, **Nilüfer Turizm** (© 0224/444-0099), based in Bursa, provides the most comprehensive bus service into Bursa. The 4-hour trip from Istanbul costs 15YTL ($13/£5.80). **Metro** (© 0212/444-3455) runs buses almost hourly from Istanbul for the same price, as does **Kamil Koç** (© 0212/444-0562).

VISITOR INFORMATION   The **Tourist Information office** (© 0224/251-1834; fax: 0224/220-1848) is hidden underneath Atatürk Caddesi in the center of town. If you're standing with Orhan Camii on your right and the Belediye (Municipal Building) on your left, the office is straight ahead of you at 12 o'clock. The PTT (post office) is located a few blocks west (to the right) down Atatürk Caddesi on the opposite side of the street.

All of the major bus companies have ticket offices around Heykel; tickets can also be purchased through any local travel agent or at the *otogar.*

ORIENTATION   The concentration of early Selçuk-inspired architecture is clustered in the commercial center of Bursa, in the area better known to the locals as

> ### *Tips* Turkish Towels & Such
>
> If you're in the market for a few fluffy towels or one of those luscious Turkish bathrobes that sell for an arm and a leg in Bloomingdale's, the price for selection at Bursa's **Covered Bazaar** (see "What to See & Do," below) can't be beat. The subtlest prints and plushest linens and towels are found at **Özdilek**, with branches in both the bazaar (exit the underground passage opposite the PTT and walk 1 block in) and a shopping center at Yenı Yalova Yolu 4, on the highway from the *otogar* (© **0224/219-6000**). Silk fabrics, such as scarves, blouses, and tablecloths, are available in shops on the upper level of **Koza Hanı,** the historic *bedesten* (covered market) next to Orhan Camii. For modern merchandise in a slick mall setting, the new glass pyramid–topped **Zafer Plaza** houses franchises such as Quicksilver, Vakko, Demirel, Mavi Jeans, and Polo Garage.

Heykel, after the equestrian statue of Atatürk commanding the plaza just a few blocks to the east (*heykel* means "statue" in Turkish). Again, using the Tourist Information office for orientation, to the west/right is **Tophane Park** and the **Hisar District,** where the conquering Ottoman armies set up their capital in the 15th century. The road leads into the posher **Çekirge** section, where ambassadors and statesmen flock for the hotels and thermal hot springs. The winter ski resort of Uludağ is located about 36km (22 miles) to the south of Bursa and reachable via a funicular from the center of town.

GETTING AROUND   In all likelihood, you will spend most of your time between the Heykel and Çekirge neighborhoods. While covering small distances on foot in either neighborhood is possible, the two are just too far apart to think about walking between them. Instead, hop on a *dolmuş*—in Bursa, *dolmuşes* are group taxis—running conveniently along the main arteries. (The street names change so many times that it's useless to mention them here.) *Dolmuşes* cost around 3YTL ($2.60/£1.15) and are distinguishable from the multiple destinations marked on the roof of the car. A taxi taking the same route will cost about 10YTL ($8.70/£3.80).

WHAT TO SEE & DO

Bursa is so jampacked with historic structures that it would be impossible to list them all here. In addition to the major sites named below, be sure to wander through the marketplace, spread out among open-air and covered streets. *Hans* are traditionally double-storied arcaded buildings with a central courtyard, usually occupied by an ornate fountain or pool or raised *mescit* (a small mosque). The *hans* are still used for trade and make lovely shaded retreats to take a coffee outdoors and poke amid the local merchandise. The **Fidan Han** dates to the 15th century and has a central pool topped by a *mescit*. The **Pirinç Han** (closed) was constructed by Beyazit II to earn the revenue necessary to cover the expenses of his mosque and soup kitchen in Istanbul. The **Ipek Han** is the largest *han* in Bursa and contains an octagonal *mescit* in the center of the courtyard. The revenue from this *han* was used to pay for the construction of the Yeşil Mosque. The courtyard of **Emir Han** has a graceful marble pool with exterior faucets to allow for ablutions.

Archaeology Museum (Arkeoloji Müzesi)   Constructed with the charm of any 1972 institutional project, this museum is worth the 30 minutes it will take to get

through, especially if you're strolling through Çekirge or into Kültür Park. The fact that the attendant trails you to turn the lights on and off is a bit unnerving (the museum doesn't see that many tourists), obliging you to react with an appropriate level of enthusiasm. The museum houses regional artifacts dating back to the 3rd century B.C., with crude pottery and tools from as far back as the Neolithic period. Particularly impressive is the collection of ceramic and glass objects from the Classical era, much of which has remained surprisingly intact. The extensive collection of coins displayed on the mezzanine is significant because notable figures had a habit of emblazoning their portraits on the face of the piece, providing a rare window of accessibility to the ancients.

Kültür Park. ℂ 0224/220-2029. Admission 2YTL ($1.75/80p). Tues–Sun 8:30am–noon and 1–5pm.

Atatürk Museum (Atatürk Müzesi)   This is one of those traditional timber mansions at which you'd love to get a closer look. The historic rooms have been left as they were when Atatürk slept here on his visits to Bursa, down to the very last particle of dust.

Çekirge Cad., next to the Çelik Palas. ℂ 0224/236-4844. Free admission. Tues–Sun 8:30am–noon and 1–5pm.

Bursa Museum of Turkish and Islamic Arts (Türk Islam Eser. Müzesi) 🎯
Housed in the former *medrese* of the Green Mosque, built in 1419 by Çelebi Sultan Mehmet along with the other buildings in the Yeşil complex, this museum is worth a look, particularly because they've gone to the trouble of providing English translations. The exhibits are intimately displayed in small rooms around a central courtyard. There's a space devoted to derviş cult objects, a *hamam* room displaying silver clogs and silk embroidered bath accessories, and a model of a traditional Turkish coffeehouse, complete with barber's chair. The collection also includes Selçuk ceramics, inlaid wood pieces, and objects in iron, copper, bronze, and wood. A visit takes under 30 minutes.

Yeşil Cad., on the left just before the Green Mosque. ℂ 0224/327-7679. Admission 2YTL ($1.75/80p). Tues–Sun 8:30am–5pm.

Covered Bazaar (Bedesten)   The covered bazaar that stands on the site is a modern version of the original that was built by Yıldırım Beyazit in the 14th century and leveled in the earthquake of 1855. There's no glitz—or tourists—here, evidenced by the distressing concentration of satin embroidered towels and bedspreads. Keep your eyes open for good-quality baby clothes and knockoff sportswear, and if you're looking to stuff a throw pillow, this is the place to do it, as stalls displaying fluffy unspun cotton of varying composition and quality abound.

Enter through Koza Hanı, or follow Çarşı Cad. from Ulu Camii. Daily 8:30am–7pm.

The Great Mosque (Ulu Camii) 🎯🎯   When this building was erected in 1396, architects were just beginning to dabble in the problem of covering large spaces with small domes, and the result is the first example of a monumental Ottoman multidomed mosque. The 20 domes, supported on 12 stout pillars, are better admired from within, where the final result comes together in the mosque's five naves and four bays.

The date of completion (802H—H is for *hicret,* the day Mohammed left Mecca for Medina) is inscribed on the pulpit door, but several waves of renovations were necessary after the invasion of Tamerlane, with major restorations completed after the earthquake of 1855.

The wooden *minbar* (pulpit) is a masterwork of carved geometric and floral reliefs, as is the banister work and other wood details. But the main focus of the mosque is the three-tiered **ablution fountain** beneath a large light well. Although this has its practical purposes, the result is an embracing sensation of serenity, and many worshipers remain on the raised platforms surrounding the fountain for long moments of meditation.

Bursa center. No phone. Free admission. Daily dawn–dusk.

Green Mosque (Yeşil Camii) ⍟   Commanding a hillside terrace above the city, Yeşil Camii takes its name from the green and blue tiles in the interior. Intent on leaving his mark on Bursa, Mehmet I ordered the construction of this mosque, built entirely of hewn stone and marble, as a monument to the victorious ending of his 10-year struggle for the throne. Although an architect's inscription over the portal gives the completion date as 1419, the final decorations were ordered in 1424 on the orders of Murad II, and the two minarets were added in the 19th century.

One of the first mosques to employ an inverted T floor plan, the building signals the dawn of a new Turkish architectural tradition. The "Turkish pleat," an ingenious geometric corner detail allowing for the placement of a circular dome atop a square base, is a design device original to Turkey, while the use of multicolored ceramic tile, an influence that arrived with Tamerlane, is intricate enough to make your head spin. The high porcelain *mihrab* (a niche oriented toward Mecca) is a masterpiece of Ottoman ceramic art, difficult to miss at an understated 10m (33 ft.) high. In the center of the *mihrab* in Arabic script is the word "Allah," mounted on the wall at a later date.

The sumptuous gold mosaics and tile of the Imperial loge were probably an overstated attempt at one-upping the loggia that served the Byzantine emperors; it is flanked on either side by the servants' quarters and the harem, and a closer look is at the discretion of the caretaker.

East of Heykel at the end of Yeşil Cad. No phone. Free admission. Daily dawn–dusk.

Green Tomb (Yeşil Türbesi) ⍟⍟   This Selçuk-influenced tomb, representing one of the noblest of its era, has become the symbol of Bursa. If you're looking for a blue building, look no further, as the tiles of this hexagonal structure are actually turquoise, topped by a lead dome resting on a plaster rim. The construction of the tomb was ordered by the tenant himself, Sultan Mehmet I, and was completed around 1421. The color glazing of the interior tile work is an outstanding example of the art, from the window pediments adorned with verses of the Koran and *hadiths* (narrations of the life of Mohammad) in Arabic script, to the tile inscriptions on the sarcophagi. It's also worth noting the workmanship of the colors of the panels on the *mihrab*, which change color according to your perspective.

East of Heykel at the end of Yeşil Cad. No phone. Free admission. Daily 8am–noon and 1–5pm.

Koza Hanı ⍟⍟   Meaning "Cocoon Inn," this caravansary was built in 1490 by Beyazit II to raise funds for his mosque in Istanbul. Built on two levels, the inn provided a place for the merchants to trade the last of their goods, as this was the final stop on the Silk Road from China. In the middle of the courtyard is a small *şadırvan* (ablution fountain) for the small *mescit* (prayer room) poised above; in the summer the verdant space becomes a peaceful tea garden. The monumental portal decorated with turquoise tiles and carvings leads into the covered bazaar. Today the Koza Hanı continues its legacy of trading in silk with shops and boutiques stocked with scarves and fabrics at exorbitant (yet negotiable) prices.

Bursa Center. No phone. Free admission. Daily 8:30am–sunset.

Muradiye Complex (Muradiye Külliye) 𝒜𝒜   Constructed by Murat II between 1424 and 1426, this complex includes a mosque, a *medrese,* a soup kitchen, a bath, and a royal cemetery amid an overgrown garden of roses, magnolias, and cypress trees. Although the entrance to the grounds is open, many of the tombs and even the mosque are locked up, but the idle-yet-earnest ticket-window attendant will catch up with you for a private tour of the grounds, proudly locking and unlocking the royal tombs.

The Murat Paşa Mosque is a typical example of early Ottoman architecture, although the *mihrab* and *minbar* are 18th-century baroque. To the right, beginning toward the rear of the grounds, is no ordinary cemetery. The 12 stately tombs serve as the final resting places of not only some of the first sultans, but a sobering number of members of the royal family as well, including Hüma Hatun (mother of Mehmet the Conqueror), Shehzade Ahmed (son of Beyazit II and crowned prince), Sultan Murat II, Mustafa (son of Süleyman the Magnificent), and Gülşah Hatun (wife of Mehmet the Conqueror). Because succession rights relied not on heredity but on survival of the fittest, it was standard, even expected, practice for the victorious leader to cover his back by strangling his brothers with a wire cord.

The most recognizable casualty of this practice was the son of Süleyman the Magnificent: Şehzade (Prince) Mustafa, who as object of a plot spun by Roxelana for the succession of her own son, was unjustly murdered at the hands of his father. Ironically, the tomb was built by Selim II, Roxelana's son and successor to the throne.

The restored opulence of the tomb's outstanding porcelain tiling radiates hues of teal and red on quartz whose production technique was, until recently, lost. In contrast, the mausoleum of Murad I, son of Orhan and third Ottoman sultan, is elegant in its simplicity. The tomb has a domed central courtyard surrounded by the traditional ambulatory. Upon the request of the sultan, an oculus was designed in the dome to allow the rains to wash over the open tomb, symbolizing his sameness with the plain folk.

After reigning for just 18 days and living the rest of his life in exile, Cem Sultan, the youngest son of Mehmed II, was brought back to Bursa to receive a royal burial in the tomb that had actually been built for Şehzade Mustafa.

The 15th-century *medrese,* now operating as a clinic, was designed around a central courtyard accessible through vaulted arches at the entrance. No one will bother you if you want to take a quick peek, but the main use for this clinic is as a tuberculosis dispensary, so it might be better to do your admiring from the outside.

The Tarıhı II Murat Hamamı next to the mosque is still in operation, with separate days designated for men and women.

Çekirge (from the town center, take *dolmu* marked MURADIYE). No phone. Free admission. Tues–Sun 8:30am–noon and 1–5pm.

Orhan Gazi Mosque (Orhan Camii) 𝒜𝒜   Constructed between 1339 and 1340 by Orhan Gazi, this is one of the most important early Ottoman constructions in Bursa. Pointed arches on the veranda show the beginnings of a particularly Ottoman detail, while the exterior brickwork recalls its Selçuk origins. The mosque was damaged in 1413 by Karamanoğlu Mehmet Bey and repaired in 1417 by Çelebi Sultan Mehmet. Note the star-shaped decorations representing the course of the sun and the marble embellishments on the eastern and western facades.

The surrounding complex is one of the first in the Ottoman tradition, consisting of a mosque, *medrese,* soup kitchen, bath, and inn. The cats apparently stay there free of charge, and the whole courtyard and mosque interior have a homey feel.

Bursa town center, across from the Municipal Building. No phone. Free admission. Daily dawn–dusk.

> **Fun Fact They Died with a Smile (or, That Joke's a Killer)**
>
> When Sultan Orhan arrived in Bursa, he immediately set out to build his mosque. He appointed a man named **Hacivat** as supervisor, who in turn hired a local blacksmith named **Karagöz** to oversee the installation of the iron supports. Hacivat and Karagöz used to pass the time with clever quips and witty conversation that kept the laborers in stitches. The two eventually had the workmen doubled over in hysterics, to the point that work on the mosque came to a complete halt.
>
> When the sultan found out about the construction delays, he had Hacivat and Karagöz hanged (or decapitated, depending on which interpretation of the oral history you hear). The decapitated version is favored, because illustrators have had a grand time depicting the two hapless jokers approaching the sultan's throne to protest with their heads under their arms. Whichever demise you choose, the outcome is the same: Orhan finds someone to relate the dialogues, until the sultan, too, is keeling over with laughter. Realizing his error, the sultan orders a local leather worker to create lifelike figures of the two, so that they can continue their legacy of comedy. This puppetlike shadow play gained momentum and grew into a popular cultural tradition, boasting as many as 200 characters in one presentation.
>
> As you drive from the center of town toward Çekirge, ask your driver to point out the **Karagöz Hacivat Memorial,** a small but colorful representation of the two folk heroes.

Tombs of Osman and Orhan ⟨𝄐⟩ This lovely park attracts local tourists as much for its tea gardens and stunning views as for the **tombs** of the two founders of the Ottoman Empire. The location in the *Hisar* (fortress), the oldest section of the city, which passed from Roman to Byzantine and finally to Ottoman hands, is a fitting one for the final resting places of Osman Gazi and Orhan Gazi.

According to Osman Gazi's wish to be "laid to rest beneath the silver dome of Bursa," his tomb was constructed on the chapel of St. Elie, the Byzantine monastery formerly on the site. The sarcophagus, surrounded by an ornate brass balustrade, is decorated with mother-of-pearl inlay. At one time, the building also contained the tomb of Orhan, but after it was partially destroyed by fire and then leveled by the 1855 earthquake, Sultan Abdülaziz had Orhan's tomb rebuilt separately. The Orhan tomb, slightly less ornate than his father's tomb, was constructed on the foundation of an 11th-century Byzantine church, from which some mosaics in the floor have survived.

Hisar District (inside the entrance to Tophane Park along Arka Sok., just west of the post office). No phone. Free admission. Daily dawn–dusk.

Uluumay Ottoman Museum ⟨𝄐⟩ The restored architectural gem that is the Sair Ahmet Medrese rivals the museum within. Located in the Muradiye Complex, this assemblage of folk art was collected from around the Ottoman Empire, including the Caucuses, the Balkans, and the home territory of Anatolia. The ample ethnographic exhibition features over 400 pieces of Ottoman-era jewelry, plus household items, saddlebags, silk scarves, and silver watch fobs, to name a few.

Sair Ahmet Paşa Medresesi, Muradiye Camisi Karşısı, Beşikçiler Cad., Muradiye. © **0224/225-4813.** Admission 3YTL ($2.60/£1.30). Tues–Sun 9am–6:30pm (closed at 6pm, Sept–Apr).

Yıldırım Beyazit Mosque (Yıldırım Beyazit Camii)   The two prominent domes, set one behind the other, represent an attempt at a design feature reminiscent of the St. Irene of Constantinople and the St. John's Basilica at Ephesus. Awkwardly juxtaposed above the three remaining domes, the larger two create a prayer hall that was to become a theme in the architecture of Ottoman mosques.

The mosque forms a part of the *külliye*, or complex, comprising a *medrese*, a *hamam*, a hospital, and the tomb of the Sultan Beyazit I, built by his son Süleyman the Magnificent in 1406.

Northeast of the town center in the Yıldırım District. No phone. Free admission. Daily dawn–dusk.

WHERE TO STAY

Çelik Palas Hotel ⊛⊛   Built in the 1930s under instructions by Atatürk, the Çelik Palas holds the title as Turkey's first five-star hotel. Until recently, this acclaimed Turkish icon was showing its dubious pedigree, but thanks to a recent upgrade, the Çelik Palas is once again at the top of its game. The best rooms—those facing the mountains—each combine the space of two rooms forming comfortably plush junior suites, with such luxuries as two bathrooms (one with a massage shower; the other a Jacuzzi tub), stylish furniture, and a sofa bed that increases the room capacity to four. Rooms in the annex are rarely used, making this end of the hotel great for groups. Best of all, there's the large, domed, **marble thermal pool,** the crowned jewel of a small wellness facility that's free for guests (see "Water, Water Everywhere: Turkey's Mineral Springs," below).

Çekirge Cad. 79, 16070 Çekirge. © **0224/233-3800.** Fax 0224/236-1910. www.celikpalasotel.com. 158 units. 270YTL ($235/£103) double; 320YTL–570YTL ($278–$495/£122–£217) suites. AE, DC, MC, V. On-site parking. **Amenities:** Restaurant; bar; large thermal pool; spa (w/*hamam*, Jacuzzi, and sauna); concierge; tour desk; car-rental desk; shopping arcade; salon; 24-hr. room service; massage; laundry service; dry cleaning; nonsmoking rooms. *In room:* A/C, cable TV, Wi-Fi, minibar, hair dryer, safe.

Kervansaray Termal Hotel ⊛   This is the preferred hotel in Bursa, one that never lets you forget you're in a town of thermal springs. There's a decorative waterfall in the modern lobby, two swimming pools, and a renovated multidomed 700-year-old *hamam*. Most rooms have a balcony with a valley, mountain, or garden view, but, frankly, are nothing to write home about. The health club's cleverly designed swimming pool is divided by a retractable window, providing for both indoor and outdoor swimming, and the water is supplied by nearby mineral springs.

Çekirge Meydanı, 16080 Çekirge. © **0224/233-9300.** Fax 0224/233-9324. www.kervansarayhotels.com/bursa. 224 units. 150€ ($210/£107) double; 250€ ($350/£178) and up suite; rates lower June–Dec, higher for religious festivals. AE, MC, V. **Amenities:** 2 restaurants; 2 bars; outdoor pool; fitness room; concierge; tour desk; meeting and banquet facilities; car-rental desk; shopping arcade; salon; 24-hr. room service; massage; laundry service; dry cleaning; historic thermal bath w/separate sections for men and women. *In room:* A/C, satellite TV, minibar, hair dryer.

Safran Hotel   The first guesthouse in Bursa, this hotel occupies a beautiful safran colored Ottoman mansion on a historic street across from Tophane Park. Rooms are characterized by old mattresses and worn flannel or print bedspreads, making the entire experience more like spending the weekend in a friend's garret. This of course assumes a minimum level of cleanliness, and the rattiness itself can be somewhat charming.

Ortapazar Cad., Arka Sok. 4, 16040 (near the gated entrance to the Osman and Orhan tombs). © **224/224-7216.** Fax 224/224-7219. http://safranhotel.sitemynet.com. 10 units. $90 (£45) double. AE, MC, V. **Amenities:** Children's playroom; laundry; dry cleaning; parking. *In room:* A/C, cable TV, minibar, hair dryer, safe.

Water, Water Everywhere: Turkey's Mineral Springs

A geologic oddity-cum-spa treat with which Turkey is uncommonly blessed is the mineral spring. Thermal baths flow freely throughout the countryside and, depending on the properties and temperature of the water, are reputed to address such varied ailments as obesity, digestive problems, rheumatism, and urological disorders. Soaking in the springs and covering yourself with mineral-rich mud are some of the country's lesser-known pleasures. You can experience the thermal springs enclosed in pamper-me surroundings or in humble out-of-the-way sites.

In Bursa, history and pampering go hand in hand, and no historical pilgrimage to this city would be complete without a long soak in a mineral-rich thermal pool. The **Kervansaray Termal Hotel's 700-year-old thermal bath** ✦✦ (p. 224) takes advantage of the **Eski Kaplıca** thermal spring, an ancient source used as far back as Roman times. The bath was built in grand Ottoman style by Sultan Murat I in 1389, and a soak here (7am–11pm) is made all the more satisfying with its multiple domes and old stonemasonry. The price of admission to the thermal baths, including massage and *kese* (sloughing), is 30€ ($42/£21).

No one knows who originally occupied the **Yeni Kaplıca** *hamam* ✦✦, Yeni Kaplıca Cad. 6, Çekirge (ℂ **0224/236-6968**; 13YTL/$11/£4.75 entrance to man's side; 10YTL/$8.70/£3.80 woman's entrance; 6YTL/$5.25/£2.30 sloughing, 12YTL/$10/£4.60 massage), built in 1555 and reconstructed for Süleyman the Magnificent by Grand Vizier Rüstem Paşa. The *hamam* (or at least, the men's side) still displays its original opulence, allowing wide-eyed tourists to feel like Julius Caesar for a day.

Separated from the Yeni Kaplıca building by a tea garden is the less-impressive **Kaynarca**, Yeni Kaplıca Cad. 8 (ℂ **0224/236-6955**; 6YTL/$5.25/£2.30 entrance, treatments extra), essentially a mud pit catering to women only. **Kara Mustafa Paşa Thermal Bath,** Mudanya Cad. 10 (ℂ **0224/236-6956**), was left over from the Byzantine era and was actually the first building on the site. There are two sections, including one where you can ooze yourself into a gravelike tile ditch full of scorching hot mud (avoid wearing a white bathing suit for this). There are also the regular bath facilities and cubicles for changing and resting. Kara Mustafa also has rudimentary hotel accommodations. Granted, it's all rather gritty, but thoroughly worth the experience. The more luxurious **Çelik Palas Hotel thermal pool** ✦✦ (p. 224; 30YTL/$26/£11 entrance for nonguests, free for guests) rests beneath a single multiple-sky-lit dome; the hotel's facility offers opulence while the others excel in local character.

WHERE TO DINE

Çiçek Izgara TURKISH   There's nothing worse than wandering around the center of a busy town and not knowing where to eat. Çiçek Izgara comes highly recommended by the locals, combining three floors of white linen tablecloths and impeccable service with the bright casualness of a cafeteria. Menu items include *peynerli köfte* (meatballs with cheese), *kabak dolması* (stuffed zucchini), and *cacık,* a refreshing yogurt soup.

Belediye Cad. (just after Orhan Camii on the left, 2nd floor). © 0224/221-6526. Kebaps and *köfte* 7YTL–12YTL ($6.10–$10/£2.70–£4.60). MC, V. Daily 10am–midnight.

Uludağ Kebapçısı ✿✿ KEBAPS   The best food is often found in unremarkable, even divelike places. Although Grandpa Iskender, the inventor of the *döner kebap,* has the historical corner on this much-loved recipe, this place has perfected it. Located in two narrow storefronts near the old bus terminal, the Uludağ Kebapçısı is arguably the best place in the world to eat the Iskender *döner kebap.* You can order it with decadent slices of steak *(bonfile),* surprisingly delicious kidney *(böbrek),* or what the owner called "back" *(kantıfile)*—but don't complain to me if your cholesterol levels shoot through the roof: Uludağ goes through 18kg (40 lb.) of butter per day. Throw caution to the wind, and top it all off with the *sütlü helva,* a heavenly milk pudding served mainly in the cooler months.

Garaj Karşısı Şirin Sok. 12. © 0224/254-7264. Kebaps 10YTL ($8.70/£3.80). MC, V. Daily 11am–midnight.

2 Iznik & Nicaea: A Pilgrimage & Some Plates

To Turks, the sleepy lakeside resort of Iznik provides a respite from the sweltering summer sun; to Christendom, Iznik sits atop modern-day **Nicaea,** the former seat of the Eastern Roman Empire and the site of the first and second Ecumenical Councils. It's also synonymous with Ottoman ceramic art, which reached its pinnacle in the 15th and 16th centuries during the reign of Süleyman the Magnificent. While you're here, you should take the time to have lunch at one of the lakeside restaurants.

GETTING THERE & GETTING AROUND

Iznik is easily reached from Bursa or via the ferries from Istanbul to Bursa (see "Getting There," p. 218). *Dolmuşes* marked "Iznik," regularly depart from Yalova, north of Bursa, from the main road that passes in front of the ferryboat landing (cross the street and hop on one headed south) as well as from Bursa itself. Once in Iznik, buses deposit passengers on the main road in front of the church. Drivers should take the car ferry from Istanbul to Yalova. From Yalova, follow the road to Bursa taking the first turnoff at Orhangazi to Iznik and follow the road along the north side of the lake.

Iznik retains the grid plan established in its Hellenistic era. Monuments are well signposted, but without a car, you'll be pounding the pavement for the better part of a day.

WHAT TO SEE & DO

Ancient Nicaea   The ancient city of Nicaea and modern-day Iznik are enclosed along the eastern edge of Lake Iznik by about 5km (3 miles) of **ancient city walls** ✿, made accessible through several ancient gates of which the **Istanbul Kapısı** ✿ is the best preserved. In the center of town are the well-preserved remains of the **Church of Aya Sofya** ✿✿ (admission 2YTL/$1.74/£1.15), an 11th-century church that served as the Patriarchate during the period of exile following the fourth Crusade. The church preserves parts of the mosaic flooring and a partially exposed fresco of the Pantocrator in the niche of the left aisle. Excavations conducted in 1935, however, revealed traces of an older structure dating to the 6th century A.D. and attributed to Justinian.

Near the southwest corner of the church (across the street) are partially uncovered outdoor tile-production workshops from as early as the 15th century. Many of the **brick and mud kilns** are still intact.

The **Yeşil Camii** dates to the late 14th century and displays a minaret covered with tiles in a colorful zigzag pattern. Unfortunately, these are not originals, as the actual tiles were destroyed. Across the street is the **Nilüfer Hatun Imareti,** built by Murat I and named after his mother, wife of Orhan Gazi and a Greek princess in her own right. Originally used as a charitable foundation and soup kitchen, the well-restored *imaret* (soup kitchen) now contains the **Iznik Museum** (admission 2YTL/$1.75/ 80p), harboring a small collection of Roman and Byzantine artifacts and remnants from nearby burial mounds. There's also a small collection of Iznik tiles, as well as several ethnological items.

Thirty years of excavations have barely made a dent in the uncovering of the **Roman Theatre,** built by Pliny the Younger between 111 and 113 during his time as governor of Bythinia. Rather than building the theater into the side of a hill, the theater was constructed using vaults.

Iznik, Bursa. Iznik Tourism Information Office. © 0224/220-1848. Provincial Cultural Directorate. © 0224/220-9926.

The Iznik Foundation   Tiles, richly decorated with floral designs and colors recalling precious gems, served as architectural decoration in the palace, mosques, tombs, and other buildings with a predominantly religious function. (The sultan was also the caliph, extending religious function to the palace.) For this reason, Iznik ceramics represent one of the most important examples of Islamic art. Sadly, with the decline of the economic and political power of the Ottoman Empire, artisans and ateliers became less and less in demand, and ultimately the techniques used to make the ceramics were lost.

Thanks to the Iznik Foundation, this great artistic tradition is enjoying a steady revival. The foundation, which consists of an educational facility, a research laboratory, and a commercial center, has invested an enormous amount of energy in researching the technologies necessary for achieving success in each complex step of production. One of the first challenges is the acquisition of the raw materials, as authentic Iznik pieces contain a high ratio of quartz, a semiprecious stone. The remaining obstacles are technical, involving the proper ratio of quartz, the chemical composition of each pigment, and the correct application of heat (each pigment must be fired at a different temperature). Ottoman artisans labored their entire lives to perfect just one aspect of the product, with one person expert in the creation of coral red, another in cobalt blue, and yet another in maintaining accurate and consistent heat to a wood-fired kiln made of brick. The foundation's finished products are faithful copies of the originals that sell at prices competitive with the inferior products sold in Avanos, a town in the interior of Anatolia. The price of a plate or tile at the foundation can reach the stratosphere, but remember, these are made of quartz, while the fakes are made of clay. The foundation office is open to visitors and is also equipped with nine guest accommodations for those wishing to stay overnight. They also have a main office in Istanbul at Kuruçeşme Öksüz Çocuk Sok. 14, Beşiktaş (© **0212/287-3243**).

Sahil Yolu Halı Saha Arkası, Iznik. © **0224/757-6025.** Fax 0224/757-5737. www.iznik.com. Free admission.

3 The Princes' Islands

The Princes' Islands are just a hop, skip, and jump from Istanbul, and a well-received respite from the chaos and scorching sun of the city. The islands were originally used as a place of exile for members of the royalty and clergy during the age of Byzantium. It was later taken over by the more clever residents of the city for their summer homes.

The atmosphere is one of pure repose thanks to the prohibition against vehicles; the only form of transportation here (besides your own steam) is the characteristic and charming horse-drawn phaeton.

Thanks to the introduction of seabuses that shorten the ferry trip by an hour, the islands are only a half-hour away, making them an accessible retreat from city life.

GETTING THERE IDO ferries to the islands depart from the Kabataş docks adjacent to Dolmabahçe Palace and make stops at Kadiköy on the Asian side, Kınalıada, Burgazada, Heybeliada, and Büyükada. The ride all the way to Büyükada takes about 2 hours and costs 2YTL ($1.75/80p) each way. The faster catamaran shortens the trip from Kabataş to Büyükada to about 45 minutes including one stop at Heybeliada (June–Sept; ✆ 0212/444-4436; www.ido.com.tr). The trip costs a mere 5.50YTL ($4.80/£2.10) each way, a pittance considering that seats are reserved compared to the body shuffle inevitable on the more crowded slow boat. From Bostancı on the Asian side, there's limited direct IDO service to Büyükada (departing at 7 and 7:30am weekdays and 9:10am on Sat–Sun). Weekend service continues on from Büyükada to the other three islands before ending at Kabataş. The one-way fare is 2.50YTL ($2.20/95p). Be sure to confirm all departure times in advance, as schedules may change.

WHAT TO SEE & DO ON THE PRINCES' ISLANDS Thanks to the absence of motorized vehicles, the islands have managed to retain their old-world charm. Horse-drawn carriages serve as local taxis, and bicycles share the meandering roads with domestic donkeys. As expected, Istanbullus inundate the islands in the summer, looking to enjoy the characteristic architecture of the many Victorian-style clapboard mansions, along with a relaxing day at the beach.

Big Island, or Büyükada, is the largest of the five islands and the one most crowded during high season. There are several good beaches, diving facilities, and the old hilltop monastery of Ayayorgı (St. George) from which you can almost see all the way back to Istanbul. To get to the monastery, take a carriage to Luna Park and take the 30-minute uphill path to Ayayorgı Peak, where you can sip their homemade wine while enjoying the panorama at the monastery's simple restaurant on the hill. To better appreciate what the islands have to offer, organize your excursion for a weekday, when the ferries are not packed like sardine cans and you can still get a glimpse of the sand beneath the blankets of the other sun worshipers. In the fall a stroll along the deserted cobblestone lanes met by the occasional donkey cart or a friendly pack of hopeful stray dogs transports you countless years back in time.

Fun Fact **A Famous Former Resident**

Leon Trotsky spent the first years of his exile from Russia on Büyükada, from 1928 to 1933.

Kınalıada was the site of a major human rights infraction—the Byzantines gouged out the eyes of and exiled Romanos Diogenes IV here for his defeat by the Selçuks in the Battle of Manzikert. The monastery built for the unfortunate general is still standing. The island was raided many times by pirates and later inhabited mainly by Armenians, but because of a harsh climate, it has attracted fewer people than the other islands. Electricity first came to the island in 1946, and it wasn't until the 1980s that the island received a water supply from the Municipality. Kınalıada is also the only one of the Princes' Islands without the services of the 19th-century phaetons.

Burgazada is the second of the Princes' Islands, originally settled as a Greek fishing village. In the 1950s the island attracted the wealthy Jews of Istanbul, who restored existing mansions or built their own. The island is also the home of a famous Turkish writer, Sait Faik, whose home has been turned into a museum. Two swim clubs are near the ferry landing, but if it's beaches you're after, you'll be better off on one of the other islands.

Heybeliada is the island closest to Büyükada and most similar in character in that the natural beauty attracts boatloads of weekenders in the summer. The waterside promenade ensures a steady stream of visitors looking to avoid the crowds over on Büyükada, but aside from a few eateries, you'll have to make this a day trip or book a room on Büyükada anyway.

WHERE TO STAY Fantasy becomes reality on Büyükada, the biggest of the islands but not so built up that you want to avoid it. That's why the listings here are all on the "Big Island." The **Hotel Splendid Palace,** 23 Nisan Cad. (turn right at the Hotel Princess and drop your jaw at the white domed mansion on your left; ℂ **0216/382-6950;** fax 0216/382-6775; www.splendidhotel.net; 120YTL/$104/£46 double), is a palatial clapboard house with views of the Marmara with peaceful gardens, a private swimming pool, two restaurants, and an on-site patisserie. It's closed November through March. The newly renovated **Hotel Princess,** Iskele Meydanı 2 (straight up the street from the ferry landing on the right; ℂ **0216/382-1628;** fax 0216/382-1949; www.buyukadaprincess.com; 110YTL–160YTL/$96–$139/£42–£61 double), is a more modest but gracious seaside lodge and is open year-round. There's a small pool overlooking the Marmara Sea for use in the summer months.

WHERE TO DINE Restaurants specializing in fish line the wharf to the left of the ferry landing on Büyükada, for breezy and atmospheric waterside dining. **Kalamar Restaurant,** Gülistan Cad. 10, Büyükada (ℂ **0216/382-1245**), is one of the first waterside restaurants that you encounter as you make your way down the wharf. **Milano Restaurant,** Gülistan Cad. 8, Büyükada (ℂ **0216/382-6352**), just a few doors down, has been here for more than 35 years and is the most famous restaurant on the island. Expect exorbitant prices for everything on the menu, and remember, you're paying for the waterfront view. More reasonable meals (minus the view) can be had in the main square at **Yıldızlar Caféteria,** Iskele Cad. 2, Büyükada (ℂ **0216/382-4360**), actually a 100-year-old cafeteria and tea garden serving *döner kebaps,* grilled cheese sandwiches, and the Turkish fast-food favorite, *lahmacun.*

4 Polonezköy

Little more than an intersection in the road, the village itself has been designated as a national park. The bucolic setting, home to several restored Polish houses set on exquisite expanses of rolling hills, makes this a fashionable weekend getaway for residents of Istanbul or foreigners with a bit of spare time.

The origins of Polonezköy go back to the mid–19th century, when the Polish exile Adam Czartoriski lobbied Sultan Abdülmecid for the creation of a colony for Polish refugees, many of whom were fleeing from the invading Russians. The sultan granted these exiles permission to build a village in a forested area on the outskirts of Istanbul. The original settlement—called Adampol after Czartoriski—had only 12 residents. Today, the settlement remains ethnically Polish.

The distinctive character of the town has attracted some foreigners with impressive credentials: Franz Liszt, Gustave Flaubert, and Lech Walesa all slept here, and even Pope John Paul II stopped in for a visit in 1994.

GETTING THERE   Getting to Polonezköy is pretty much impossible unless you have a car. To get there from the European side, drive across the Fatih Sultan Mehmet Bridge north of the city and follow the highway to the Beykoz/Kavaçık exit. Follow the road through Açarlar after which it's about another 15 minutes through Turkish suburbia and the winding village road into Polonezköy. (The total time from Taksim is about 30 min.)

EXPLORING POLONEZKÖY   This forested retreat is a perfect place to spend a weekend outdoors or an afternoon by the fire. In summertime, a festive weekend produce market draws locals in traditional Polish dress, and plenty of onlookers. A nature lover's path runs from near the Adampol Hotel through the woods, and most of the hotels have bikes for their guests. Best of all is the possibility to wander around town and negotiate the hire of a pony for an enjoyable, if not authentic, pastoral experience.

WHERE TO STAY   The recently restored **Polka Country Hotel,** Cumhuriyet Yolu 36 (© **0216/432-3220;** www.polkahotel.com), is rustic and romantic. A garden swimming pool enjoys pastoral hillside views, while in cooler weather stone fireplaces in several buildings encourage guests to rekindle the romance. A dry sauna is also tempting after a windy afternoon along the forest trails. The hotel is owned and operated by Hakan Ozan, an architect whose vision for the building is simple and tasteful. All rooms have telephones and TV, but try to nab one of the two top "penthouse" rooms, made slightly more rustic thanks to slanted roofs. (These also have air-conditioning.) Rooms are 100YTL ($87/£38) on weekdays, 150YTL ($131/£57) on weekends (breakfast not included).

WHERE TO DINE   Continuing the village tradition, **Leonardo Restaurant,** Polonezköy 32, Beykoz (© **0216/432-3082**), is the only restaurant in town to serve Polish food. It's also one of the few places you can get pork or even wild boar, but they also serve steaks, grills, and schnitzel at prices that hover around 28YTL ($24/£11) per dish. The Sunday buffet lunch is a hugely popular event for weekend getaways and costs around 45YTL ($39/£17) per person with drinks. The restaurant is in the restored home of one of the first Polish immigrants and has a splendid outdoor garden for Indian-summer evenings. Bring a bathing suit and towel in summer, because Leonardo has a pool in the garden.

Appendix A: Istanbul in Depth

The history of Istanbul reads like an encyclopedia of ancient and modern civilizations, as virtually every major player, from Greece's Alexander the Great, to Persia's Cyrus, to the long lineup of Roman, Byzantine, and Ottoman emperors and sultans—fought and won control of this city on the Straits. Notwithstanding the pillaging, each ruler left his (and sometimes her) mark on the city, and as recent excavations show, it's impossible to swing a trowel without hitting archaeological pay dirt. Below is a brief intro to help you navigate the centuries.

1 History 101

ISTANBUL IN PREHISTORY

During the ice age, the Sea of Marmara and the Black Sea were mere freshwater lakes, separated by two valleys now known as the Bosphorus and Dardanelle Straits. Around 6000 B.C., with the melting of the ice caps, the sea rose up to overflow its banks; discoveries in prehistoric settlements in the Kadiköy, Fıkırtepe, and Pendik districts of Istanbul include organic remains of life that could survive in both fresh and salt water. Prehistoric settlements were also discovered under the Hippodrome (in excavations taking place in 1927–29), at the Hagia Irene and Archaeology Museum, and more recently, at Yenikapı, Üsküdar, and Sirkeci, during the excavations of the stations to serve the future Marmaray Rail. The discoveries at Yenikapı alone, which date to the 4th century B.C., have unceremoniously reset the clock on Istanbul's ancient history.

EARLY GREEK SETTLEMENTS

According to historical sources, the earliest settlements in the region we now call Istanbul were founded by migrants from the Greek town of Megara around 660 B.C. The earliest historical reference we have of this time is of the Persian King Darius' conquest of the city in 512 B.C.—at that time, the "city" amounted to settlements in Calchedon (modern Kadiköy) and on the "promontory"—probably the hill that is now Sultanahmet.

In the latter half of the 4th century B.C., **Alexander the Great** swept through the settlements on the Bosphorus in his campaign against the Persians to annex all of Anatolia under **Macedonian/Greco** rule. Almost 2 centuries after his death, around 146 B.C., the city on the straits came under Roman domination.

NEW ROME

Under Roman rule, the city's early fortunes ebbed and flowed. When Septimus Severus (A.D. 197–211) encountered resistance to his self-proclamation as emperor of Rome, he simply razed the city to its foundations. It was during the rebuilding following these events that the Hippodrome and Obelisk were constructed. Under Severus' son, Caracalla, the city was known as Antonia or Antoniana. Emperor Valerian (A.D. 253–260) was confronted with raids by the Goths, while Diocletian (A.D. 284–350), instituted a doomed system of governmental reform, dividing the empire into two administrative units. It was a system destined to collapse into civil war; but the long-term effect was a more theological schism, as Christianity grew and took hold throughout the Empire. In the wake of Diocletian reform, **Constantine** (A.D. 324–337) emerged to establish his capital over that of previous Roman emperors, rebuilding the city to equal if not surpass the splendor of Rome. Six years later, in A.D. 330, its architectural eminence realized and a sizeable population of around 200,000, the city was baptized "New Rome." The city was renamed Constantinopolis (or Constantinople) in honor of the emperor.

CONSTANTINOPLE, CITY OF THE WORLD'S DESIRE

By the time Constantine had established imperial Roman power in Constantinople, his acceptance of Christianity was complete, having publicly espoused the faith in the Edict of Milan in A.D. 313, which mandated the tolerance of Christianity within the Roman Empire. Under **Theodosius,** paganism was outlawed and Christianity, by this time already widespread, was made the official religion of the state. By Theodosius's death in A.D. 395, the eastern and western provinces had grown apart ideologically, and the Roman Empire was divided in two. When Rome fell in A.D. 476, Constantinople emerged the dominant capital of the empire. But although predominantly Greek and Christian in culture, citizens of what we will now call Byzantium considered themselves Roman, and the leadership maintained a thoroughly Roman administration.

The reign of Emperor **Justinian** and his Queen **Theodora** (A.D. 527–565) inaugurated a period of great prosperity. Justinian's construction of the majestic Ayasofya (Church of Holy Wisdom) established Constantinople as the spiritual center of Christendom. Justinian commissioned new buildings and conducted restorations all across the empire—an undertaking so vast that it thrust the empire into economic crisis after his death.

Around the end of the 9th century A.D., a rivalry emerged between the Orthodox Church and the Papacy over the veneration of icons. The worship of idols was first condemned by **Emperor Leo III** in A.D. 726 and then reiterated by successive emperors. In 1054, over this and other theological disagreements, the pope severed any ties that had united Byzantium with the West.

Distracted by religious and bureaucratic disputes, the Byzantines were unprepared for the arrival of nomadic Turkish warriors raiding the empire's lands in the east. In response to the growing Turkish presence, Byzantine Emperor **Alexius Comnenus** turned to the Christians of western Europe for aid against the increasing threat of the Turks, warrior tribes originating from the steppes of Mongolia who expanded westward into present-day central Asia, the Middle East, and Anatolia. And the first Crusade was launched.

The Selçuk Turks triumphed over the second Crusade in 1147, eventually setting up **The Sultanate of Rum** at Konya and achieving significant cultural growth and territorial expansion. But the Crusades were by no means a cure-all. Tensions arose because the Crusaders had no specific mandate from the pope, little sympathy toward the Greek Orthodox religion, and no agreement on the nature of their association with the Byzantine Empire. Allied with Venetian merchants who had an eye on the riches of the East, the Crusaders sacked and plundered Constantinople in 1204 in the **fourth Crusade,** creating the Latin Empire of Constantinople and widening the schism between the churches of the East and West. Driven from Constantinople, the Byzantine court established a small empire in exile at Nicaea, creating a balance of power with the flourishing Selçuk Sultanate of Rum.

Michael VIII Palaeologus, ruler of the empire in exile, succeeded in reclaiming

Byzantine Constantinople

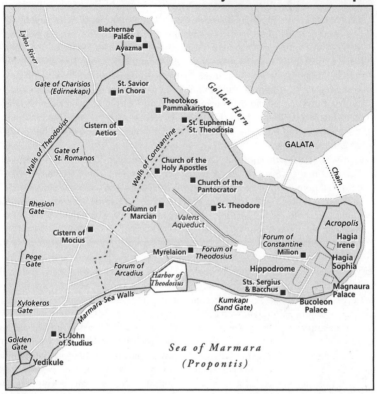

the city of Constantinople in 1261. Though their territory was drastically reduced, subsequent Byzantine emperors repeatedly tried to reunite the Orthodox and Catholic churches against the threat of invading Turks. This proved futile, and in 1453, **Mehmet II,** leading an army of Ottoman Turks, circumvented the Byzantine defenses of the Golden Horn by having his fleet carried, ship by ship (by means of a brilliantly engineered "moveable path") over land, behind the Byzantine navy. After centuries of decline and decay, the Byzantine Empire had come to an end.

OTTOMAN ISTANBUL

With his victory over Constantinople, Mehmet II acquired the title of *fatih,* or conqueror, and established his new capital, naming the city Istanbul, probably after having heard the Greeks say *"eis ten polin"* (to the city). His troops were permitted 3 days of looting and pillaging, and then the city was restored to order. He immediately began reconstruction, converting churches into mosques and repopulating the city with artisans, merchants, and farmers from all over the empire. The importance of sea power was not lost on Mehmet, who established control over the Black Sea and managed to capture some of rival Venice's islands in the Aegean. The city's importance as a naval and trading center was confirmed. Istanbul quickly became an international

(Fun Fact The Tulip Period

While wandering Topkapı Palace, or even through the Grand Bazaar, you will see spindly tulips in designs on everything from Iznik tile to silk scarves. The early 18th century in Ottoman history is known as **Lâle Devri,** or the Tulip Period. The word "tulip" is actually derived from the Ottoman Turkish word for gauze *(tülbend),* which was used to wrap turbans—which bear a striking resemblance to a tulip in full bloom. The Tulip Period is not only associated with a flowering of the arts but also with court society's collective obsession with the flower. Tulips, which are native to central Asia, became the dominant decorative motif, filled the gardens of the Ottoman elite, and were the source of endless festivals.

It was actually through the Ottomans that the tulip first came to western Europe. In the 16th century, a Dutch ambassador to the Ottoman Empire returned home with a few bulbs and touched off a fad that has forever since associated Holland with the tulip. By 1637, Holland had developed a sophisticated tulip bulb market, in which batches of bulbs were worth more than the average Dutchman's yearly income.

city with a mixture of cultures as Christians, Greeks, Armenians, and Jews all were welcomed by the sultan. After all, these diverse peoples brought with them a wealth of knowledge—and new tax revenues.

The long reign of Mehmet II's great grandson, **Süleyman,** was the golden age of the Ottoman Empire, distinguished by military successes, administrative organization, economic prosperity, social order, and cultural greatness. Both the city and the empire flourished under his direction;

the population grew, road and caravansary networks were extended, trade prospered, and his military machine enjoyed success after success.

He expanded on the Turkish and Persian traditions of justice to protect the lowest members of society from unfair governmental practices or excessive taxation; state decrees were posted publicly to discourage officials from instituting fraudulent or arbitrary laws. The people responded by hailing him as Süleyman the Lawgiver.

Dateline

- ca. **4000** B.C. Modern excavations in and around Üsküdar, Kadiköy, Sirkeci, and Yenikapı provide evidence of prehistoric settlements. Late Bronze Age fragments discovered under Hagia Irene and the Archaeology Museum point to 2000 B.C.
- ca. **1200–700** B.C. Migration of Greeks to Aegean coastal regions.

- ca. **660** B.C. Earliest documented settlement in Istanbul is founded by Greek settlers from Megara.
- ca. **499** B.C. Persians, led by Darius, sack the city and drive out the Greeks.
- **334** B.C. Alexander the Great drives out the Persians.
- **146** B.C. The city on the straits comes under Roman rule.

- A.D. **197–211** Septimus Severus consolidates power; punishes the city by razing it to the ground; the Hippodrome and the Obelisk date to this time.
- **268** Visigoths attack the city and fail.
- **284** Diocletian reforms Roman administrative system.
- **313** Edict of Milan establishes official tolerance of Christianity.

OTTOMAN ADMINISTRATIVE STRUCTURE

The Ottoman ruling class was organized into five Imperial Institutions, the most important of which was the military. Almost as important as the military were the scribes, or "men of the pen," whose primary function was the collection of revenue, in addition to their formidable duties in general record-keeping. Religion and culture were the dominion of the *ulema,* Muslim leaders educated in theology and law assigned the task of religious leadership, education, and justice. Finally, the Inner and Outer Palace Services took care of the general day-to-day administration of the palace and care of the sultan.

In theory, all lands belonged to the sultan, who by divine right could claim all titles, revenues, and property. The actual administration was bureaucratic, and the sultan's newly acquired territories were controlled through a *timar* system adapted from the Selçuks and Byzantines. A *timar* was a province assigned to a military administrator who, in exchange for the land and its revenue, provided military services and assistance in the administration of the territory. With time and expansion of the empire, the *timars* were converted into tax-paying farm units, and one-fifth of all property, goods, and captives became royal possessions.

In contrast to the Christian policy of lands passing along generational lines, *timars* were assigned according to merit. Christians and prisoners provided the sultan with a steady supply of loyal subjects under the *devşirme* (literally, collection), where teams were sent to conquered territories in search of the best and most promising young boys. Families often hid their children, but on the whole, the opportunity for a distinguished career of service to the sultan was appealing. Candidates between the ages of 8 and 15 were selected and sent to Istanbul, where they were converted to Islam and educated in the palace school. The finest of the *devşirme* were chosen for continued education and placement in high palace positions while the majority of the trainees entered into the elite military corps of Janissaries. By 1700 the Janissaries (*yeniçeri;* literally "new troops") had swelled to over 100,000 from 12,000 during the reign of Mehmet the Conqueror, ultimately becoming more powerful than the government they served and inciting frequent rebellions.

The Turkish aristocracy, comprised of Muslims, Turks, Arabs, and Iranians, shared the rank of *askerî,* with the newer *devşirme* class of Christian converts making up the ruling class. During Süleyman the Magnificent's reign, this internal

---

- **330** Constantine establishes his capital at Byzantium, renaming it New Rome, then Constantinople. Restoration of Hagia Irene.
- **360** Constantine builds the first Ayasofya.
- **412–422** Building of the city walls.
- **441–451** The Huns attack the city.
- **476** Fall of the Roman Empire; Constantinople emerges as sole religious and cultural capital of the Eastern Roman Empire.
- **491** Construction of Blachernae Palace begins.
- **527** Justinian and his Queen Theodorsa ascend the throne.
- **537** The foundations of the Ayasofya are laid.
- **553** Earthquake damages dome of Ayasofya.
- **675** Eyüp Sultan leads Arab siege of the city.
- **726** Leo III rejects the idea of icons.
- **1054** Catholic and Greek Orthodox churches split.
- **1071** Selçuks defeat Byzantine army at Malazgirt.
- **1204** The city is sacked and falls under Latin rule as a result of the 4th Crusade; Byzantine court establishes capital at Nicaea (Iznik, near Bursa).
- **1261** Michael VIII Palaeologus reclaims Constantinople.

continues

rivalry was expertly maneuvered to ensure honesty and obedience.

From the time of Mehmet II, sultans attended sessions of the Imperial Council, a meeting of the sultan's viziers, judges, and department heads (seated on a cushioned platform later simply known as the *divan*) in Topkapı Palace. At meetings 4 days a week, all government business was conducted; public petitions and complaints were heard in the morning and executive issues were addressed in the afternoon.

Driven by the *gazi* guiding principle of *jihad* (struggle), the Ottomans had transformed themselves from plunderers into conquerors.

THE OTTOMAN DECLINE

Several factors, both foreign and domestic, contributed to the progressive deterioration of the Ottoman Empire over the subsequent 2½ centuries. Although Süleyman left a legacy of territories on three continents and the splendor of an empire without equal, he also left behind a scheming widow—Roxelana, the Circassian-born concubine he took as his wife and trusted advisor. Roxelana manipulated her husband, his sons, and the court with sometimes fatal results. She orchestrated events culminating in the murder of Süleyman's favorite sons, Mustafa and Beyazit, thus clearing the path of ascension

for her utterly incompetent son, Selim II. Nicknamed Selim the Sot, he preferred the pursuits of physical pleasure to governing the empire and left his grand vizier in charge of decision making. The grand vizier assumed more responsibility, but simultaneously set an unfortunate precedent of bribery, favoritism, and corruption. And taking a page from Roxelana's book, members of the harem (that is, mothers of prospective heirs) exerted more and more control over the workings of the government; this culminated in the mid–17th century with an era recognized as "The Sultanate of Women."

The abandonment of the traditional practice of fratricide contributed to the weakening of the system as well. Rather than kill off all potential heirs and risk the endangerment of the line, sultans, beginning with Mehmet III in 1595, adopted the practice of imprisoning their sons and heirs instead of assassinating them. Isolated from daily life, inexperienced in the ways of the government or military, accustomed to excess, they either went crazy or emerged completely unprepared for the demands of leadership.

Meanwhile, in the Janissary Corps, celibacy had long been abandoned, and Selim II decreed that sons of Janissaries—who were born free Muslims—could enroll. Eventually this paved the way for

- **1453** Mehmet the Conqueror takes Constantinople.
- **1481** Reign of Beyazit II begins.
- **1492** Columbus discovers the New World.
- **1512** Reign of Selim I begins.
- **1517** Selim returns victorious from Egyptian campaign, laden with holy relics. Istanbul becomes the center of Islam.
- **1520** Reign of Süleyman begins.
- **1566** Reign of Selim II begins.
- **1574** Reign of Murad III begins.
- **1622** Osman II assassinated by the Janissaries; Ahmed I restored to throne.
- **1687** Reign of Süleyman II begins.
- **1774** Reign of Abdülhamid I begins.
- **1789** Reign of Selim II begins; education becomes obligatory.
- **1826** Janissary massacred and corps abolished; medical and military schools opened; and Tanzimat Reforms.
- **1839** Reign of Abdülmecid begins; establishes parliamentary system and laws.
- **1854** Britain and France support Ottomans against Russia in the Crimean War.

other free Muslims to join, and by the mid–17th century the Janissary Corps had grown to 200,000, squeezing the state for the payroll to support the increase in numbers. The purchasing of office undermined the merit system, and although the palace school continued to function, the *devşirme* was abandoned. During times of peace, without a paycheck, with no active duty and no prospects of conquest or booty, the Janissaries would often turn to moonlighting or to the looting of their own locally governed lands. Already feared by the state structure, they continued to exert an influence on politics to further their own financial interest. Osman II recognized this threat in 1622, but was assassinated by the Janissaries after an effort to control them. Nevertheless, the internal deterioration of the Corps was inevitable as was the weakening of Ottoman military might.

The organization of the *timer* (feudal-like system of government) was not left unaffected by this internal degeneration. To meet the needs of an expanding empire, the *timer* system was converted to a tax-based system of farm units, requiring administrators to send a portion of their tax revenues to Istanbul. Local administrators treated the land as private property, siphoned tax moneys, and removed any incentive for the peasant population to produce. The effects were not only economically disastrous, but this weakening of the centralized government also encouraged local bandit raids and peasant revolts, consequences that the government was ill-equipped to control.

With the government decentralized, corrupt, and morally hollow, the Ottomans were unable to deal effectively with outside threats or absorb the economic pressures of a Europe in Renaissance. Vasco da Gama's circumnavigation of Africa opened up new trade routes to the east; the East India Company of London could therefore sell their goods in Istanbul for less than the Ottomans would pay for direct trade with India. And with new sea trade routes, merchants no longer paid levies for passage through Ottoman territory. Meanwhile, a Western industrial revolution produced cheaper goods that flooded the Ottoman market, thanks to Süleyman's Capitulations (see "Süleyman the Magnificent: Pragmatic Statesman," below). Silver and gold mined in the Americas drove up prices, the cost of living rose, and peasants abandoned their villages, which had disastrous effects on agricultural production.

Obviously not all sultans and administrators proved to be indifferent, ineffectual, and corrupt, but those who weren't were the exceptions. Although a technically

- **1856** Treaty of Paris; Ottoman Empire accepted as a European state.
- **1861** Reign of Abdülaziz begins.
- **1875–85** Loss of most European territories, Tunisia, Egypt, and East Rumalia.
- **1876** Reign of Abdülhamid II begins; establishes first constitution; then, frustrated with parliamentary gridlock, imposes an autocracy.
- **1878** The "Sick Man of Europe" progressively deteriorates; Britain occupies Cyprus.
- **1881** Mustafa Kemal born in Salonika.
- **1908** Coup d'état led by Young Turks; Abdülhamid is deposed.
- **ca. 1908–09** Mehmed V installed as lame duck sultan.
- **1914** Ottoman Empire enters World War I as ally of Germany.
- **1915** Under leadership of Mustafa Kemal, Turkish forces successfully repel Anzac forces at Battle of Gallipoli.
- **1918** Reign of Mehmed VI begins; Turks surrender; Allied forces enter Istanbul.
- **1919** Mustafa Kemal leads national resistance for sovereignty; occupational Greek army lands at Smyrna.

continues

Süleyman the Magnificent: Pragmatic Statesman

In 1520 Süleyman ascended to the Ottoman Empire throne and immediately launched invasions into Europe. In 1521 he gained control of Belgrade and the Danube. He then turned his attention to Rhodes, the last Crusader stronghold and bastion of the Knights of St. John—the island that stood between him and his Egyptian territories, not to mention Mecca and Medina. Süleyman triumphed after a 145-day siege and mercifully released all the Knights and mercenaries, thus gaining the admiration of much of Europe (though he'd come to regret this act later in his career). Eight years later the Knights were granted Tripoli and the Island of Malta in a charter sealed by Holy Roman Emperor Charles V to thwart movement of Ottoman fleets in the Mediterranean.

Süleyman insinuated himself into the politics of Europe and attempted to destabilize both the Roman Catholic Church and the Holy Roman Empire; he believed that any power in those hands was a threat to Islam. Urged on by Francis I of France, Süleyman defeated the young Hungarian king, Louis II (nephew of Charles V), in 1526 at the battle of Mohács. In 1529, at the request of the appointed king of Hungary, he returned to confront Archduke Ferdinand of Austria. Süleyman drove Ferdinand back to Vienna but was unable to penetrate the city's defenses—a failure that would become a recurrent theme for the Ottomans.

Although Süleyman's reign was characterized by almost constant war, he brought peace to the lands that he conquered. Süleyman was said to have embodied perfectly the characteristics of *adale* (justice), much like his namesake, King Solomon. Conquered lands often fared better once he took over.

inferior Ottoman navy was defeated by a coalition of Western states at Lepanto in 1571, the Ottoman navy was able to reestablish its naval presence by taking Cyprus from Venice later the same year.

The gradual decline was arrested later that century with the reign of **Murat IV**

- **1920** Grand National Assembly created in Ankara with Mustafa Kemal as president.
- **1922** Greeks driven from Anatolia; sultanate abolished; Abdülmecid named as caliph only.
- **1923** Treaty of Lausanne, Mustafa Kemal establishes the modern Republic of Turkey; Kemal is elected president; Ankara replaces Istanbul as capital.
- **1924** Caliphate abolished and all members of the Ottoman dynasty are sent into exile.
- **1924–38** Mustafa Kemal Atatürk institutes programs of modernism, secularism, and reform.
- **1934** Voting rights established for women.
- **1938** Atatürk dies in Dolmabahçe Palace; Ismet

Inönü becomes republic's second president.
- **1945** Turkey issues a last-minute declaration of war on Germany.
- **1946** Turkey becomes charter member of United Nations.
- **1950** Inönü's Republican People's Party defeated in first free election. Adnan Menderes's Democratic Party takes over.

Looting was forbidden, and the sultan gained respect by placing provisions along the route of a carefully planned military campaign so as not to take anything from the local peasants along the way. Kings were retained as vassals of the sultan, and as long as the tributes (taxes) were sent to Istanbul, life continued as before.

Above all, Süleyman was a pragmatic statesman. In 1536 he signed a treaty with Francis I of France, conceding commercial privileges to the French in exchange for an informal alliance against their common enemy, the Habsburgs. With these "Capitulations," the French were exempt from Ottoman taxes and were permitted to fall under French jurisdiction. In response to this French-Turkish cooperation, the Habsburgs urged the Persians to wage war against the sultan. Turning his attentions East, Süleyman wrestled Iraq from Persian control, arriving as far as the Persian Gulf. Here the Portuguese dominated trade with the East—a presence he was never able to repress.

The Mediterranean Sea was another source of annoyance; despite Süleyman's conquest of Tripoli in 1551, the Knights of Malta (including many of the Knights released after the sultan's victory over Rhodes) were aggressively cutting off Ottoman sea routes. Süleyman began his siege of Malta in 1565, but the Knights fought back ferociously, the battle dragged on to winter, and Süleyman was forced to stand down.

The Ottoman armor was beginning to show weakness, provoking Süleyman, at age 72, to reassert his empire's superiority by taking Vienna once and for all. But he died in his tent during the campaign on the Danube. According to tradition, his heart is buried in Szigetvár on the spot where he passed away.

and his grand vizier, **Köprülü,** who maintained a policy against corruption and a return to the more centralized system of government. The *gazi* spirit was reignited, inspiring decades of new campaigns toward further expansion. Köprülü was so effective that the position of grand vizier was handed down to his

- **1952** Turkey joins NATO.
- **1960** Military coup overthrows Menderes, who is executed the following year.
- **1961** Army restores parliamentary government.
- **1964** Turkey granted associate member status in European Union.
- **1965** Demirel's Justice Party wins elections.
- **1971** Demirel resigns after army intervention.

- **1973** Republican People's Party wins elections; Bulent Ecevit becomes prime minister.
- **1974** Turkey sends troops to northern Cyprus.
- **1980** Military coup d'état; General Kenan Evren leads government.
- **1983** Turgut Özal elected prime minister.
- **1989** Özal elected president.
- **1991** Süleyman Demirel elected prime minister.

- **1993** Özal dies; Demirel becomes president; Tansu Çiller becomes Turkey's first female prime minister.
- **1996** Çiller steps down as prime minister.
- **1999** Bulent Ecevit elected prime minister again. Kurdistan Workers Party (PKK) leader Abdullah Ocalan captured in Kenya, convicted of treason, and sentenced to

continues

son and his grandson, Kara Mustafa; this was the first dynasty associated with the post.

The Ottomans were determined to capture Vienna, and in 1683 **Kara Mustafa** led the army's second doomed attempt (the first having been Süleyman the Magnificent's failed siege of the city in 1529) to take the Austrian capital. The Ottomans were no match for new European artillery and were soundly defeated by an alliance of European forces—a miscalculation that Kara Mustafa paid for with his life. The army's retreat was met by ambushes and further defeats, ending in the 1699 **Treaty of Karlowitz,** which granted Austria the provinces of Hungary and Transylvania, and marked the first time in history that the Ottoman Empire actually relinquished territory.

The 18th century was, for the most part, characterized by wars with Austria and Russia. Victories against the Austrians served to stabilize borders along the Danube, but the Russians were pushing into Muslim territory in an attempt to become a Black Sea power. In the first half of the century, the Ottoman military met with many successes, not the least of which was the defeat of **Peter the Great** at the Prut River in 1711. Nonetheless, two additional clashes with Russia culminated in the **Treaty of Küçük Kaynarca,** which followed a 1774 victory by Catherine the Great. (She, as champion of the Christian Orthodox faith, actively encouraged revolt in Russian-populated Ottoman territories.) The treaty was an enormous blow to the Ottomans, demonstrating that the Ottoman Empire was no longer the great power it once was. In addition to annexing European territories, the Treaty of Küçük Kaynarca granted the Russians extensive commercial privileges in the Black Sea, a diplomatic presence in Istanbul, and the protection of the Orthodox Christian faith on Turkish soil. The desire for territorial and economic dominance, along with the trafficking of loyalties, would characterize the Russian-Turkish conflict well into the 20th century.

REFORM ATTEMPTS

It was obvious to Selim III that reform was needed. Inspired by the American and French revolutions, he created a new corps, the *nizam-i jedid* ("the new order"), on Western models, even adopting European-style uniforms. The Janissaries revolted to what they saw as a loss of power and privilege, and in a conciliatory gesture that cost him the throne, Selim dissolved the *nizam-i jedid* in 1807. In the next few years, the Janissaries executed many of the reformers as well as Selim's successor, Mustafa IV; **Mahmud**

death. Two major earthquakes rock northwestern Turkey in August and November, killing an estimated 18,000 people.

- **2000** Former prime minister Necmettin Erbakan sentenced to 1 year in prison for challenging Turkey's secular rule.
- **2002** Turkey lifts bans on education and broadcasting in Kurdish.

- **2002–03 and 2005** Turkish troops join Security Assistance Force in Afghanistan.
- **2002–03** Justice and Development Party (AKP) wins landslide victory at the polls; prohibition against Recep Tayip Erdogan running for Parliament lifted; Abdullah Gul steps aside allowing Erdogan to assume post of Prime Minister.

- **2003** Terrorist bombing at Neve Shalom synagogue in Istanbul. Days later, the British Embassy and HSBC Bank are targeted. More than 250 are killed.
- **2004** Turkey abolishes death penalty. PKK announces end to cease-fire.
- **2005** E.U. Accession talks officially launched but later put on hold because of

II was spared only because he was the sole surviving Ottoman prince. Proceeding with caution, Mahmud's first action was to deal with the anarchy that had taken root in the provinces, but as nationalist uprisings in Serbia, Greece, Algeria, and Romania saw the empire eroding at its borders, it was clear that the Janissaries were of little use in the defense of the empire. This allowed Mahmud to gain enough support to finally have the corps destroyed. On June 15, 1826, in a staged massacre, Mahmud II had the Janissaries surrounded and "dissolved." Taking their place was a new army trained in European techniques by German military advisors.

Finally rid of the Janissaries' influence, Mahmud II, followed by his successor, **Abdülmecid,** was able to embark on significant modernization that would last for 40 years. The period of **Tanzimat** (literally, "reordering") was ushered in, aimed at strengthening the power of the government while encouraging an economic and social structure similar to that of Europe.

Influential during this period was the arrival of telegraph lines into Istanbul in 1855, facilitating a literary renaissance that would develop into an incubator for new nationalistic ideas. Supporters of this patriotism were called "New Ottomans,"

whose objectives of preserving territory and limiting autocratic rule would be attainable through the adoption of a constitution. Considered dissidents, many of these supporters were forced to flee, pursuing their nationalistic aims from posts abroad.

The reforms, however, failed to alleviate a worsening financial crisis brought on by a flood of foreign products, ending in a Franco-English monopoly on tobacco, salt, alcohol, silk, and other essentials. Loans to foreign banks were bankrupting an empire that had degenerated so much as to be known as "the Sick Man of Europe." European powers used this weakness to manipulate political balances. This foreign domination was no more evident than in the Ottoman participation in the Crimean War (1854–56), when the Ottomans granted the Catholic French the right to protect Christian sites in the Ottoman-held Holy Land. The Orthodox Russians found the excuse they needed to further their territorial ambitions and declared war on the Sultanate. Britain and France entered the conflict to protect their commercial interests, and the Russians were ultimately defeated. Even though the outcome was territorially favorable to the Ottomans, the empire was demoralized, having gone from imperial power to political pawn in less than 300 years.

Ankara's refusal to allow traffic from Cyprus into Turkish ports/airports.

■ **2006** Ribbon cutting on new Baku Tblisi Ceyhan pipeline.

■ **2007** Nomination (and subsequent election) of Abdullah Gul for president sparks outrage between secularists and Islamists and is met with official condemnation by the military. Tensions heat up on the border as Turkey threatens cross border raids into Northern Iraq in response to PKK attacks on Turkish military in the south of Turkey.

Roman & Byzantine Emperors

Roman Emperors	Reign A.D.		
Constantinus I	330–337	Constance II	641–668
Constantinus II	337–360	Constantinus IV	668–685
Julien l'Apostat	360–363	Justinianus II	685–695
Jovien	363–364	Leonitus	695–698
Valens	364–378	Tiberius II	698–705
Gratien	378–383	Justinianus II (2nd time)	705–711
Theodosius I	383–395	Tiberius III	711–711
Byzantine Emperors		Phillipicos	711–713
Arcadius	395–408	Anastasius II	713–716
Theodosius II	408–450	Theodosius II	716–717
Pulcheria	450–453	Leon Isauros II	717–741
Marcianus	450–457	Constantinus V	741–775
Leon Flavius I	457–474	Leon IV	775–780
Leon II	474–474	Constantinus VI	780–797
Zenon	474–491	Irene	797–802
Anastasius I	491–518	Nikephoros I	802–811
Justuinus I	491–527	Mikhail I	811–813
Justinianus I	527–565	Leon V	813–820
Justinus II	565–578	Mikhail II	820–829
Tiberius Constantinus I	578–582	Theophilos	829–842
Mauricius	582–602	Mikhail III	842–867
Phokas	602–610	Basileios I	867–886
Heraclius	610–641	Leon Sophos IV	886–911
Constantinus III	641–641	Alexandros	911–912
		Zou Carhopsina	912–919

Abdülhamid II succeeded in temporarily reinvigorating the failing empire, but it was too little too late. In 1875 he was confronted with a rebellion by a Russian-backed Pan-Slavic movement in the Balkans. Battered and driven back almost to Istanbul, the Ottomans were forced to sign the disastrous **Treaty of San Stefano** in which much of the Ottomans' European territory was lost. Anti-Russian powers swiftly united behind Britain to force a modification of the treaty in 1878 at the Conference of Berlin. Nevertheless, the damage had been done. European imperialism was costing the Ottomans more losses: Tunisia to the French in 1881, Egypt to

the British in 1882, and East Rumalia to Bulgaria in 1885.

Abdülhamid II responded by reaffirming his designation as caliph and beginning a policy of reinvigorating Islamic unity. With nationalistic tendencies developing among the Arab groups and Albanians, he hoped to create a sense of solidarity geared at holding the empire together.

Succumbing to external and internal pressures, he reluctantly instituted the first written constitution establishing a parliamentary system modeled on those in the West. For the first time in the history of the empire, absolute Ottoman rule had been relinquished, but as a condition to accepting the document, Abdülhamid

Romanos I	919–944	Andronicos I	1183–1185
Constantinus VII	944–959	Isaacios II	1185–1195
Romanos II	959–963	Alexios III	1195–1203
Nikephoros II	963–969	Alexios IV	1203–1204
Jean Tsimiskes I	969–976	V. Alexios	1204–1204
Basileios II	976–1025	**Latin Occupation**	
Constantinus Viii	1025–1028	Theodoros I	1204–1222
Romanos III	1028–1034	Jean Ducas III	1222–1254
Mikhail IV	1034–1041	Theodoros II	1254–1256
Mikhail V	1041–1042	Jean Ducas IV	1256–1258
Zoe & Theodora (the sisters rule jointly)	1042–1042	**Byzantine Emperors** Michael VIII	
Constantinus IX	1042–1055	Palaeologus	1258–1282
Theodora (2nd time)	1055–1056	Andronicos II	1282–1328
Mikhail VI	1056–1057	Andronicos III	1328–1341
Isaacios I	1057–1059	Jean V	1341–1347
Constantinus X	1059–1067	Jean VII	1347–1355
Romanos IV	1067–1071	Jean V (2nd time)	1355–1376
Mikhail VIII	1071–1078	Andronicos IV	1376–1379
Nikephoros III	1078–1081	Jean V (with grandson)	1379–1391
Alexios I	1081–1118		
Jean II	1118–1143	Manuel II	1391–1425
Manuel I	1143–1180	Jean VIII	1425–1448
Alexios II	1180–1183	Constantinus XI	1448–1453

insisted on retaining the right as final arbiter on unresolved issues. When the opposition became too outspoken in 1877, he simply neglected to reconvene the parliament and ruled autocratically for the next 30 years. Harshly criticized for repression, censorship, and paranoia of conspiracy, he was nevertheless effective in his Westernization of the empire, concentrating on public works, economic development, education, and communications. The telegraph, which provided access to information from beyond the empire's borders, was also useful to his network of spies, providing Abdülhamid with a means for controlling potential insurgencies from within.

The strengthening of the ideal of nationalism, both within the empire and among the provinces, had important negative consequences. Armenian revolutionary groups were springing up in response to a new sense of national identity. Concerned with another separatist movement and suspicious of an Armenian allegiance with European powers, Abdülhamid suppressed these insurgencies in a series of brutal massacres in which an estimated 300,000 Armenians were killed. More separatist movements arose: Greeks in Crete demanding unification with Greece rebelled, resulting in the loss of the island, while Bulgar aggression in Macedonia was inciting unrest among the Greeks there.

European response to Abdülhamid's regime was less than positive, but the Ottomans continued to receive consistent support from the Germans, who, along with the concessionary rights to a Berlin-to-Baghdad railway, enjoyed substantial commercial privileges.

Abdülhamid's crushing policy of censorship was unable to staunch the flow of new ideas. In the late 1880s an organized movement called the Committee for Union and Progress (CUP), made up primarily of military officers and rebels in Macedonia, was organized. In the name of "Liberty, Justice, Equality, and Fraternity" these **Young Turks** orchestrated a successful nonviolent coup d'état in 1908 designed to reinstate the constitution. Abdülhamid was deposed and his brother **Mehmed V** was released from prison as token head of state.

THE YOUNG TURKS

The constitution once again in place, the Young Turks, led by a triumvirate dominated by **Enver Paşa,** had gained control but lacked a clear objective other than controlling autocratic rule and territorial integrity. Ottomanism was no longer a viable ideology given the rise of nationalistic tendencies in the troubled provinces. Solidarity based on a policy of **Pan-Islamism** was especially popular as a way to cement people across national lines, but proved to be too racially narrow. The ideal of **Pan-Turkism,** the uniting of all Turkish-speaking peoples, gained popularity but gave way to **Turkism** as the new national identity, which merged a modernized Islamic tradition with European cultural influences. In spite of these parliamentary disagreements, the effects on administration were significant: a political structure based on European models; a transformation in the role of the press; the engagement of European advisors in agricultural, law, and military matters; increased public works; and the establishment of individual and women's rights.

The social effects of these institutions were lasting, but internal conflict was seen as an opportunity by foreign powers. In 1911 Italy seized Libya and the Dodocanese Islands. Even more devastating was the loss of the remaining European territories in the first Balkan War to an alliance among Bulgaria, Serbia, Greece, and Montenegro. Some European territory was regained 2 years later in the second Balkan War, but the situation was enough for the CUP to mutate into a military dictatorship controlled by a triumvirate of Enver Pasha, Mehmet Talat, and Ahmet Cemal.

WORLD WAR I

Although the Turks favored neutrality in the conflict germinating between the Central Powers of Germany and Austria and the allied countries of England, France, and Russia, Enver Pasha, who declared himself war minister in 1914, favored cooperation with the Germans. Business is business, however, and two battleships were commissioned from the British, destined to restore pride to an outdated navy. Fearful of Turkish entente with their adversaries, the British withheld consignment of the ships, and the Germans shrewdly came to the rescue with the delivery of two battleships, the *Göben* and the *Breslau,* complete with a German crew sporting fezzes.

In the summer of 1914, Enver Pasha signed a secret peace treaty with the Germans promising naval assistance in the face of Russian aggression in the Black Sea. Two months later, flying the sultan's flag, the *Göben* and *Breslau* attacked Russian ports and the Ottoman Empire was dragged into a war. The Russians retaliated by land through the Caucuses, while the British had successfully organized Arab revolts in the eastern provinces, leaving the Turks surrounded by hostile forces. Mustafa Kemal Atatürk's legendary defense of Gallipoli in 1915 succeeded in saving the Straits, and therefore

Istanbul, from invasion. Nevertheless, Turkish forces were no match for Allied tanks, automatic weapons, and airplanes and on October 30, 1918, the CUP government agreed to an armistice with England and France. Two weeks later British and French troops were occupying the sultan's palace. Enver Pasha, Mehmet Talat, and Ahmet Cemal fled the city on German warships, leaving the Allied forces to decide how to divide up the empire's few remaining territories.

Under the Treaty of Sèvres, all European territories were lost except for a small area around Istanbul. Armenia and Kurdistan gained autonomy, Greece was assigned the administration of the region around Izmir, and French and Italian troops were left to occupy portions of the rest of Anatolia. The Capitulations, suspended shortly before the war, were restored and control of Turkish finances was taken over by the Allies. The government of **Mehmet VI** signed the treaty August 20, 1920, but its destiny was to be short-lived.

THE NATIONALIST MOVEMENT

Spurred on by defeat and foreign occupation, nationalists established pockets of resistance called "Defense of Rights" groups. **Mustafa Kemal** (the name Kemal, meaning "perfection," was given to Mustafa by a school instructor for his exceptional achievement; "Atatürk" was added later) was already an active nationalist, having taken part in the CUP overthrow of 1909. He had subsequently distanced himself from the CUP, but his outspokenness had made him many enemies. Mustafa Kemal was sent to Samsun on May 19, 1919, with nebulous military orders, but instead began organizing various nationalist factions, formally resigning from military service shortly after. His goals in leading the resistance were inflexible: the recognition of a national movement and the liberation of Anatolia from foreign occupation.

That same year two important nationalist congresses were convened at Erzurum and Sivas, forming the basis for the **National Pact.** The first conference called for an independent Turkish state, while the second defined the objectives of the movement. Presiding over these meetings, Mustafa Kemal called for the rights to all remaining Ottoman territories, control of Istanbul and the Straits, the guarantee of minority rights, and rejection of foreign intervention in Turkish affairs. Unwilling to alienate the loyalists and conservatives, Mustafa Kemal reasserted the movement's allegiance to the sultan-caliphate, maintaining that until the sultan was free of foreign control, the committee would act on behalf of the people. In response, the sultan declared Mustafa Kemal a rebel, and a *fetva*—the killing of a rebel as a religious duty—was issued. Mustafa Kemal and his followers established themselves in Ankara, far from the reaches of their enemies, voting on August 23, 1920, for the creation of the **Grand National Assembly.**

In the fall of 1919, the Greeks got greedy and began moving inland, arriving as far as the Sakarya River (about 81km/ 50 miles west of Ankara). Troops led by **Ismet Paşa** (General) beat the Greeks back to Izmir, and in several decisive victories, Mustafa Kemal succeeded in driving the Greek troops completely off the peninsula. This last victory in the war for independence earned Kemal recognition by foreign governments as de facto leader of the Turks. The Soviet Union was the first power to sign a treaty with the nationalists in 1920, establishing set boundaries between the two countries. As nationalist troops approached Thrace, France begged off a confrontation with a complete withdrawal of French forces. Although the British remained in Thrace, they were unwilling to get caught up in a battle on behalf of the Greeks and instead arbitrated the Armistice of Mundanya, requiring the Greeks to retreat behind the

Maritsa River. Kemal had succeeded in retaking possession of Istanbul, the Straits, and Thrace, essentially nullifying the Treaty of Sèvres, and it was clear that a new treaty would have to be drawn up. The Allies invited both the Ottoman government (to be represented by the sultan) and the Grand National Assembly to participate in the creation of the **Treaty of Lausanne,** but fearing that divided representation would only weaken his cause, Kemal declared the sultanate abolished and sent Ismet Paşa as sole representative of Turkey. Mehmet VI was smuggled to Malta on a British ship where he remained in exile, putting the final nail in the coffin of the Sick Man and ending 6 centuries of an empire. The role of caliph was given to his cousin Abdümecid, heir to a defunct Ottoman dynasty.

In 1923 the Treaty of Lausanne (which replaced the earlier Treaty of Sèvres and thus nullified, among other things, the formation of an independent Kurdistan), recognized Turkey as a sovereign nation. The nation's borders as proposed by the National Pact were established except for the concession of Mosul to Iraq and that of Alexandretta and Antakya (now the Hatay) to France as part of a Syrian mandate. The treaty also called for Greece and Turkey to exchange their respective minority populations, excluding those in Istanbul and western Thrace. This was meant to improve relations between the two countries in the long run, but tragically uprooted almost two million people from their adopted homelands.

Success at Lausanne was immediately followed by the Grand National Assembly's proclamation of the Republic of Turkey and the election of Mustafa Kemal as president.

MUSTAFA KEMAL ATATÜRK & THE REPUBLICAN PERIOD

At the beginning of the war for liberation, Kemal saw a country in ruins. Kemal's vision for the republic was Westernization, modernization, solidarity, secularization, and equality for all Turks. Kemal governed as an inflexible yet benevolent autocrat, asserting that a transitional period was necessary in securing effective reform. To this end he formed the Republican People's Party (RPP), which became the exclusive political vehicle for his programs. When Abdümecid indicated a desire to expand his role as caliph into the political sphere, Kemal, wary of opposition from anti-reformers and traditionalists, abolished the caliphate and banished all members of the house of Osman.

In 1924 the Grand National Assembly drew up a constitution establishing guaranteed civil rights and a legal framework for the government. Formally elected president by the assembly, Kemal selected Ismet Paşa as his prime minister, handpicked his cabinet, and set out virtually unobstructed on a path of brisk modernization.

To Kemal, secularization was essential in a modern system and vital in dealing with a European world. He closed the religious courts and ordered all religious schools secular. His rapid reforms were not without opposition—both from those who wanted a larger role for Islam in the government as well as those who grew disillusioned with Kemal's pervasive cult of personality. The Progressive Republican Party (PRP) was formed from an opposition consisting of former supporters and associates. Kemal, in a willingness to experiment with open dialogue, admitted the party into the system, even replacing Ismet Paşa with the PRP's Fethi Bey.

An uprising in the southeast put a hasty end to this experiment. An insurgency led by Sheikh Said of the Nakshbendi Order of the Dervişes in the Kurdish southeast had broken out, intent on restoring the caliphate. Kemal responded by invoking an emergency law (the Maintenance of Order Law), reinstated Ismet Paşa as prime minister, and swiftly crushed the rebellion. The sheikh was condemned and hanged along with more than 40 other rebels; newspapers were closed down, journalists arrested, and the PRP outlawed.

Years earlier on a trip to Europe, Kemal had been the brunt of ridicule for his tasseled red felt hat; so, in 1925 the fez, symbol of Ottoman oppression, was outlawed. Stating that "civilized men wear civilized hats," Kemal chose to wear the more modern Panama hat, much like how Mehmet the Conqueror had replaced the turban with the more "modern" fez.

Derviş orders were outlawed (but not completely suppressed). The praying at tombs was prohibited. Honorary titles were abolished. It seemed to the people that Kemal was determined to sever all ties with the past and with tradition, and the people in the outlying regions rioted. Mindful that a drastic measure such as banning the veil would enrage his critics, he opted for discouragement instead. Women in Istanbul and in the other cities began to appear in public without the veil, but the practice caught on less quickly in the rural areas.

The legal code was overhauled, taking its examples from the Swiss, Italian, and German systems. Civil law, previously the dominion of the religious leaders, was secularized, which had a particularly profound effect on women's rights. In a move toward equality, polygamy was outlawed and marriage became a civil contract, depriving husbands of the absolute right provided by Islamic law to divorce for any reason. Women were also granted equal rights in matters of custody and inheritance, while education for women on the secondary level was recognized as equal in importance to that of men. By 1934, women's rights had extended to universal suffrage, and Turkey won the distinction of being the first country in the world to have elected a woman to the Supreme Court.

Kemal's flurry of reform angered many Muslims, and in 1926 a plot to assassinate the president was uncovered. Fifteen conspirators were hanged, including members of the extinct Peoples' Republican Party and a former deputy, while others were either tried and exiled or acquitted. In 1928 a constitutional provision declaring Islam as the state religion was deleted, completing the secularism of the Republic of Turkey.

A census, which was the first systematic accounting of the people of Turkey, brought to light gaping holes in the needs of the population. Only 10% of the people over the age of 7 were literate while even a smaller percentage of children were even in school, prompting significant reforms in education in the next few years.

Kemal's next task was aimed at both engendering Turkish pride and uniting his polyglot nation under one tongue. By the 1920s, Arabic, Persian, and French words made up 80% of language use, and Kemal ordered his scholars to the task of constructing a pure Turkish language purged of foreign influences. Arabic script was replaced with Latin characters. To quiet the voice of his critics, Kemal personally traveled around the country teaching the new alphabet in public squares when necessary. Not even Islam was spared: In 1932 the state made it mandatory for the traditional call to prayer to be broadcast from the loudspeakers in Turkish instead of Arabic, the language of Islam.

All this modernization and bureaucratic reorganization only served to underline yet another need for change. Keeping track of all these Mohammeds, Mahmuts, and Mehmets was getting confusing, and it was obvious that a better method of identification would be necessary. Up to this point, villagers were called by their first names; now, the people were ordered to select a last name, lest they be assigned one less imaginative. Mustafa Kemal was given the name Atatürk ("father of the Turks") by the Grand National Assembly. Ismet Paşa (the Paşa meaning "general") adopted İnönü, the site of one of his victorious battles, while others selected surnames from the less original Bey ("Mr.") to something more creative along the lines of "great slayer of mountains." Old habits die hard, however, and even today it is common practice to address a person by his first name, followed by the respectful "Bey."

Atatürk's presidency was characterized by six guiding principles later to be known as the "Six Arrows." In addition to the three early principles of Republicanism, Nationalism, and Secularism, Atatürk worked toward emphasizing the ideals of Populism, Reformism, and Etatism. Populism was based on the principle that all (men) were equal, but just as important was that all men were Turks, emphasizing the sovereignty of the people over their nation. Reformism confirmed their responsibility toward rapid modernization, while Etatism embraced the government's role in economic development. "Political and military victories cannot endure unless they are crowned by economic triumphs," said Atatürk, and in 1934 a 5-year plan for achieving economic sovereignty was inaugurated. The Ottoman economic legacy was one of agricultural stagnation and little public confidence in the quality of Ottoman products. A British saying went, "If you want to hang yourself, do it with English rope." Atatürk reversed these trends by developing agricultural and industrial production, raising Customs tariffs to protect the local industry, buying up the foreign railroad concessions, and determinedly avoiding the foreign debt trap. Nevertheless, growth was slow and the people began complaining of a low standard of living. The labor law of 1936 set up provisions for the rights of workers: Strikes were outlawed but a method of arbitration was set up. A state insurance program providing for accidents, for unexpected death, and for seniors was established, furthering the government's support of the labor force.

Atatürk fostered a policy of peaceful foreign relations, subscribing to his enduring ideal: "Peace at home, peace abroad." For the first time in Turkish history, antagonism and warfare were not central to the government's approach to its borders. He signed pacts with Greece, Romania, Yugoslavia and the Balkans, Iran, Iraq, and Afghanistan, and entered into friendly status with the Soviet Union, the United States, England, Germany, Italy, and France. In 1932 Turkey became a member of the League of Nations and in 1936, in response to Mussolini's aggression in Ethiopia, Atatürk successfully lobbied at the Montreux Convention for Turkish fortification of the Straits.

In 15 years of presidency, Atatürk transformed a feeble dictatorship into a modern, reasonably democratic, forward-thinking republic. On November 10, 1938, his efforts finally took their toll, when, after years of drinking, he died of cirrhosis of the liver, but not without naming İnönü as his successor. The League of Nations offered tribute at his death by calling him a "genius international peacemaker." Atatürk's legacy lives on and even to this day, the time of his death is always observed with a minute of silence.

FOREIGN POLICY & WORLD WAR II

Having served as prime minister from the beginning, having fought alongside Atatürk in the war of independence against the Greeks, and having represented Turkey at the Lausanne Conference, Ismet İnönü's appointment to the presidency by the Grand National Assembly the next day was a mere formality. But no sooner did İnönü take office than he was confronted with an international crisis of unprecedented proportions.

The Soviet Union's relentless lust for unfettered access to the Bosphorus Straits made it a continuous threat, while Hitler's appetite for the Balkans boded badly for Turkey. Sandwiched between two great and potentially hostile powers, Turkey entered into a "declaration of mutual guarantee" with Britain followed by a treaty of nonaggression with France. The Nazi-Soviet pact of nonaggression signed in August 1939 presented a difficult problem for Turkey, as it pitted the Soviets against Britain and France. Turkey sent an envoy to the Soviet Union in an attempt to secure a peace treaty with them, but to no avail. Betting on security in numbers, Turkey entered into a "treaty of mutual assistance" with Britain and France stipulating that no action would be required of Turkey that might lead to an eventual involvement in a war with the Soviet Union. The arrival of the Germans on Turkey's doorstep with Hitler's invasion of Greece prompted Turkey to initiate a preemptory nonaggression treaty with Germany, stipulating nonaggression with either Britain or France. Four days later Germany invaded the Soviet Union, an almost irresistible turn of events for the Turks, given their historically acrimonious relationship with the Russians. Still, Turkey managed to stay out of the fight, including denying the Germans access to the Straits or passage on or over Turkish land. After Germany's defeats in Egypt, North Africa, and Stalingrad seemed to confirm the inevitable defeat of the Germans, Turkey finally took sides when at a meeting with Roosevelt and Churchill in Cairo, Inönü relented to a request that Turkish military facilities be made available to the Allied forces.

Inönü's fence-sitting allowed Turkey to maintain its neutrality at least until February 1945, when a declaration of war on Germany became a prerequisite for admittance into the San Francisco Conference (the precursor to the United Nations, of which Turkey was one of the original 51 members).

Nevertheless, war took its toll on the Turkish economy. During the war years, inflation rose significantly, and to feed the war debt, the government imposed a capital levy on the Turkish people. Contrary to the government's posture of absolute equality, the levy was applied arbitrarily and mercilessly, and was particularly biased against rich Greek, Armenian, and Jewish merchants. Deadlines for payment were often harsh, and default was punishable by property seizures, arrest, and deportation into forced labor. To this day, Turkey acknowledges this as a shameful episode in its history, attributable to the extraordinary pressures of war.

There were postwar problems to address as well. The discovery of wartime documents revealed the Soviet Union's enduring desire for control of the Bosphorus and the Dardanelles. Historically a European issue, the United States joined with Britain to support Turkey against Cold War pressures, expanding Turkey's scope of "Europeanization" to now include the United States. The Truman Doctrine of 1947 confirmed a United States–Turkish friendship with the United States' contribution of $400 million toward strengthening the security of Turkey and Greece against Soviet aggression. Turkey later demonstrated its support of Western policies by sending an infantry brigade to Korea to serve under United Nations command in the 1940s and 1950s.

In a postwar desire for political stability and national security against Russian aggression, Turkey pursued a policy of friendship with its neighbors, signing the Greece-Yugoslav Alliance, the Turkish-Pakistani Mutual Security Pact, and the Baghdad Pact, in addition to its membership acceptance by NATO. Turkey's recognition of Israel provoked outrage among its Arab neighbors, but because Arabs still had the stigma of being Ottoman subjects, they were simply ignored.

MUSICAL CHAIRS IN TURKEY'S POLITICS

Pressure mounted in postwar Turkey over the state's increasingly authoritarian rule. Responding to spreading dissension, Inönü yielded to his critics and authorized multiparty activity, permitting access to a democratic process. In 1946 four of the dissenters, Jelal Bayar, Adnan Menderes, Refik Koraltan, and Fuad Koprulu, founded the Democratic Party, and despite bribery, scare tactics, and even suspicious ballot handling, the Democratic Party gained unexpected popularity in the general elections and a voice in the decision-making process. By the election of May 1950, the Democratic Party had attracted enough of the displaced minorities to win a sweeping majority, appealing to private business owners, Islamic reactionaries, and the struggling rural population. In a first-time stunning example of Turkish democracy at work, Inönü stepped down peacefully to lead the minority People's Party. Bayar was elected president, Menderes was chosen as prime minister, and a period of relative prosperity was inaugurated. Economic initiatives were taken to relax government controls and to encourage private enterprises, and Menderes' alliance with the United States resulted in the arrival of American aid, agricultural assistance, equipment, and countless John Deere tractors. In a move to appease their Islamic supporters, the Democratic Party approved the reinstatement of religious instruction as an optional educational program and reversed Atatürk's decree requiring Turkish as the language of the call to prayer.

Despite a brief period of progress in the early 1950s, Turkey's economy took a nose dive. To finance its poorly managed reforms, the government was forced to take out foreign loans, and Turks began seeking employment beyond their borders. Meanwhile, in a move to return to a one-party system, Menderes began undermining his opposition by banning political meetings, invoking censorship, and creating a special Democratic Party to "investigate political activity," a sufficiently vague mandate for random arrests. Although Menderes maintained a high degree of popularity, the military elite and the foreign-educated intelligentsia began to sow the seeds of rebellion. In response, Menderes imposed martial law. Within a week, students were demonstrating in the streets and cadets from the military academy were staging protests. Cemal Gürsel, a commander of the ground forces and one of the leaders of the movement, decided it was time to act, and in spite of a lack of a clear plan, set the military machine into motion. On May 27, 1960, in a nonviolent coup d'état, the armed forces—as self-appointed guardian of Atatürk's Republican legacy—arrested President Bayar, whose later sentence of death was changed to life in prison. Menderes was hanged on charges of treason, along with hundreds of members of the Democratic Party (DP). The Committee of National Unity, composed of high-level military officials who had participated in the coup, dissolved the Democratic Party government and took over. The people, jubilant of the overthrow, were rewarded with a new constitution; Gürsel was elected president of the Assembly, and former President Inönü, 37 years after his first appointment as prime minister, assumed the position again, along with the task of constructing the Second Republic.

Four political parties offered candidates in the 1961 election, of which only four won seats: the Atatürk-influenced Justice Party (JP), led by Süleyman Demirel; Inönü's social democratic RPP; the right-to-moderate Turkish Workers

Party; and the communist Confederation of Progressive Trade Unions. Despite Inönü's popularity, the RPP lost ground, while the JP, plumped up by displaced members of the late DP, made gains. Nevertheless, neither was able to summon a majority and legislation was paralyzed. After a year and a half, the military handed over control of the state to civilian rule but maintained a watchful eye on the government in the ensuing years. In 1965 the JP was successful in acquiring a majority in the Grand National Assembly, sidelining the RPP for the first time since 1961 and providing Demirel with enough votes to end the coalition-style government in favor of a cabinet.

MODERN TURKEY & THE THIRD REPUBLIC

In spite of the new structure, bickering, crossing of party lines, and splinter groups plagued the political machine. Confidence in the system plummeted, as did the value of the Turkish lira, resulting in unemployment, poverty, hunger, and ultimately social repression. The social and economic situation deteriorated so much so that in 1971, in what became known as the "coup by memorandum," Demirel was forced by the military to resign.

The 1970s were a reactionary time in Turkey, much as the 1960s were in the United States, with Marxist and Leninist doctrines clogging impressionable minds. It wasn't long before antigovernment organizations turned to violence in order to further their cause. The left-wing Turkish People's Liberation Army resorted to political assassinations, kidnappings, and fantastic bank robberies, while the Grey Wolves, the terrorist arm of the Islamic-minded National Salvation Party, made standing in a bus line a potentially fatal activity. By mid-1979 the death toll attributed to terrorist violence had reached 20 a day. The military again stepped in.

The military coup of 1980, led by army Chief of Staff General Kenan Evren, was greeted with relief by the general population as well as by concerned members of NATO. Two years later, just as they did after previous coups, the military restored civilian government, although they did only offer one candidate for president: Kenan Evren.

The new government found a secure identity in the Motherland Party, led by Turgut Özal, an economist with a proven track record in economic policy. Atatürk's policy of étatism was removed in favor of private enterprise. Unfortunately, two particularly volatile situations impeded Özal from achieving significant progress in building a free market and boosting foreign trade. Tensions in the east were mounting among the Kurdish nationalists, while Turkey's involvement in the Korean War only further drained the country's resources. Yet despite these impediments, plus the additional challenge of governing a system with the reinstatement of opposition parties, Özal succeeded in making headway in areas of foreign policy and economics. Nevertheless, some of Turkey's nouveau riche got accustomed to the excesses of the 1980s, although not always by legitimate means. Upon Özal's death in 1993, Demirel, representing the True Path Party (Doğru Yol Partısı or DYP) composed of former members of the now defunct JP, made yet another political comeback as Turkey's seventh elected president.

TURKEY AT THE TURN OF THE 21ST CENTURY

Although Turkey has been vigilant in guarding its secularism, it has not been without a constant struggle. An increasingly corrupt government was bound to provoke resistance, and a return to traditionalism gave credibility to Islamic activity. Educational and welfare programs made possible through endowments from

Saudi Arabia gave rise to religious fanaticism, reinforced in the wake of the 1979 revolution in Iran. By 1995, with pro-Islamic sentiment on the rise, the Islamic partisans, having formed the Welfare Party, had gained enough votes in the parliamentary elections to make the coalitions stand up and take notice. With Necmettin Erbakan at the helm, the Welfare Party obtained legitimacy through a coalition with the majority DYP, an alliance that most factions had tried to avoid. Erbakan was appointed to serve alternating years as prime minister with the current prime minister, making him the first Islamic leader in the history of the Turkish Republic.

Erbakan's participation as prime minister was an outright affront to the 1982 constitution's prohibiting of "even partially basing the fundamental, social, economic, political, and legal order of the state on religious tenets." Erbakan was widely criticized, especially by the military, which later forced him to resign. The Welfare Party was accused of being antisecular and was banned in 1998 along with Erbakan, who was prohibited from participating in politics until 2003. The Justice and Development Party (Adalet ve Kalkınma Partısı or AKP in Turkish), formed in August 2001, took over where the Welfare Party left off, claiming a new, moderate stance and a willingness to work within the secular system. The AKP was propelled into power in 2002 with more than 34% of the vote, in no small part as a result of the ineptitude of the government in power to handle the 1999 earthquake, which claimed the lives of over 20,000. It is a well-publicized fact that much of the destruction caused by the earthquake could have been avoided had adequate building methods been employed, and that poorly constructed buildings were a result of corrupt business practices. The vote was also seen as a backlash against institutional corruption as well as dissatisfaction with the crumbling Turkish economy. Reccep Tayıpıdp Erdoğan, the former mayor of Istanbul whose leadership of the party was delayed as a result of incendiary remarks he had made in 1997 *("Mosques are our barracks, domes our helmets, minarets our bayonets, believers our soldiers")*, has been at the helm since 2003, and apparently the Turks are more than satisfied with his performance. In 2004, the AKP received an unprecedented 44% of the vote and its popularity just keeps growing. In the summer of 2007, however, the military perceived the pendulum swinging a little too far right when Erdoğan nominated Abdullah Gül for president and released a public statement of warning. Gül's wife wears a headscarf, you see, and this issue in itself is one of the most explosive ones in contemporary Turkish politics. The ban on headscarves in all public buildings (which includes government offices and public universities), is part of Atatürk's reforms, making it particularly incendiary for the wife of the president to wear one. Meanwhile, secularists view the lifting of the ban—portrayed by the religious right as a human right—as the slippery slope toward complete Islamization of the country.

In spite of the tensions between the religious conservatives and the secular progressives, Turkey has experienced a historic level of economic stability and progress in the past few years. Erdoğan has also been at the forefront of Turkey's push for full admittance into the E.U., a process that will take at least a decade.

2 Architecture, Art, Music & Language

First impressions of Turkey reveal a society much more European than one expects, but echoes of a strong, proud and decidedly oriental heritage shine through in the arts, culture, music, and folklore. Tourists flock to those "Turkish Nights" shows expecting to cram in a few hours' worth of "authentic" folklore. But while a belly dancer in a glittery harem hat may seem the epitome of exoticism, this ritual crowd-pleasing is anything but a Turkish invention.

Turkish culture developed by absorbing the artistic traditions of conquered lands, so more than any one defining style, the Turkish arts are characterized by layers and layers of complexity. From the time the Turkish tribes spread through Anatolia in the 11th century until the end of the Ottoman Empire, the Turks had incorporated decorative and architectural styles from the Sassanids (a pre-Islamic Persian dynasty), the Romans, the early Christians, the Byzantines, and Renaissance-era Europeans.

ARCHITECTURE

The architectural and decorative arts of Turkey are closely linked to the Islamic faith, which gave major importance to mosques, *medreses* (theological schools), and mausoleums. Almost all mosques follow the plan of Mohammed's house, which was composed of an enclosed courtyard surrounded by huts, with a building at one end for prayer and an arcade to provide shade. Whereas in Mohammed's time the call to prayer was sung from the rooftops, minarets were added later for convenience and style.

The main objective reflected in Selçuk architecture was the proliferation of the purist Sunni orthodoxy, which was achieved by concentrating its efforts on the construction of *medreses* and other public works such as mosques and baths. To provide a means of safe passage for trade as well as the means for communication from one end of the empire to another, the Selçuks built a network of fortified caravansaries. Although Rum Selçuk architecture at first reflected the influences of the Iranian Selçuks, over time they developed

a distinct style, incorporating features like pointed arches from the Crusaders and lofty arched spaces from Christian Armenians and Syrians employed under the sultan. They also developed the squinch, a triangular architectural device that allowed the placement of a circular dome atop a square base, laying the groundwork of what was later to become an outstanding feature of Ottoman mosque architecture. The Selçuks also combined traditional Arabesque styles with indigenous Anatolian decorative motifs that literally flowered into a unique style of geometric architectural ornamentation.

A defining feature of Ottoman architecture became the dome, a form that expanded on earlier Turkish architecture but was later haunted by the feat of superior engineering accomplished in the soaring dome of the Ayasofya. As the Turks conquered Christian lands and churches were converted into mosques, traditionally Byzantine ideas were crossing cultural barriers and finding their way into the Selçuk and Ottoman vocabulary.

Ottoman architecture reached its zenith in the 16th century under Süleyman the Magnificent, in the expert hands of his master builder, Sinan. In the service of the sultan, Sinan built no fewer than 355 buildings and complexes throughout the empire, including the Süleymaniye, whose grand and cascading series of domes has become not only a defining feature of the Istanbul skyline but also a pinnacle in Ottoman architecture. (Sinan succeeded in surpassing the Ayasofya with the Selimiye in Edirne, a destination not covered in this guide.)

Although Ottoman architecture is primarily defined through monumental works and along a historical continuum, certain aspects of domestic architecture developed over time that gave the Ottoman house a number of distinctive features. Early Ottoman houses were timber and wood frame construction. Later,

15th- and 16th-century building used masonry or brick infill, lending the houses a decidedly Teutonic feel. The most recognizable (and enchanting) characteristic is the protruding enclosed verandas, often with bowed windows.

In certain towns, in unusually large structures or among the upper classes, the Ottoman house followed the oriental model of separating the private quarters (for the women) from the administrative rooms (in a home, this would have been where the head of the household greeted male guests, men and women always being kept separate). But this was more the exception than the rule, and Ottoman houses were owned and inhabited by the entire cross section of cultures and religions represented by citizens of the Ottoman Empire. Sadly, whatever one's vision of the traditional Ottoman house, the Republican break with all things Ottoman abruptly turned these treasures into a thing of the past.

ART

Whereas Byzantine art featured elaborate religious interiors and the use of luxury materials like gold and silver, Islamic *hadith* frowned on the use of luxury items in its mosques, favoring instead unpretentious items like ceramics, woodcarvings, and inlay. Additionally, because of the Islamic prohibition against the representation of religious images of living creatures, Turkish decorative arts were channeled into alternative features like flowers, geometric forms, and Arabic script.

The Selçuks introduced the use of glazed bricks and tiles in the decoration of their mosques, and by the 16th century, the Ottomans had developed important centers of ceramic production at Iznik and Kütahya. Ottoman tiles incorporated a new style of foliage motifs and used turquoises, blues, greens, and whites as the dominant colors. Spectacular uses of tile can be seen all over the country, in mosques, palaces, *hamams* (Turkish baths), and even private homes.

Woodworking and mother-of-pearl or ivory inlay were primarily used in the decoration of the *minbar* (pulpit), but this craft extended to the creation of Koran holders, cradles, royal thrones, and even musical instruments.

Calligraphy is intimately related to the Islamic faith and dates back to the earliest surviving Koran manuscripts. Over the centuries, different styles of calligraphy emerged, with one of the basic requirements being that the text is legible. The Selçuk period brought about a more cursive graceful script, while the earlier Arabic script was more suited to stone carving. The ornamentation of holy manuscripts became an art in itself, as seen in pages that are gilded with gold leaf or sprinkled with gold dust, and in script whose diacritical marks are accented with red ink.

Besides the use of calligraphy in religious manuscripts, under the Ottomans the application of an imperial seal or *tuğra* (pronounced *too*-rah) on all official edicts became customary. The earliest example of a *tuğra* can be traced back to Orhan Gazi on a 1324 endowment deed, with each successive sultan creating his own distinct and personal representation. Today these seals are significant works of art, bearing price tags that stretch into the hundred- or even thousand-dollar ranges.

The art of marbled paper is another traditional Anatolian art that flourished under the Ottomans. Known as *ebru,* the art of marbling calls for natural dyes and materials, and a precise hand to create a collection of spectacular, one-of-a-kind designs.

The art of carpet weaving has a complex heritage that goes back for thousands and thousands of years. Based on the necessity of a nomadic existence, carpets had more practical functions: warmth and cleanliness. As tribes migrated and integrated, designs and symbols crossed over borders as well. Carpet designs parallel those of the other artistic media, with geometric patterns a common feature of the 13th century.

Wool carpets provided warmth for the harsh winters, while *kilims,* also placed on the ground, provided coverings for cushions in a *şark*-style (Oriental-style) setting that could later be used to transport the contents of the tent. Prayer rugs, identifiable by a deliberate lack of symmetry (the "arrow" will always be lain in the direction of Mecca) continue to be one of the more beautiful categories of traditional Turkish rugs.

Although Turkish carpets became one of the more coveted trappings of status in Europe, appearing in the backgrounds of many a Renaissance artist such as Giovanni Bellini and Ghirlandaio, the more ornate and sophisticated designs preferred by Europeans were the creation of non-Turkic (mostly Armenian) craftsmen. Today, however, even these stunning pieces are part of the traditional Turkish carpet-weaving lexicon.

MUSIC

Much like the art, architecture, and even food of Turkey, Turkish music blends a wide range of styles and cultures, from Anatolian troubadours on horseback to the commercially successful tunes of arabesque at the top of the charts. Different combinations of styles and genres have given rise to countless new sounds that despite being modern still sound unfamiliar to a Western ear untrained in Eastern modes. An irregular meter called *akşak,* typical to Turkish folk music that originated on the Asian steppes, may sound strange to ears trained on the regular cadences of double, triple, and 4/4 time.

This style was kept alive by lovelorn troubadours singing the poetic and humanistic words of folk icons like Yunus Emre or Pir Sultan; only recently was the music written down. Folk music endures in the rural villages of Turkey and is a regular feature at wedding celebrations, circumcision ceremonies, and as part of a bar or cafe's lineup of *canlı muzik* (live music).

Classical Turkish music began as the music of the Ottoman court, and in an empire composed of a patchwork of cultures, the top composers were Greeks, Armenians, and Jews. Turkish classical music has its origins in the Persian and Arabic traditions, and eventually the music of the Mevlevi became a major source as well.

Military music had an important role in the successes of the Ottoman Empire, with its thunderous use of percussion aimed at demoralizing an enemy before battle. The Janissary band influenced 18th- and 19th-century European music, in *alla turca* movements written by Mozart and Beethoven, and operas written by Lully and Handel.

The "Europeanization" of the Ottoman Empire in the 19th century brought many foreign musicians to the court, including Giusseppe Donizetti, brother of the more famous Gaetano Donizetti, who was given the position of head of the Imperial Band in 1831.

Pop music took hold of Turkey in the 1950s and 1960s, much as it swept the Western world. But pop in Turkey took on a different form, first with the popularity of the tango in the 1950s, and then with the re-recording of Western favorites using Turkish lyrics. It wasn't long before Turkish musicians began composing their own forms of pop. In the 1970s, as the rural population began to migrate to the cities in search of their fortunes, a widely disparaged form of music called *arabesque* swept the nation off its feet, with the sounds of unrequited love, sentimentality, and even fatalism. Arabesque was a fusion of the new pop, folk, and traditional music that developed into a new and highly commercial style; today, these both exotic and catchy phrases blare from every taxicab, long-distance bus, and discothèque.

LANGUAGE

Turkish is the official language of Turkey, uniting not just its citizens, but also a diaspora of Turkish-speaking peoples throughout Asia. The Turkish language originated in the highlands of the Altay Mountains of central Asia and is heavily spoken in lands stretching from Turkey to China, including Azerbaijan, Turkmenistan, Özbekistan, Turkistan, Kazakistan, Kirgizistan, Tajikistan, and Northern Cyprus. At the height of the Ottoman Empire, the Ottoman language was a mélange of outside influences heavily infused with Arabic, the language of religion and law; Persian, the language of art and diplomacy; and French, well, just because it's French. Pure Turkish, spoken primarily in the home, was considered inappropriately informal and familiar for public use.

Atatürk was convinced that pride in one's language was critical in instilling a sense of nationalism in a people, and one of his landmark reforms was to uplift Turkish to its rightful and preeminent role as a national language. He began by purging foreign influences from the Turkish language and introducing the Latin alphabet. Words of Arabic origin still maintain a tremendous presence in daily usage, especially concerning religious matters, and knowledge of some foreign languages will nevertheless come in handy in places like the *kuaför* (coiffeur), the *asensör* (elevator, in French), or the *likör* (liquor) store. English is slowly creeping into the language, particularly in the area of technology, with words like *telefon, Internet,* and the less high-tech *seks.*

Turkish is an agglutinative language, which means that words (and sometimes whole sentences) get formed by tacking stuff on to the root. Each suffix has some grammatical function but also provides for a discreet amount of flexibility in shades of meaning. To make matters worse, the suffix must follow rules of spelling and phonetics, so that there are eight ways of expressing the word "of."

In 1924, when Atatürk introduced the mandatory use of the Latin alphabet, Turkish became a phonetic language and is pronounced exactly as it is written, making it relatively easy to read. Is it hard to learn? Compared to what? Will a novice's pronunciation be any worse than an American's attempt at getting his lips around French? Probably not. But Turks are so uncommonly adept at languages that in all likelihood your contact with Turkish will be kept to a minimum. In most major tourist areas and many secondary ones, the local merchant population speaks English, along with French, German, Spanish, Italian, Danish, and even Russian.

Even so, it's absolutely the minimum of courtesy to put yourself out there in an attempt to communicate a few words in the native land of the country you are visiting, and knowing a few basics will help you feel less isolated and helpless. See appendix B, "Useful Turkish Terms & Phrases," for a glossary of common phrases and terms, with a pronunciation guide.

The history of Islam dates to the beginning of the 7th century A.D. in the city of Mecca, in today's Saudi Arabia. At the time, Mecca contained what was believed to be the first holy shrine built by Adam and Eve. Later, after Abraham was spared the task of sacrificing his only son, he rebuilt a temple on the same spot and dedicated it to the One True God. This shrine, constructed in the shape of a simple cube (hence the word *Kaaba,* from the Arabic word *muka'ab,* or cube), attracted the devotion of a host of pagan cults and, by the end of the second half of the first millennium, contained over 360 types of statuettes and cult objects. Pilgrims representing a broad range of cults flocked to the city, and the wealthy and influential members of the community were delighted with the revenue that these pilgrimages brought.

Mohammed was born in Mecca around A.D. 570 (or CE, for "Common Era") and grew up in a monotheistic family tradition. A naturally pious man, Mohammed often headed off into the hills for moments of isolated contemplation and prayer. On one of these occasions, Muslims believe that the angel Gabriel appeared with a message from God, a revelation that is accepted as the first verse of the Koran (*Koran* means "The Recitation"). The Koran forms the foundation of the Islamic faith and is believed by Muslims to be the direct word of God.

In a world of inequality, poverty, and misery, Mohammed's preachings of purity of heart, charity, humility, and justice gained a devoted following well beyond the borders of Mecca. The tribesmen of Mecca, perfectly content with the economic benefits of the status quo, grew alarmed and hostile at these developments, eventually forcing Mohammed and his followers to leave Mecca in fear for their lives. The town of Yathrib welcomed Mohammed and gave him an honored position as leader, changing its name to Madinat al-Nabi or "the town of the Prophet." The town was later to become known simply as Medina.

Many of the misconceptions of Islam come from models that are related to culture and not religion. The basic principles of Islam are quite admirable, and every requirement has a practical purpose. The act of prayer sets specific time aside for the recognition of a greater power, and the act of physical prostration is a constant reminder of one's humility and man's equality. Practically speaking, regular prayer develops a sense of peace and tranquillity, of punctuality, obedience, and gratitude. Furthermore, the setting aside of 5 minutes five times a day for introspection and meditation can only have positive effects on one's overall health, especially in the face of the stresses that the modern world has to offer. The month of ritual fasting, or Ramadan (*Ramazan* in Turkish), reinforces principles of discipline and teaches people to appreciate what they have and to understand what it's like to do without. Ramadan also brings families and communities together in a feeling of brotherhood and unity.

Islam is a socially conscious religion that attends not only to inner growth but to external affairs as well. The concept of charity is implicit in Islam, which calls for a specific contribution to be made to those less fortunate (2.5%) unless doing so would cause undue hardship to the giver.

Sadly, people tend to dwell on the concepts of polygamy, unequal treatment of women, and terrorist activity associated with the Islamic idea of *jihad*. These concepts, when examined in historical context, have pure motives that have been manipulated through the ages to further the self-interest (or vision) of individuals. (This manipulation took different forms under different authoritarian Muslim regimes.) For example, the idea of multiple wives gained ground at a time when wars were creating an abundance of widows whose only alternative for survival would have been prostitution; the humanitarian solution at the time was for a man to provide a home for as many wives as he could afford.

Islam preaches modesty, and in many societies, particularly in Saudi Arabia and Iran, this concept has been taken to extremes, requiring women to wear a black chador in public. Ironically, there is absolutely nothing in the Koran or any of the *hadiths* (tradition based on the life of the Prophet Mohammed) that requires a woman to wear any specific garment. In fact, the requirement of modesty applies to men as well. To force or coerce a women (or anyone) in matters of religion goes against the true spirit of Islam. (Here's a solution: Blindfold the men.)

A divisive issue in Islam dates back to the death of Mohammed and relates to the succession, an area of disagreement that spreads into ideology. **Shiite** Muslims believe that the true line of *imams* (or spiritual leaders) is one based on genealogy, and that the rightful representatives of Islam descend from Ali, Mohammed's cousin and son-in-law. Shiites believe that part of the imam's inheritance is divine knowledge passed between relatives. Armed with a direct line to God, Shiites often exhibit a tendency toward blind adherence.

Sunni Muslims interpret Mohammed's ideology more democratically and acknowledge the line of succession as one based on merit and "the consensus of the community."

Turkey, whose Muslims are predominantly Sunni, is the only Muslim country in the world to allow its citizens the freedom to decide their own level of observance. While the political atmosphere in Turkey represents both liberal and conservative extremes (and everything in between), Atatürk's reforms regarding secularism provided the country with the basis for personal freedoms not available to other Muslim countries where national law is based on an interpretation of *shariah* (the way of Islam).

The universal reaction of Westerners arriving in Turkey is the revelation that Islam is not synonymous with terrorism, and Muslims are just people like you and me living their lives, celebrating their families, and worrying about the bills. And they are thinking the same thing about us. While it's true that throughout the history of Islam (and Christianity, and others . . .) religion has been manipulated for political purposes, it's edifying to learn that Islam represents a generosity of spirit, a gentleness of heart, and the practice of good, clean altruistic living. The Anatolian influences in Turkish culture add some rich traditions and folklore into the mix, the result being that many Turks have found a way to adapt to the contradictions inherent in a changing world.

4 Recommended Books & Films

Because Turkey is the custodian of a past so densely packed with history's most critical eras, if you don't do your homework before you go, you'll wind up simply wandering through pretty piles of rocks and stone.

BOOKS

The definitive modern interpretive work on the history of Turkey is by the renowned Middle East historian Bernard Lewis, in *The Emergence of Modern Turkey* (Oxford University Press, 2001).

First published in 1961, the latest edition addresses current issues confronting Turkey, including involvement in NATO, Middle East politics, E.U. accession, and the recent and increased presence of political Islam in Turkish politics.

Turkey Unveiled: A History of Modern Turkey (Overlook Press, 1999) was written by Hugh and Nicole Pope, two journalists working for the *Wall Street Journal* and *Le Monde,* respectively. In *Turkey Unveiled,* the Popes give us insights into the most divisive issues of Turkey today. A more recent analysis of modern problems and trends in Turkey written from a Western insider's point of view is provided by Stephen Kinzer, former Istanbul bureau chief of the *New York Times,* in *Crescent and Star: Turkey Between Two Worlds* (Farrar Straus & Giroux, 2001).

John Ash approaches the history of the city in *Istanbul: The Imperial City* (Penguin, 1998) by casting a lens on the more than 20 pivotal historical events or periods beginning with the pre-classical era through to the present day. The author's special connection with the place not only makes this an easy read, it's also chock-full of references and anecdotes that couldn't fit into this book.

Another great read on the Byzantine empire is *A Short History of Byzantium* (Vintage Books, 1998), John Julius Norwich's condensed version of a three-volume epic about one of the most enduring empires on Earth.

Ottoman Centuries: The Rise and Fall of the Turkish Empire (William Morrow & Co., 1988), by Lord Kinross, has established itself as the definitive guidebook on Turkey during the Ottoman Empire. In a thoroughly readable prose, Kinross leads you through history while providing the contexts for understanding Turkey today.

Another book by Kinross is *Atatürk, the Rebirth of a Nation* (titled *Atatürk: A Biography of Mustafa Kemal, Father of*

Modern Turkey in the U.S. and currently out of print), also respected as *the* handbook on the man who single-handedly reconstructed a nation. Also see Andrew Mango's more recent *Atatürk* (John Murray Pubs, 2004).

Constantinople: City of the World's Desire, 1453–1924 (Griffin Trade Paperback, 1998), by Philip Mansel, provides an accurate and colorful history of the Ottoman Empire while sprinkling the pages with attention-grabbing little morsels of lesser-known trivia.

Coverage of terrorist actions committed by militant Muslims has prejudiced much of the Western world against anything Islamic, causing many tourists to Turkey to be unnecessarily apprehensive. *What Went Wrong* (Oxford University Press, 2001), a balanced and scholarly work by Bernard Lewis, guides readers through the transformation of Islam from a cultural, scientific, and economic powerhouse to a significantly tarnished underdog. Follow this up with *What's Right With Islam* (Harper San Francisco, 2004), in which Feisal Abdul Rauf argues how the violence perceived by the West to be at the heart of terrorism has, in fact, nothing to do with religion and everything to do with economics and politics.

Mary Lee Settle's *Turkish Reflections* (Touchstone Books, 1992) and Jeremy Seal's *A Fez of the Heart: Travels Around Turkey in Search of a Hat* (Harvest Books, 1996) are two excellent travelogues that have established themselves as de facto reads for anyone interested in Turkey. *Turkish Reflections,* although accused of being outdated, succeeds in providing an accurate portrayal of the Turkish people and vivid images of the physical landscape. Interesting little snippets of trivia are sprinkled throughout the text and are especially entertaining as supplements to a historical perspective, but as a read, may be more suitable for post-voyage reminiscences. In *A Fez of the Heart,* Jeremy Seal succeeds in capturing the sights and smells of his destinations while ostensibly on the hunt for the legacy left by the fez. Seal tosses in bits of history while you're not looking and throws in unexpected episodes of hilarity that will garner you unwanted attention in public places.

For Orhan Pamuk, *Istanbul: Memories and the City* (Alfred A. Knopf, 2005) is a (tedious) personal reflection on life growing up in the "melancholy" of an Istanbul in transition. Descriptions of faded apartment buildings, and the tension between tradition and convention are as much a self-portrait as a window into the city at the crossroads of civilization. The book also includes dozens of black-and-white photos of the city, allowing a glimpse of Istanbul before major investments in restoration.

For a modern woman's view of what it's like to work, live, and travel in Turkey, pick up the recently compiled and released *Tales From the Expat Harem: Foreign Women in Modern Turkey* (Seal Press, 2006). It's a compilation of essays, stories, and travelogues by various non-Turkish women.

In fiction, obviously, the most insightful reads will be those books written by native Turks, and in recent years, several Turkish authors have created mesmerizing works of fiction set within a vivid Turkish reality. Orhan Pamuk made quite a splash well before he won himself a Nobel Prize

in 2006 for literature. Irfan Orga's *Portrait of a Turkish Family* (Hippocrene Books, 1989) is a poignant account of a simple Turkish family caught between the Ottoman Empire and Atatürk's Republic. Journalist and leading satirist Aziz Nesin spent much of his life in prison, where he penned a large portion of his highly biographical essays—colorful images of growing up in a traditional Turkish family at the beginning of the 20th century.

FILMS

The Turks rigorously resent the unfair characterization of Turkish people in the 1978 film *Midnight Express* (see "*Midnight Express:* Fact or Fiction?" in chapter 1), a movie that has been accused of encouraging prejudices in Westerners. They point out that the movie was financed by Greek cinema magnate Kirk Kerkorian and filmed using actors of predominantly Greek and Armenian origin—two nations notorious for their bad blood with Turkey. Nevertheless, it's a movie classic, it did win an Oscar, and it *was* set in Istanbul.

Coming soon to a theater near you is Part II of *The Thomas Crown Affair,* with Angelina Jolie and Pierce Brosnan sparring over the disappearance of the illustrious Kasikci (Spoonmaker's Diamond). Called *The Topkapı Affair,* the movie is based on the book *Light of Day* and adapted from Ustinov's 1964 film *Topkapı.*

Appendix B:
Useful Turkish Terms & Phrases

1 Pronunciation Guide

VOWELS

a like the "a" in father
â like "ya" (the circumflex adds a diphthong)
e like the "e" in bed
i like the first "i" in indigo
ı like the "e" in the
o like the "o" in hope
ö like the German "ö" or like the "u" in the English word further
u like the "u" in super
ü like the French "u" or like the "u" in the English word funeral

CONSONANTS

c like the "j" in Jupiter
ç like the "ch" in church
g like the "g" in gather
ğ is silent and indicates that the preceding vowel should be elongated (dağ becomes "daaah," meaning "mountain")
h is *always* aspirated
j like the "s" in pleasure
s like the "s" in simple
ş like the "sh" in share

2 Basic Vocabulary

NUMBERS

1	bir	11	onbir	90	doksan
2	iki	12	oniki	100	yüz
3	üç	20	yirmi	101	yüzbir
4	dört	21	yirmibir	200	ikiyüz
5	beş	30	otuz	1,000	bin
6	altı	40	kırk	2,000	ikibin
7	yedi	50	elli	1,000,000	birmilyon
8	sekiz	60	altmış	2,000,000	ikimilyon
9	dokuz	70	yetmiş		
10	on	80	seksen		

DAYS OF THE WEEK

Sunday   **Pazar**
Monday   **Pazartesi** (literally, "the day after Sunday")
Tuesday   **Salı**
Wednesday   **Çarşamba**
Thursday   **Perşembe**
Friday   **Cuma**
Saturday   **Cumartesi** (literally, "the day after Friday")

MONTHS OF THE YEAR

January   **Ocak**
February   **Şubat**
March   **Mart**
April   **Nisan**
May   **Mayıs**
June   **Haziran**
July   **Temmuz**
August   **Ağustos**
September   **Eylül**
October   **Ekim**
November   **Kasım**
December   **Aralık**

EXPRESSIONS OF TIME

1 hour   **bir saat**
Afternoon   **Öğleden sonra**
Morning   **Sabah**
Night   **Gece**
Today   **Bugün**
Tomorrow   **Yarın**
What time is it?   **Saat kaç?** (literally, "how many hours?")
Yesterday   **Dün**

USEFUL SUFFIXES

ci, cı, çi, çı, cu, cü, çu, çü   indicates the seller of something
i, ı, u, ü   indicates "of something" (an "s" is added after a vowel)
ler, lar   makes a word plural
li, lı, lu, lü   indicates the presence of something; "with"
siz, sız, suz, süz   indicates the absence of something; "without"

USEFUL WORDS & PHRASES

Check, please!   **Hesap, lütfen!**
Cheers! (drinking)   **Şerefe!**

Closed   **Kapalı**

Do you have any dishes without meat?   **Etsiz yemek var mı?**

Excuse me   **Pardon** (French pronunciation) or **Afadersınız**

Gate (travel)   **Kapı**

Goodbye   **Güle güle** (said by the one staying); **Allahaı Smarladık** (said by the one leaving)

Goodbye   **Hoşça kalın** (an all-purpose goodbye)

Good day   **Iyi günler**

Good evening   **Iyi akşamlar**

Good morning   **Günaydın**

Good night   **Iyi geceler**

Hello   **Merhaba**

How are you?   **Nasılsınız?**

How much?   **Kaç para?** (literally, "how much money?") or **Ne kadar?**

I'm fine, thank you.   **Iyiyim, teşekkür ederim**

Is there . . . ?   **Var mı . . . ?** (question of availability, as in "süt var mı"—do you have any milk?)

Is there any meat stock in this dish?   **Içinde et suyu var mı?**

No   **Hayır** *(higher)*

One ticket, please   **Bir tane bilet, lütfen**

Open   **Açık**

Please   **Lütfen**

Pleased to meet you   **Memnun oldun**

Thank you (formal)   **Teşekkür ederim** (try to remember: "tea, sugar, a dream")

Thank you (casual)   **Sağol**

Thank you   **Mersi**

There isn't any; no; none   **Yok**

Very beautiful   **Çok güzel** (said also when the food is good)

Welcome!   **Hoş geldiniz!** (response: **Hoş bulduk**)

Well done!   **Bravo!** or **Aferin!**

Where? Where is it?   **Nerede?**

Where's the toilet?   **Tuvalet nerede?**

Yes   **Evet**

3 Glossary of Terms

Acropolis   Highest part of a Greek city reserved for the most important religious monuments

Ada(sı)   Island

Ağa   Arabic title given to commanders in the Ottoman military

Bahçe(sı)   Garden

Bayanlar   Ladies

Baylar   Gentlemen

Bayram   Arabic term meaning "feast," denoting several of the Muslim holidays

Bedesten   Covered inn or marketplace

Bey   Turkish title of courtesy following a man's first name meaning "Mr." as in "Mehmet bey"

Bulvarı   Boulevard

Büyük   Big

Caddesi   Avenue

Caldarium   Hottest section of a Roman bath

Caliph   Literally "successor" to the prophet Mohammad; in the past, the title was held by the religious leader of the Islamic community and was known as "commander of the faithful"

Cami/camii   Mosque; derived from the Arabic *jama* meaning "place of reunion"

Caravansary   A fortified inn; Turkish spelling is *kervansaray*

Çarşı(sı)   Market; bazaar

Celebi   Nobleman

Çeşme   Fountain

Cıkış   Exit

Cumhuriyet   Republic

Cuneiform   Linear script inscribed into tablets; used by the ancient Mesopotamians and in Asia Minor

Deniz   Sea

Dervish   A member of a mystical order of Islam

Divan   Word used to refer to the Ottoman governmental administration

Dolmuş   Minibus, minivan, or any car that operates as a group taxi

Döviz   Foreign currency

Eczane   Pharmacy

Efendi   Turkish title of courtesy following a first name meaning "sir" or "ma'am"

Emir   Arabic title for a military commander or governor of a province

Ev/evi   Home, house

Fatih   Conqueror

Frigidarium   The cold room of a Roman bath

Gar   Station

Gazi   Literally, "warrior"

Giriş   Entrance

Gişe   Ticket window

Hadith   Traditions based on the words or actions of Mohammad

Hamam(ı)   Turkish bath

Han(ı)   Inn or caravansary

Hanım   Address of respect meaning "lady"

Harem   Women's quarters of a house (literally: "forbidden")

Havaalan(ı) or **hava liman(ı)** Airport

Hegira Literally, "the emigration"; *see* hicret

Hicret The date in 622 when Mohammad left Mecca for Yathrib (Medina) to escape local hostilities; this event marks the beginning of the Islamic calendar

Hijab From the Arabic *hajaba* meaning "to conceal"; used to mean any modest covering worn by a Muslim women

Hisar Fortress

Iconoclasm 8th-century A.D. Christian movement that opposed all religious icons

Imam Literally "leader"; an educated religious guide

Iskele(sı) Wharf, quay, or dock

Janissaries The select corps of the Ottoman army

Jihad Literally, "struggle" or "striving" (Arabic; in Turkish: *cihad*)

Kaaba Muslim sacred shrine in Mecca

Kale(si) Castle or fortress

Kat Floor (of a building)

Kervansaray *See* caravansary

Kilim Flat weave rug

Kilise Church

Konak/konağı Mansion

Koran The holy recitations of the Prophet Mohammad; Muslims believe that these revelations are the direct words of God

Küçük Small

Kule Tower

Külliye(sı) Religious and social complex consisting of mosque, school, and buildings for public use

Kümbet Literally, "cupola" or "dome"; synonym for *türbe*

Liman(ı) Port

Mahalle(sı) Neighborhood

Medrese Muslim theological school

Mescit Small prayer space; mini-mosque

Mevlana Title of respect meaning "Lord" (Arabic)

Meydan(ı) Public square

Meyhane Tavern, pub, or rowdy restaurant

Mihrab The niche in a mosque oriented toward Mecca

Minaret The towers of a mosque from which the *muezzin* chants the call to prayer

Minbar Pulpit

Muezzin The Muslim "cantor" of the call to prayer

Necropolis Ancient Greek or Roman cemetery

Oculus Round "skylight" in the top of a dome

Oda(sı) Room

Otogar Bus station

Pansiyon Pension, guesthouse

Paşa Title given to commanders in the Ottoman army (close to general) and to governors of provinces

Ramadan Islamic month of ritual fasting; Ramadan (*Ramazan* in Turkish) follows the lunar calendar, so that the festival is not confined to one season

Şadirvan Literally, "reservoir"; used for ablution fountains

Şarap Wine

Saray(ı) Palace

Şarcüteri Delicatessen

Satrap Persian governor of a province

Şehzade Crowned prince

Selamlık In a traditional Turkish house, the part reserved for the men and the reception of guests

Sema Mystical dance of the Mevlevi order of the dervişes

Seraglio Sultan's palace

Sokak/sokağı Street

Stele Ancient tombstone

Sublime Porte Originally the main door of the palace where meetings of the divan were held; the term was eventually used to refer to the government, and the entire Ottoman Empire in general

Tepidarium The tepid room of a Roman bath; used for relaxation

Tuğra Sultan's imperial seal

Türbe(si) Turkish monumental funerary tomb

Ulu Great

Yalı Traditional wood Ottoman house, usually a secondary residence, built on the sea

Valide Sultan Turkish title equivalent to Queen Mother

Yol(u) Road (karayolu: highway or autobahn)

Yurt Nomadic tent, traditionally made of felt

4 Menu Guide

WHAT IS IT?

Alabalık Trout

Ananas Pineapple

Ançuez Anchovy

Balık Fish

Barbunya Red mullet

Beyin Brain

Bezelye Peas

Biber Pepper (kara biber: black pepper)

Bıldırcın Quail

Bonfile Filet of beef

Çam fıstığı Pine nut

Ciğer Liver

Çilek Strawberry

Çorba Soup

Çupra Sea bream

Dana Veal

Domates Tomato

Domuz Pork

Dondurma Ice cream

Ekmek Bread
Elma Apple
Enginar Artichoke
Erik Plum
Et Meat
Fasulye Bean
Havuç Carrot
Hindi Turkey
İspanak Spinach
Istravrit Mackerel
Jambon Ham
Kabak Squash (zucchini, pumpkin, and the like)
Kalkan Turbot
Karides Shrimp
Karnıbahar Cauliflower
Karpuz Watermelon
Kavun Melon
Kayısı Apricot
Kaz Goose
Kefal Gray mullet
Kılıç Swordfish
Kiraz Cherry
Köfte Meatball
Kuzu Lamb
Lağus Grouper
Lavaş Grilled unleavened bread
Levrek Sea bass
Limon Lemon
Lüfer Bluefish
Mantar Mushroom
Marul Lettuce
Meyva Fruit
Meze Appetizer

Mezgit Cod
Mısır Corn
Mürekkep balığı Squid
Muz Banana
Ördek Duck
Palamut Bonito
Patates Potato
Patlıcan Eggplant/aubergine
Peynir Cheese
Pide Flatbread
Pilaf (pilâf) Rice
Piliç Chicken
Portakal Orange
Salatalik Cucumber
Sardalya Sardine
Şeftali Peach
Şeker Sugar
Sığır Beef
Soğan Onion
Som Salmon
Sosis Sausage
Tarak Scallop
Tatlılar Sweets
Tavuk Hen (for stewing)
Tereyağı Butter
Ton Tuna
Torik Large bonito
Tuz Salt
Un Flour
Üzüm Grapes
Yumurta Eggs
Zeytin Olive
Zeytinyağı Olive oil

HOW IS IT PREPARED?

Buğulama Steamed
Çevirme Meat roasted on a spit
Çiğ Raw
Doğranmış Chopped
Dolma Stuffed
Ezme Paste
Fırın Roasted or baked; oven
Füme Smoked

Guveç Earthenware dish; casseroles cooked in this pot
Haşlama Cooked, boiled
İzgara Grilled
Islim Braised
Kavurma Fried or roasted
Kebap Roasted
Pane Breaded and fried

Püre   Purée
Rosto   Roast meat
Saç   Iron griddle for cooking over wood fires
Sahanda   Fried

Şiş   Skewer
Sote   Sauté
Tandır   Clay-lined oven
Taşım   Boiled
Tava   Fried

DRINKS

Ayran   Yogurt drink made by the addition of water and salt
Bira   Beer
Çay   Tea
Kayısı suyu   Apricot juice
Kiraz suyu   Cherry juice
Kola   Cola
Maden suyu or soda   Carbonated mineral water
Meyve suyu   Fruit juice
Portakal suyu   Orange juice

Rakı   Alcoholic drink made of aniseed and diluted with water
Şarap   Wine
Şekerli   With sugar
Şekersiz   Unsweetened
Şişe suyu   Bottled water
Soğuk içecekler   Beverages
Su   Water
Süt   Milk
Suyu   Juice

APPETIZERS

Ara sıcak   Hot appetizers (translated literally, "in the middle hot")
Arnavut ciğeri   Spicy fried liver with onions
Beyin haşlaması   Boiled brain
Beyin kızartması   Fried brain
Börek   Flaky pastry, either baked or fried
Cacık   Salad of yogurt, cucumber, and garlic; often served as a soup
Çiğ köfte   Spicy raw meatballs
Çoban salatası   Salad of tomatoes, peppers, cucumbers, onions, and mint in olive oil and lemon
Ezme salatası   Spicy relish of chopped tomatoes, cucumbers, peppers, hot green chili peppers, onion, and parsley
Fesuliye piyası   White bean with onion salad

Havuç salatası   Carrot salad
Hibeş   Spread of chickpeas, red pepper, onion, and yogurt
Humus   Chickpea purée
Patlıcan salatası   Purée of roasted eggplant (also served warm; also refers to eggplant sautéed with tomatoes and peppers)
Sigara böreği   Fried filo "cigar" pastry filled with cheese
Soğuk mezeler   Cold appetizers
Su böreği   Baked filo filled with meat or cheese
Talaş böreği   Puff pastry filled with meat
Yalancı dolması   Stuffed grape leaves (no meat)
Yaprak dolması   Stuffed grape leaves (sometimes with meat)

SOUPS

Balık çorbası   Fish soup
Domatesli pirinç çorbası   Tomato and rice soup
Et suyu   Consommé
Ezo gelin çorbası   Red lentil soup with bulgur and mint

Işkembe çorbası   Tripe soup (also kokoreç)
Mantar çorbası   Mushroom soup
Mercimek çorbası   Lentil soup
Sebze çorbası   Vegetable soup

MEATS & KEBAPS

Adana kebabı Meatballs of spicy chopped lamb flattened and grilled on a skewer

Böbrek Kidney

Çöp kebabı Same as çöp şiş

Çöp şiş Small lamb cubes grilled on a skewer; also called çöp kebabı

Döner kebap Thin slices of lamb roasted on a vertical revolving spit

İçli köfte Corn or bulgur balls stuffed with minced lamb (boiled or fried)

İskender kebabı Sliced *döner kebabı* served on a layer of pide, tomatoes, and yogurt, and covered with melted butter

Izgara köfte Grilled meatballs

Kadın budu köfte "Lady's thigh," meatballs of lamb and rice, deep fried

Karışık ızgara Mixed grill

Kuzu budu rostosu Roasted leg of lamb

Kuzu pirzolası Grilled lamb chops

Şiş kebabı Marinated lamb cubes grilled on a skewer

DESSERTS

Aşure Thick sweet pudding of whole wheat, mixed fruits, and nuts

Baklava Flaky pastries soaked in syrup or honey

Çukulatalı pudding Chocolate pudding

Fırın sütlaç Baked rice pudding

Hanım göbeği Honey-soaked flour pastry

Helva National favorite of semolina, sesame paste or flour, sugar, and nuts

Kaymaklı kayısı tatlısı Poached apricots stuffed with cream

Krem karamel Crème caramel

Künefe Butter-soaked pastry filled with melted cheese, soaked in syrup, and served hot

Muhallebi Milk pudding

Revani Honey-soaked semolina

Sütlaç Rice pudding

Tatlılar Sweets or desserts

Tavukgöğsü Sweet chicken pudding

OTHER FAVORITE DISHES

Damat dolması Squash stuffed with ground lamb and nuts

Domates doması Stuffed tomatoes

Etli biber dolması Stuffed green peppers

Gözleme Folded savory pancake filled with potato, cheese, or meat

Hunkar beğendi Eggplant purée topped with lamb cubes (literally, "the sultan was pleased")

Imam bayıldı Stuffed eggplant (literally, "the imam fainted")

Lahmacun Fast food of thin crust dough topped with minced lamb, tomato, and onion

Mantı Meat dumplings topped with warm sauce of yogurt, garlic, and chile oil

Menemen Wet omelet of beaten eggs, tomato, and green peppers

Musakka Casserole of eggplant, vegetables, and ground lamb

Peynirli tost Grilled cheese sandwich (also called tost)

Simit Sesame seed–coated soft pretzel

Index

See also Accommodations and Restaurant indexes, below.

Yeni Kaplica *hamam* (Bursa),
    225
Yeni Marmara, 211
Yeni Valide Camii (Yeni Camii;
    New Queen Mother's
    Mosque), 146
Yeraltı Camii (Underground
    Mosque), 168, 185
Yerebatan Sarnıçı (Yerebatan
    Cistern), 33, 141, 182
Yeşil Camii (Green Mosque;
    Bursa), 221
Yeşil Camii (Nicaea), 227
Yeşil Türbesi (Green Tomb;
    Bursa), 221
Yildirim Beyazit Mosque
    (Yildirim Beyazit Camii;
    Bursa), 224
Yıldız Palace and Park (Yıldız
    Sarayı ve Parki), 151–152
Yıldız Park, 7
Yogurt
    Kanlica, 8
    Tarihi Kanlıca Yogurdu, 173
Young Turks, 244
Youth & Sports Day, 15
Yüksek Kaldirim, 177

Zafer Bayrami (Victory Day),
    16
Zafer Plaza (Bursa), 219
Zeyrek, 161
Zeyrek Camii (Church of the
    Pantocrator), 161
Zoë, Empress, 120
Zulfaris Museum (Jewish
    Museum of Turkey), 181

ACCOMMODATIONS

Airport Hotel, 83
A'jia, 59, 82
Anemon Galata, 77
Ansen 130, 76
Antik Hotel, 70
Apricot Hotel, 59–60, 69
Arena Hotel, 63
Ayasofya Konakları, 64
Bentley Hotel, 79
Çelik Palas Hotel (Bursa), 224
Ceylan Inter-Continental, 71–72

Cihangir Hotel, 59, 75
Çirağan Palace Hotel Kempinski
    Istanbul, 6, 80
Deniz Konak, 69
Dersaadet Oteli, 66
Eresin Crown Hotel, 63
Fehmi Bey, 66–67
Four Points by Sheraton, 83
Four Seasons Hotel, 6, 63
Four Seasons the Bosphorus,
    7, 63, 80–81
Galata Antique Hotel, 77
Germir Palas Hotel, 72, 74
Grand Hotel Ayasofya, 69
Hotel Armada, 67
Hotel Empress Zoe, 67
Hotel Erguvan, 67
Hotel Niles, 70
Hotel Princess (Büyükada), 229
Hotel Splendid Palace
    (Büyükada), 229
Hyatt Regency, 74
Kervansaray Termal Hotel
    (Bursa), 224
Lady Diana Hotel, 64
Lares Park, 74
Les Ottomans, 7, 59, 81
Lush Hotel, 59, 74–75
The Marmara Istanbul, 72
The Marmara Pera, 77–78
Mauısafir Suites, 74
Mavi Ev (Blue House), 64
Misafir Suites, 59
Naz Wooden House, 68
Ottoman Hotel, 68
Park Hyatt, 74
Pera Palas Hotel, 59, 76
Pera Rose, 76
The Point, 75
Polka Country Hotel
    (Polonezköy), 230
Radisson SAS Bosphorus Hotel,
    81–82
Richmond, 78
Ritz-Carlton Istanbul, 72
Safran Hotel (Bursa), 224
Sapphire, 70–71
Sarı Konak, 68
Sheraton Istanbul, 83
Sirkeci Konak, 71
Sofa, 79
Sude Konak, 71
Sultanahmet Palace Hotel,
    64, 66
Sultanhan Hotel, 66
Sultan Hill, 68
Sultan's Inn, 70

Sumahan, 7, 60, 82–83
Swissôtel, 79
Villa Zurich, 75–76
W Istanbul, 81
WOW Convention Istanbul, 83
Yenişehir Palas, 76–77
Zeugma Hotel, 69

RESTAURANTS

Adigüzel Restaurant, 105
A'jia, 109
Anemon Galata Hotel, 178
Asitane, 84, 96
Balıkçı Sabahattin, 92
Banyan Seaside, 108
Beymen Brasserie, 106
Beyti, 98
Boncuk, 102
Borsa, 84, 106
Buhara 93, 94
Café du Levant, 107
Carne, 106
Çiçek Izgara (Bursa), 225
Çiya Sofrası, 109–110
Da Mario, 108
Darüzziyafe, 95
Degustasyon Lokantası, 103
Deli-Bakkal, 104
Del Mare, 109
Develi Restaurant, 84, 98
Divan Lokantası, 100
Doğa Balık, 85, 102
Dubb, 94
Eminönü Belediyesi Sosyal
    Tesisleri, 94
Enginar, 105
Felafel House, 101
Feriye Restaurant, 107
Fes Café, 95
Flamm, 103
Galata House, 105
Gelik Balık, 85, 96, 98
Hacı Abdullah, 100
Hacı Baba Restaurant, 100
Hamdi Et Lokantası, 90, 92
Havusbaşı Çay Bahcesi, 140
House Café, 84–85, 102
Hünkar, 106
Istanbul Modern Restaurant
    and Café, 38
Kalamar Restaurant
    (Büyükada), 229
Köfteçi Arnavut, 191
Konyalı Topkapı Sarayı
    Lokantası, 93, 131

Yedikule (Seven Towers
    Fortress), 45, 154–155
Yenikapi, 45